Opening Up Education

Opening Up Education

The Collective Advancement of Education through Open Technology, Open Content, and Open Knowledge

Edited by
Toru Iiyoshi and M. S. Vijay Kumar

Foreword by John Seely Brown

The Carnegie Foundation for the Advancement of
Teaching

The MIT Press
Cambridge, Massachusetts
London, England

For information about special quantity discounts, please email special_sales@ mitpress.mit.edu

This book was set in Sabon by SNP Best-set Typesetter Ltd., Hong Kong.

Printed and bound in the United States of America.

Library of Congress Cataloging-in-Publication Data

Opening up education : the collective advancement of education through open technology, open content, and open knowledge / edited by Toru Iiyoshi and M. S. Vijay Kumar.
    p. cm.
  Includes bibliographical references and index.
  ISBN 978-0-262-03371-8 (hardcover : alk. paper)
  1. Distance   education—Computer-assisted   instruction. 2. Education,
Higher—Effect   of   technological   innovations   on. 3. Educational
technology. 4. Open learning. I. Iiyoshi, Toru. II. Kumar, M. S. Vijay.
LC5800.O678 2008
378.1′758—dc22
                                                                    2007039375

10 9 8 7 6 5 4 3 2 1

To our wives and sons—
Hiromi, Rukmini, Ken, Suhas, and Taku
—whose support and encouragement makes this important work
possible.

Contents

Foreword: Creating a Culture of Learning   xi
   John Seely Brown
Acknowledgments   xix

**Introduction: An Invitation to Open Up the Future of
Education   1**
   Toru Iiyoshi and M. S. Vijay Kumar

Section I: Open Educational Technology   11

  1 Section Introduction: "Open Educational Technology: Tempered
    Aspirations"   13
    Owen McGrath

  2 "Designing Open Educational Technology"   27
    David Kahle

  3 "The Gates Are Shut: Technical and Cultural Barriers to Open
    Education"   47
    Stuart D. Lee

  4 "Does an Open Source Strategy Matter? Lessons Learned from the
    iLabs Project"   61
    Phillip D. Long and Stephen C. Ehrmann

  5 "Evaluating the Results of Open Education"   77
    Edward Walker

  6 "A Harvest Too Large? A Framework for Educational
    Abundance"   89
    Trent Batson, Neeru Paharia, and M. S. Vijay Kumar

7 "Digital Libraries, Learning Communities, and Open Education"   105
Clifford Lynch

8 "Open Source in Open Education: Promises and Challenges"   119
Christopher J. Mackie

Section II: Open Educational Content   133

9 Section Introduction: "Open Educational Content: Transforming Access to Education"   135
Flora McMartin

10 "Widening Participation in Education through Open Educational Resources"   149
Andy Lane

11 "Building Open Learning as a Community-based Research Activity"   165
Candace Thille

12 "Extending the Impact of Open Educational Resources through Alignment with Pedagogical Content Knowledge and Institutional Strategy: Lessons Learned from the MERLOT Community Experience"   181
Tom Carey and Gerard L. Hanley

13 "Why Understanding the Use and Users of Open Education Matters"   197
Diane Harley

14 "OpenCourseWare: Building a Culture of Sharing"   213
Steven R. Lerman, Shigeru Miyagawa, and Anne H. Margulies

15 "Challenges and Opportunities for the Open Education Movement: A Connexions Case Study"   229
Richard G. Baraniuk

16 "2005–2012: The OpenCourseWars"   247
David Wiley

17 "Revolutionizing Education through Innovation: Can Openness Transform Teaching and Learning?"   261
Catherine M. Casserly and Marshall S. Smith

Section III: Open Educational Knowledge   277

18 Section Introduction: "Open Educational Knowledge: More than Opening the Classroom Door"   279
Cheryl R. Richardson

19 "Inquiry Unplugged: A Scholarship of Teaching and Learning for Open Understanding"   289
Richard A. Gale

20 "The Middle of Open Spaces: Generating Knowledge about Learning through Multiple Layers of Open Teaching Communities"   303
Randall Bass and Dan Bernstein

21 "Open Teaching: The Key to Sustainable and Effective Open Education"   319
Diana Laurillard

22 "Promoting Technology-enabled Knowledge Building and Sharing for Sustainable Open Educational Innovations"   337
Toru Iiyoshi and Cheryl R. Richardson

23 "Scaffolding for Systemic Change"   357
Barbara Cambridge

24 "Learning Design: Sharing Pedagogical Know-How"   375
James Dalziel

25 "Common Knowledge: Openness in Higher Education"   389
Diana G. Oblinger and Marilyn M. Lombardi

26 "Open for What? A Case Study of Institutional Leadership and Transformation"   401
Bernadine Chuck Fong

27 "What's Next for Open Knowledge?"   417
Mary Taylor Huber and Pat Hutchings

Conclusion: New Pathways for Shaping the Collective Agenda to Open Up Education   429
   Toru Iiyoshi and M. S. Vijay Kumar

About the Authors   441
Index   451

Foreword: Creating a Culture of Learning

How could I say no? When approached by Toru and Vijay to participate in the workshop bringing the authors of this influential book together to discuss their preliminary chapter drafts, I was intrigued. After all, the challenges that we face in education today are daunting, and the editors had assembled quite an impressive company who were struggling to find ways through education to respond to those challenges. The world becomes more complex and interconnected at a lightning-fast pace, and almost every serious social issue requires an engaged public that is not only traditionally literate, but adept in a new, systemic literacy. This new literacy requires an understanding of different kinds of feedback systems, exponential processes, the unintended consequences inherent in evolving social systems, etcetera. In addition, the unrelenting velocity of change means that many of our skills have a shorter shelf life, suggesting that much of our learning will need to take place outside of traditional school and university environments. It is also unlikely that sufficient resources will be available to build enough new campuses to meet the growing demand for higher education, at least not the sort of campuses we have traditionally built for colleges and universities. Nor is it likely that current methods of teaching and learning will suffice to prepare students for the lives they will lead in the twenty-first century.

In response, we need to find a way to reconceptualize many twentieth-century education models, and at the same time reinforce learning outside of formal schooling. There may be powerful ways to blur the distinction between formal learning and informal where both turn on the social life of learning. Of course, we need to get back to basics—refining the most effect modes of teaching, mentoring, and coaching, but we also should put some thought to informal teaching to support the inevitability and necessity of informal learning.

Fortunately, the networked age might be the "silver bullet" that will provide a way to both improve education and to set the stage for a necessary culture of learning. In the digital age, communities self-organize around the Internet, which has created a global "platform" that has vastly expanded access to all sorts of resources including formal and informal educational materials. The Internet has also fostered a new culture of sharing, one in which content is freely contributed and distributed with few restrictions.

The latest evolution of the Internet, the so-called Web 2.0 has blurred the line between producers and consumers of content and has shifted attention from access to information toward access to other people. New kinds of online resources—such as social networking sites, blogs, wikis, and virtual communities—have allowed people with common interests to meet, share ideas, and collaborate in innovative ways. Indeed, the Web 2.0 is creating a new kind of participatory medium that is ideal for supporting multiple modes of learning. Two of those include social learning, based on the premise that our understanding of content is socially constructed through conversations about that content and through grounded interactions around problems or actions. The focus is not so much on *what* we learn but on *how* we learn.

The second, perhaps even more significant, aspect of social learning, involves not only "learning about" the subject matter but also "learning to be" a full participant in the field. This involves acquiring the practices and norms of established practitioners in that field or acculturating into a community of practice. By entering into this community, you are required to assimilate the sensibilities and ways of seeing the world embodied within that community. And this is exactly what happens if you want to join an open source community with their key practices and expected contributions.

A culture of sharing, augmented with a culture of participation now made more feasible than ever with the Internet and Web 2.0 platforms will most likely start with the students themselves, as we see so vividly in both the complex massively multiplayer game worlds and the power of study groups—whether conducted face-to-face or virtually. But the culture of sharing and participation must also involve content. MIT broke the ice when then President Chuck Vest launched the bold Open-CourseWare (OCW) project. Other universities quickly followed MIT's lead, and both the content and the means of accessing class materials and remixing and repurposing them for different audiences grew. But it is time that we move beyond merely considering content. We must begin to determine ways in which this content can encompass multiple kinds of instructional or learning activities within it. It is, after all, the combination of things we do with content that creates learning platforms.

Technology, of course, is key, and I want to dwell on only two aspects of how technology can now transform our learningscape: immersion and intelligent tutoring systems. Immersion is a concept that has received all too little attention in the learning literature. Consider, for example, how every one of us has learned the immensely complex system that is our own native language. We learn language through immersion and desire. Immersion comes from being surrounded by others talking and interacting with us and is furthered facilitated by our deep desire to interact, be understood and express our needs. We learn language fearlessly and constantly. Nearly everyone with whom we interact is a teacher for us—albeit an informal teacher, encouraging us to say new things, correcting us, extending our vocabulary, and so on. This simple form of immersion is fundamentally social in nature.

In today's high tech, graphically rich world we now have almost limitless opportunities to leverage immersion. We can now build simulation models of cites, historic events, atomic structures, biological and mechanical systems to name just a few. Our challenge becomes how to share the vast simulations and data bases that already exist and share them in a way that others can extend, remix and compose them in order to expand their reach and scope. I still dream of a virtual human system where I can explore any aspect of how our bodies function from organs to cells to membranes. There are promising signs, but as of yet we have no real framework for constructing and sharing modules of such a system. But if we can entertain the semantic web, perhaps we could entertain a vast and recursively interconnected web of simulations. No one group can build it all, but many could contribute, including students themselves.

Although richly visual, immersive three dimensional simulations will help the *born digital* student master complex topics, that will not be enough. We need to augment these systems (as well as the more passive course material) with computer-based intelligent tutors. Intelligent tutoring systems have had a long history stretching back to the 1970s where, in fact, I first became engaged in the issues of education and training. Some of our systems were pretty impressive as long as you overlooked the fact that they required a million dollar computer per student for our most advanced systems. But now we have machines 10,000 times more powerful, and in the last few years we have experienced the commoditizing of computing where vast amounts of computer power can be rendered cheaply through cluster or utility computing or even more recently, cloud computing. This means that our past dreams for building intelligent tutoring systems that could afford open-ended learning under the skillful eye of a tutor/coach/mentor is now becoming realistic. Indeed, the prior work of Carnegie Mellon University (CMU) and now their Open Learning Initiative (OLI), wonderfully described in this book, have reignited interest in this direction by demonstrating the power and utility of such systems.

The third category I want to dwell on is knowledge. For decades we have worked to create better theories of learning and successful models of teaching. We collect small fragments of data and struggle to capture context from which this data was extracted, but it is a slow process. Context is sufficiently nuanced that complete characterizations of it are extremely difficult. As a result, educational experiments are seldom definitive, and best practices are, at best, rendered in snapshots for others to interpret—see the description of the KEEP Toolkit in Toru Iiyoshi's and Cheryl R. Richardson's chapter in section III for the best and most evocative example of this. But we can do more.

If there was one thing I took away from the Carnegie meeting, it was that no one pedagogical or technical approach is the answer to ensuring that students are engaged and prepared. We need to be catholic in our point of view. There are thousands of colleges and universities worldwide, as well as many other institutions of learning, including training centers and technical schools. In addition, there are tens of thousands of institutions that support "informal" learning. And as the section headings in this book illustrate, we need to think about how technology, content, and knowledge about learning and teaching can be creatively combined to enhance education and ignite students' passions, imaginations and desires to participate in constant learning about (and sense making of) the world around us. And we need to collect shared, distributed, reflective practicums in which experiences are vetted, clustered, commented on, and tried out in new contexts, as several of the authors here posit.

Again, in the spirit of sharing and participation, how might we start to instrument our learningscapes and to start collecting massive amounts of data about what is working and what is not and why. Consider OCW. There may well be millions of students using this material, but we need to ask what we're learning from them. Are there particular paragraphs or problems (in a problem set) that are routinely misinterpreted? How are test questions being misinterpreted? What sequence of materials appears to be working best? Are any systematic error patterns showing up? Can we model these errors? These queries barely scratch the surface of the information we need to collect, but readers who are particularly interested in these questions will be especially informed by Diana Laurillard's chapter. And of course, just as Amazon does in their Web site, experiments can be designed and continuously run and the data collected to see what works best for a class of users. When enough micro experiments are run and the data is continuously collected and analyzed automatically it can lead to some surprising breakthroughs.

But if we do all the above along with all the ideas expressed in this book—will it be enough to meet the educational challenges we currently face? I would suggest we need to extend our thinking around open education to include more of a Learning 2.0 (based on Web 2.0) perspective. There are two primary reasons why this might be true. The first turns on a question first posed to me by John King, associate provost of University of Michigan. He asked how many students I thought that University of Michigan (Ann Arbor) taught each year. I knew that the university had approximately 40,000 students give or take a few thousand, so that was my answer. He responded that 250,000 was closer to the actuality, adding that I had gotten UM's enrollment right. What you forget, he said, is that each year the incoming students bring their social networks with them. These networks reach back into UM students' communities and schools. Using the social software and social network tools of SMS, IM, Facebook, MySpace, they extend the discussions, debates, bull sessions and study groups that naturally arise on campus to encompass this broader constituency, thus amplifying the effect the university is having across the state.

Now I doubt that there is hard evidence regarding the extent this is currently happening, but nevertheless it does draw attention to the broader learning milieu or learning landscape we need to consider, and it brings attention to extended forms of participation offered by the Internet. These extended forms start to merge tools for doing research with tools for learning—a boundary that needs to be blurred ever more. As a simple example, consider how many students pick up the practice of writing software by joining an open source community of practice such as Linux, Apache, etcetera. There may be small groups on a campus, but generally these communities of practice are highly distributed. Joining one of these communities entails first becoming a legitimate peripheral participant working on a small project improving or extending some piece of code and slowly building up a reputation from the work you do to moving into more central tasks and challenges in the community. Participants are learning new techniques about software practice from watching the work of their peers, defending their own work and participating in community discussions about emergent problems. This peer-based learning process is about *learning-to-be* a practitioner rather than just *learning about* software. Today's students don't want to spend years learning about something before they start to learn-to-be a practitioner in that knowledge domain. Of course, this happens to some extent on today's campuses in the form of practicums and laboratory exercises, but these are usually labor intensive in terms of the instructor's time and effort. They are also labor intensive for the student. But time spent on learning is a funny commodity. If the student is passionately engaged in acquiring the practice, then time seems to disappear. Passion is the key, which brings us to our last point.

Today the Web offers students incredible opportunities to find and join niche communities, niches that make up much of what Chris Anderson in 2004 in *Wired* magazine termed the "Long Tail." Finding and joining a niche community that ignites their passion sets the stage through productive inquiry and peer-based learning to acquire both the practice of and knowledge about a field. Nearly all the resources discussed in this book, along with the millions of niche amateur (from the Latin word *amateur* meaning lover of) communities could provide a powerful learningscape for life long learning that is grounded in the learning practices acquired on campus. Not only would this provide real leverage for open education, but it would be a major step toward creating a culture of learning for the twenty-first century.

John Seely Brown

Acknowledgments

This volume is a product of a journey that started one and half years ago and would have been simply impossible to commence or complete without the scaffolding of support, encouragement, effort and plain old fashioned commitment, so freely offered by so many to whom we are profoundly grateful. As we take this opportunity to recognize several of them we are profoundly conscious that it has taken a village.

First of all, we have greatly benefited from the wisdom and generosity of our authors. We are indebted to them for willingly giving of their experience, expertise, and vision to this endeavor. We deeply appreciate their patience and flexibility, which was challenged on more than one occasion over the course of this production, and of course, we were thrilled to have many stimulating exchanges of ideas and engaging discussions with them.

We were extremely fortunate to have as part of our core editorial team, the talent and energy of Owen McGrath, Flora McMartin, and Cheryl Richardson, as section editors. Whether coaxing and cajoling our authors to meet impossible deadlines, providing critical reviews, or working to bring coherence to the disparate contributions, these three colleagues brought invaluable dedication, professionalism, and scholarly perspective to this effort.

We are deeply obliged to Gay Clyburn for guiding us, gently but firmly, through the publishing process. We are also thankful to her and the copy editors, Ellen Wert, Kristen Garabedian, and Lori Low for their tireless and uncomplaining efforts to help produce a finished volume out of a rich but sometimes rough collection of essays. We are grateful to

Ellen Faran and her colleagues at the MIT Press for their valuable help with this publication.

Our note of thanks would be incomplete if we did not recognize some people whose work and thinking have been important influences in this field: Hal Abelson at MIT, Joseph Hardin from the Sakai Foundation and the University of Michigan, Larry Lessig from Stanford University, Ira Fuchs from the Andrew W. Mellon Foundation, and Marshall Smith from the William and Flora Hewlett Foundation are among the people who have always urged us to think hard about the non-trivial issues of being "open" in education.

We are very conscious of the significance of our institutional surround in this effort. The supportive environment at the Carnegie Foundation and MIT, who in their own distinctive ways are engaging deeply in establishing the value of open and innovative educational practices, has been valuable. We are grateful for the support and encouragement from the leadership of our organizations, including Lee Shulman, Pat Hutchings, John Barcroft, and Ann Fitzgerald at the Carnegie Foundation and Dean Daniel Hastings at MIT.

The book project would not have been launched had it not been for the encouragement at the outset from John Seeley Brown, provocateur and thinker at large, who recognized the significance of undertaking this collective scholarly effort at this time and put his intellectual weight behind it.

Finally and foremost a note of deep gratitude and genuine admiration for a "Most Valuable Player"—Emily Crawford from the Carnegie Foundation, for shepherding this exercise—coordinating the myriad calls and meetings (working closely with Mary Curtin at MIT), organizing the online project workspace, communication, and overall project management that was absolutely critical to execute this complex production effort, and for good measure helping us with proofreading the manuscripts and providing helpful feedback.

Toru Iiyoshi and M. S. Vijay Kumar

Opening Up Education

Introduction

Toru Iiyoshi and M. S. Vijay Kumar

It's almost as if a window was opened through which the future was very clearly visible. "See that?" he said. "That's the future in which you are going to live your life."
—Albert A. Gore, *An Inconvenient Truth* (2006)

Al Gore first realized what the future might look like when one of his undergraduate professors showed him how human activity—unless changed—would lead to the acceleration of global warming, resulting in serious harm to the environment and all life on earth. Alerted and intrigued, but most importantly motivated, Gore began working to change the future. The window was opened to him as a young man, and together with people around the world, he began to take action, both individually and collectively, to bring about a preferred future.

Similarly, our motivation for embarking on this book has been to open a window for our readers into the future of education. We hope that as you read through its chapters and see visions of what is possible, you will be alerted, intrigued, and motivated to start taking steps, in your own capacity, towards a preferred future for education.

A Perfect Storm

Before we jump into that future, though, let us quickly look back and remind ourselves that education's history is one of expansion and innovation. As the number of people participating in education has increased, so has the number of ways in which we learn and teach. In other words, the history of education is a narrative on *opening up education*. Over the last few decades, new media and information communication technologies have enabled faculty, students, and educational institutions to advance education in many ways. Computer-Assisted Learning, Intelligent Tutoring Systems, Computer-Supported Collaborative Learning, interactive multimedia, telecommunications, and the Internet have not only transformed how we learn and teach but have also extended educational opportunity.

Today, a confluence of events is creating the perfect storm for significantly advancing education. With a growing inventory of openly available educational tools and resources, and with an increasingly engaged and connected community, transformative opportunities for education abound. We see a proliferation of new initiatives, many with the potential to radically change the ecology and the economics of education. However, to date, many innovative educational endeavors still remain in isolated and closed domains, rarely shared across classrooms, disciplines, or institutions. Thus, educators find it difficult to advance their pedagogical practice and knowledge as a community.

The good news is that the emerging open education movement in higher education and beyond is beginning to change the way educators use, share, and improve educational resources and knowledge by making them open and freely available.

We are cognizant that the term "open education" can have multiple interpretations and the movement has multiple dimensions.

Rather than propose one more definition, our reference to open education embraces the many dimensions of this movement as well the many interpretations of the term "open" as it has been applied to education over time, such as increased access, greater choice, and flexibility. What we offer instead is an extension to these definitions that emphasizes the value of collectivity leading to an assertion (more in the nature of an aspiration) that a key tenet of open education is that *education can be improved by making educational assets visible and accessible and by harnessing the collective wisdom of a community of practice and reflection.*

There are several indicators of how the open education movement is affecting the educational landscape. For example, tens of thousands of course Web sites and other educational materials are now freely available from hundreds of institutions, organizations, and projects from thousands of educators around the world, representing an unprecedented upsurge in access to educational resources. At the same time, hundreds of educational institutions have joined international consortia and alliances to develop and share open educational technologies, resources, and repositories, creating new models of collaboration for the production and distribution of educational resources. Furthermore, some of these groups are moving toward the collaborative construction, extension, and revision of course materials across disciplines, indicating that "building upon each other's work," which has been a valued common practice in research over centuries, finally starts gaining momentum in teaching and learning.

Perhaps the most significant sign of open education's promise of deep transformation is that it is becoming an essential part of the discourse on educational opportunity and change at institutional, national, and international levels. Forums sponsored by OECD (See *Giving Knowledge for Free: The Emergence of Open Educational Resources* at http://www.oecd.org/cer) and UNESCO (See http://www.unesco.org/iiep/virtualuniversity/forums.php), and conferences hosted by developing countries, actively explore the effectiveness and viability of open solutions to address large-scale educational reform. Teacher training and faculty development efforts are areas of particular interest, along with opportunities for continuous education. Meanwhile, institutions in developed countries are beginning to grapple with how the open education movement can bring vitality and relevance to curricula through new models of learner participation, and through cross-disciplinary and global perspectives. These institutions are also beginning to rethink their educational infrastructure in order to better support open education.

Yet, despite the increasing interest in open education and the availability of these growing collections of educational tools and resources, we risk missing the transformative and innovative opportunities, be it for improving teaching and learning in a single classroom or creating the necessary educational capacity for nation building. As a global educational community, we can benefit from a deeper understanding of how open educational tools and resources are being created and used in ways that build upon one another's experience and practical knowledge. It is vital that we continue to explore possible synergies and sustainability strategies for all these current and future open education efforts and promote a "culture of openness" across boundaries and borders.

We believe that the timing is right for the engagement exercise called for in this book. The movement has advanced far enough for us to articulate the visions and conditions necessary for opening up education in ways that can dramatically advance learning and teaching. It is our hope that the experience and wisdom captured in this volume will help to make such visions and conditions tangible and move us forward.

Building This Collection

As a collection of 30 reflective and generative essays by 38 prominent leaders and thinkers involved in open education initiatives, this volume explores the *challenges* to be addressed, the *opportunities* to be seized, and the potential *synergies* to be realized from the various efforts in the movement for enhancing educational quality and access. The authors are faculty, researchers, academic technology experts, directors of major open education projects, administrators, leaders of professional organizations, and program officers and scholars from granting and research foundations, so, as you can imagine, the perspectives, ideas, and visions they provide are broad, diverse, and, of course, thought provoking.

From the inception of this project, our goal was to engage the authors in a collective exercise of critical reflection on the open education movement. With the aforementioned key tenet of open education as a foundation, we presented our authors with a framing question: "How can we take full advantage of open educational technology, content, and knowledge to create opportunities to improve the quality of education?" Finally, in order to establish coherence within and across the sections of this volume, we urged our authors to consider the following dimensions in addressing the framing question:

• The educational value proposition and implications of open education initiatives;

• The micro and macro factors that would accelerate these initiatives towards having a larger impact on education; and

• The means and mechanisms for iteratively and continuously improving the quality of teaching and learning through effective development and sharing of educational innovations and pedagogical knowledge.

We also used several elaborated questions for each of these statements to help the authors better reflect on and respond to these issues (Appendix A).

In September 2006, the authors and the editorial team convened the Open Education Summit at The Carnegie Foundation for the Advancement of Teaching in Stanford, California, to launch the book project. The summit brought together many of the book's contributors to collectively explore and articulate their visions for open education and the issues they saw emerging in this rapidly growing area. The intent was not only to bootstrap the publication project but also to identify future research and development agendas. Questions emerged relating to understanding and promoting the impact of open education efforts.

• How can we enable and encourage learners and educators to participate in open education?
• What does open education mean as an agency for both formal and informal education?
• How can niche learning communities take advantage of open education?
• What support needs to be provided?
• What are the different types of warranting mechanisms underlying the different types of certification we currently have?

In addition, many possible indicators of transformation, significant risk and challenges, and synergy were suggested from multiple perspectives during the Summit (Appendix B).

The Organization of This Book

Even though many of our authors have been closely associated with various significant open education initiatives, this volume is neither a collection of reports on open education projects nor up-to-date summaries of their successes. Instead, the authors have shared their critical analyses and reflections on the strategic underpinnings of past and current open education efforts, exploring issues and possibilities, and building upon their own and others' experiences. They have delved into the implications and visions for future work in three areas: open educational technology, content, and knowledge of practice.

We took this three-section organization (technology, content, and knowledge) largely as a convenient and easily understood framework. Naturally, the three categories are not mutually exclusive. In fact, their natural interrelationships become evident from the very beginning, and as you read through these chapters you will find that many of them discuss possibilities and challenges across these dimensions, exploring critical implications and synergies not just for one area but also for the entire realm of open education.

Each section opens with a section editor's introduction that includes: a brief definition(s) of the area and the scope of the section; major issues and topics in the area; a sample of the main ideas and viewpoints presented in the chapters of that section, and some perspectives from the section editors, along with some navigational guidance. A set of chapters then addresses the multiple dimensions of the impact that various open education efforts have had and could have on the form and function of education. Finally, each section ends with a chapter contributed by leaders from a funding or research foundation that has devoted significant effort toward advancing open education.

Throughout this volume, perspectives are offered on how "lessons learned" from these ambitious open education efforts can achieve a collective vision, characterized by an abundance of sustainable and transformative educational opportunities and not merely pervasive use of technology-enabled tools and resources.

The book implicitly celebrates the success of the initiatives that have helped invigorate the open education movement. But it is also an invitation to explore areas of discomfort as we reflect on the limited impact so far and the potential for remarkable change.

Our intent, finally, is to issue a wake-up call to the education community to not miss the boat and under-explore the potential for reinventing and energizing education. Otherwise, the open education movement will be ephemeral and will not make substantial impact on learning and teaching. Accordingly, we close the volume with a chapter in which we share some concrete recommendations for shaping the collective agenda for open education's future.

What Readers Should Look For

We anticipate that the readers of this book—as educators committed to innovation and change, students interested in how technologies can help bridge living and learning, and leaders interested in shared resources, planning, and policy making—will be concerned with the future of education.

For us as editors, assembling this volume and working closely with the section editors and authors has been a tremendous adventure and rewarding journey. We invite you, the readers, to join and extend this excursion as you make your way through the book, taking your individual paths and making stops along the way depending on where you want to go and what you might be seeking. We encourage you to cross the borders of the book's sections on technology, content, and knowledge.

As you navigate your way through this collection we urge you to consider the role of open education in helping to explore solutions to the critical challenges that we all face everyday as learners, practitioners, educational researchers and planners. And we invite you to grapple with questions such as these: How can we make teaching and learning more stimulating and engaging? How can we make good teaching and learning practices visible and shareable? How can we harness educators' inspiration and passion for better teaching and learning?

We hope your intellectual journey through this book is an engaging, productive, and rewarding experience that will assist you as you join others to construct an ideal future for education.

Bon Voyage!

Reference

David, L., Bender, L., Burns, S. Z. (Producers), and Guggenheim, D. (Director). (2006). *An Inconvenient Truth* [Motion Picture]. Based on the book *An Inconvenient Truth: The Planetary Emergency of Global Warming and What We Can Do About It* by Al Gore. United States: Paramount Classics and Participant Productions.

Appendix A. The Questions Used to Promote Authors' Reflections

In Your Field . . .	The Educational Value Proposition and Implications of Open Education Initiatives	The Micro and Macro Factors That Will Move These Initiatives from Their Current Stage to Whatever Their "Golden" State Might Be	Approaches to Share Effectively, as a Community of Practice and Reflection, the Innovations and Pedagogical Experience and Knowledge to Improve the Quality of Teaching and Learning in Various Contexts and at Many Levels
In Your Field . . .	What are the unique value propositions of your initiative(s)? What are the educational or other motivations behind your initiative(s)?	If there was only one thing you could change about ways your initiative is organized, what would it be? Given your initiative's current standing and your goals, what more will it take to achieve them?	What kind of community do we need in order to build, leverage, and take advantage of open education and for what purposes? How can we encourage and support effective adoption and adaptation of open educational tools and resources to promote local pedagogical innovations?

	What are your critical and candid reflections on what you and others have done in the field so far (in terms of successes, obstacles, problems, and impact)?		Given their "open" nature, what do you see as key risks to the quality of open educational tools and resources? And, what are effective mechanisms to ensure their quality? How can we take advantage of open tools, resources, and knowledge to transform and improve teaching, learning, and educational systems?
Thinking broadly . . .	What is the potential for open education to change educational outcomes? Why? What are constructive ways of evaluating the effectiveness of open educational assets in teaching and learning?	How can we make open education sustainable? How can we make open education scalable? Why is interoperability and standardization of format critical? What are major challenges?	What have you learned from others' successes and challenges (within your field and across fields)? How could these fields and initiatives collaborate and intersect to achieve greater goals?

Appendix B: Select Indicators of Transformation, Significant Risk and Challenges, and Synergy from the Open Education Summit

1. Indicators of Transformation
• Virtual "meta" universities created which offers access to cross-linked educational resources.
• Curriculum approval processes include criteria about re-use/adaptation of the most appropriate resources and expertise from other teachers and learners
• Students keep the record of their own learning that has been validated in a variety of ways by a variety of educators.
• Greatly expanded and accepted pathways to learning anything and everything
• 100% of students finish college who enter college.
• Contribution to research on teaching of their subject is necessary criterion for promotion to full professor in top universities.

2. Indicators of Significant Risk/Challenges
• Lack of meaningful methods of assessing and validating what someone has learned.
• Failure to integrate open education initiatives into other institutional approaches to enhance faculty development.
• Reluctance to participate in open education because of financial, sustainability, and preservation concerns.
• Less coherence in many individuals' education through decreased guidance, feedback, structure, warranting of choices.
• The cultural communities that surround causes are fractured and not replaced leaves a growing anomaly associated with participation in the learning process.

3. Indicators of Synergy
• Partnering across institutions or systems to offer subscription based education.
• Wider and more economical access to textbooks and other educational materials.
• More flexible means of pursuing teaching and learning goals.
• Productivity of educational organizations increases while redundant work is reduced and energy shifted to more creative work with learning and teaching.
• Funding for teaching innovation is dependent upon re-use of existing teaching innovations as in the research domain.

Section I

Open Educational Technology

1   Section Introduction

Open Educational Technology: Tempered Aspirations

Owen McGrath

The chapters in this section grew out of initial proposals and a culminating day-long meeting at which participants gathered to discuss issues of openness in educational technology, resources, and scholarship. These authors have led higher education projects, initiatives, or organizations involved in aspects of design, development, adoption, policy making, standards setting, or evaluation of open technologies used in higher education teaching and learning settings. For them, the term "open educational technology" has broad meaning that extends well beyond any lowest-common-denominator definition such as "open source software for education." While the terminology may be new, the sharing and cooperation it denotes are not. More novel, perhaps, is the broader scale of organization, development, and adoption attempted in these projects.

Across the variety of perspectives on open educational technology represented, these authors are all concerned with promoting and sustaining openly distributable information technologies that hold potential for improving and extending the reach of higher education. Their shared aspirations for this work go far beyond using technology to support the status quo. Along with design and adoption of open technologies in these projects are also open approaches to teaching and learning that look for cultural barriers to tear down and traditional instructional arrangements to reconfigure. The projects described here offer views of teaching and learning that are about much more than economical transmission of information on the Internet. The technologies discussed serve educational initiatives whose goals and scope of inquiry are not solely concerned with spreading more knowledge. Instead, broadened notions of teaching and learning underlie these technology initiatives—some explicit, most implicit—that see, for instance, the learning situation of university-level students as being about the communities and activities in which they participate.

Major Issues/Questions

At the meeting that led to this book, the authors in this section agreed that initiatives such as theirs would not catch on widely if they could not show results. White papers and manifestos alone will not sustain an open education movement. But how to study and evaluate such projects? Here these authors were quick to agree that conventional approaches are often inadequate. Approaches using cost-benefit analyses and benchmark comparisons of impact, though admirable and sensible, often cannot tell the full story. Some of these projects, for instance, involve an impressive variety in implementation across sites, with the focus adjusted to local activity and communities of learners. In such cases, evaluation might have to look like rigorous descriptions concerned with learning as a local, socially constructed amalgam of shared meaning and community activity.

While emphasizing design and evaluation, these authors also identify institutional and cultural barriers to the advancement of open education. Especially in this first section of the book, there is an awareness of not only external barriers but also internal challenges to the processes of creating open educational technology. Several of these chapters point to issues posed by the scale and organizational processes involved in creating, maintaining, and extending open source technology. Observers of the open source software phenomena in general tend to agree on the importance of analyzing the organizational processes involved—not just the code produced. The same holds true in these chapters about open educational technologies, as we'll see.

In offering a brief description of the chapters, I will point out some of the ways they converge around the issues of design and evaluation, and also offer some background context for certain technological and organizational issues raised by the authors. Whether considering design, development, or implementation, the authors of these chapters share a focus on the problem of scale: the organizational and process challenges common to large-scale, cross-institutional open education technology projects.

In reading the chapters, a few fundamental questions to keep in mind include:

1) How should open educational technology be built, extended, and maintained in the large cross-institutional and international efforts?

2) How can the teaching and learning activities supported by the technology be evaluated in an open way?

3) How do the perspectives of teachers and learners inform these projects?

A Principled Open Design

David Kahle (2008) provides some answers to the first two questions by setting forth design considerations for those who would build and extend open educational technologies. Based on his experience developing the Visual Understanding Environment (VUE) at Tufts, Kahle describes principles to consider when building or extending open education technologies. As Kahle points out, these guidelines are very general. In thinking through specific implications of Kahle's principles, we can appreciate how they point us to key areas where conventional design approaches need to be adapted in order to work for open educational technology.

The emphasis on ownership, which Kahle defines in terms of extendibility, entails one such breakaway from conventional software design approaches. Where open source applications are being developed, extended, and owned by large international consortia of institutions, new questions arise as to who the users and stakeholders are, how to gain their input in the design process, and how to balance local and community needs when they diverge. The design and development process becomes especially challenging when determining and reconciling the needs of one institution's users with those of the wider community. Also, the teachers and students who would use the technology are often not readily at hand. Instead, ideas, requirements, feature requests, bug reports, etcetera, often only find their way into the development process after percolating up from within remote member institutions. While the conventional approach to the requirements process has been to interact with users and stakeholders in the information-gathering phase, a far-flung community like VUE's user base makes such direct interaction challenging or even impossible.

The temptation, then, is to rely heavily on one's access to users at the local institution. In the case of VUE, as Kahle mentions, such reliance would have led to a tool shaped to meet the specific needs of one institution at the expense of the needs of the wider community. Instead, Kahle's principled approach entailed developing VUE for interoperability with the OKI (Open Knowledge Initiative) digital library connections, for flexibility in how categories are added, and for customizability for interface layout. All are examples of generalized features for which more parochial design alternatives would have met one institution's needs while rendering the tool unserviceable for many others.

Opening Up Institutional Connections

Kahle's advocacy of design principles such as accessibility and ownership resonates in Stuart Lee's (2008) discussion of Oxford University's decision to adopt Bodington, an open source learning management system originally developed by Leeds University. Of the various open educational technologies mentioned in this section, one of the more recognizable is the learning management system. Across the many commercial and open source choices, these systems encompass a fairly similar suite of tools integrated into one package with a simple if familiar role hierarchy of instructor, teaching assistant, and student.

It is particularly this role hierarchy that troubles Lee, but his critique of role-based control structures goes beyond merely pointing out a mismatch with contemporary teaching and learning arrangements within Oxford. Adopting a hierarchy in which roles are organized primarily around the concept of instructor-led courses would also close many gates to the outside world, he argues. In an era in which institutional, national, and international initiatives herald technological opportunities to open up education on a whole new scale, something as seemingly minor as a role-based authorization system could preempt new possibilities for access.

Bodington imposes few limits. Rather than pre-assigned roles for users, it allows for hierarchies, groups, and access control to be added to individual sites as needed. Users do not have roles. Instead, the groups they join have access permissions assigned for resources, thereby accommodating a flexible, multi-way dissemination of materials such as files and documents. With arrangements spanning across the teaching and learning continuum from personal spaces to whole "societies," most of Bodington's educational resources remain open to viewing by anyone on the Internet.

Lee's focus on overcoming potential sequestration and barriers, we see, applies not just to students but also to teachers. In the pilot study described at the end of the chapter, literature lecturers were surveyed about their attitudes on sharing lecture notes, slides, and reading lists. From the brief description of the survey responses, one gains a different conceptual angle—quite different from official accounts offered by institutional or national initiatives—on the *sense* of the lecturers' movement within their communities of teaching. The lecturers' candid perspectives reveal perceptions of conflict and autonomy that are important to hear in discussions of open education. Bodington's technical affordances for sharing teaching materials within and across institutions may open up possibilities for supporting this less-visible community of teaching—a topic relevant to the third section of this book. But the example also gives a strong hint that group interests and perspectives need careful accounting if open education initiatives are to generate change in the organizational lives of these institutions.

Tools, Tasks, and Time

Where Stuart Lee describes the propping open of electronic gates at Oxford, Phil Long and Steve Ehrmann (2008) recount a story of technological openings attempted within another privileged realm: undergraduate engineering education at MIT. To appreciate the iLabs project, it's useful to notice from the start that a hoped-for goal was to let students "try out the identity of being a professional." This conception of learning as identity-building guided the project in ways that might urge us to consider which theoretical perspectives on learning can provide a full account of these lab activities coordinated around research equipment. The chapter also invites us to reconsider the taken-for-granted "chalk and talk" arrangements so familiar in traditional higher education math and science settings. In iLabs, instruments and equipment—

though big and expensive resources used by researchers—are made available to students for extended periods of time. Since instrument time is costly and demand for research access a priority, there might have been little reason or incentive for giving access to undergraduates without the clever economizing made possible by the Web services broker. As the project matured, iLabs activities involved new participation structures and access to partly structured, open-ended inquiry for students. When connected to electronic laboratory tools, the suite of iLabs programs enabled students to encounter problems similar to those typically encountered by expert researchers.

According to the evaluation report conducted by the TLT Group (referenced in the chapter), the analyses were often of the kind researchers typically grapple with: Things just don't behave as one would expect. Framed in terms of whether access to the tools enabled students to experience authentic engineering practice, the initial phase of iLabs might be classified as offering simply some changes in the what and how, such as the instrumental conditions and handling aspects of the students' lab activities. Merely giving the students access to these instruments did not represent much of an overall change in their access to joint participation in real laboratory activity, as the disappointing results of the early pendulum labs would seem to confirm.

In fact, a variety of lab procedures were attempted. A tacit model of learning as joint participation seems to have evolved during this project. Assessing the students' results in these labs was no longer to be considered a separate and final phase. Opportunities for teachers and students to participate together in redesigning and refining the lab experiments would seem to constitute a new kind of activity system, especially where taking on the improvements together may have offered students a new perspective on their instructors' understandings of how to practice science.

Evaluating Open Educational Technology

The kind of detailed retrospective evaluation seen in the iLabs project is exemplary in both depth and methodology. Ed Walker (2008) yearns for a day when open technology projects rise or fall based on this kind of evaluation. For open education technology to succeed, argues Walker, initiatives cannot be about just making more source code open, but must also concern opening up the evidence of learning progress in the activities the software supports.

A cynic might ask why open educational technology should be held to such lofty standards when for so many years equivalent commercial systems have seemingly not. Though somewhat true, the cynic's complaint misses more subtle implications in Walker's entreaty. Walker's chapter touches on areas where open educational technology initiatives need extra care: especially around issues of data collection, or "tactical gathering of data" as he calls it. Here lurks a potential problem in many open technology projects due in part to the way these large-scale, cross-institutional open source development projects are often organized. Many open educational technology projects risk falling short in providing functionality for capturing and monitoring user activity—information that is key to Walker's metric and method components.

A corollary evaluation problem touched on in Walker's chapter deserves consideration here. As if all the data-gathering issues were not enough, evaluation of technology innovation in higher education has always faced two other lethal foes: span and scope. Unlike areas of educational research where longitudinal studies are feasible, technology-related evaluation efforts often suffer from acutely small time spans within which to deliver results that will be deemed relevant. Fast development cycles and short adoption curves make a mockery of many well-intentioned technology investigations. Even when attaining scientific rigor and careful deliberation, investigators deliver their results often to find that the particular technologies under study have already become widely adopted or supplanted by something new.

Pursuing a line of inquiry that involves asking what general "effects" a technology has on students' learning turns out not to be fruitful. A major reason involves the often wildly dramatic differences in study findings across settings. Some researchers will conclude that a given technology has a significant positive effect on learning; others quickly follow with a conclusion exactly opposite. And in between these two shores usually flows a river of studies exhibiting what is known as the "no significant difference" phenomenon. As one seasoned evaluator observed, what vexes evaluation efforts usually turns out to be not the technology being studied, but the questions being asked. The kinds of evaluations that do end up making a useful difference are rarely about universal impacts, but often are about how different adaptations of a technology idea might work in different ways across settings (Ehrmann, 1998).

Visions of a New Learning Ecology

Counterpoised to Walker's entreaty for rigorous evaluation based on careful assessment is the chapter by Batson, Paharia, and Kumar (2008), who proclaim that the advancement of open education is, if not inevitable, so compelling that what is needed now is not more evidence but raised awareness of the "enablers" that can help overcome key remaining institutional "barriers" to progress. Open educational technology's distinguishing features cluster around aspects of visibility, social interaction, shared meaning-making, and unfettered access to resources. Educational activities made possible in open educational environments are characterized by the opportunities for collaborative participation and creative exchange. Freed technologically from resource scarcity around which higher educational institutions have traditionally organized, according to Batson, Paharia, and Kumar, the new era of information abundance requires transformed approaches to teaching and learning.

For Batson, Paharia, and Kumar, a key conceptual shift necessary in realizing the possibilities of open educational technologies is to see how they restore the "social" character of learning that has so often been suppressed in the past. The chapter traces the beginning of this restoration back to the rise decades ago of the ability to link students by networked computers. Those early conversations and dialogues over networks, the authors point out, offered a variety of new communicative situations that fell in between speaking and writing—a kind of public "persistent conversation" made possible by a communication medium not readily available in traditional composition classrooms (Bruce, Peyton, and Batson, 1993). As simple as the technology appears to us today, the kinds of visible conversations made possible by these early real-time conferencing programs led to some of the first educational experimentation with open arrangements and collaborative technologies that are commonplace today.

Going further, Batson, Paharia, and Kumar point to another new area of abundance: increased technological connectedness outside the classroom. From these authors' open learning perspective, paying attention to students' extracurricular digital practices is not simply about spanning a generation gap. It's about leaving behind many traditional teaching arrangements in favor of something better. Barriers to teaching and learning innovation can be seen in the traditional assumptions that students must operate within solitary instructional performances. In other parts of their lives, students participate in networks that promote "remix," such as imitation, sharing, and collaboration. That issues of authorship and ownership are organized and handled so differently in those many other online settings creates a provocative challenge to conventional institutional wisdom, the authors suggest.

Unbound Books vs. Unbound People

This oscillating interest—shifting from how students participate in activities to how pedagogically to structure activities—emerges as a key analytical issue for the authors in this section, as they consider how to promote open educational technologies (and plan, design, build, and adopt the information technologies that will support them). Another dimension of the relational character of learning comes into relief in Clifford Lynch's (2008) critical analysis of the popular proposition about open education: a sort of universal education for all made possible by connecting more and more information resources with more and more people. The views offered in Lee's, Long and Ehrmann's, and Kumar's chapters—of learning being characteristic of a person's participation in ongoing activity—are brought further into relief by Lynch's argument that to equate access to information resources and access to education is to miss the fundamentally social character of education.

Echoing the previous chapter's message that it would be premature to start closing down traditional institutions of higher education just yet, Lynch's chapter reminds us that teaching and learning are not simply about the transmission of information and acquisition of knowledge. His chapter makes this point in several ways: by emphasizing the social nature of education and by warning against a superficial notion of what "social" entails, especially in the context of digital libraries. This chapter offsets simplistic views of networked information technology as an irresistible change agent in education. Even careful analyses of emerging decentralized social production offer expansive views on the potential transformation of economic and political relations but tend to focus solely on higher education's role in publishing (Benkler, 2006). As Lynch points out, well-intended plans to expand the reach of university education often overestimate the value of open Internet technologies in supporting "communities" around resources such as digital libraries. While Lynch speculates on how communities might be successfully organized around content-based practice, he also perceives profound changes in education that would need to attend the advent of truly open higher education online.

As with the other chapters in this book, Lynch's arguments point to the need for more critical understanding of how digital content actually gets taken up and used by people (Brown and Duguid, 2000). What should also be clear by now is that Lynch's argument is not a call for evaluative studies to measure the impact or general learning outcomes brought about by digital libraries. Thankfully, the literature on educational uses of digital library resources is not strongly characterized by a concern with identifying and measuring general effects produced by the technology. Any such attempt would confront even greater obstacles than those of other open educational technology realms: not only the difficulty of interpreting across a variety of research designs but also an endless variation in the technologies used.

Productive Consumption

Where other authors write from their particular positions on the open learning stage, Christopher Mackie (2008) offers insights from his perspective behind the scenes as a grant officer for the Mellon Foundation, a major funder of open educational initiatives. Like the others, Mackie wants to see profound change in the traditional institutional culture of higher education. Obviously not willing to settle for piecemeal engineering of teaching and learning settings, he wants wholesale changes in the way digital technologies and media are produced and consumed in higher education. His alternative and much more ambitious approach to improvement entails a sort of new political economy of open learning.

In Mackie's view, the culture of universities needs to change fundamentally to allow for the kinds of open technology development and resource sharing described by authors in this book.

While the pathways to such change might not be clear, the outcomes of its progress are easier to imagine, as Mackie considers what the changed nature of institutional engagement with making and sharing open educational opportunities could look like. The shift in the locus of software development away from proprietary commercial companies and into loosely organized consortia of higher education institutions, as Mackie sees it, has led to noticeably different processes and results in the production of community source software. Indeed, most of the software projects featured in this book are more like cathedrals than bazaars, to use Eric Raymond's metaphor (1999). Unlike the larger open source movement described by Weber, programming here is carried out predominantly by paid staff who work within fairly traditional organizational structures (2004). Behind the community source projects are evolving organizations still experimenting with management structures that might allow them to better coordinate distributed software development.

However, as Mackie points out, many of the same simplicity principles—loose coupling, lightweight data standards, shared code repositories—that make community source projects successful do not apply conveniently when it comes to making and sharing open educational content. How best to cultivate and sustain the production and consumption of educational resources on a broad scale has become a major focus of open education advocates, as the chapters in the second section of the book reveal.

Implications

My final purpose in this overview is to suggest some criteria for choosing among theoretical traditions that might help in allowing us to account for the range of design and evaluation issues raised in these chapters. To end by prescribing one particular theory of teaching and learning would, it seems, be contrary to this book's general theme of openness. So I offer at least two.

In reading these chapters, it is worthwhile to notice how these projects question conventional notions about learning and instruction. From a comparative point of view, learning to become an engineer or a writer of compositions is not considered here simply as being an effect of, response to, or outcome of instruction per se—whether in a lab, classroom, or online. In these chapters, the units of analysis for teaching and learning extend well beyond instruction of individual students. Instead, the institutional organization of teachers and students coordinated around technology-mediated activity in communities seems to be the preferred norm here.

Two allied viewpoints, social practice theory (Lave and Wenger, 1991) and cultural historical activity theory (Cole, 1996), offer approaches to describing and accounting for many of the interesting observations and questions found in these chapters. By treating teaching and learning as sociocultural processes, both theoretical positions take an interest in learning as being about changing participation in socially situated practices and activities. Being able to account for how and why it is that some formal educational situations can be organized in ways that, oddly enough, appear at times even to militate against learning is another strength of both viewpoints. Both also offer interesting ways of talking about key observations made in several of these chapters: the prevalence of conflict, problems of access and sequestration, and the formation of learners' identities (Lave, 1996). And as many chapters in this book indicate, overcoming institutional and cultural barriers requires much more than technology solutions; it requires an approach to understanding how barriers get socially organized in the first place (Goldman, Chaiklin, and McDermott, 1994).

Our choice of theories to use for the design, study, and evaluation of open education will, as always, make available certain kinds of questions for the asking and certain stories for the telling (Shulman, 2007). For the authors in this section and the book as a whole, the narratives worth telling often unfold from variations on questions like "Who is doing what?" instead of simply "Who knows what?" As raised in several chapters, questions about the long-term trajectory of learners and of the production of their identities open up a line of inquiry that is central to social practice theory and cultural historical activity, as well. And where several chapters turn a critical focus on traditions of resource scarcity— educational haves and have-nots—both theoretical perspectives offer ways of examining institutional policies and arrangements, especially the extent to which they limit access. Finally, both perspectives see learning as an inseparable feature of the shared understandings that people generate together when engaged in culturally meaningful practices—technology-mediated or otherwise.

References

Batson, T., Paharia, N., and Kumar, M. S. V. (2008). A Harvest Too Large?: A Framework for Educational Abundance. In T. Iiyoshi and M. S. V. Kumar (Eds.), *Opening Up Education: The Collective Advancement of Education through Open Technology, Open Content, and Open Knowledge*, pp. 89–103. Cambridge, MA: MIT Press.

Benkler, Y. (2006). *The Wealth of Networks: How Social Production Transforms Markets and Freedom*. New Haven, CT: Yale University Press.

Brown, J. S., and Duguid, P. (2000). *The Social Life of Information*. Boston: Harvard Business School Press.

Bruce, B., Peyton, J. K., and Batson, T. (Eds.). (1993). *Network-Based Classrooms*. New York: Cambridge University Press.

Cole, M. (1996). *Cultural Psychology: A Once and Future Discipline*. Cambridge, MA: Harvard University Press.

Erhmann, S. (1998). What outcomes assessment misses. Presented at the 1998 AAHE Assessment Conference in Cincinnati, OH. Retrieved July 21, 2007, from http://www.tltgroup.org/programs/outcomes.html

Goldman, S., Chaiklin, S., and McDermott, R. (1994). Crossing borders electronically: Mentoring students via e-mail. In G. Spindler and L. Spindler (Eds.), *Pathways to Cultural Awareness: Cultural Therapy with Teachers and Students* (pp. 247–283). Thousand Oaks, CA: Corwin Press.

Kahle, D. (2008). Designing Open Education Technology. In T. Iiyoshi and M. S. V. Kumar (Eds.), *Opening Up Education: The Collective Advancement of Education through Open Technology, Open Content, and Open Knowledge*, pp. 27–45. Cambridge, MA: MIT Press.

Lave, J. (1996). Teaching, as learning, in practice. *Mind, Culture, and Activity*, 3(3), 149–164.

Lave, J., and Wenger, E. (1991). *Situated Learning: Legitimate Peripheral Participation*. Cambridge, UK: Cambridge University Press.

Lee, S. D. (2008). The Gates are Shut: Technical and Cultural Barriers to Open Education. In T. Iiyoshi and M. S. V. Kumar (Eds.), *Opening Up Education: The Collective Advancement of Education through Open Technology, Open Content, and Open Knowledge*, pp. 47–59. Cambridge, MA: MIT Press.

Long, P. D., and Ehrmann, S. C. (2008). Does an Open Source Strategy Matter?: Lessons Learned from the iLabs Project. In T. Iiyoshi and M. S. V. Kumar (Eds.), *Opening Up Education: The Collective Advancement of Education through*

Open Technology, Open Content, and Open Knowledge, pp. 61–75. Cambridge, MA: MIT Press.

Lynch, C. (2008). Digital Libraries, Learning Communities and Open Education. In T. Iiyoshi and M. S. V. Kumar (Eds.), *Opening Up Education: The Collective Advancement of Education through Open Technology, Open Content, and Open Knowledge*, pp. 105–118. Cambridge, MA: MIT Press.

Mackie, C. J. (2008). Open Source in Open Education: Promises and Challenges. In T. Iiyoshi and M. S. V. Kumar (Eds.), *Opening Up Education: The Collective Advancement of Education through Open Technology, Open Content, and Open Knowledge*, pp. 119–131. Cambridge, MA: MIT Press.

Raymond, E. (1999). The cathedral and the bazaar. *First Monday*, 3(3). Retrieved July 21, 2007, from http://www.firstmonday.org/issues/issue3_3/raymond/

Shulman, L. S. (2007, January/February). Counting and recounting: Assessment and the quest for accountability. *Change*, 39(1), 20–25.

Walker, E. (2008). Evaluating the Results of Open Education. In T. Iiyoshi and M. S. V. Kumar (Eds.), *Opening Up Education: The Collective Advancement of Education through Open Technology, Open Content, and Open Knowledge*, pp. 77–88. Cambridge, MA: MIT Press.

Weber, S. (2004). *The Success of Open Source*. Cambridge, MA: Harvard University Press.

2

Designing Open Educational Technology

David Kahle

A common observation made by those skeptical of the open educational technology movement is, "you get what you pay for." The implication is that products developed without the benefit of sustained commercial investment, and lacking the control structures and accountability identified with centralized, for-profit incentives, will be certain to disappoint.

While investment and organizational practice certainly have an impact on product outcomes, assessing a technology's value in terms of finance and governance models alone fails to recognize another, perhaps more accurate, predictor of open technology success—design. Rather than "you get what you pay for," the sentiment "you get what you design for" may be a better characterization of open educational technology's potential to positively affect teaching and learning. Simply put, design matters. Designers have a greater influence on outcomes to a much greater extent than is often recognized.

Design is a highly influential, value-laden and reflective practice which, within our context, must mirror, accommodate, and reconcile the values and assumptions intrinsic to open education. A number of values, or principles, often associated with open education may serve as a foundation for open technology design theory and practice. These principles include access, agency, ownership, participation and experience. Highlighting the core values of open technology and defining these as principles of design practice is an important first step toward accelerating the production and ultimately the adoption of innovative educational software that honors the complex needs and interests of educators and learners alike.

The Primacy of Design

In understanding the role of the designer in open educational technology development, it is helpful to begin with an inclusive rather than restrictive notion of design and to recognize how directly theories and ideas regarding design influence practice. Starting with an expansive, holistic approach to this topic—the idea of design at large and the general relationship among design values, theory and practice—encourages us to appreciate design as both a product and process that has a residual effect on educational environments, resources, and the activities they support.

Design as Practice and Problem Solving

Design can be seen as pragmatic, rooted in problem solving, reflective, and consequential. Often the impetus and motivation for design springs from problems, conundrums, and challenges. These may be as grand a challenge as providing universal access to education or more personally focused, such as integrating an open educational technology into one's own curriculum. When we are deliberate in our approach to articulating a solution to a problem which faces us, we actively engage in the process of design and we become, in a very real sense, designers.

And the design of effective educational technologies is something we can pursue, control, and take responsibility for. It is our approach to design, however, our methods of identifying and addressing the issues surrounding open educational technology that determines a design's effectiveness, relevance, and elegance.

Design Theory and Values

Approaching technology design as a common activity rooted in problem solving is to see the design process and its outcome as a means to an end. It is these "ends" that consciously, and at times unconsciously, inform our approach to problem solving and our practice of design. Goals and values shape the design theories that, in turn, guide our approach to technology development. Therefore, understanding design within the context of open educational technology development necessarily requires an awareness of the roles and origins of those design theories that inform our practice. Where such a theory is lacking, as I believe is the case with open technology development, there is a need to make explicit a set of principles, goals or values that can serve as the basis for a useful design theory.

The role of design theory is to introduce frameworks for prioritizing and analyzing design problems. The twentieth-century Swiss architect Le Corbusier, speaking in reference to his Modulor system of proportions, captures the general purpose of design: "Architects everywhere have recognized in it, not a mystique, but a tool which may be put in the hands of creators of form, with the simple, aim . . . of 'making the bad difficult and the good easy'" (Le Corbusier, 1966, p. 5). Creators of open educational software are also in need of a tool, a theory of design, to guide their practice in this important area. It must, however, be based upon suitable principles.

Design Theory and Open Education

Open education brings with it its own set of goals, values, and aspirations that transcend any specific project or functional quality of technology. Open education, open content, and open source as a collective idea is often discussed as a means to liberation (Unsworth, 2004), empowerment, and democratization (Vest, 2006). Equal access to current knowledge and a standing invitation to everyone to participate in advancing new ideas are common themes of the open education movement. How can any design theory informed by such a grand set of values be, at the same time, of any practical use to developers of open education technology?

Adaptable Design Principles

Perhaps the answer to this question lies within the idea of open education itself. Rather than attempting to derive a narrowly prescriptive theory of design for all open educational technology projects, articulating a small set of adaptable design principles may prove more practical. A design theory that could flexibly co-exist alongside multiple approaches to educational technology design, one that does not attempt to subsume or oversimplify the complex practice of educational software development would stand a better chance of adoption and, in turn, be more influential.

Those creating educational software often draw upon multiple descriptive and prescriptive theories, depending upon their specific set of instructional or learning objectives (Reigeluth, 1999). These may include cognitive theories that describe how humans process information, instructional design theories that offer guidance on the necessary components of a learning activity, or visual design theory that guides interface development. A design theory for open educational technology is intended to supplement these important design considerations.

This new design theory would raise an additional set of questions (problems) based on the values of open education that are best addressed (resolved) during the design process. Again, rather than advocate for a "one best theory" for educational technology, the goal is to broaden existing design and development practices through translating some key values of open education into pragmatic design principles. Toward this end, I propose five principles of design that I believe to be critical to the success of open educational technology. While not exclusive to open technology design, these qualities reflect some of open education's highest values:

1. Design for access.
2. Design for agency.
3. Design for ownership.
4. Design for participation.
5. Design for experience.

Although principles alone do not produce useful and open educational technologies, the ideas associated with this basic set of design principles can serve as a guide to technology creators.

Open Technology Design Principles and VUE

The Visual Understanding Environment (VUE) project currently underway at Tufts University serves as a case study to illustrate the benefits and challenges of adopting these design principles for open educational technology.

VUE is an open source application designed to facilitate thinking, teaching, and learning with digital resources. An important goal and challenge of the project is to develop an uncomplicated, highly flexible and adaptable toolset for structuring information in support of the widest range of scholarly interests and activities.

VUE provides users with a flexible, visual interface for locating, annotating and establishing relationships among local and networked information, including Web resources. VUE has been described as concept mapping meets digital libraries and figure 2.1 supports this characterization.

While the functionality of VUE 1.5 reflects the open technology design framework presented earlier, some of the features described below are currently being implemented as part of the VUE 2.0 scheduled for release in fall 2007.

Guiding the VUE project is a strong desire to create tools that make working and thinking with digital resources intuitive, instructive, and enjoyable. A common educational challenge facing teachers and students is that well established approaches to organizing and managing print material in support of scholarly activities are either cumbersome or impossible to implement when working with digital content (Sellen and Harper, 2002). We regularly rely on margin annotations, Post-it notes,

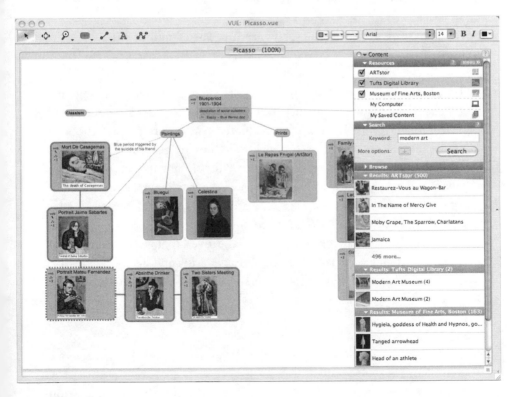

Figure 2.1

and even carefully arranged stacks of papers as a means of processing and integrating new material and ideas into our work. While today we have many powerful applications for locating vast amounts of digital information, we lack effective tools for selecting, structuring, personalizing, and making sense of the digital resources available to us.

In addition, many of our most popular learning management systems accommodate only highly generalized educational contexts where the primary design goal is the efficient distribution of content rather than student engagement with and exploration of new material. Such technologies limit how content is organized around complex concepts, how information is presented, and the degree to which students may interact with instructional material. Restricting access to information, limiting engagement and participation, and providing learners and instructors with little control over the learning activity, materials, or processes creates a demotivating experience. It is this condition that the open technology design framework attempts to address.

Designing for Access, Agency, Ownership, Participation, and Experience

This basic theory of design provides a beginning framework against which the myriad design questions that occur as part of design and development processes may be evaluated and addressed in an open manner. The intent of this framework is not to be prescriptive or to provide specific guidelines for software development, but to increase awareness of a few key ideas that greatly influence the openness, flexibility, and value of technology for education. Though each design quality is treated separately below to elaborate its specific merits, in practice these principles are highly interrelated and overlapping. They are influenced by existing approaches to technology design and, to a large degree, may be viewed simply as different perspectives on a common set of open technology design values.

Design for Access
While each of the design principles presented within this framework deals in one way or another with access, highlighting access as a primary design consideration for open education speaks directly to the question

of "open for whom?" Approaching access from the perspective of open education compels us to think more holistically about potential barriers to obtaining, operating, and thinking effectively with technology and information than is often the case with strictly open-source technology initiatives.

Traditionally, the idea of access as it relates to open technology has been cast in terms of ubiquity and affordability. Software or content that is priced beyond the reach of educators and learners or which requires a sophisticated technical infrastructure available only to a few can hardly be considered open. However, simply because a resource is free or readily available does not mean it is accessible and useful to individuals.

Design for access in this context not only enables the acquisition of open resources but effective thinking, learning, and doing with them. Beyond simply addressing technical and economic obstacles to technology adoption, design for access challenges us to recognize, accommodate, and design with individual cognitive and physical differences in mind. Existing design theories such as *universal design* and its latter extension to education, *universal design for learning*, address these dimensions of accessibility and offer useful guidance to designers and developers of open educational technology. A goal of universal design (UD) as articulated by Mace (2006) is to design "products and environments to be usable by all people, to the greatest extent possible, without the need for adaptation or specialized design." Qualities such as "flexible in use," "equitable use," "simple and intuitive," and "tolerance for error" are emphasized in universal design. In a similar spirit, universal design for learning (UDL) stresses access to learning over simple access to information by accommodating student differences in cognition.

Many educational software applications such as VUE are designed for general educational purposes and may not approach accessibility from a specific curricular objective. However, even open content and technology destined for integration into varied learning contexts can be designed for access. Standards such as those advanced by the W3C's Accessibility Guidelines Initiative and Section 508 of the U.S. Rehabilitation Act outline reasonable measures that can be taken to accommodate individual cognitive and physical differences. Applying such standards and leveraging the inherent flexibility of digital media to provide users with alternative ways of engaging with resources and of enabling integration with other assistive technologies defines open access in terms more meaningful to a diverse learner audience.

Through Flexibility, Access to Knowledge   In support of open access as defined above, VUE is designed to assist individuals in making information meaningful by supporting processes beyond simply locating or acquiring data. Perhaps most importantly and in direct support of individual differences, VUE does not assume how information will be organized, but rather offers teachers and learners the flexibility to structure content in any manner that suits their needs. This flexibility provides access to knowledge in at least two ways.

First, VUE supplies learners with a rich environment within which to establish, explore and reason about important relationships among ideas and information in their own terms and, second, at the same time, it captures this process in a form visually accessible to others. The design goal of making information visible and accessible to diverse learners participating in a range of educational contexts required a design approach that abstracted and simplified the manner in which digital content—whether local files, Web-based resources, text, or multimedia—was represented and manipulated. Guided by this priority, concept-mapping conventions consisting of simple links and nodes were identified as a suitable foundation for VUE's graphical user interface to digital resources. By adopting a simple but flexible visual language for expressing complex relationships among ideas and information, VUE's value as a tool for thinking with and about digital content accommodates a variety of user communities.

One challenge to designing for access lies in reconciling the practical importance of appealing to general interests and cognitive similarities across populations with the desire to address individual differences. The design of VUE's feature set is meant, in part, to address this challenge and, to date, progress toward this goal is encouraging. VUE provides alternate methods of viewing and working with digital resources and tools for scaffolding the development and presentation of content maps.

For example, VUE directly supports visual thinkers through its rich graphical controls for expressing complex relationships among digital resources and, at the same time, supports the manipulation of this map content via editable hierarchical lists for those more comfortable working with text. Likewise, while many learners appreciate the freedom of a blank map canvas, others benefit from more structure. Educators may scaffold mapping activities using imported ontologies to guide the types of concepts and relationships used in exploring a topic. Maps constructed with such controlled vocabularies may then be analyzed computationally as another means of assessing similarities and differences among student understandings.

VUE's tools for interactive presentations also reflect a commitment to access to knowledge by addressing the difficulties people often experience when trying to integrate complex information. Noting the inherent limitations of common, linear presentation tools, Edward Tufte writes, "The slide serves up a small chunk of promptly vanishing information in a restless one-way sequence" (2003). Designing for access led the VUE team to development mechanisms by which people could focus in on a specific piece of information as part of the presentation while maintaining a sense of its place in context.

Design for Agency

While design for access focuses our attention on expanding access to technology across multiple dimensions, designing for agency highlights design's influential role in determining the degree of user action and control over these open educational resources. This focus on agency compels developers of open technologies to consider the broader social and political context within which a technology will likely be used and how design decisions ultimately impact that environment. Designing for agency anticipates technology's conditions for adoption, its flexibility, and its potential for adapting to local needs and requirements. Here, openness of technology is measured by the degree to which it empowers users to take action, making technology their own, rather than imposing its own foreign and inflexible requirements and constraints.

Those with even limited experience in deploying new technologies within an academic community are highly aware that the conditions for success extend well beyond the technical. The phenomenon of unintended consequences surrounding technology integration is partially a symptom of naïve design processes that view technology as neutral and fail to recognize the downstream sociopolitical consequences of technical design decisions.

As one example of the larger impact of technical design and choice, Langdon Winner cites the development of the mechanical tomato harvester in the 1940s. "To accommodate the rough motion of these harvesters in the field, agricultural researchers have bred new varieties of tomatoes that are hardier, sturdier, and less tasty than those previously grown." Winner continues by noting that the size and cost of the harvester favored highly centralized forms of agriculture and reshaped control, authority, and social relationships within California's agrarian communities (1986, p. 26).

Colleges and universities have implemented their own "tomato harvesters" with the best of intentions. The design and subsequent implementation of many campus-wide course management systems (CMS) impose their own hidden but consequential requirements that directly impact the nature of online education. These include the need for centralized administration and control over what and when new tools will be introduced, inflexible notions of the relationship among students and teachers, and a limited view of what a course is and how information should be organized. Failing to consider agency as a design criteria for open educational technology increases the likelihood that new educational tools may bring with them requirements at odds with the values and ideals of open education. They may unintentionally limit rather than expand options for a technology's deployment and use.

Designing flexible and adaptive technologies that minimize technical and organizational overhead and which place students and educators at the center of control harnesses technology's transformative potential for education. The value of simple and versatile tools is not lost on learning communities. Today, students and educators are eagerly adopting, adapting, and combining smaller online tools such as blogs, wikis, and instant messaging applications in support of teaching and learning scenarios not possible with larger monolithic systems. Likewise, the popular Google Maps application which offers only a limited set of features out of the box but which provides an open programming interface enabling extension and adaptation has inspired many innovative and educational mapping applications. Such design approaches, which assume that a large part of a technology's value lies in its capacity to be extended and combined with other applications, are worth emulating in open educational technology development. Design for agency encourages the development of smaller components and smart tools that clearly express what they do, rather that imposing how they should be used. Designing interoperable tools with personal agency in mind empowers individuals and institutions to build, adapt, and integrate custom educational solutions in a manner that best meets their needs.

Meeting Individual Needs   The VUE project approached the principle of agency by first suspending assumptions as to how scholars prefer to work with digital resources. While a number of use cases guided the application's development, VUE is ultimately designed as a small and flexible tool for individuals and in support of individual needs. There was no single use case or imagined educational context around which VUE was designed. The design process recognized that while the central challenge of selecting, structuring, and personalizing digital resources en route to understanding is common to many, its precise form or expression is highly dependent upon individual teaching and learning preferences, specific educational settings, and working contexts.

For this reason, VUE was designed as a general-purpose utility. Its many features and functions, which are quite useful within formal educational contexts, are equally helpful outside of the classroom and in support of informal learning needs. This flexibility is pervasive in VUE and results in considerable user control. Rather than implementing VUE as an interface to a single digital library, the application is resource agnostic, designed to accommodate an ever-increasing range of digital information sources. The guided mapping described above is also designed to accommodate individual interests. Based on common standards such as RDF Schema and OWL for defining ontologies and CSS for styling the appearance of map objects, it allows for unbounded support of domains and educational activities. Finally, VUE has been designed as a portable client application to be owned and managed by individuals that does not require extensive or coordinated technical infrastructure and support.

Design for Ownership

The ability to literally own a technology or collection of resources is almost a given with open source software and content. Various licensing agreements adopted by producers of open educational resources permit users to acquire and adapt source code and educational materials to their liking. Designing for ownership assumes a future of educational resources assembled in part from the earlier work of many designers and developers. This approach anticipates that any given product may become part of a future application or resource and, in so doing, will become transformed into something quite different.

This proposition is not always easy to accept for designers of educational resources who contribute significant time and energy toward developing new tools. An important role for open education initiatives is to establish practices that reward the original creators of material with proper acknowledgement and that cultivate a sharing, global community that blurs the line between producers and consumers of open resources. As the supply of high-quality open technologies and resources increases, it is likely that producers of new educational tools will also be the direct beneficiaries of earlier efforts.

Designing for ownership is also closely linked to fostering individual agency and participation and the ability to define a technology in one's own terms. People are far more motivated to invest in adopting or extending an educational resource if they share in its ownership and evolution. Designing for ownership speaks to the importance of locality in determining a technology's use and meaning (Nardi and O'Day, 1999, p. 54). The opportunity for a group or individual to make a technology personally meaningful is to own it. Co-ownership and shared responsibility for a resource's development, a characteristic of so many open technology initiatives, is advanced by the most flexible software architectures and licenses. However, even with such provisions in place, an ongoing challenge for many projects is to maintain this degree of open ownership once a community has been defined, empowered and institutionalized.

To Modify Is to Own   Ownership is often expressed through adaptation and modification. And as a modular and open source product, VUE lends itself to further refinement and extension by future developers. However, beyond making the code widely available, the VUE design team built a number of the application's core components around the Open Knowledge Initiative software standards. By adopting common technical standards, owners of VUE may more easily extend the application and integrate those resources and repositories most meaningful to specific domains, tasks, and educational activities. VUE's standards-based design enables educators and students to incorporate an increasing variety of digital repositories and resources as needed. Further, offering various options for exporting VUE content maps in open formats has fostered adaptation and integration into numerous information management workflows and external systems.

On the surface, designing for ownership requires little more than adopting truly open licensing agreements which encourage future use, adaptation, and open sharing. In support of this goal, VUE 2.0 is licensed under Educational Community License. However, designers can make ownership more meaningful to future adopters by allowing for the easy decomposition of resources and technologies to fit an individual's environment and to enable new derivative works. This may involve creating, exposing, and documenting function-specific components in the case of educational software or allowing educators to extract a sub-set of educational content from an online course.

Design for Participation

If the design of educational technology facilitates broad access and fosters personal agency and ownership, participation in adopting and evolving a new application is likely to occur. The forms of participation in open educational technology presented here refer both to community involvement in developing or extending an educational resource as well as pedagogical designs which recognize the values of an individual's engagement with the educational resource itself: active learning. Thus, essential to the success of open education projects from the perspective of participation is the establishment of representative communities capable of informing the design process, designs which encourage contributions, and an understanding of the importance of active participation in learning. The broader question raised by this value is how open is the technology to participation in its development and use.

Community is readily associated with open technology, and there are many examples of open source projects that benefited greatly from sustained, active communities. Participation in these communities, however, has largely consisted of those invested more in the technology's development than its use. Design and development processes that invite partnerships with intended audiences may lead to technologies that are highly accessible and oriented toward user action and control. Early experiences with *participatory design* involving the collaborative development of computer systems by managers, union workers, and technology designers provide models still relevant to today's open education initiatives. This design approach, originating in Scandinavia in response to broader social goals of democratizing the workplace, enlists intended users of a technology as active members of its design team (Ehn, 1993). Rather than simply identifying user likes and dislikes, such design practices take seriously user concerns and their existing environmental conditions.

More recently, an awareness of the degree to which social interactions among user communities influence technology development highlights the necessity of more inclusive design practices. Design practices that account for the social construction of technology by encouraging the participation of multiple user communities are emerging and inform open educational technology development (Gay and Hembrooke, 2004). Emphasizing inclusive design processes in no way minimizes the important role that purely technical choices play in enabling future participation over time. The benefits of open interoperability standards discussed earlier in regards to flexible technology integration apply to participation as well. Such standards permit external development communities to extend technologies to meet local needs and to advance the original product.

Another design consideration for those developing educational applications is provisions that encourage and support student participation and interaction—with each other and with educational resources. While not every tool used in support of the academic mission is directed toward learning, those that are will be more effective if grounded in educational practices that promote social and active learning (Bransford, Brown, and Cocking, 2000, p. 209).

Too often, however, many so-called open educational technologies are designed as unidirectional conduits for delivering more information faster, and therefore, fail to support the forms of student interaction, engagement, and reflection necessary to advance understanding. By seeking the involvement of students, teachers, and instructional designers in the open design process, designers of open educational technology may create truly innovative, highly participatory applications that advance teaching and learning. Taken together, encouraging broad participation in the design process and prioritizing designs that foster active learner participation enables the positive transformation of both the educational technologies and the educational communities that adopt them.

Collaborative Design for Wider Participation   The principles of design for participation have been a central part of the VUE development process. Concerning community involvement in VUE's design, over the course of the project faculty, students, instructional designers, and technologists have been invited to participate in design discussions and to review the application at various stages of development. Many of the features currently under development for VUE 2.0, including the presentation tools and ontology supported scaffolds, are in direct response to input from the academic community. The formal methods of soliciting participant input as part of VUE's design process are complemented by including additional menu options within the application to solicit feedback and to invite users to participate in online discussions. These options provide an easy mechanism for a broader audience of participants to contribute ideas and comments to the VUE project team.

Participation among technology developers has also been enabled by VUE's standards-based open architecture and flexible toolset. A number of organizations external to the VUE project team have adopted the Open Knowledge Initiative (OKI) standards as a means of making their digital content accessible through VUE and other OKI compatible software. To facilitate this activity, the VUE team, in collaboration with MIT's OKI project, established an online registry for developers to describe and post their digital repository modules. As a result, VUE users can query and install plug-ins to a variety of digital collections directly from within the application. Activity around these standards has been mutually beneficial, as VUE adopters gain access to a greater variety of digital resources, and content publishers offer their subscribers a flexible tool for viewing, structuring, and managing their educational material.

Supporting Active Learning   VUE is designed for participation from a student-centered, educational perspective as well. The tool's design encourages students to take an active, leading role in structuring, annotating, and manipulating digital content in support of their learning. Furthermore, these content maps are not digitally frozen, as are so many online resources. A VUE map created by an instructor to present key resources about a complex concept or topic may be downloaded and easily extended by students seeking to add their own resource nodes, links, and annotations. This form of active engagement with materials is critical to the learning process and assists students in personalizing and integrating new concepts and ideas. Designing for participation with learners in mind presents opportunities for VUE to move beyond simply making educational material accessible to providing information in a flexible format accompanied by tools that allow for further manipulation, extension, and refinement.

Design for Experience

Designing for user experience is usually the last consideration of many open educational technology projects. This is unfortunate, as a technology's look, feel, and the messages it conveys are as important to community adoption as is its depth of content and sophisticated functionality. Design for experience recognizes that all participants, particularly busy educators and students, quickly form opinions as to what resources are interesting, helpful, and worth their investment of time.

Design for experience is a form of human-centered design, an approach to technology with a long history. However, rather than focusing solely on the usability of a product, designers interested in the more affective qualities of their applications must also consider its appeal. "Does this tool attract attention? Is the experience of using the resource enjoyable and satisfying?" are questions that stem from designing for experience.

In *Emotional Design* (2004), Norman describes three styles of design that prompt or motivate user reactions to everyday tools. *Behavioral design* addresses the usability of a software application (Is the interface intuitive and effective?). *Visceral design* relates to an object's surface appeal (How does it look and feel? Is it eye catching, attractive or repulsive?). *Reflective design* addresses one's satisfaction with a tool and the self-image its use projects. Taken together, these three styles of design influence our emotional response to technologies and acceptance or rejection of them. Norman concludes that attractive things simply work better. Tools that engage us and are enjoyable to use induce qualities of mind favorable to creative thinking and problem solving.

Open educational resources and technology have long been high on substance and low on appeal. However, it is this affective dimension of a tool, its attraction, that when combined with thoughtful instructional content and design motivates learners, capturing their attention and engaging the mind. One need only observe the considerable draw of video games and online social networking and role-playing environments to understand the potential of technology to engage an audience. Designing for experience recognizes the instructional benefit of creating open technology and resources that are at once substantive and attractive, compelling and a pleasure to use.

An Appealing Experience   While VUE may not successfully compete for attention with today's most popular virtual gaming environments, great effort has been taken to design an attractive, appealing user interface (UI)—to design for experience. The VUE team dedicated considerable effort to reviewing the strengths and weaknesses of existing user interface models for managing and visualizing digital information.

Because available UI code libraries did not support the quality of user experience desired, additional resources were allocated to create custom interface components to accommodate VUE's specific requirements for user interaction. Attention was also dedicated to how maps look, feel, and function. What may appear to be small design decisions affecting only surface appeal actually serve to guide or scaffold clear communication and presentation of ideas using VUE. Such examples demonstrate the often hidden but nevertheless highly influential role of design in mediating educational activities, understanding, and experiences (Pea, 1991). Perhaps most importantly for the VUE project, the value of designing for experience was recognized early in the process and the role of designer was identified and established as an integral part of the development team. Positive user feedback regarding VUE's ease of use and clear presentation of information suggests that this extra effort was justified.

Advancing Education

The purpose of working toward a theory of design for open educational technology is not to prescribe but to guide development practices. Recognizing that design matters, that the values and goals of open education can be either hindered or advanced through design choices, is the primary motivation for establishing design principles. Those presented here—access, agency, ownership, participation, and experience—provide a basic but generative framework for evaluating various design options for open educational technology. While it is impractical for any one application to meet all possible considerations stemming from these principles, the Visual Understanding Environment provides an illustrative example of how attending to even a few conditions extending from these principles can have a positive impact on the development of educational software. Given the current enthusiasm for and investment in open content and open technology initiatives, now is the perfect time to develop design methods that will deliver educational resources consistent with open values.

References

Bransford, J., Brown, A. L., and Cocking, R. R. (Eds.). National Research Council (U.S.) Committee on Developments in the Science of Learning, and National Research Council (U.S.) Committee on Learning Research and Educational Practice. (2000). *How People Learn: Brain, Mind, Experience, and School* (Expanded ed.). Washington, DC: National Academy Press.

Csikszentmihalyi, M. (1991). Thoughts on education. In D. Dickinson (Ed.), *Creating the Future: Perspectives on Educational Change* (pp. 83–86). Aston Clinton: Accelerated Learning Systems.

Ehn, P. (1993). Scandinavian design: on participation and skill. In D. Schuler and A. Namioka (Eds.), *Participatory Design: Principles and Practices* (pp. 41–77). Hillsdale, NJ: Lawrence Erlbaum Associates.

Gay, G., and Hembrooke, H. (2004). *Activity-Centered Design: An Ecological Approach to Designing Smart Tools and Usable Systems*. Cambridge, MA: MIT Press.

Le Corbusier. (1966). *The Modulor: A Harmonious Measure to the Human Scale Universally Applicable to Architecture and Mechanics* (2nd ed.). Cambridge: Harvard University Press.

Mace, R. (2006). About universal design. Retrieved January 5, 2006, 2006, from http://www.design.ncsu.edu/cud/

Nardi, B. A., and O'Day, V. (1999). *Information Ecologies: Using Technology with Heart.* Cambridge, MA: MIT Press.

Norman, D. A. (2004). *Emotional Design: Why We Love (or Hate) Everyday Things.* New York: Basic Books.

Pea, R. D. (1993). Practices of distributed intelligence and designs for education. In G. Salomon (Ed.), *Distributed Cognitions: Psychological and Educational Considerations.* Cambridge: Cambridge University.

Pinch, T., and Bijker, W. (1984). The social construction of facts and artifacts: Or how the sociology of science and sociology of technology might benefit each other. *Social Studies of Science,* 14, 399–441.

Reigeluth, C. (1999). What is instructional-design theory and how is it changing? In C. Reigeluth (Ed.), *Instructional-Design Theories and Models: A New Paradigm of Instructional Theory.* Mahwah, NJ: Lawrence Erlbaum Associates.

Rose, D. H., and Meyer, A. (2002). *Teaching Every Student in the Digital Age: Universal Design for Learning.* Alexandria, VA.: Association for Supervision and Curriculum Development.

Sellen, A. J., and Harper, R. (2002). *The Myth of the Paperless Office.* Cambridge, MA: MIT Press.

Tufte, E. R. (2006). *The Cognitive Style of PowerPoint.* Cheshire, CT: Graphics Press.

Unsworth, J. (2004). The next wave: Liberation technology. *Chronicle of Higher Education,* 50(21).

United States General Services Administration (2007). Section 508: the road to accessibility. Retrieved January 5, 2007, from http://www.section508.gov/

Vest, C. (2006). Open content. *Educause Review,* 41(3).

Winner, L. (1986). *The Whale and the Reactor: A Search for Limits in an Age of High Technology.* Chicago: University of Chicago Press.

World Wide Web Consortium. Web Accessibility Initiative Home Page. Retrieved January 5, 2007, from http://www.w3.org/WAI/

3

The Gates Are Shut: Technical and Cultural Barriers to Open Education

Stuart D. Lee

In Thomas Hardy's *Jude the Obscure*, Jude Fawley dreams of overcoming the social and cultural barriers of the day by gaining a place at the University of Christminster (Oxford). Jude studies hard but does not enjoy the privileges of class. Despite his hard work, all his attempts to get a place at a college are rejected. In one letter, the Master of Biblioll College declares: "You will have a much better chance of success in life by remaining in your own sphere" (Hardy, 1998). Destroyed by the rejection, one night Jude drunkenly takes to the city: "At ten o'clock he came away, choosing a circuitous route homeward to pass the gates of the college whose head had just sent him the note. The gates were shut, and, by an impulse, he took from his pocket the lump of chalk which as a workman he usually carried there, and wrote along the wall: 'I HAVE UNDERSTANDING AS WELL AS YOU; I AM NOT INFERIOR TO YOU: YEA, WHO KNOWETH NOT SUCH THINGS AS THESE?'— Job xii. 3" (Hardy, 1998). Getting into higher education was a seemingly impossible task for those of a certain social class, despite their obvious ability.

Thankfully, over the hundred or so years since then, the barriers to entering university and education have been systematically removed. Education for all, matched by networks of schools, colleges, and universities has been a major political ambition of most developed countries. The UK, for example, saw early experiments in a different type of Open Education in the 1970s (Giaconia and Hedges, 1982; Holt, 1990; Huitt, 2001; Lessig, 2003; Mai, 1978; Rathbone, 1971). The recent target by the UK's Labour Government to reach a 50 percent participation rate by all school-leavers in higher education illustrates this.

As access and opportunities opened up, the next fortress to attack was that of the mono-disciplinary approach—the barriers this time were to be found within the institution. Traditional degrees focused on single subjects, and it proved extremely difficult to cross these boundaries. Yet this has changed over the years with the proliferation of joint honors, foundation degrees, and the rise of interdisciplinary degrees.

The rise of open education, the very subject of this book, seems like the next natural step in this progressive development. By harnessing the new technologies, we are in an unprecedented position to make educational material available to everyone at any time, regardless of social or national background.

Yet all is not well. As we have striven with reasonable success to achieve these goals, technical and political events have overtaken us. Separately these have contributed to an erecting of new barriers. If Hardy were here to update his novel, Jude would surf the Web, come across a university site, only to be prohibited from accessing its resources because he did not have a username or password. How did we get to such a situation? And more importantly, how can we reverse it?

The Technical Gates Are Shut

Technically, the clearest example of the closing down of education lies in the commercial learning management system (LMS, aka the "virtual learning environment" or VLE). The underlying model used by these systems causes concern. First, the user is usually defined as falling into one of three roles—(system) administrator, tutor, or student (or similar nomenclatures)—with the limitations of what one can do in the system defined by this role. These are rigidly observed: Once a student, always a student, and never a tutor be. For many people, this may not present a concern. However, if you wish to turn areas over to students so they can lead their learning, create their own learning experiences, or peer-review, it can be problematic. The systems are driven by the Student Record System (SRS) or some external identity management application that then populates the LMS. Understandably, these favour robustness and accuracy over flexibility, but above all simplicity—and a single role per user—is as simple as it comes. These are notorious for running into issues with the variant roles people play in a higher education institution.

This is then perpetuated by the LMS. Taking its feed from the SRS, the pigeonholing becomes established across all areas and functions of the system. Although some commercial systems now claim to accommodate multi-roles for users, this can only be said to be true if a user can choose or be given different access privileges at any point in the system. To simply say you can be both a student and tutor is not enough. Privileges do not map neatly to roles. For example, a "tutor" can wear many hats: teacher, mentor, examiner, administrator, etcetera. In one area tutors may be allowed to do whatever they want (their own area related to their course, for example), but in others it might be more secure to allow them only to read some material, such as exam results, rather than to have editing rights. This complexity is not the exception to the rule; consider these potential privileges:

• see the title of a resource
• view or download a resource
• upload a resource
• alter the information about an area
• post a message
• fill in a questionnaire
• analyze the results of a survey
• change access rights

Now consider the various roles people occupy in a university: lecturer, tutor, personal mentor, course designer, head of subject area, head of department, committee member, financial controller, research project manager, pro-vice chancellor, dean, graduate, teaching assistant, undergraduate, student project leader, student society head, etcetera. Mapping these with the previously listed privileges one might want in areas within the LMS effectively illustrates how complicated the concept of multi-roles truly is.

Additionally, although these systems may have originated from academic projects within universities, many are now multi-million dollar international companies. Higher education is a large part of their market, but that is not the sole, or necessarily prime, driving force. One can also see that commercial online training is the main customer base being targeted—bringing training courses and modules to the workplace (including the military). Here the problems arise. Online training profits from courses where access is controlled and where access is only granted if money changes hands. Unless access to the modules can be restricted to specific cohorts, such as those who have paid, the system will be of little to no use.

How does this manifest in higher education? Apart from the issue of set roles, noted above, it is common to find students logging onto their LMS and being presented with a list of the modules they are registered on. This is presented as "personalization," which in the confusion of most higher education syllabi can be seen as a good thing for students (who immediately see the information most relevant to them). What would happen, though, if in a seminar the tutor (who may have greater access to the system) detects an opportunity for an interdisciplinary approach and directs the student to resources in other departments? When the student logs on they may well find their way barred, the gates closed, because the system only recognizes them as a student of one discipline. Educational resources then, even within the institution, are not "open." They are controlled, managed, restricted, and channeled.

The situation can become even worse when we look at opening education up beyond the walls of the institution. Again we need to examine the economic factors. Primarily this is a case of licensing. LMS systems are usually licensed according to the number of full-time equivalents (FTEs) who will use the system. Therefore, if the institution wants to expand access to members of the public (like Jude), or share areas with another institution, it may well need to renegotiate the license (usually at a higher cost). At what point, the vendor may ask, does allowing accesses from other institutions to a single LMS go beyond the extension of an individual licence and actually become two separate licenses? It is true that most systems do allow some means of making areas publicly accessible or usable as "tasters," but these are just hints of what might be available: an *ersatz* experience.

That "controlled access" is sold as a virtue of the system is understandable when we start to consider cultural barriers, but these issues are now beginning to filter into the procurement process of LMSs. In a recent survey on the UK's relevant discussion list (vle@jiscmail.ox.ac.uk), several respondents noted that they would have to renegotiate their license if they wished to expand the number of FTEs, and suggested that this was increasingly making them look at an open source solution (predominantly Moodle). As one respondent argued: "There will be a need to open up the VLE to 'non-students'—parents, students 14–16 in schools, employers—which won't be covered by our current license . . . it is something we'll have to deal with at some stage."

As noted above, one possible solution is the adoption of open source software. Here the licensing restrictions are not aimed at limiting use or development (outside of commercial exploitation). This is not a panacea though. It is perfectly feasible to build an open source product with all the restrictions noted above concerning the tyranny of the SRS. Open source solutions can just as easily pigeon-hole users into defined roles with set functions, and create barriers to access just as capably as their commercial counterparts.

Perhaps conscious of the fact that it was our college walls that Jude scribbled on, when selecting the LMS for Oxford University ease of access and exploration was paramount. The teaching system necessitates this in that the important educational relationship is built up in the tutorial (often on a one-to-one basis). The individual student gets a personalized, albeit human, education through the tutor; it is the latter's duty to guide the student to appropriate material, but more importantly to provide encouragement if the student wishes to research other areas. Every student is entitled to attend any lecture, and in many cases is positively encouraged to explore outside of his or her traditional discipline. This is a guiding principle of the original thinkers in open education.

When looking to procure an LMS, Oxford needed an inherently flexible and open system. We are increasingly looking to alternative forms of assessment, like peer review, or to encourage our graduate students to gain teaching experience. Thus the traditional roles of student/tutor/system administrator which are the *de facto* in many LMSs, including Moodle, were not appropriate. A system was required that broke free of the concept of roles, and also allowed the system to suddenly open up access at key sublevels. It also needed to accommodate the growing pressure to share resources (teaching and research) with colleagues and students at institutions other than Oxford.

This is key. Here the underlying pedagogical principle was one of openness (at least within the university), and this dictated the choice of platform. If the system we were to choose required a change to this ethos and accepted practices, it would be doomed to failure from the outset.

Thankfully, such a system existed: the Bodington LMS, developed at the University of Leeds. This is open source (see www.bodington.org) and is currently being merged with the SAKAI code (see http://sakaiproject. org/). For the purpose of this article, however, the underlying design principles behind Bodington helped throw open the gates to education.

Bodington's key assumptions important to this discussion are:

1) Rights, such as the ability to perform certain actions, should be attached to resources not people;

2) People have different roles in different parts of an institution. In some areas they may only be categorized as standard users, while in others they may need more advanced rights;

3) Many institutions are devolved, and central top-down impositions of rights will often jar with the bottom-up realities;

4) Institutions stretch beyond the standard central authentication systems to include commercial partners, colleagues, or students at other universities, etcetera. Any system must therefore be able to accommodate these;

5) A system should be inherently open, for access to the system and for access across the system, with the ability to restrict access at key points— not the other way around.

In practice, this means the following: Although an instantiation of Bodington will include all members of the institution, the groups themselves are not labeled as student/tutor/admin with associated rights. Instead, at each resource level, like an area of Bodington, the creator is free to select any group or create an *ad hoc* grouping and say "these people will have these rights in this section." These rights can be cascaded, but do not affect the rights that the group or individual has elsewhere in the system. Thus by adopting this model, you can easily open the whole system to all users. At other areas you can close it down to specific, controllable cohorts like committee members or tutorial groups. More importantly, you do not need to log on to the system until you reach a place with restricted access. Pointing a browser at www.weblearn.ox.ac.uk, for example, allows you to immediately access Oxford University's instantiation of Bodington, and browse until you reach a restricted area. This provides two benefits. First, it allows search engines like Google to index the site up to the point of restriction. Second, suddenly in the same system you can easily have an "open education" area (making certain modules open to visitor access) and a "closed education" area (restricted to students or staff within your institution).

The Pedagogical Gates Are Shut

Some of the above clearly goes beyond the limitations of the technology, however. It points to more fundamental issues. First, the pedagogical practices of the institution, which have nothing to do with any system purchased or developed, may impose barriers between disciplines. If the institution does not support interdisciplinarity, for example, then a closed system might be acceptable. Or if lecturers feel that an open system where all the resources are available may confuse students, a "locked-down access by module" approach would be appropriate. Neither, however, in the view of this author could ever be defended as open.

The Cultural Gates Are Shut

Cultural barrier(s)—an even greater hurdle—must still be overcome if we are to achieve the vision of openness. This includes both the policy decisions (local, national, and international) and attitudes of individuals.

Many longstanding issues surround the sharing, or opening up of access to, resources or content via electronic means. The most prominent and often-cited is that of copyright and intellectual property, which works adversely in two ways. First is the obvious infringement of copyright in teaching material. In the analogue world, lecturers undoubtedly photocopied handouts with copyright material contained therein under the assumed umbrella of fair use and educational use. For them to consult a legal adviser at each point would have been impossible; regardless, the chances of getting "caught" were slim. Even when lecturers moved into the digital world by assembling teaching material electronically for presentation (PowerPoint slides, for example) they undoubtedly copied images and other digital objects without ever fully considering the copyright issues. Again though, as the presentations were not circulated as such (unless on paper handouts), the chances of having legal action issued against them were often nonexistent. When we move into the open education arena, however, the chances of being on the wrong end of a legal settlement soar, and thus increase reluctance to go "open." This has certainly been one side effect of the Copyright Licensing Agency's (CLA) Higher Education Trial Licence in the UK (see http://www.cla.co.uk/support/he/HE_TrialPhotocopyingandScanningLicence.pdf). This is a worthy attempt to tackle the issue of staff digitizing or reusing copyrighted material for teaching without clearing it, but at the same time recognizing that this goes on and will continue to go on. Under this proposed agreement, lecturers can digitize up to 5 percent or one chapter (whichever is greater) of a book, and up to 5 percent or one article (whichever is greater) from a single journal issue. This material can be made available in the LMS, but:

1) the institution must keep detailed records of all items scanned;
2) the scanning may only be carried out by the person(s) designated to do so;
3) material must be held in a password-protected environment accessible only to students on the relevant course;
4) material needs to be presented in a form as close as possible to the typeset original;
5) a specific disclaimer at the beginning of each item must be included;
6) the licence does not cover material already in digital form.

One can only imagine the messages the above will send to academics, and especially the effect that point 3 has on open education. One also questions how realistic the above is, and why there is such concentration on the already impoverished area of education when the millions of deposits in YouTube show an almost Wild West attitude to copyright laws. Unless the open education process is backed by copyright lawyers, this is a real impediment to academics wishing to embrace the ideals of open education. They will be simply too afraid to do it.

This can also work the other way. In many countries the academic work produced by individuals in their research and teaching remains the copyright of their employer, such as the academic institution. Therefore by giving this away, lecturers may in fact be assigning rights over material they do not actually have control of. If we take the example of the UK's Jorum national repository (see http://www.jorum.ac.uk), the heavily bureaucratic procedure to register and deposit material stems mainly from the project creators' desire to protect themselves against legal actions by institutions.

Copyright and Intellectual Property Rights (IPR) then present major obstacles that can affect both the willingness to share material in the open education world, and the willingness to assist in disseminating the information deposited by others. This clearly is a policy decision, outside the control of individuals, and can only be addressed at the government level or by controlling bodies of universities.

When we consider individuals, however, and what is within their control, we come across the major problem of attitudes to sharing. Do people really want open education? By "people" we mean the practitioners, the holders of the material, namely the academics themselves. Clearly the Master of Biblioll College in *Jude the Obscure* would have no truck with such nonsense. Yet even with the "democratization" of higher education from the 1960s onwards, can we really detect an appetite for sharing and openness amongst our colleagues?

Authors grapple with this topic throughout the book, but for the purposes of this chapter we will concentrate on the sharing of material between academics. In the UK, at least, this has been high on the agenda. This stems primarily from two perceived advantages: 1) efficiency, since lecturers and teachers can simply re-use material, and 2) proliferation of best practice. Initiatives such as the Design for Learning Programme (see http://www.jisc.ac.uk/index.cfm?name=elp_designlearn) run by the Joint Information Systems Committee, the growing interest in LAMS (see http://www.lamsinternational.com/) and similar tools, and the launch of a national learning object repository (Jorum, see http://www.jorum.ac.uk/) all represent a growing interest in concepts of sharing best practice and materials. Yet how substantial are the foundations for this?

As one respondent to the LMS survey noted above stated: "Staff do not like having their materials accessible by anyone else . . . [they] seem to fear the critique that could occur if anyone could look at their work—'Look, they're teaching that all wrong!—and especially fear their line-managers seeing their day-to-day teaching materials. . . . There is a tendency by some staff to do as little as possible to complete their contractual obligations and no more. Sharing work via a VLE is seen as 'helping management.' "

It is undoubtedly true that the concept of sharing lesson plans, etcetera, is promoted in primary and secondary level education in the UK (the schools sector, in other words). Partly this stems from the training teachers get in educational best practice, but it is also driven by the need to achieve common goals usually set by a national curriculum. This is not so clear-cut when one moves into post-16 education and particularly to higher education, however. The diversity one sees between curricula in universities, the prized notion of academic freedom (to teach, research, and say what you want), and the pressure of achieving tenure or a good assessment grade through publications creates a melting pot of individuality. This in turn can lead to a sense of ownership and competitiveness which can be unhealthy in terms of open education. Economic forces driving universities can also worsen the situation. Departments are being pressured into recruiting more students, especially from overseas, and to get better research results. This, despite everyone's best intentions, is creating a feeling of "us vs. them" with *them* being the other universities competing for exactly the same students and the same research funds. Understandably, to try arguing for openness and sharing of material seems to be at best a case of poor timing, at worst like King Lear railing against the storms.

To test this, we conducted a small project to explore attitudes towards sharing amongst literature lecturers across three UK universities: Oxford, Oxford Brookes University, and Leicester University. Not only did we investigate how easy it was to reuse someone else's work (based on LAMS sequences, see http://www.lamsinternational.com/) but also attitudes to sharing material, namely making one's lecture notes, slides, reading lists, and so on, freely available to people outside of his or her institution to reuse (see http://www.english.heacademy.ac.uk/explore/projects/archive/technology/tech10.php). The results were interesting. In summary, they presented a positive view of sharing in that people were still able to overcome any idea of competitiveness and were willing to make their material available to those inside and outside of their home institutions. The main barrier to this was preparation of the material. Many academics use learning objects as *aide memoires* and rarely have the time to fully decontextualize their material and make it of general use. Additionally, there is no career incentive to do this, and in particular to make the material fit for use.

Nevertheless the willingness was there, if not the effort. When questioned as to why this was so, it arose that academics regularly share ideas and collaborate in thriving communities between institutions. These usually work on the level of the subdiscipline (lecturers who teach Shakespearian studies in different universities all know each other, for instance), and it is as common for a lecturer to say "I'm a specialist in X," as "I'm a member of X University." If these subdisciplines can be expanded to include all sectors in education and the general public, and provided with facilities to easily share material, then it is possible that the cultural barriers to open education that clearly are an issue can be prised apart.

Here then we have an opportunity. If people are willing to share resources within meaningful communities to advance their discipline (but not for some common good of education), then if we provide the tools to create these networks that cross academia and open up to the general public (ignoring national boundaries), we can begin to realize our goals. Academics are willing to release their material if they are a) protected from litigation; b) protected from criticism; c) given an incentive to do so; and d) furthering their discipline. This is an emerging philosophy, exposed so readily by the folksonomy community sharing tools that have exploded onto the Web, such as MySpace, Flickr, and YouTube.

Conclusion

So where can we go from here? Considering the discussions above, we could look at pursuing a few goals that would help to push the gates back open and would help to further the cause of open learning:

1) Open learning can only work if it has support from both ends—top and bottom—such as policy makers all the way to government level and practitioners, including lecturers and teachers.

2) Open learning as a concept is not new. The aspirations of previous scholars show that a deep-rooted desire to pursue this agenda fortunately exists, but the mistakes of the past in terms of over-stretching should be recalled. Moreover, the constraints of the present, which were not as evident perhaps 30 years ago (such as the emerging competitive nature of academia) must be recognized.

3) Our IT choices can force the agenda. More worryingly perhaps, if our choices are based purely on technical specifications and finance, we can in fact be unwittingly working against the cause of open learning.

4) Therefore, learning management systems, repositories, etcetera, should be built in a flexible manner that allow for the easy exposure of material to all system users and to people external to the system. The key component with such systems is access control and the ability to fine-tune this.

5) Such systems must recognize the complexities inherent in educational institutions and the shifting sands of the roles of individuals. The simplistic pigeonholing of tutor and student is about 30 years out of date already, so to see it replicated in IT systems developed this century indicates a major flaw in the design process—namely a gap between system designers and practitioners, or more probably highlighting a different target market.

6) Identity Management (IDM) systems that feed the LMS must also recognize this complexity. Increasingly this requires a federated approach to IDM, where the roles of individuals which differ from unit to unit are federated and thus recognized and not reduced.

7) Licenses that are based on FTE numbers within the local institution, and demand any renegotiation of this should the unit wish to open up content to others outside of the university or college must be resisted.

8) To mitigate against point 3 above, when an LMS or similar system is chosen, the practitioners must be involved in the selection process from the beginning. Selection should be based on their needs arising from their daily workflows.

9) Within these systems, academics should be encouraged to share material and make it open at least within the institution. An attitude of openness needs to be engendered at even the local level.

10) The existing willingness of the academics to share material wider than their institution amongst existing networks, usually based on a subdiscipline, should be built upon. In particular, using the key lessons from folksonomy applications, simple systems should be developed that allow existing academic networks based on subdisciplines to quickly share and expose their material for others to use.

References

Giaconia, R., and Hedges, L. (1982). Identifying features of effective open education. *Review of Educational Research*, 52(4), 579–602.

Hardy, T. (1998) *Jude the Obscure*. London: Penguin.

Holt, J. (1990). *How Children Fail.* Harmondsworth: Penguin.

Huitt, W. (2001). Humanism and open education. *Educational Psychology Interactive.* Valdosta, GA: Valdosta State University. Retrieved October15th, 2006, from http://chiron.valdosta.edu/whuitt/col/affsys/humed.html

International Council for Open and Distance Education. (n.d.). Retrieved May 30, 2007, from http://www.icde.org/oslo/icde.nsf

Lessig, Lawrence. (2003, May). *Open Education Interview.* Retrieved October 15, 2006 from http://www.elearnspace.org/Articles/lessig.htm

Mai, R. P. (1978, April). Open education: From ideology to orthodoxy. *Peabody Journal of Education, 55*(3), 231–237.

Rathbone, C. (1971). *Open Education: The Informal Classroom.* New York: Citation Press.

4

Does an Open Source Strategy Matter? Lessons Learned from the iLabs Project

Phillip D. Long and Stephen C. Ehrmann

As the rich collection of creative and effective open source projects described in this Carnegie volume demonstrates, innovation comes in all shapes and sizes in higher education today, enabling access to resources, pedagogy, and devices. This chapter describes one particular type of open source innovation—middleware called iLabs (supported largely by the Microsoft-MIT iCampus Alliance; see http://icampus.mit.edu) that enables users to run experiments remotely over the Web. First, we will briefly describe the development of remote labs at MIT and the development of the iLabs middleware. Then we will discuss some of the factors that have hindered the spread of this potent use of the Web, and draw a few tentative conclusions about how these issues affect the dissemination of educational innovation based on open source software.

Remote labs, such as those made available via iLabs, extend access to laboratory experiments, making them available 24/7 whenever students wish to use them. They also enable faculty to bring experiments into lecture to explore real "what if" scenarios, without needing to have laboratory equipment in the classroom. Remote labs can provide laboratory experiences with devices that otherwise would be impossible for students to manipulate (for example, controlling expensive or dangerous equipment). Sharing expensive laboratory resources can provide students with more opportunities to interact with experiments and confront the messiness of real data, not simulations. This is a crucial step if the intent of the experiment is to give students the opportunity to experience the difference between modeling the world versus understanding how the real world actually works.

Yet with all of this potential, the wider adoption of remote labs generally, and iLabs in particular, has been limited. This is the case even after financial incentives have been offered to faculty and institutions around the world to adopt iLabs-supported remote labs and pilot their use in courses.

Why has the dissemination of open source iLabs middleware received such limited uptake and interest? We will return to that question. First, however, we need to summarize the history of iLabs development at MIT.

Remote Labs—History at MIT

Accessing remote instruments through the Web has been an interest since the first Internet browsers were developed (Berners-Lee and Cailliau, 1990). Various programs to provide Web-based remote access to scientific instruments quickly emerged (for example, Aktan et al., 1996; Goldberg et al., 1994).

In 1998, Professor Jesus del Alamo, an electrical engineer, was unaware of these fledgling educational innovations. Like most engineering faculty at research institutions, his collegial connections around the world, his reading, and his conference participation were oriented toward engineering research, not education. Del Alamo, an experimentalist, had what he thought of as a "bit of a crazy idea" for one of his courses: to allow students to create and run a real experiment, not just a simulation, by using a Web browser to control the apparatus. It was already becoming common for students to use lab instruments by programming a computer sitting next to the instrument, without ever touching the instrument itself. LabView (National Instruments, See http://www.ni.com/) provided access to experimental equipment for students sitting next to the devices. Why not extend that an arbitrary distance through the Internet?

Economic motives existed alongside the pedagogical reasons to consider remote use of laboratory equipment. In a traditional laboratory course serving 40 students, students might come for two hours and work in pairs on experiments (so 20 identical equipment setups would usually be needed). Staff would have to be available to set up this expensive equipment for students in advance (20 setups for each class session); the equipment would then lay idle, obsolescing, until its next use. The expensive space devoted to the laboratory would also lay idle (See Pope and Anderson, 2003, for an economic analysis of undergraduate engineering laboratories at the University of Pennsylvania, as well as an analysis of the alternative approach to organizing laboratories developed there). And lab assignments could only be done during the brief class period allotted for work in the laboratory; experiments that might require student attention periodically over many hours simply wouldn't work in a traditional undergraduate course. Small wonder that lab work is rare.

By contrast, an iLab would allow students to use a single piece of equipment, one after the other, 24/7. For lecture courses like del Alamo's, a remote lab would enable true experiments to become part of the course's homework. Del Alamo realized that, with such a strategy, students could do research with the same equipment that professionals used, rather than affordable, simplistic student versions of the real thing.

In March 1998, del Alamo used a small grant from Microsoft to hire an undergraduate student through the Undergraduate Research Opportunities Program (UROP; MIT has an extensive program to encourage faculty and others to engage undergraduates in professional work in exchange for money or academic credit; about 85 percent of all MIT undergraduates have participated in at least one such UROP project.). This student, Lane Brooks, designed the architecture for Web control of a Microelectronics Device Characterization Laboratory in just a few months, using equipment from del Alamo's research to do the actual experiment and a donated computer to control the experiment. The iLabs project has used productively and widely the talent among MIT undergraduates in the development of the iLabs software architecture.

Impressed and excited, del Alamo decided the new laboratory setup was reliable and solid enough to use in the fall term with Integrated Microelectronic Devices, a graduate student class of over 30 graduate and undergraduate students from EECS and the Materials Science Department.

In spring 1999, del Alamo used an improved version of this lab with an undergraduate class of about 90 students, Microelectronic Devices and Circuits. Although reactions were somewhat mixed and students had discovered new ways to break the lab, del Alamo was nevertheless encouraged. Del Alamo applied for funds from the MIT Alumni Fund for Educational Innovation program to continue his work in developing Web labs. The success of his first lab also enabled him to apply successfully for a donation of equipment from Hewlett Packard. This equipment donation allowed him to run his Web labs on a different machine than was used for his research. The results of this foray encouraged him to delve more deeply into evolving the idea.

Later in 1999, Microsoft Research and MIT began the $25 million iCampus Project (See http://icampus.mit.edu/). iCampus's goal was to support the development of new technologies to support teaching and learning. Five iLabs were funded with separate iCampus grants, each to a different faculty member, including del Alamo's work in electrical engineering. These included a heat exchanger experiment in Chemical Engineering, a polymer crystallization experiment in Chemical Engineering, a "flagpole" sensor experiment, and a "shake table" experiment in Civil Engineering.

Because the developers of these early projects made their own decisions about design, their programs for doing common tasks (for example, creating accounts for students, authorizing access to the experiments, and storing results of experiments) were each developed independently and in different ways. This is a common consequence of innovations developed by separate labs or developer teams, even when working on the same content area—one that characterizes many open source projects.

Scalability in Online Experiments
The initial iLabs experiments followed a pattern that is typical in academe: Each lab was built by a team consisting of a lead faculty member (the domain expert), developers, and related technical experts (usually students). They used the technology and design approaches most familiar to them without regard to the other teams building experiments in their respective discipline areas. They created useful and functional labs. Yet each required a mechanism for authenticating the user, authorizing access to the experiment, and managing the resulting data sets generated. And each did this in a reasonable but unique way.

Building experiments in this fashion is a time-honored tradition. But it makes the cost of constructing the $n^{th}+1$ experiment no different from the nth experiment. Support for these experiments, and maintenance of the software, is usually the responsibility of the faculty member who developed the lab, because the software is likely to be unique and perhaps not well-documented.

The problems multiply if the faculty member wants to share access to the experiment with colleagues, because the developer faculty member must manage the external accounts, pay attention to the course schedules of faculty from around the world using the experiment (faculty who may be in different time zones and may not speak the same language as the developer), and manage data created and stored on servers. In other words, when the developers each create their own infrastructure, there are enormous disincentives for sharing experimental equipment over the Web.

The iLabs Architecture

The central contributions to the iLabs shared lab architecture (Harward et. al., 2004; Harward et. al., 2006; Harward et. al.,2006b are 1) a distributed design and 2) a set of reusable Web services to provide functions required of any online remote lab.

Distributed Design The fundamental insight into a sustainable and scalable proliferation of remote labs was to divide the responsibilities inherent in managing these labs into two parts.

1. One set of activities revolves around the actual experimental equipment and the domain expertise associated with instrumenting the experiment for network access.
2. The second focuses on management of the access to the remote lab, account creation, use policies, and data sets resulting from use. Connecting the experiment to the network is properly the responsibility of the owner of the lab equipment being shared. However, the experiment owner should be shielded from and not responsible for users beyond her or his own students. The latter ought to be in the hands of the user community accessing the equipment, wherever in the world they reside.

This division of responsibilities is built into the iLabs architecture shown in figure 4.1.

The iLabs Service Broker is responsible for accounts, usage policies, and data collected from batch-oriented experiments. The owner of the

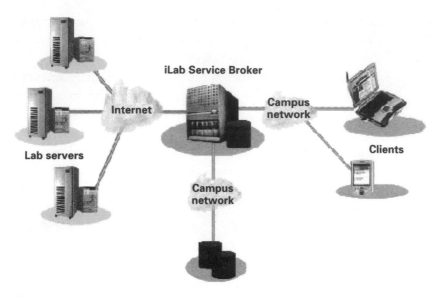

Figure 4.1
The iLabs architecture

lab experiment puts it online using a dedicated lab server. The Service Broker enables lab owners to share excess capacity of their experiments without being penalized for their willingness to do so (where "excess capacity" is a result of experiments that have short execution times relative to the user interaction required to configure them). Where does this excess capacity come from?

Students do homework, whether problem sets or remote lab experiments, the same way around the world. They often wait until the last minute before the homework is due before doing their experiments. Figure 4.2 shows the pattern of students accessing the microelectronics experiment during the week, with the due date at 2:00 p.m. on Friday (the arrow). Peak server load on the experiment server immediately precedes that deadline. The remote lab designer needs to plan for spikes in peak usage to accommodate this behavior.

Here's the good news: Creating capacity to meet occasions of peak demand creates unused capacity for all the other hours and days. That's "found" capacity that can be potentially shared with other instructors or learners who might need to use this equipment.

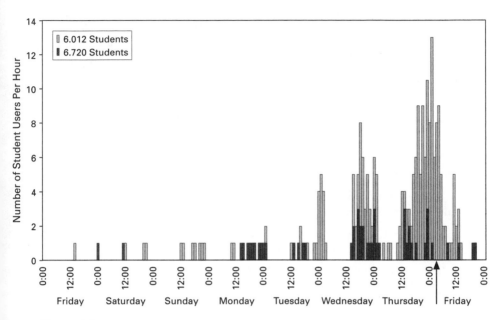

Figure 4.2
Creating sharable capacity

Table 4.1
Web services in the batch iLabs architecture

Web service	Description
Authentication	Validate who can access the experiment
Authorization	Determine if a given user has permission to access a particular experiment
Experiment data storage	Manage individual user data storage and persistence
Workflow	Policy management

Web Services When building experiments for remote access, common requirements are encountered. For these the iLabs team has designed and coded a reusable set of Web services (see table 4.1.)

In a typical configuration, a campus using iLab-based experiments will run a Service Broker administered by local IT staff. This Service Broker can access multiple lab servers located both on one's local campus as well as on campuses remote from the users. The students' accounts and their experiment storage reside on their own Service Broker regardless of where the experiment itself is executed. The lab server team need not be aware of which student is using the equipment at any given time, but may be assured that the student comes from an approved campus.

Authentic Tools and Interface Design   The options offered by remote labs also include the ability to use the same research equipment that professionals use. It is hoped that students will thereby begin to try out the identity of being a professional and, from there, take other steps to enter the profession. The Center for Authentic Science Practice in Education (CASPiE) project at Purdue University is anchored around this notion of authentic learning with professional tools and student engagement in "real research with real tools" as central to their work.

However, the software written for the practicing professional is often designed to provide great flexibility and granular control—desirable attributes for the practicing scientist but frequently a learning curve of significant incline to the novice learner. The iLabs environment allows a great deal of latitude in how the student learning experience is presented, though it affords this at a cost in development time and expertise.

Adding value through thoughtful interface design, an example   The University of Queensland (UQ) teaches a third-year engineering course in control theory. In this course, a significant laboratory exercise is presented through the introduction of an inverted pendulum experiment. This experiment requires students working in teams to write a program (using MatLab™, in this instance) to control an electric motor from which hangs a pendulum arm. The pendulum has two sensors connected to it to provide exact information on its position. The student's task is to write a program that swings the pendulum arm back and forth until it inverts to the vertical position, and when it reaches this point, to change the inputs to the controlling motor to try and balance the pendulum arm in the vertical position (see figure 4.3).

Typically the students spend five weeks in the engineering lab to perform this experiment. The data the students receive from the instrumented beam are the two angles that describe the beam's position. By observing the outcome of their experiment, they must adjust their control program and rerun the code to see if they have brought the beam closer

Figure 4.3
The inverted pendulum experiment by the University of Queensland (Joel
Carpenter, student developer; Geir Hovland and Mark Schulz, faculty project
coordinators)

to vertically balancing. Data from UQ indicate that about 5 percent of
the teams successfully complete the application and get the beam balanced, though much learning is accomplished.

Joel Carpenter, a third-year undergraduate who had never taken the
course, began the task of creating an iLab implementation of the inverted
pendulum experiment. Carpenter brought two key insights to the task,
having recently sat in front of the apparatus and watched students struggling to complete the experiment. The first was to add a state diagram
to the user interface so that when the program failed, there was a starting
point to look at the code to make adjustments. Just knowing what state
the pendulum was in when it failed gave insight into where to attack
revising the program.

The second insight was born from the frustration of the real lab experience. When running the code and observing the behavior of the pendulum, then changing the code again, the feedback is largely numerical.
You can see the pendulum swinging differently in response to each code
modification for each run, but comparing across runs is impossible. Or
is it?

With a webcam on the experiment, you can observe each run as
though you were in the lab. That's useful. But the insight Carpenter
brought to the problem was recognizing that the actual pendulum arm
could be digitally removed and replaced by an animation of the arm

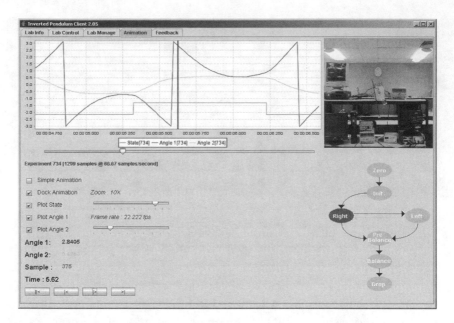

Figure 4.4
The user interface for the iLabs inverted pendulum experiment. Note that the pendulum arm is actually an animation overlaid onto the Webcam image driven by the data being collected. This allows multiple runs of the experiment to be visually compared, assisting in the debugging of the control code.

driven by the data. If this can be done, then it's also possible to overlay the image with several animations of the arm controlled by data from multiple runs of the experiment. One can see the impact of code changes by comparing one run to another visually. The application interface is shown in figure 4.4.

This insight provides a pedagogically more useful learning environment than that available from the interface of the original experiment. This is a key attribute of learning-centered application design that can add value to the student experience beyond that provided by the original equipment configuration. Assessment of the students using the inverted pendulum experiment led to the observation that using iLabs "was better than being there." Students received more useful feedback from the thoughtfully designed interface than they had in the "real" equipment on the lab bench. One result of this implementation was that the percentage of students completing the experiment increased to 30 percent in the five weeks.

The iLab made possible a large increase in the number of experiments performed.

In the traditional two-hour lab, the experiment could only be run a few times because each run has many steps: equilibrating the equipment, running the experiment (several minutes), data analysis, data interpretation, altering the code, and trying the experiment again.

In the iLabs implementation, the experiment execution time remains the same. The efficiencies gained in having more insight into how to edit the experiment increases student efficiency. But the big factor affecting the volume of experiments is its availability 24/7. Instead of 80 experiment runs completed in a week's worth of lab time, the iLabs implementation ran 580 times. The volume of experiments led to wear and tear on the equipment. So those students who procrastinated had to account for shaft slippage in addition to everything else in writing their code to balance the beam. This radical increase in use included students who used the iLabs experiment in the lab. After running the experiment directly a few times in the traditional way, most students then began using the online version instead because the information presented was simply more useful for interpreting data.

Limitations of Remote Labs: Issues of Scale

Not all experiments are suitable for delivery via remote labs. Some require crucial unique steps that cannot be abstracted in any educationally meaningful way through a remote interface. Experiments may consume chemicals or other agents that must be provided through some form of automated delivery system in the remote lab context. Finally, the mechanisms by which equitable sharing of remote labs is enabled is only just being confronted.

Does It Matter That the Software Was Open Source?

"Open Source" is a term with several relevant definitions. Fundamentally, the essence of open source revolves around distribution of the source code for software with the freedom to modify change and redistribute the resulting work. The variations around open source usually focus on the resulting constraints imposed on the redistribution activity—does it require attribution of the original author(s) and how? Is it redistributable to anyone or to only others who work in nonprofit areas? And in the most liberal interpretation, can a commercial version of the code be derived for sale? This latter point is where much of the open source world "forks," to borrow the source code phrase that describes a significant branch in the original code base.

Did it matter that the software was open source and did not come with strings attached? Yes. The iLabs project, as with most of the iCampus family of educational technology R&D efforts, allows for the derivation of new commercial alternatives, even as it encourages keeping the code fully accessible to the public as open source. It is interesting to see what impact the open source nature of the project has had. On several occasions over the course of the project, the mere possibility that the adopter's own work to develop or adapt iLabs could be taken commercial has led to a "second look" that otherwise would not have been given.

For example, colleagues at The University of Queensland were much more open to exploring the potential of iLabs when the opportunity to create and distribute their own implementations unencumbered by inherited intellectual property (IP) rules was emphasized. No one has taken iLabs and tried to derive a commercial version, but the vision of that option has opened minds and gained attention. The chance to make money, even when that isn't in the end of much use, gave an incentive to look a second time. While the iLabs team has no interest in this direction and is committed to maintaining an open source code repository, if wider access to experiments were reached by significantly enhancing the core code base and successfully disseminating it commercially, a goal of the iLabs project would be achieved.

Did it matter that authors could see how MIT's code was written as they wrote their own? Yes. The first experiment contributed by the UQ community, the inverted pendulum experiment, was implemented using the openly disseminated "time of day" test as a template. Through creative "play" with this example code, the student developer first taught himself the skills required to develop an experiment client, and then from this template added his innovative insight to enhance the students' understanding of the experiment (in this case the active state diagram and data-driven pendulum arm animation, allowing comparisons of multiple experimental "runs"). This typifies the power of open source as a vehicle for learning as well as a platform for creativity. Open source is the scientific method brought to software. As in science, it is an engine of innovation for technological as well as human development.

Is it critical for projects like iLabs to be pure open source efforts? No. Open source is, in our view, a pragmatic consideration as much as a philosophical orientation. Where commercial tools add value to otherwise open source projects, we see no reason not to leverage that value. For example, the interactive architecture of iLabs gives the adopter the choice of building a client in the language of his or her choice (C# or Java, for instance) or to leverage a widely distributed commercial software, LabView™, which is often found in teaching labs today. If the adopters have already invested in controlling teaching instruments in their labs with this interface, a plug-in to connect it to the iLabs architecture leverages this investment.

Closing Thoughts

We see serious barriers to widespread adoption of any faculty-developed innovation in technology, including the fact that instructors are rarely prepared, supported, or rewarded for finding innovations to adopt (Ehrmann et al., 2007). The results of huge software investments are often wasted when educational software fails to build a wide base of users that can sustain it before its technological clock strikes midnight. Too often software becomes technically or educationally obsolete before it can attract the support needed for its upgrade and continued growth (Morris et al., 1994).

Open source is no panacea to this decades-old problem. In fact, for some potentially popular software, open source could prevent it from obtaining private sector investment for formative evaluation, marketing, user support, and continuing upgrades. However, in our judgment, software such as iLabs does not offer a sufficient profit motive for commercial sustainability.

An open source strategy seems the best chance, and it offers several benefits.

First, iLabs has the potential to provide "minds-on" access to the seminal experiments that mark creative achievements in different science and engineering disciplines. The open source nature of the software is in the spirit of science itself. When we have approached other institutions about iLabs, the open source nature of the project seems to reassure them that MIT's motives are consistent with theirs. This advantage seems real, even for institutions that have no reason to rewrite code. The open source character of the project also increases the chances that faculty will invest time in building labs, for some of the same motives drive them to do other research. The more likely an institution is to reward faculty for using research to improve teaching, the more compelling this motive would be.

Second, the open source nature of the code creates more freedom of action for user institutions, companies, and governments that may wish to enter into a sharing relationship with one another. They can create, adapt, or purchase their own software to link their experiments to the iLabs infrastructure. They can even create new versions of iLabs components.

Although such steps are not sufficient to assure widespread use of iLabs, we believe that an open source approach is a necessary condition for building a multi-institutional, multi-national environment for sharing laboratory equipment and experiences.

References

Aktan, B., Bohus, C., Crowl, L., and Shor, M. H. (1996). Distance learning applied to control engineering laboratories. *IEEE Transactions on Education*, 39(3), 320–326.

Berners-Lee, T., and Cailliau, R. (1990). *WorldWideWeb: Proposal for a HyperText project*. Retrieved on February 26, 2008, from http://www.w3.org/Proposal.html

Ehrmann, S. C., Gilbert, S. W., and McMartin, F. (2007). *Factors Affecting the Adoption of Faculty-Developed Academic Software: A Study of Five iCampus Projects*. The TLT Group. Retrieved on February 26, 2008, from http://icampus.mit.edu/projects/Publications/TLT/iCampus_Assessment_Full.pdf

Goldberg, K., Mascha, M., Gentner, S., Rothenberg, N., Sutter, C., and Wiegley, J. (1994, September–1995, March). *Mercury Project: Robotic Tele-excavation*. University of Southern California. Retrieved on February 26, 2008, from http://www.usc.edu/dept/raiders.

Harward, J., del Alamo, J. A., Choudary, V. S., deLong, K., Hardison, J. L., Lerman, S. R., et al. (2004). *iLabs: A Scalable Architecture for Sharing Online*

Laboratories. International Conference on Engineering Education 2004, Gainesville, FL, October 16–21, 2004. Abstract available online at http://mtlweb.mit.edu/~alamo/pdf/2004/RC-104.pdf

Harward, V. J., Mao, T., and Jabbour, I. (2006). *iLab Interactive Services—Overview.* Center for Educational Computing Initiatives, MIT. Retrieved on February 26, 2008, from http://icampus.mit.edu/iLabs/Architecture/downloads/downloadFile.aspx?id=54

Harward, V. J., Northridge, J., Zbib, R., Naamani, L., Jabbour, I., and Mao, T. (2006b). *iLab Interactive Ticketing and Integrated Management—Overview.* Center for Educational Computing Initiatives, MIT. Retrieved on February 26, 2008, from http://icampus.mit.edu/iLabs/Architecture/downloads/downloadFile.aspx?id=56

Morris, P. M., Ehrmann, S. C., Goldsmith, R. B., Howat, K. J., and Kumar, M. S. V., (Eds.). (1994). *Valuable, Viable Software in Education: Case Studies and Analysis.* New York: Primis Division of McGraw-Hill.

Pope, D., and Anderson, H. (2003). Reducing the costs of laboratory instruction through the use of on-line laboratory instruction. In S. C. Ehrmann, and J. Milam (Eds.), *The Flashlight Cost Analysis Handbook: Modeling Resource Use in Teaching and Learning with Technology, Version 2.0.* Takoma Park, MD: The TLT Group.

5

Evaluating the Results of Open Education

Edward Walker

The standpoint of this chapter is that more attention to evaluation will be necessary in order to increase and sustain the scale and impact of open education. By evaluation, I mean the systematic collecting and analyzing of results to corroborate hypotheses about cause and effect. By open education, I mean education that is available to virtually any learner, is within his or her means, and results in meeting his or her learning objectives. From the perspective of an evaluator, it is evidence that a resource contributes to these measures, not its provenance, that is of concern. Therefore, I assume that open education will make use of both open and non-open content, software, and delivery technology. I believe that relevant data and their insightful interpretation will play an increasingly essential role in making all types of educational resources available enough, affordable enough, and effective enough to enable ubiquitous educational opportunity.

Moreover, I believe that the ultimate and inspiring goal of open education is not just to put shiny new goods on easier-to-reach shelves, but also to create categorical improvements in educational opportunity and educational outcome; that is, education that is both more efficient and more efficacious. For the open education movement to have substance and be durable, the educational experiences that it provides will need to be a better value because those experiences have higher pedagogical quality and produce more satisfying results.

Increasingly, the proponents of open education are being asked to provide concrete evidence of gains in the productivity and efficiency of teaching and learning interactions that are due to open education. Some of this evidence is in hand. Educational technology and academic content, as well as the standards they employ, are successful innovations. More sophisticated learning experiences and more effective educational systems are being created and used every day. This trend is bound to continue as more and more educational infrastructure falls into place, and more and more learning content is created and used. Both learners and providers can expect that educational resources will be universally available and more affordable because digitization, computing, and networking are making education easier, faster, and cheaper to provide and to get.

Economic forces will respond to differences in performance, cost, benefit, and risk, and thereby will evaluate any gains in productivity and effectiveness due to open education. With luck, everyday teachers will provide higher quality educational experiences, and everyday learners will realize higher quality educational outcomes as those economic forces lead to a continuing increase in the scale of educational access and success—even after the current enthusiasm for change and initial impulse of funding has passed.

But modifying educational practice and business models to exploit lower cost and greater scale in order to deliver more worthwhile educational experiences will require accountability and predictability for educational opportunity and outcome. Accountability and predictability are essential ingredients of good practice. They depend on the collective will to develop and use good methods for quantifying and comparing the benefits and costs of alternative approaches to teaching and learning. In addition, the open education movement will need to self-evaluate in order to substantiate the claims it makes and defend its results against professional error and inappropriate interpretation. Thus, evaluation will be necessary in order to identify, interpret, replicate—and defend—results.

The evaluation of open education is immature. In part, this is because the phenomena of educational inputs and outputs are complex, and the underlying psychological and physiological processes are yet to be understood. Measuring results and postulating what led to them is difficult for any multidimensional, longitudinal behavior, and establishing that a meaningful change in such behavior really did occur requires real evidence that really is hard to obtain. Furthermore, in a new field such as open education, practitioners are inclined to justify assumptions and demonstrate differences from existing practice, rather than make comparisons that are based on measures and metrics which are themselves evolving and as likely to result in professional embarrassment as to produce insight.

But nothing less than the painstaking unraveling and reweaving of complex cause and effect is required if collections of content and sequences of experiences are to be consolidated into strategic designs for learning and if business processes and software applications are to be integrated into efficient and effective systems for delivering those designs.

Approaching Evaluation Strategically

The first step in evaluation is simply to accept both that measures must be meaningful, and that meaning must be measured. Meaningful evaluation in part involves tactical recording of data and reporting of results about efficiency and productivity that feed planning and estimating processes. It also involves testing pedagogical hypotheses against quantifiable outcomes by systematically and critically analyzing those outcomes in order to determine under which circumstances which factors do and do not corroborate the hypotheses.

Strategic evaluation, then, includes both describing conditions and results systematically and explaining why the conditions matter and the results make sense. Three components are involved in this practice.

Meaning.   Evaluation is meaningful when it is performed by experts and informed users who use precise and public criteria, evidence from repeatable procedures and outcomes, and measures that are based on everyday use under everyday conditions.

Metrics.   Nothing improves without being measured. Metrics by which not only the complete learning experience and the entire cost of providing that experience can be quantified, but also the specific benefit due to content, software, and pedagogical paradigms can be quantified are the raw material of evaluation.

Method.   Methods for collecting and analyzing data are the unifying force and balance point between meaning and metrics. Rigorous procedures impart trustworthiness and relevance to data, consolidate exploratory activities and preliminary findings into best practice, and augment reporting with explanation.

Kinds of Activities, Data, and Interpretation

The cultural habit of evaluation eventually becomes self-reinforcing. However, before a community has developed the habit of evaluation, the practical pressures on individual organizations and fear of failure discourage testing or technique building beyond the immediate needs of the local environment. Moreover, disclosing the results of evaluation is risky when there is a lack of shared criteria for evaluation, and irrelevant or simplistic comparisons are possible. It is ironic that because of such factors, practitioners do not participate in collaborative evaluation. The potential savings in time and money, as well as greater insight, to be gained from exploiting techniques that others have developed or from not repeating mistakes that others have made is obvious.

If field-wide evaluation is not likely to emerge spontaneously, what brings together a critical mass of participants so that metrics, method, and meaning can escape the boundaries that individual organizations impose?

Generally, what leads to the development of common methods of evaluating and routine publishing of results is pressure for accountability and predictability—pressure that is exerted by such third parties as professional communities, policy organizations, and funding bodies. Provided these third parties have sufficient authority and integrity, the pressure they bring to bear raises the marginal utility of sharing results and developing standard benchmarks and analytic procedures. Once community evaluation starts, the collaboration produces continuous improvement both in results and in methods.

Activities

The tools of evaluation and the procedural techniques for using them in a consistent, systematic, and repeatable level of professional practice are developed in three distinct kinds of activity.

• Studies and projects
• Field and laboratory experiments
• Marketplace use of products and services.

These activities are complementary, and they are not mutually exclusive. The same terminology often is applied to all, but each imparts different constraints on the kinds of variables that can be manipulated, the kinds of measures that can be made, and the kinds of inferences that are justified by the data they produce. The factors that distinguish them are differences in scale, expected lifetime, and intent.

Studies and Projects: Proofs of Concept   Further work may be planned from the outset, but studies and projects tend to be relatively short, small-scale activities that are focused on answering particular, circumscribed questions and are not intended to produce a long-term activity or a deployable product or service. The activity typically is constituted by proofs of concept and feature demonstrations. The objective is innovation or testing, and a negative or surprising outcome may be as useful and informative as the hoped-for result.

The audience for reporting results is peers, not users or customers. Results are reported primarily through meeting presentations and publications. For example, the initial objective of the MERLOT project was to provide a means for peer review of learning objects and support community interaction necessary to develop expertise in their use. The initial purpose of the project was to demonstrate this function and its appeal to faculty members. Except for the limitations imposed by the project itself, how much the reviews "cost" to produce and validating "why" people participated in MERLOT were not primary considerations. Thus, simple metrics such as the number of reviews posted and the number of participants in MERLOT, etcetera, could be used to evaluate the project.

Trials and Experiments: Proof of Utility   An experimental product or service generally is less complete than a deployed product, and the context of a laboratory or engineering trial does not address non-crucial dimensions of a production environment. To save time and expense, trials and experiments may have artificial performance requirements or may use simulated data or processes. Although they deliberately abstract away from some conditions that are not relevant to the question at hand, and they may apply resources that would not be used in a production environment, they are intended to be real where it counts and, thus, to produce results that support detailed evaluation and conclusions that can be replicated and translated to production environments. Activities such as the Plugfests conducted by the Advanced Distributed Learning Laboratory (ADL) and the Joint Information Systems Committee (JISC), the IMS alt-i-lab events, or the Pew Learning and Technology Program, mimic crucial dimensions of the real world as closely as possible.

Results are gathered and reporting takes place in public, scenario-based, proof-of-practice demonstrations such as the Plugfest or alt-i-lab events, or in documented field trial conditions like those from the Pew Initiative studies. The intent is that success in the experiment or trial will accelerate transition to and reduce the risk of full-scale use, as well as provide greater understanding of the causes that underlie results. Therefore, the activities require substantive participation by both suppliers and consumers, and they gradually adopt more formal methods for collecting data and for evaluating both efficiency and efficacy.

Products and Services: Proofs in Practice   Production quality content and software and real-world teaching and learning paradigms have to be complete and robust, well-integrated with their context, and supported for long-term everyday use. Their use can produce extensive data, and detailed reporting of results for products and services takes place in venues and publications that communicate performance in the marketplace—broadly defined as the place where educational resources are provided, acquired, and used. Thus, the measures of product and service activity include sales, numbers of users, attempts to use student success rates, and satisfaction.

Because of the modifiability of software, the adaptability of digital content, the realism of simulated environments, and the configurability of modern enterprise environments, marketplace activity is not clearly separate from corresponding experimental or laboratory activity. In fact, many experiments are carried out in marketplace environments, and many products and services are, effectively, experiments or tests with real-world outcomes.

Data

Accomplishing an objective involves complex and holistic effort. Individuals and organizations can be both suppliers and consumers in this effort. For example, an educational institution might consume software products and academic content from its suppliers in order to supply educational experiences and a variety of services to its student consumers. Thus, measures of efficiency or productivity have little value unless the several factors that might have contributed to them are disentangled. Terminological fashion aside, data of four general kinds make up the raw material of evaluation: performance, cost, benefit, and risk. Some high-level descriptions of the kind of performance, cost, benefit, and risk metrics that suppliers or consumers use are listed below.

Performance

• **Supplier** The time, labor, or resources expended or saved to produce a result; the frequency with which that result is used; the number of times and number of application domains in which it is re-used.

• **Consumer** The time or effort required or avoided to realize an outcome; the frequency with which that time or effort must be expended; the number of different outcomes that can be realized with that expenditure.

Cost

• **Supplier** The immediate and lifetime costs of producing, installing, maintaining, and using a capability, including collateral costs of its use; the degree of difficulty and level of expertise required to obtain results using the capability.

• **Consumer** The cost of acquiring, upgrading, and using a capability, including collateral costs of its adoption and use; the degree of difficulty and level of expertise required to achieve outcomes using the capability.

Benefit

• **Supplier** Business targets, marketplace objectives, or customer satisfaction—measured immediately and longitudinally; choice of business partners and marketing options; faster and cheaper response to new opportunities.

• **Consumer** Institutional and personal targets, business process objectives, and end-user satisfaction—measured immediately and longitudinally; choice of suppliers and deployment options; faster and cheaper response to changing business requirements.

Risk

• **Supplier** Correlations between planned and actual results, identification of factors driving and blocking outcomes, expense of risk management—compliance tests, the size and quality of the community of use, the availability of staff.

• **Consumer** Correlations between educational objectives and actual outcomes, identification of factors driving and blocking outcomes, expense of risk management, certification outcomes, the size and type of the community of use, the readiness and performance of staff.

The complexity and precision of data of these four types will increase as implementations of open education accumulate, and the community of practice consolidates its know-how with its knowledge and refines and extends practice and understanding.

Interpretation

Activities produce data and artifacts of practice such as examples, procedures for managing risk, a body of tools, standard techniques, and benchmark tests. Interpretation is required to relate these to hypotheses about cause and effect, and explain how the results support them. That is, understanding what the data mean and why the practice works requires theories and models that go beyond mere description to have predictive and explanatory power. Interpretation also is necessary to establish that data and the methods that produced them can be trusted to reflect the effect of specific and relevant causes.

For an interpretation to be both politically useful and scientifically meaningful, it must answer two fundamental questions: "What is being compared to what?" and "Can the comparison be trusted?". For example, the MERLOT Consortium makes open resources available to faculty members and students. If such resources are made more available, affordable, and effective—in other words, more open—then it is logical to hypothesize that over time more faculty members will use more MERLOT resources more efficiently. Providing evidence that supports this hypothesis is not straightforward. Consider the data in table 5.1.

One purpose of interpretation is to reduce the risk of making wrong conclusions or inaccurate predictions based on interpretations of such data. In this table, the number in the "Users" row is larger every year, and the numbers in the "Items" and "Time" rows are not larger in 2005 than in 2004, but are larger in 2006 than in any preceding year. To trust the interpretation that some improvement in the openness of MERLOT resources caused more people to use more items, we first need to know that other obvious interpretations are not valid. For example:

Table 5.1
Raw data from web site visits

	2003	2004	2005	2006
Users	22,824	30,110	46,355	55,725
Items	8	10	10	22
Time (in minutes)	5:19	5:03	4:35	7:20

Note: These data were invented for the purpose of the discussion that follows. They do not reflect actual usage of MERLOT resources.

Did what constituted a faculty member change?

Did the way data were collected change?

If such changes in context did occur, then we cannot conclude that "more openness" caused the observed changes in the data for 2006. Even if the meaning of the labels and the way the data were collected were consistent from year to year, we still need to establish that some other cause did not produce the apparent changes. Some of these causes can be addressed by further analysis. For example:

Chance: are the differences statistically likely or unlikely?

Global trends: are the differences correlated with some external trend such as an increase in the general use of online resources or a change in faculty demographics?

Only if the differences in the data from year to year are not likely to be due to some accidental factor or extraneous cause can sophisticated questions about the impact of openness be addressed. For example:

Is the increase correlated with the amount or kind of open content available in MERLOT?

Did new categories of faculty members begin to use MERLOT resources?

Did faculty members begin to use MERLOT resources differently?

The scenario of interpretation outlined above is just a rudimentary sketch of the kind of systematic method that is required to relate meaning with metrics. The point of the example is that hardly any interesting comparative question can be answered and hardly any interesting "next question" can be asked unless the methodology for collecting and evaluating results provides reasonable assurances that accidental or extraneous factors were not at work and that the evidence at hand is consistent with predictions from relevant hypotheses about causation.

Applying the Strategy

It has been asserted above that the meaning of open education can be measured, and that outcomes from open education can be evaluated by using supplier and consumer metrics of performance, cost, benefit, and risk, and systematic method of interpretation. The methods for making measurements and for using them to make comparisons of interest are certain to increase in precision and utility once the practice of evaluation is adopted by the community of practice. Other metrics will be incorporated in the framework, and the framework of measures will change.

How can the threshold of community adoption be reached? Three ongoing projects offer an unusual opportunity for bringing into being a cultural practice of strategically motivated evaluation for open education. Each project has explicit objectives for increasing the availability, affordability, and effectiveness of education—that is, for meaningfully improving education through greater openness. In addition to their collective general relevance to open education, the projects are devoting complementary special effort to three distinct central concepts of openness. The California State University's eLearning Framework will provide significantly more open academic content. The Open University's project will provide significantly more open collaboration between and among students and faculty. And the Sakai Foundation's activities will provide significantly more open configuration of educational technology.

These three projects will evaluate their success on internal terms, and each is likely to develop a rich set of measures and procedures for applying them for such self-evaluation. The data that each project will collect and use for its internal purposes will span the kind of complete educational environment illustrated by the performance, cost, benefit, and risk metrics that were listed above. These data will provide the basis for direct and detailed comparison with benchmarks from prior or alternative practice, and the projects are of sufficient scale and duration to allow for the evolution of their methods of evaluation. The work products of the projects will provide a continuing stream of results and interpretation. A concerted effort to consolidate the internal metrics and methods of these three projects easily could provide the basis for introducing community evaluation of open education.

A simple way to begin would be to cast the measures of inputs and outcomes that are now being used by the individual projects in the common performance/cost/benefit/risk framework provided here. For example, all three projects will generate before and after data on such global benefits of open education as the breadth of resources available, student success rates, and improved allocation of faculty/student time, as well as provide benchmark metrics for organizational cost and performance in delivering educational experiences. Because of their emphasis on different aspects of open education, each will provide unique evidence for comparing the cost to provide and the beneficial impact of more open content, collaboration, and configuration. Metrics for performance and cost among the projects are likely to fit the framework readily and be straightforwardly comparable across projects once terms are translated, whereas metrics for educational quality and organizational risk are more likely to require study and development to consolidate individual differences or differentiate individual requirements.

It is possible, but not very likely, that these individual projects (or others) will generalize their methods of evaluation or consolidate their procedures for evaluating and reporting results with others of their own accord. It is more likely that tailoring evaluation to meet local needs and the exigencies of schedules and budgets will preclude such "extra" work on results and methods—unless third parties act to provide the additional impetus and resources necessary to produce meaning, metrics, and methods for open evaluation of open education. The time and the circumstances are right for them to do so.

At least one reader will point out that such evaluation has a dark side. Indeed it does. Measures can be inappropriate, results can be "produced," and inferences can be mistaken. Many variables that don't have much to do with education, such as technical change, funding pressure, or individual motivation, may have a lot to do with educational outcomes. Nevertheless, it is wrong-headed to infer from the risk of error or the possibility of irrelevant influences that there are no appropriate measures, no genuine results, or no valid inferences. That mistakes are possible means only that evaluation itself must be subject to evaluation.

Conclusion

The impact of networked computing on supply-chain management and retailing is evident, as are the changes in organizational practices brought on by this technology across several disciplines and several types of organization. Change that is similar in kind and scope is taking place in education.

The common trait of groups that reach their objectives in times of change seems to be a shared and persistent commitment to excellent performance, open communication, and group accomplishment. This commitment depends on well-articulated (right or wrong) hypotheses about cause, *and* on routinely measuring outcomes and comparing results to determine whether the hypotheses are consistent with them. Those who succeed in transforming education will have such a commitment.

A lot of evaluation is going on now in education. But much of it seems oriented toward merely justifying assumptions and describing data, rather than toward explaining outcomes or decomposing their causes. In contrast to other fields, there seems to be less skepticism about whether the data are trustworthy and analytical comparisons are meaningful. Consequently, less attention is paid to methods for collection and analysis than is necessary to understand results or predict future outcomes.

This brief essay is intended to provide a rationale for more, and more systematic, evaluation of open education. It suggests that methodology is the critical component of such evaluation, and provides a superficial description of the kinds of activities, data, and interpretation that are involved in evaluating open education.

Developing and using accepted methods of evaluation will expose hypotheses about cause and effect to support or disprove. As a side effect, it will result in better recognition of contributors and their contributions to the field, as well as discourage the sequestering of lessons learned. Strengthening the role of evaluation in the ecosystem of open education will result in a deeper understanding of gains in practice.

6

A Harvest Too Large? A Framework for Educational Abundance

Trent Batson, Neeru Paharia, and M. S. Vijay Kumar

The *plethora* of educational resources in digital form at the present time can seem overwhelming. 225,000 hits for a Google search, or 140 emails in your email queue in the morning, lead many of us to just walk away or shut our computers off. Our culture is at "glut stage" in all ways, and the same is true of higher education. But open education approaches, some tested over the decades before we reached flood stage, may offer ways to turn glut into plenty.

The term "open education"[1] has had many flavors over the years such as learning by doing, informal learning, a holistic approach, real-world learning ("authentic learning") and many others. However, it has always meant that teachers and students should be open to varieties of teaching approaches, which turns out to be perhaps the most useful historical framework for understanding the current challenges of network learning and digital abundance. In the predominant lecture-classroom of past decades, open education has often seemed merely a counterculture alternative (remember the "open classroom"?). Now, however, as we move more fully into the age of digital knowledge, what was just an alternative is now an imperative. The Internet and the Web along with a host of available educational resources are making "open" the necessary default. Overnight, "open" is on steroids and has taken on new meanings:

• Teachers are becoming facilitators in a charged, multivocal, online, and onsite learning discussion that is multicentered and which they no longer control.

• Publishing is freed of many traditional gate-keepers and therefore disciplinary content is revised constantly.

• All educational design principles are giving way to the mandate: "be open to multiple possible users and uses."

Exciting, yes, but also bewildering. The abundance of information and interaction opportunities can overwhelm and be underexploited by an educational system whose practices are cast in a framework of scarce resources. Higher Education, with a culture that has comfortably settled over the centuries on one dominant model of formal academic learning wedded to paper and print, as well as physical tools such as lab instruments, is highly situated (that is you learn where the tools are), reflecting this model of scarcity. Students pay tuition to have access to the scarce resources of faculty and learning tools located in one place. This scarcity is monetized through a seat-time measure.

The manifesting nature of learning via the Internet, open education, starts with abundance—abundance that will only multiply over time. Philip Slater, an anthropologist and author of *In Pursuit of Loneliness*, saw the post-war abundance in America as a root cause for the "revolution" of the 1960s, when baby-boomers, enjoying the wealth of their parents, who had grown up during the depression, could not understand their scarcity-based beliefs (1970). Their poverty assumptions—lie low, hide your wealth lest it be stolen, do not display emotions, life is full of danger—enraged their Dionysian offspring. "Let's celebrate life, not suspiciously guard our riches" was translated into "don't trust anyone over 30," to paraphrase Slater. We now appear to be facing the same cultural fissure 40 years later: Open educational resources (OER) are so abundant that the scarcity-based assumptions of educators are challenged.

Now, instead of scarcity of educational resources, in this new technology age we are faced with open content, open resources, open learning, open architecture in design of physical and virtual spaces, open source, and open knowledge, all of which have blossomed in the last ten years. Academia is responding. "Charged" open academic discussion spaces are leading to better understanding and accommodation for social aspects of learning. The flood of new academic content is being directed into new communities of "remix." Designers of physical and virtual learning spaces—including the basic architectural concepts of software design—are learning to accommodate the ongoing volume, variation and innovations.

In short, we are moving toward a knowledge ecology characterized by unfettered access to educational resources, choice, and change in the

Table 6.1
Analysis of trends toward open learning in higher education

Scarcity-based/ Inertial frameworks	Trend Indicators	Abundance-based/ Enabling frameworks
Individual learning	Collaborative learning, whole student development, internships, service learning, experiential learning, field work, recognition of "real-world" work	Open learning: embracing the social aspects of learning
Conveying knowledge; content is a thing	Reconsidering legal definitions of knowledge	Open learning: codeveloping knowledge with students; and students with students; content is a process
Design must support predictable processes	Open architectures in software design, learning spaces, and organizational structure	Design supports unintended innovation

context and clientele of higher education. Table 6.1 shows how higher education is already moving toward open learning:

The "trend indicators" in the second column are positive trends toward a more varied approach to teaching and learning. Yet, we wonder if these positive trends can become robust enough to truly engage the learning opportunities now presented by network learning. Can higher education fully exploit the abundance of open education opportunities available?

Open Learning as Visible Work in Process

It is a challenge for educators to understand what is happening inside students' heads while they are learning. Without that understanding, it is hard to assess the value of the teaching approach. Open learning makes the processes of teaching and learning visible, more apparent as work in progress.

Consider a familiar scenario, the writing classroom. You might recall the typical college composition course: Following directions from the teacher, the students would write papers, hand them in, and then get them back a few days later with red marks. To guide them in their writing, the students would look at models of good writing and try to remember various principles that the teacher provided. But writing is thinking, a process of discovery, invention, and drafting. How can writing teachers participate in and guide that process? How can they coach students during the process instead of only at the beginning and the end? How can they make the process open?

One approach is to adopt a studio-writing approach. Each student, using a computer, engages in "social writing," via chat or other real-time and asynchronous social software, with the teacher also present in the group discovery (brainstorming) phase of writing. The studio writing approach is a natural outgrowth of this new abundance of student content. With technology's ability to handle multiple simultaneous inputs and arrange them into a readable dialogue, writing students need no longer write alone during the first stages of the writing process.

For example, a teaching approach called Electronic Networks For Interaction (ENFI), (See http://endora.wide.msu.edu/1.2/coverweb/ cmcmday.html) has been widely adopted in composition programs around the country. Teachers can see ideas develop in the dialogue, can get to know their students' writing better, and can guide the discovery phase of writing in a new way. This is a valuable aspect of open education abundance: learning through practice in a social setting with guidance from a teacher, with the whole process visible and open to scrutiny. Writing by hand on paper is often a slow process and hard to share; writing on a computer is fast and highly sharable.

Now consider a student's learning over time: how might that be captured and shared? We find a similar example in the Open Source Portfolio (OSP), a tool within the Sakai collaborative learning environment (See www.sakaiproject.org). Portfolios allow completed student drafts of work (visual, textual, symbolic and the like) to stay with the student over a course, a series of courses, a full certificate or degree program, or over a lifetime of lifelong and "life-wide" learning.

Electronic portfolios of any stripe are at the heart of open education. If students' work (their "assets"), their reflections on it, and faculty members' comments on it are Web-accessible for those with permission to view, student learning in response to a syllabus is visible and open to scrutiny. The conversation around this student-generated content can then be extended electronically in space and time. In fact, this conversational remixing of content and comments can be as valuable as the original content creation itself.

These two approaches, ENFI and the use of portfolios, suggest how digital abundance offers new views that can lead to increased learning and better-informed assessment of learning.

Open Learning: Learning from Peers

As the examples would suggest, student-generated content is now easier to include as part of the "text" of the course. As students comment on each other's work in process, guided and influenced by teacher comments, they and the teacher are bringing to life a vital new kind of social learning: conversation (part oral and part sharing of work done on computers) with each other, which, in itself, is the work of the course. The conversation can (and does) continue between classes.

This new kind of interaction engages students and faculty in ways that demand a new set of skills. However, faculty think of "net-gen" students and may not know how to work with net-gen social-learning capabilities—of the technology or of the students. It might be helpful to think, instead, of the "selves" open education can bring together. Darren Cambridge, a faculty member at George Mason University, describes a "network self" that has a strong social aspect in his forthcoming book (2008). Cambridge's network self is comfortable with abundance and finds ways to use digital abundance. Social use of the network in turn engages the "entrepreneurial self," the open, playful self. This self loves to collect (aggregate) and create new connections. It lives in the infinite space of the (social) mind and learns through relationships.

The network self and entrepreneurial self open a much larger social context for teaching and learning. This is the self who revels in abundance and who is open to learning how to be a smart, life-long consumer of abundant open education resources. Higher education needs to learn how to best use social-learning opportunities.

Content, Community, Creativity, and the Commons

As we see that abundance of student-generated course work can lead to new ways to leverage the social aspects of learning, we then wonder how faculty and researchers can similarly use the new digital abundance in support of traditional academic values. They, too, find themselves in a swirl of new ways to search and create disciplinary content. As a result, higher education leaders are grappling with issues of who owns the content, how to certify which content has been vetted within the disciplines, how to use the abundance of content in the classroom, and how to sustain a coherent community of learning. Creative Commons (See http://creativecommons.org/) has addressed these concerns in imaginative and powerful ways.

Creative Commons
After releasing it open-copyright licenses in late 2002, Creative Commons began a massive effort to gain adoption of the licenses and build a vibrant sharing economy between creators on the Internet. The potential and the vision for a robust sharing system were clear. Under a sharing paradigm, a musician could easily remix a song that she found online and then share her creation; a math teacher in Vietnam could easily download, translate, and redistribute a lesson plan that someone in India posted online long before, and a scholar in Nigeria could access findings of cutting-edge research found online and apply them to her local setting. Without open licenses, these uses and others like them would be difficult, even if the original authors wanted to share their work, all because copyright got in the way.

Creative Commons designed a three-step framework that supported its vision: (1) grow licensed content, (2) make that content searchable, and (3) enable communities of remix and collaboration. This framework was followed, and continues to be followed, in order to build and evolve the commons. This framework created a vital feedback loop for society via the Internet—create, aggregate, help users find items of interest, encourage recontribution, and the original creation lives on. This process has worked for centuries but at a much slower pace, and with far fewer potential participants. Creative Commons reimagined how the creative force within society could work in a digital age.

The last step of the Creative Commons framework, building communities of collaboration and remix, offers an unprecedented opportunity to leverage this growing abundance of resources to educational advantage. By focusing on this step, open educational resources can be used to their maximum potential, both improving the quality of these resources, and increasing the reach of who can access knowledge. Much more is possible, both across projects, and in deeper ways.

Consider the example of ccMixter, a "community music site featuring remixes licensed under Creative Commons where you can listen to, sample, mash-up, or interact with music in whatever way you want" (See http://ccmixter.org). Here, musicians engage in a musical conversation to better each other's content. ccMixter is much more than a site that hosts music: It is a community of musicians who post their songs, remix other people's songs, and give feedback and commentary to each other.

When a remix of a song is made, the system creates an automatic link between the two songs. If one song has twelve remixes, all of those remixes are linked from the original song, making it possible to explore different expressions and evolution of the original song. The overall "composition" of music is constantly evolving as it includes the participation of more and more distributed people through remixes, and comments. Contests are held on the site periodically, where the whole community both comes together, and competes, to make the best mixes from the tracks available on the site. Authors of winning mixes are chosen to be put on special CDs, or are given recording contracts so they could receive more exposure and social credit for their efforts. The site is licensed under Creative Commons, so musicians are able to remix without having to worry about copyright.

Community for Educators

Imagine how features on ccMixter might be applied to create an OER "mixer" for teachers. Educators could post their lesson plans to a Web space, the OER Mixer, in a transformable text, audio or video format. Other educators could build upon or alter these works to add content, tailor it to meet the needs of their local community, or add pedagogical material. They can repost their new versions, and the software would create a visible connection between the original work and the new work. Thus, if I wanted to add a video component to John's lesson plan in geometry, I could connect my video to John's original lesson plan.

Building communities for educators means building "mixers" where educators can remix an abundant amount of content created by their peers to produce better, and more collaborative open educational resources.

Community for Researchers: AcaWiki

One of the primary functions of higher educational institutions is to research cutting-edge social, scientific, and cultural issues in order to progress society forward. But, because of copyright law and academic culture, most findings from academic research are published in proprietary journals that require costly subscriptions in order to gain access. Oftentimes it is only those affiliated with a well-funded university who can gain access. Though there is an abundant amount of existing scholarly research, unfortunately, most of it is not accessible.

Forthcoming efforts like AcaWiki (See http://icommons.org/node/acawiki) use open licensing, community, and the Internet specifically to more widely disseminate research findings for the public. AcaWiki leverages the power of social software to produce Creative Commons-licensed, summaries of academic papers in language accessible for the lay reader, for the education and use of the general population. The project aims to get a community of graduate students and academics to write short (two- to three-paragraph) magazine-like summaries of academic papers and contribute them to the AcaWiki pool. Because copyright applies only to the written work, and not the ideas or data behind it, summaries of academic papers can be written and licensed under a Creative Commons BY (Attribution) license and freely distributed on the Internet and in hard copy throughout the world.

To add more value to the information, other contributors will be able to annotate, discuss, or append information to the original entry, perhaps adding analogies, pictures, videos or other devices to make the information more easily understandable. Community members can also add value by creating "playlists" of summaries by stringing them together with segues to show how a particular stream of research has evolved over time so they can more quickly understand the "big picture." Researchers, experts in the field, graduate students, and the public will be able to link through to a discussion section for each of the articles where they can debate or post supplementary materials. Beyond these primary features, summaries of academic works can be translated into other languages so that people around the world can have access to them. Further, summaries can be marked up with machine-readable metadata so that machines can derive understanding from the content. With such a resource available, individuals, educators, and society benefit from increased access to scholarly research.

Design: Open Design Provides Flexibility and Choices

How do we apply these "mixing" principles to design of new learning environments, both real-world and virtual? And will this mixing—achieved through open source or open standards communities or through enlightened design of physical learning spaces—result in designs that themselves invite free exchange and social learning?

In a typical lecture hall, the teacher is up front and the students sit in chairs that are fixed to the floor. Such physical inflexibility restricts how the teacher can interact with students and students can interact with each other. Software design has followed a similar pattern, favoring tools that support faculty, rather than student, management in digital space. A traditional course management system, for example, reinforces the segmented learning experience of students, where their work ("learning assets") is rarely used in a subsequent semester or across a series of courses.

The design and development of educational applications, even if they are open source, often lead to limited educational value and fragile viability. Technical design aspects have often limited the portability and interoperability of learning resources and consequently inhibit the kind of flexibility that leads to support of diverse pedagogy and sharing of learning materials. For example, the tight coupling of the user interface to learning components (as in a monolithic learning management system) constrains the use of learning objects in different contexts or to address different learning goals.

An open architecture project such as MIT's Open Knowledge Initiative (O.K.I) (See http://www.okiproject.org/) addresses two critical attributes for technology tools and platforms to be educationally productive: choice and sustainability. Enabling and supporting choice is an essential goal in light of some "givens" of the nature of technology and educational environments:

• Educational value is derived through multiple modes and diverse tools. For example, an instructor might want to support a class with a sophisticated simulation engine and a rather ordinary discussion list while administering tests on paper. The platform must support easy transition from one to the other.

• The technologies on which we build our infrastructure will necessarily change. In the near term, educational software frameworks must foster a "marketspace" of tools and content, both proprietary and open source, so that educators and learners can pick and choose the functionality that best meets their needs.

The distinction between proprietary, open source, or "let's-build-our-own" applications have become blurred as OKI-inspired ideas and technologies are changing how applications are created and maintained. Increasingly, open applications that embrace open standards that enable prudent combinations of open source and proprietary solutions are being seen as the norm.

Open application architecture and design are crucial enablers for an environment rich with remix opportunities and where higher education, industry, and standards groups bring different contributions further accelerating education technology innovations and diffusions. The technical and legal framework of these systems should allow the participation and contribution of different actors based on their specific strengths, to be leveraged. For instance, the Sakai and OSP initiatives have embraced the community source approach to leverage both the creative values of academia and the ongoing maintenance and marketing abilities of industry through the engagement of community corporate partners, such as rSmart (See http://www.rsmart.com) among others.

A sustainable educational ecology requires this diversity of participants and a sense of safety to innovate. If a code contribution can lead to a timely improvement in application functionality, then it seems safe to continue to contribute. If the community is organized to preserve the contribution process over time and support the application, then it seems safe to use.

Flexibility in design of tools and spaces, both virtual and "real" life, helps both faculty and students take advantage of the greater number of choices they now have for communication and collaboration, visualization, access to resources, archiving and searching, blended classes, and rethinking course design. The open technical and organizational frameworks that support such flexibility are in a sense a natural extension of the open learning and research architecture that higher education has attempted to present over time, albeit with mixed results, in order to allow the integration and interoperation of new and diverse ideas and research.

Rethinking Education for the Open Learner

The initiatives referred to so far illustrate that the functionality of open educational resources can be extended: Content can be altered and improved upon, pedagogical methods can be shared, along with the possibility of learning gains, and new communities can collaborate constructively through open design and practices. They suggest that the silos we all know about in higher education are under assault in the new world of remixing. When allied around a common goal of producing the best application for academic use, trust and familiarity develop and a common discourse emerges. People learn to talk to each other and the silos start to dissolve. Open source communities such as Sakai or Apache or Kuali, and open knowledge communities such as OCW or OKI, are prime examples of how the interests of ownership and of social creativity are being rebalanced within the open world.

We can see that new affiliations are developing around the core knowledge-creation process in higher education and that technology applications on the Internet are literally creating academic culture and space in the virtual.

Can we then also imagine an educational model that productively leverages this abundance to offer structured learning opportunities to the networked learner beyond, or even instead of enrollment in a higher education institution?

Before leaping enthusiastically into constructing the possibilities, it is instructive to remind ourselves that existing academic institutions do help to navigate through the human sea of knowledge. They organize it into majors and requirements to make the decision process much easier and more goal oriented. They provide a teacher and classmates to both guide and motivate. They provide a structure and a social context to help bridge students from beginning stages of learning toward maturity. They help students address issues of finalizing work by providing a schedule of "deliverables" (assignment sets), of matching the learner with the job market, of certifying the value of students' learning, and the general issues of being a young person away from home.

Though an online structure could not offer the full array of brick-and-mortar institution services, we might be able to define online communities that offer some of them.

Community for Student: P2PU

Let us imagine a vibrant Web community of learners at something called Peer-To-Peer University, or "P2PU." P2PU would not be a "real" university, but rather, a group of self-learners and tutors who work together to emulate some of the functions an academic institution would carry out, in a peer-to-peer fashion. Providing degree tracks would help self-learners navigate the vast terrain of OER resources in a goal-oriented way. P2PU would define "degrees" by assembling OER materials from different repositories that, together, would suffice as a "degree" in that subject. For example, P2PU might specify 15 physics courses, available across the various OER project sites, which one would have to complete in order to get a P2PU physics degree. Since many OER resources contain components that are not free and open, such as textbooks and academic papers, P2PU would only use courses that either have all the components available, or will find alternatives. Thus students might take Physics 101 from MIT OCW, and Physics 202 from Tufts OCW.

Beyond specifying degree tracks, P2PU would organize scheduled "courses" where groups of learners would come together and learn the material for a course. Participants could also have profile pages that detail their interests, occupations, and show which courses they have completed. Posting the names of students and the OER courses somewhere on the site could provide an additional incentive for having students complete classes at P2PU. It may be that one day an employer would recognize a "Net Degree" from P2PU to be as valuable, or even more valuable, than a traditional university degree. Inherent in the system, P2PU students—who are comfortable with their "network selves"—would be recognized as resourceful self-starters and group learners. A "Net Degree" from P2PU would be valuable in its own right, and soon begin to take on its own meaning of accreditation.

Barriers to Realizing OER's Potential

Though such possibilities are inspiring, does the current architecture of higher education allow for opportunities such as P2PU? Or is the inertia of passive learning perpetuating a disinclination, on the part of students as well as faculty, to enter a "discomfort zone" of remixing? Do students even like decentralized authority? Between faculty and students, which group is really risk-aversive when it comes to imaginative use of technology and open education?

We could easily believe that faculty who themselves are exploring new means of participating in remixing communities in their own fields would naturally apply this experience in the classroom. Even then, while some faculty members may boldly go where open education leads them, some students, despite their expertise in some uses of the Internet and IT tools, can be very conservative in their expectations in the classroom. They may come to college expecting that regardless of the IT toys on campus, in the classroom itself, their teachers will still tell them what to know and then test them on what they have been told.

This technology-conservative view, of course, is not the popular view about the "net-gen." (See, for example, http://www.centerdigitaled.com/story.php?id = 103831.) However, we wonder if current generalizations about the net-gen really play out in the classroom. Chatting on your smart phone in class does not necessarily mean you, as a young student, are ready to be immersed in energy-demanding, non-directed collaborative work. Facility with technology and focused intellectual work are still very different cognitively. And, perhaps the students' high schools have been held to national standards that run counter to the new culture of abundance. Students may "have the hippie in them," but they do not really expect it to be in their teachers. Have we created a mental mold called "the classroom" that has us in thrall?

Perhaps part of the current puzzle about open education lies in this question: if the remixing process is speeded up and a million eyes replace "gatekeepers," then is knowledge enriched or watered down? How do we certify this accelerated process of learning and creating knowledge? Faculty members have served for centuries as a knowledge filter, providing interpretations of disciplinary knowledge, guiding students toward important ideas and methods of inquiry so they themselves can gain expertise. Rather than defining a rigid course, are faculty ready to become more like facilitators, guiding students through the "raw" disciplinary remixing?

Poised for Change?

We are at the very beginning of a millennial shift in higher education. How do all the parties involved—faculty, students, designers, institutional and corporate leaders, and others—best adapt to network learning and accept learning as a work in constant progress? How do faculty best include the now-available, just-in-time student work in the open-education academic conversation? How can their own classrooms become as vital as the remixing sites described here?

Formalizing and certifying network learning will take time, as we are learning through work with electronic portfolios. Electronic portfolios formalize the process of in-class remixing, but to use them well, faculty must reexamine the often-implicit learning goals underlying their courses and see how these goals play out in the new "student-work-in-progress" portfolio world that is a microcosm of the larger open-education world. How can their students progress toward those learning goals in a way that includes the vast learning opportunities opening before them like a bright dawn? How can students engage in disciplinary content creation and remixing using new digital tools under the guidance of their teachers? And how can their curriculum, learning spaces, and tools be designed to seamlessly incorporate ever-new learning opportunities? How can they join the dance of digital abundance?

Perhaps we are leaving behind the time when change in higher education can continue to be incremental and are instead entering a period of disrupted equilibrium.

Note

1. See W. Huitt (2001), Humanism and open education, *Educational Psychology Interactive* (Valdosta, GA: Valdosta State University). Retrieved Jan 8, 2008, from http://chiron.valdosta.edu/whuitt/col/affsys/humed.html. This study summarizes other studies to support the claim that "open education" approaches in the 1990s resulted in only mixed results, and that "facilitative teaching"—used as a direct instruction method—produced better results. Aspects of facilitative teaching:

- response to student feeling;
- use of student ideas in ongoing instructional interactions;
- discussion with students (dialogue);
- praise of students;
- congruent teacher talk (less ritualistic);
- tailoring of contents to the individual student's frame of reference (explanations created to fit the immediate needs of the learners);
- and smiling with students.

Using technology tools now allows instructors to achieve all of these—except the last—to be more "facilitative" without having to use a direct instruction method if they adopt traditional open education approaches. Still, the cautions from this study of seven years ago are important.

References

Cambridge, D. (In press). Two faces of integrative learning. In D. Cambridge, B. Cambridge, and K. Yancey (Eds.) *Electronic Portfolios 2.0: Emergent Research on Implementation and Impact.* Herndon, VA: Stylus Publishing.

Slater, P. (1970). *The Pursuit of Loneliness: American Culture at the Breaking Point.* Boston: Beacon Press.

7

Digital Libraries, Learning Communities, and Open Education

Clifford Lynch

A century and a half ago, Thomas Carlyle famously wrote that "the true university today is a collection of books."[1] If indeed the true university is a library, then the unprecedented capability of the Internet and the World Wide Web to open up access to almost incomprehensibly large storehouses of information should be tantamount to throwing open the doors of a new, global university. This would greatly advance the dream of universally available open education—the dream of making as many educational opportunities available to as many people worldwide as possible, with minimal economic barriers other than access to basic information technology and network infrastructure.

Access to education is not the same thing as access to information, although the two are intimately related and might often reasonably be viewed as two endpoints of a continuum. Unquestionably, access to information, knowledge, and educational resources offers opportunities for learning, but gaining education from these opportunities may be more elusive.

Further, *access* is not the same as *open access*, and the economics here are important. Open access to information in the digital world has nearly zero marginal cost (basically incremental cycles and bandwidth), with virtually all of the expenses in the first copy of the information resource. Traditional educational offerings in both the physical and digital world have substantial marginal costs in terms of teacher-student interaction. While technology can perhaps help teachers to manage a few more students per class effectively, fundamentally, more students in these settings mean more scarce and expensive teachers.

To really make the economics of large-scale open education work, we need to minimize or even completely eliminate the traditional teacher-student interaction in favor of learner interaction with digital content and software. This suggests to me that for the foreseeable future, while open education offerings may substantially increase in quality, they will continue to lag behind the best educational offerings financed under more traditional models. And we should also recognize that the Internet is greatly broadening access to both informational resources and educational opportunities that are *not* open along with those that are, at least in relatively wealthy nations.

It is important, then, to explore the relationship between information access and access to education in the digital world, consider how digital libraries and other advanced information technologies may bring us closer to the goal of high-quality open education, and understand some of the gaps and shortcomings in potential.

Before going further, I want to immediately clarify that my focus here is on higher education, or at least education at a level that assumes basic reading, communication, mathematical, and analytical skills are already in place to provide a reasonable foundation for further learning; that there is sufficient fluency with information technology so that using local computational resources and the network, and information, tools, and services that are available through the network, do not present a major barrier. Also, I do not consider here the very real obstacles that language—most likely, lack of fluency in English—may present the would-be learner.

Libraries, Learning Opportunities, and Educational Opportunities

A difficult and subtle distinction between *learning* and *education* is actually central to questions about open education and to understanding why the treasure troves of material on the Internet do not "solve" the open education problem.

The collections available on the Internet represent a fabulous opportunity for learning. A smart, highly motivated, and disciplined learner with the right mindset and learning style can indeed gain a fine, though perhaps not complete, education in many subjects just by studying this material. Likewise, academic and research libraries, as we have traditionally understood them, offer rich learning opportunities but not typically educational opportunities, except in very limited areas such as information literacy or education about disciplinary information resources in academic settings.

So, whether in a library or on the Internet, it can be hard going for the learner, particularly if he or she is studying in isolation. For educational opportunities are more than just learning opportunities: There is some implication of responsibility by a teacher or educational institution for enabling effective, responsive, appropriate learning opportunities that are personalized to the learner. There is a sense of agency on the part of the educator. And, as I discuss later, some educational opportunities, of course, offer additional expectations, such as certification of learning.

Textbooks or videos of lectures represent a sort of halfway point: There is clearly an intention on the part of the author or lecturer to provide an educational opportunity but without the interaction, adaptation, evaluation, and personalization that characterizes full-fledged delivery of quality education. So, one way to frame the open education challenge is to ask how far beyond textbooks and instructional videos we can affordably go by intelligent use of technology and appropriate educational content; when these techniques are likely to be fruitful (for what educational needs and in what disciplines); and how closely their outcomes compare to those of traditional human teacher-intensive educational approaches. It is also worth asking the question in reverse: How much better does a traditional higher education institution do when it offers a lecture course to 500 undergraduates?

Changing the Model

The range of educational offerings—whether delivered face-to-face or via distance education through established institutions, through new commercial players, or through open education initiatives—is changing and diversifying in response to a wide range of social, demographic, and economic pressures. While the comfortable, familiar model of the college course as the unit of education springs to mind, it seems likely that we will see both larger and smaller quanta of educational opportunity offered, as well as the traditional course, in open education initiatives and elsewhere.

A wide range of motivations and goals will be driving people to these educational offerings. We already see people who want to learn some specific set of skills or master a body of facts, achievement of which is fairly easily tested. Others seek much deeper levels of professional or scholarly competence, which is more difficult to assess. While some people are pursuing leisure and recreational learning in areas like the arts, genealogy, home repair, and local history, others are seeking just-in-time, highly focused learning in response to personal or business pressures, for example concerning disease and treatment options or specific technical or regulatory questions.

The topics of interest will be much more diverse than the offerings of today's typical university, and even when the topics are familiar, the context may be radically different from the usual university courses and degree programs. For some topics, universities are natural reservoirs of knowledge and expertise; for others, we'll see the entrance of new players who may also want to become participants in the creation of open education offerings.

We may see people expecting and seeking educationally oriented approaches to what are more appropriately viewed as (or at least have historically been relegated to) independent study or personal research projects. This will raise interesting questions: Individualized independent study or guided research under faculty supervision is something we have little idea how to support in an open education environment, other than perhaps by introducing what are now unsupervised learners to each other to work together. But when one can aggregate interest in very specialized topics on a global basis, explicitly constructing educational offerings may occasionally become viable where it has not been in the past.

Educational Delivery in the Digital Environment

Clearly, the central core of an education experience, or a learning experience, is deep, thoughtful, and reflective study and engagement with a body of knowledge in a multiplicity of forms—facts, techniques, algorithms and practices, analytical frameworks, evidence. The engagement can be relatively tidy, constrained and structured—for example, working through a series of learning objectives embodied in a single textbook. Or it can be highly unstructured and open-ended, as the learner engages an anarchic body of primary evidence, and conflicting analysis of this body of evidence, and struggles to make sense of it all.

The amount of digital material available to support and engage learners is already massive and continues to grow. Yet this huge corpus is still skewed and limited in numerous ways, and calls for some critical analysis and assessment.

The Limitation of Digitized Libraries

Google's program to digitize major university libraries at institutions such as Stanford, the University of Michigan, and Oxford has received a great deal of publicity and inspired a great amount of excitement. What is not as broadly understood as it should be is that because of copyright constraints, only the public domain works from these libraries (to a first approximation, those published before 1923) will be available for reading in the foreseeable future. For almost everything else, the user will at best be able to see a couple of sentences (a "snippet") in response to a search, and then follow links to perhaps purchase a copy of the book or borrow a physical copy from a library (most likely through interlibrary loan).

In both cases, this is almost completely useless in most open education settings, particularly outside the United States. So the digitization of these great research libraries will not, as many assume, make the majority of their contents widely and openly available. There are many other digitization programs underway, such as the work of the Open Content Alliance, but they, too, will be able to offer access to only older, out-of-copyright works, or to limited collections of in-copyright works that are being made available online with the specific permission of the rights holder (for example, some university press publications, particularly out-of-print ones).

So, while a vast amount of historically interesting source material is going to be available, most monographic scholarship and most textbooks from the last three quarters of the last century will not be publicly available. Huge swaths of the primary documentary evidence of the twentieth century—audio and visual, as well as textual materials—are locked up by copyright and often inaccessible even to students and researchers at our leading universities through their research libraries, as well as to the broader public seeking information on the Web.

The Open Access Movement

On the more positive side, there has been a major move, often called "the open access movement," to open up the research journal literature. The net effect is that many journal back files are becoming publicly accessible without barriers; only the most recent six months or a year of material is locked up, and many of those papers are available in preprint or other forms through institutional or disciplinary repositories (Suber, n.d.; Willinsky, 2005). This development opens a tremendous wealth of information, and the constraints on access to the most recent materials is likely to be a problem predominantly for active researchers and very advanced students rather than the broad community of learners, though there are some very important exceptions involving patient care, for example. Indeed, in the last few years, the open access movement has gained a great deal of traction, and the trend towards more open access to the research literature seems clear.

Over the past decade, growing numbers of scholars have also been making both research and instructional resources freely available over the Web in growing numbers. These include open access textbooks, reference databases, collections of learning objects, course notes and exercises, and video and audio of lectures and related material. Some of this is targeted mostly at other teachers who will want to adapt and reuse the materials (for example, the collections of highly granular learning objects represented in projects like MERLOT are not likely to be of much help to the self-guided learner). Other materials, like the OpenCourseWare project initiated by MIT and now joined by other leading higher education institutions, are used both by teachers in their own educational work and by individual learners seeking educational materials.

Cyberinfrastructure

The growth of e-science or cyberinfrastructure approaches to scholarly work are making possible engagement with extensive observational and experimental data a real possibility for learners at all levels (National Science Foundation Cyberinfrastructure Council, March 2007). Parallels in the humanities include extensive digitized collections of primary source materials from archives, library special collections, and museums (American Council of Learned Societies, December 2006). These developments point out how increasingly diffuse the boundaries between learning and research are becoming in the networked environment. They also suggest the possible development of new, content analysis–oriented learning communities centered on these new information resources.

Challenges to the Learner

The complex and uneven nature of the available corpus of information is very challenging to the isolated and self-directed learner. There is a great burden in evaluating available information resources, determining what is likely to be obsolete, how well various materials have been vetted, and the like. But there is also a very high payoff in learning to master these evaluation skills: They are, in effect, part of learning how to learn on a continuing basis.

Yet the learner faces considerable problems attendant to a lack of coherence of available resources: How and when should one move from one to the next? Which sources cover the same ground—possibly from different perspectives? Where are the interdependencies among resources?

Some of these problems could be addressed, fairly inexpensively, by developing and maintaining high-quality, carefully reviewed study guides to various subjects and disciplines. An educational program typically structures a coherent body of knowledge to be engaged, a specific set of skills to be mastered; it seeks to offer viewpoints that, if not comprehensively diverse, are at least widely and informatively varied. It is very hard for a learner engaging an overwhelming mass of information and knowledge resources to do this for him or herself. Opening up large numbers of course syllabi and reading lists for review on the network—as OpenCourseWare has done—is a very valuable beginning and foundation for addressing this problem, and indeed in building linkages between courses and the literature. Indeed, formal and informal guides to the literature in various subjects, bibliographies, pathfinders, and other tools may also take on expanded importance in an open education environment.

Note, however, that the realm of questions I imagine the learner as grappling with is related to, but different, from more basic questions of evaluating individual information resources. Consider the difference between deciding that a specific document expresses a credible opinion on something and being able to conclude that the collection of documents that you have examined constitutes a reasonably comprehensive sampling of the diversity of opinions on the topic. Many reasonably mature self-learners can do the former fairly well; the latter is much harder and represents an important step towards mastering a subject.

Other Aspects of the Learning Experience

Beyond engagement with learning materials, there are a number of other components that can legitimately be defined as part of an educational experience.

Social Interaction

Educational experiences can and often do incorporate a very rich and sometimes centrally important social component. This can range from basic team and social learning, group study and problem solving as an option for the learner who finds this useful, to educational experiences that deliberately emphasize the development of communications and group work and problem solving skills as a key part of the curriculum. The continuum extends to what might be considered a form of professional socialization: learning to think, for example, like an architect, doctor, lawyer, mathematician—learning, that is, the habits of mind of the professional (J. S. Brown and L. S. Shulman, personal communication, September 15, 2006).

In an educational setting the faculty will make choices about how important the social components are. In a learning experience, it is likely that the learner will seek social interactions only to the extent that he or she finds them helpful in assisting individual learning. (This helps to explain why professional socialization typically cannot be achieved simply by learner-directed study of information resources.)

Group Management   The Internet, of course, can aggregate groups that share common educational interests. In cases where large numbers of learners are studying the same thing, it can aggregate into cohorts based on skill level, geography, and a variety of other factors. In cases where only a small number of people are studying a given topic worldwide, it can form a group that could never have existed when education was physically constrained to a specific university campus.

But there are many issues to consider in the open education context that have been poorly explored to date—and the answers vary from one type of educational experience to another (Lynch, 1999). For example: How big should a learning community or cohort be? How long should it be kept together? How important is cohort coherence: Should people be able to join an existing community on a rolling basis, or wait for the next one to be launched? How large a diversity of competence should be permitted within a learning community? For example, do we want to combine students studying algebra with those studying calculus with graduate students studying mathematics? How much weight should be given to geography? It helps with time zones, and thus with options for synchronous as well as asynchronous participation in the learning community, and also creates the possibility of allowing learners to meet physically if they wish. How heavily should we emphasize linguistic and cultural homogeneity within a cohort? Can we do bottom-up learning community formation for learners outside of formal educational settings? (Here, I think the evidence is strong that we can).

The social questions about group management are very important. When education is based in an institutional setting (whether it is being conducted in a physical classroom or a virtual space), having a faculty member in charge provides a framework for managing disruptive class participants. In an open education framework, much more complex social norm and community management practices need to be established, which can be very time consuming and distract from the educational goals at hand.

Assessing and Certifying Learning
Arguably, education also involves a trustworthy, nuanced, ongoing assessment of the learner's work and level of understanding, combined with some highly targeted and personalized efforts to correct misunderstandings and to deepen knowledge and skills. At least in some areas, there is promising work on personalized tutoring and evaluation systems.[2] Other areas—think about learning how to writing analytic essays—are much harder to support through automated means alone.

Sometimes education involves not just a managed learning process but also a certification of the outcome of that process—a degree or similar certificate. Some of this can be achieved by standardized testing, though it is not clear that the opportunity to take such standardized tests will be free or inexpensive or widely available. And the deeper the level of knowledge or skill being tested, the more likely it is for human experts to become deeply involved in the administration of the tests and evaluation of the test results.

Prospects for Improving Open Education

Perhaps one fruitful way to think about open education is in terms of progressive improvements to meet the needs of learners, better define and exploit educational resources, and better provide assessment of learning.

Meeting the Needs of Learners

There have always been learners for whom the library was enough, or nearly enough: They can largely work alone, and if they can find the books, articles, and other materials they need, they can learn, perhaps supplemented by some very modest guidance from human experts. The Internet, and the growth of the information base accessible through the Internet, has greatly benefited this class of learners. The introduction of large amounts of multimedia material—audio and video of lectures, for example—has further enhanced the opportunities for this group of learners, as well as helping to accommodate a greater diversity of learning preferences.

The question of "very modest guidance from human experts" is an interesting issue in the network context. Certainly the widespread availability of electronic mail has made it easy for learners to reach out to experts, but it is less clear how often or how much such experts are willing to donate their time to help random learners, or what can be done to make such donations of time and expertise more effective. Certainly one sees some appallingly bad practices (for example, faculty telling students to e-mail a prominent person in a given field and ask them a basic question) that destroy social capital. It would be helpful to get a better picture of faculty practices in this area, and to consider how faculty willingness to contribute some limited amount of time might best be leveraged in responding to legitimate needs here.

Another kind of learner works much more effectively in a peer group, cohort, class, or other social situation: Working and studying together is very important, though the presence of a teacher as well as the peer group may be relatively insignificant. The various social technologies supported by the Internet now allow us to aggregate interested learners and allow them to collaborate together using the network in a wide variety of ways.

And what of the roles of teachers, educators, and scholars in this new open education environment? A few things seem clear, such as the emergence of scholar-curators associated with data and primary content information resources serving as guides and teachers to individuals and learning communities wanting to directly engage these resources in cyberspace. They will likely form the nexus of new teaching communities that want to exploit these information resources in their own teaching. Similarly, those authoring open education resources will likely offer to manage and moderate teaching communities forming around these resources.

An Opportunity for Growth   While there has been vast investment in this area in the context of institutional higher education (for example, learning management systems and collaboration environments) there has been, to the best of my knowledge, very little investment in the context of free, extra-institutional, open education opportunities. Also, I suspect that too much of our thinking is dominated by experience in older technologies such as newsgroups, mailing lists, and learning management systems rather than newer extra-institutional models like MySpace, Facebook, or perhaps most interestingly, Second Life.

Defining and Exploiting the Tools

There is ongoing debate about exactly what constitutes a digital library. Clearly there is an information corpus, a collection. Clearly there are also tools to analyze and work with this collection, though there is a debate about how extensive and "active" these tools should be—the extent to which they should include the ability to make and publish annotations and commentaries related to the underlying connection, for example. Related to this question is the extent to which a good digital library should also incorporate social or community tools and services to allow people working with the collection to learn about, communicate with, and collaborate with each other—recommender systems, collaboration environments, and the like (Bishop, Van House, and Buttenfield, 2003; Lynch, 2002, May). Here digital libraries tend to go beyond traditional library collections, the facilities that house them, and the organizations that manage them in building and managing community around a collection—which is different than community around a set of learning goals and interests.

But many of the tools should be common, and when we look at the extra-institutional nature of open education, perhaps collection-oriented tools will provide useful insights to complement the strongly institutionally based tools from the learning management tradition.

Improving Assessment

Similarly, while there has been a great deal of investment in automated diagnostic, testing, and tutoring systems within the context of specific courses and specific institutional settings, I am not aware of much investment in the context of extra-institutional open education opportunities.

I suspect that one of the problems here is that of context. The systems are fairly tightly designed to fit within a specific curriculum, a carefully structured and explicit set of learning objectives and skills to be mastered. They codify extensive experience with learners engaging this curriculum and are also intended to co-exist with highly skilled human teachers (and often a peer group learning community) as part of a structured educational experience. Some investment in exploring if, when, and how these tools can be generalized might be a very helpful contribution to the open education agenda.

Meeting the Compelling Need

I want to be clear that rather than denigrating, I am celebrating the enormous value and importance of the straightforward learning opportunities that are multiplying along with the information resources and knowledge spaces accessible through the Internet. The learning opportunities are real, and they can address some educational needs as well. But our digital libraries and knowledge spaces will not fully meet the societal need for enhanced and broadened access to educational opportunities.

I do not believe that it is feasible today to provide large-scale, free, open access higher education that is anywhere near as good as the educational opportunities our best universities can currently offer, or that this gap will close in the foreseeable future. But we must be mindful of the overwhelming scale of the unmet need, particularly from a global perspective. There is a compelling call to do the best we can today to respond to this need, and hope that we will be able to respond more effectively in the future.

What does seem likely is that with some very manageable investments we can go a considerable distance beyond simply providing learning opportunities, and the economics of these kinds of educational offerings scale up gracefully. They also enhance the value and utility of the underlying and complementary knowledge and information resources. They pave the way for a number of new modes of interacting with content that go beyond the traditional (mostly solitary and mostly non-interactive) models of pure learning opportunities. Many of these technologies are already starting to become well established in the learning, research, and practice communities that have grown up around digital libraries (in the broad sense of information systems). Further exploration and understanding of the interactions here can, I believe, benefit both the development of open educational offerings and digital libraries.

However, we must be ready to address public policy issues. It is all too convenient for politicians looking for financial savings to argue that more and more of the functions of higher education are being provided by access to the "universal library" available through the Internet and thus does not require separate investments—that the Internet offers a properly motivated learner all that he or she needs. If we are going to see this potential fulfilled, we must be able to articulate clearly the differences between *access to information resources* and *access to education*.

Notes

1. Joan Lippincott and Cecilia Preston provided very helpful comments on an earlier version of this chapter; I am also grateful for the patience, comments and encouragement from Toru Iiyoshi and his colleagues.
2. See, for example, Rice University's Connexions project, the Math Emporium at Virginia Tech, and Carnegie Mellon University's Open Learning Project.

References

American Council of Learned Societies. (2006, December). *Our Cultural Commonwealth: Report of the American Council of Learned Societies Report on Cyberinfrastructure for the Humanities and Social Sciences*. Retrieved September 12, 2007, from http://www.acls.org/ex-cyber_report.htm

Bishop, A. P., Van House, N., and Buttenfield, B. (Eds). (2003). *Digital Library Use: Social Practice in Design and Evaluation.* Cambridge, MA: MIT Press.

Lynch, C. (1999). Civilizing the information ecology: views of information landscapes for a learning society. In S. Criddle, L. Dempsey, and R. Heseltine (Eds.), *Information landscapes for a learning society: Networking and the Future of Libraries 3* (257–268). London: Library Association Publishing.

Lynch, C. (2002, May). Digital collections, digital libraries and the digitization of cultural heritage information. *First Monday, 7*(5). Retrieved September 12, 2007, from http://www.firstmonday.org/issues/issue7_5/lynch/index.html

National Science Foundation Cyberinfrastructure Council. (2007, March). *National Science Foundation Cyberinfrastructure Vision for 21st Century Discovery.* Retrieved September 12, 2007, from http://www.nsf.gov/publications/pub_summ.jsp?ods_key=nsf0728

Suber, P. (n.d.). Open Access news. Retrieved September 12, 2007, from http://www.earlham.edu/~peters/fos/fosblog.html

Willinsky, J. (2005). *The access principle: The Case for Open Access to Research and Scholarship.* Cambridge, MA: MIT Press.

8

Open Source in Open Education: Promises and Challenges

Christopher J. Mackie

He who does not live in some degree for others, hardly lives for himself.
—Montaigne

Openness begets openness; that is the hope. But can openness sustain itself? That is an essential question. Both open educational content (OEC) and open source software (OSS) have generated cultures of openness among the institutions and individuals who have embraced them. The members of those cultures have discovered new efficiencies, new opportunities for productivity ("social production"), new forms of organization ("coopetition"), new markets ("the long tail"), new pathways to learning, and new models for engaging with their colleagues and others around the sharing and collaborative construction of intellectual property. However, the jury is still out on whether these two cultures are each sustainable, and whether they can help each other to achieve sustainability.

This chapter discusses some of the challenges facing OSS development and attempts to draw lessons from them for the OEC community. It makes a few key points: that multiple models of both OEC and OSS are possible; that each model has different strengths and weaknesses; and that the approaches one takes to sustainability will depend in important ways on the models of openness that one wishes to encourage.

My program's grantees and other partners inform the analysis in this chapter; however, the views expressed here are my own. Openness is a controversial topic. Even people who agree on its desirability can disagree over what openness really means and how best to achieve it. My colleagues and grantees hold diverse views on the various openness movements, as reflected in the diversity of the Foundation's openness initiatives, which range from the development of OSS through Mellon/ RIT, to the information accessibility and digitization initiatives of the Mellon Scholarly Communication Program, to the subscription models of Mellon-supported organizations such as JSTOR, ARTstor, Aluka, and Portico, to Mellon's extensive support of the OpenCourseWare initiative. Many of us hope that openness can be achieved broadly and deeply throughout the educational sphere, but the analyses and evaluations on which the recommendations in this chapter are based do not necessarily reflect the views of my colleagues or the Mellon Foundation.

OSS Limitations and CSS

For all that the OSS movement has produced some runaway successes, including projects like Perl, Linux, and Mozilla Firefox, there appear to be certain types of challenges that are difficult for OSS to tackle. Most notably, voluntaristic OSS projects struggle to launch products whose primary customers are institutions rather than individuals: financial or HR systems rather than Web servers or browsers; or uniform, manageable desktop environments rather than programming languages or operating systems. This limitation may trace to any of several factors: the number of programmers having the special expertise required to deliver an enterprise information system may be too small to sustain a community; the software may be inherently too unglamorous or uninteresting to attract volunteers; the benefits of the software may be too diffuse to encourage beneficiaries to collaborate to produce it; the software may be too complex for its development to be coordinated on a purely volunteer basis; the software may require the active, committed participation of specific firms or institutions having strong disincentives to participate in OSS; and so on. Any of these factors might be enough to prevent the successful formation of an OSS project, and there are many useful types of enterprise software—including much of the enterprise software needed by higher education institutions—to which several of them apply. In short, however well a standard OSS approach may work for many projects, there is little reason to believe that the same model can work for every conceivable software project.

Some higher education and other nonprofit institutions, recognizing the limitations of the classic OSS strategy, have evolved a variant that attempts to launch OSS projects for environments in which the classic model appears impossible. This variant brings to the fore the patronage dynamics, governance supports, and incentive structures obscured in the classic model and makes them the centerpiece of the strategy. Under this new model, several institutions contract together to build software for a common need, with the intent of releasing that software as open source. The institutions form a virtual development organization consisting of employees seconded from each of the partners. This entity is governed cooperatively by the partners and managed as if it were an enterprise software development organization, with project and team leads, architects, developers, and usability specialists, and all the trappings of organizational life, including reporting relationships and formal incentive structures. During and after the initial construction phase, the consortial partners open the project and invite in anyone who cares to contribute; over time the project evolves into a more ordinary OSS project, albeit one in which institutions rather than individual volunteers usually continue to play a major role. This variant is sometimes called "directed open source" but is becoming better known as "community source software" (CSS).

The relative deprecation of altruism as a value by CSS, and its replacement with an emphasis on intelligently structured incentives, has implications for how CSS projects organize themselves. CSS products typically take several years to reach market, and partners need to be confident that each participant organization will continue to contribute for the duration. As one CSS partner put it, "if we get a new Provost tomorrow who wants to know why our people are being paid by us and taking up our space but reporting to someone at another university to build software that we're going to give away for free, I can't respond by talking about altruistic benefits to higher education or the virtues of open source: I need to have a spreadsheet that shows clearly why it is in our institutional interest to keep doing this." Statements like that strike some OSS supporters as mercenary, but essentially the same calculus—perhaps better hidden from view—informs institutional patronage of OSS projects as well. CSS is not fundamentally different from OSS; rather, it recognizes the hidden sustainability dynamics of OSS and harnesses them more explicitly.

CSS has demonstrated its ability to build enterprise-scale software that can compete on features with commercial offerings; examples include the Sakai collaborative learning environment and the newer Kuali Financial System. Sakai is now in use or in pilot at more than 100 institutions and is growing more rapidly in adoption than many commercial systems. Kuali Financials offered its first public release only a few months ago, and a few smaller institutions are already adopting it; the rest of the projects are still pre-release. The initial successes of CSS have been visible enough that other projects are currently underway. Kuali, in particular, has already spawned projects to produce research administration tools and student information systems, and there is reportedly some interest in building a Kuali HR system and a library automation system as well.

The institutional orientation of CSS may be a powerful stabilizing and sustainability factor. CSS as a concept is substantially newer than OSS, however, and the jury remains out. Advocates argue that the institutional commitment is itself a guarantee of stability. Institutions do not replace these systems quickly, so a community of supporters is guaranteed for at least the medium term, making CSS potentially even a safer bet than a commercial product from a vendor that may be bought-out at any moment. The advocates have logic on their side, but many higher education CIOs understandably want to see empirical evidence that the logic is sound before they commit to joining these projects.

OEC Differences from OSS, CSS

If we have learned one thing about sustaining openness through the work of Mellon/RIT, it is that project sustainability results from the careful alignment of producers' and consumers' interests, so that each party gains something of value from the cooperative project. Traditional OSS usually aligns those interests straightforwardly, because the producers of the software are generally also its users. In cases where producers and consumers are not the same people but are both members of the same organizations, CSS may prove to work better because it makes the organizations, rather than the individuals, both producers and consumers. Other models for sustainability have been attempted, but if one cannot align producer and consumer interests effectively, then the only other demonstrated way to keep a project viable is by means of an ongoing, outside cash infusion, as when a commercial vendor adopts an OSS project. This makes the donor a single point of failure for the entire project, and if the donor is a commercial entity, it may also introduce important conflicts of interest.

One significant difference between OSS and OEC is that the alignment of producer with consumer interests in OSS production is voluntary, while the alignment of interests in CSS and OEC production usually is not. Once an institution chooses to join a CSS initiative, it assigns staff to the project as it would to any other software project; some voluntary choice may be involved, but staffing a CSS project is a job, not a hobby. Similarly, an institution may choose to join an open content initiative and may even ask for faculty volunteers. So far, at least, institutions usually end up compensating or subsidizing faculty in some way for participation—and I know of no institution that gives students the choice of whether or not to have open content in their curricula, any more than institutions ask students to choose their textbooks.

Both CSS and OEC production therefore require institutions to mobilize and align internal incentives for their stakeholders while also aligning their organizational interests with those of their consortial partners. This makes CSS particularly interesting for people seeking a sustainability model for OEC. With its leveraging of organizations to cut through the voluntary alignment problem, CSS points to at least one possible way to address OEC's similar dilemma. However, the interests surrounding OEC production are, if anything, even more challenging to align. Faculty may lose some revenue or career rewards by diverting content out of traditional publishing channels and into OEC; the content usually requires some refinement or additional processing to be useful as OEC; some portion of its processing, such as copyright clearance, is tedious and requires expertise that most content creators do not possess; and little, if any, of the work required is of tangible benefit to the content creator or his or her employer. An effective alignment of incentives therefore requires that producers be compensated for some portion of the OEC creation process, along with additional compensation of others whose time and expertise is required to shepherd content through the OEC production process. Perhaps most important, if the creator's employer is going to broker all of this organized activity, there should be something in it for the organization as well. Not all compensation need be monetary, but some adequate incentive must be found for each contributor and each piece of content.

A second difference between OSS and OEC involves community dynamics and the way the products are used. Software grows more powerful and capable through continued refinement, so there are significant benefits, as well as significant community pressures, to contribute derivative work back to the main project. Content, on the other hand, is highly contextual. An instructor will tend to acquire a piece of OEC and adapt it to his or her localized needs via language translation or more substantive amendment. The instructor can then contribute back the derivative work, but it is not usually merged into the ongoing OEC project in the same way that a software patch is merged into an OSS project, because the original creator is unlikely to need modifications targeted at different contexts. In fact, it is difficult to know how one might merge derivative content productively back into an original. If one encrusts an object with all of its possible contextualizations, the compound object will quickly become unwieldy. On the other hand, if one uses the new contextual information to remove context-specific dependencies in the original, the resulting streamlined object will tend to become so abstracted as to be unusable. As David Wiley notes, in OSS, "forking" the project into independent derivatives is usually considered a disaster; in OEC, it is the central value proposition (personal communication, May 26, 2007).

Context dependency also introduces difficulties in measurement for OEC that OSS/CSS projects do not face. The need to compile or interpret computer program code simplifies context, making relatively universal judgments about performance or quality easier to reach. The contextuality of teaching and learning styles and situations has the opposite effect, making it difficult to evaluate a piece of content without detailed reference to how it will be used, when, and by whom. This distinction can easily be overdrawn, because many aspects of software development (such as usability and programming style) are also highly contextual, and many aspects of content quality, like grammar and spelling, transcend local context to at least some degree. Notwithstanding those similarities, however, the lack of any OEC equivalent to a software compiler at the heart of the project makes it very difficult to develop broadly acontextual quality standards for OEC.

The absence of shared measures of quality in OEC matters for several reasons. First, it complicates the creation and alignment of incentives for producing high-quality OEC. It is difficult to structure incentives to produce consistently excellent work if the standard of excellence is ambiguous; instead, one must either create incentives for all producers, paying only limited attention to quality, or else one must pick some particular definition of quality, create incentives around it, and hope that enough producers and consumers share the definition to make the incentives worthwhile. Second, the absence of objective measures of quality confuses consumers as well—particularly in the realm of OEC, where consumers are looking for content precisely because they don't feel that they know enough about a subject. Finally, the lack of objective quality standards removes one foundation of the meritocratic culture upon which OSS/CSS communities depend. The example of Wikipedia, where conflict over the merits of anonymous editing have created schism, suggests that this can encourage not just the forking of content but also the fragmentation of the entire community.

All of these differences appear to work to the disadvantage of OEC versus OSS/CSS, at least in terms of sustainability. At the same time, however, OEC has at least one profound advantage over OSS/CSS: The skills required to create open content are broadly, even universally, distributed among higher education faculty, staff, and students. The pool of potential OEC contributors is orders of magnitude larger than the pool of potential contributors to a software project. It is difficult to judge the relative weights of these advantages and disadvantages, but as someone who works very hard to identify five or six institutions out of thousands that are prepared to join together to build a particular piece of software at some mutually agreeable moment, I envy OEC advocates the opportunities afforded by their large pool of potential participants.

OSS Lessons for OEC

The lessons that one may wish to draw from OSS to help OEC initiatives grow and become sustainable depend greatly on one's mental model of OEC production: Is OEC more like OSS, or more like CSS? Before reading on, answer that question for yourself—and then reflect on your answer in order to understand better your own assumptions about OEC. Do you think about OEC primarily as a voluntaristic project in the collective pursuit of maximal human freedom to learn? Or do you think about OEC primarily as an institutional effort to achieve reliable educational returns by reaping the benefits of cooperation, albeit in a way that shares the resulting value with the world rather than hoarding it? The difference is important in many ways, but real-world OEC initiatives sometimes jumble both visions in ways that make it difficult to think incisively about either.

Among other consequences, one's answer to the question has powerful implications for sustainability. Those interested in pursuing voluntaristic OEC will want to study OSS projects for strategies to reduce the need for patronage and create the greatest quantity and diversity of non-monetary, ego/status incentives for individual participants. Those interested in pursuing institutional OEC strategies will want to study OSS to get below the surface and look hard at the patronage, governance, and incentive arrangements that have aligned complex interests and permitted sustainability at scale—and should probably look even harder at CSS projects for examples of how those lessons can be incorporated explicitly into formal institutional models of open production. Institutional OEC advocates will need to pay a great deal of attention to the questions of what type(s) of virtual organization(s) make sense for OEC, and how those organization(s) should be governed and sustained.

Whatever the sustainability model they adopt, OEC advocates must also find a way to reward the production of high-quality content. This is no small challenge under any approach to OEC production. High quality, broadly usable OEC demands production values that exceed those applied to most educational content in regular use today, as evidenced by the sums spent refining existing course content to produce the material on MIT's OpenCourseWare site. Content must be edited to replace cryptic or institution-specific information; it may need interstitial information that was provided by other means in the actual course; it must be checked for copyright; it must be provided in a location and a format that permits easy access by others; and metadata must be added to help others find more precisely the content that they are seeking. For greatest efficiency, these procedures should be standardized across disciplines and institutions, so that users need not master parochial nuances in order to take advantage of content from different places. And of course, all this effort must be sustained somehow by conferring benefits on those doing the work.

If these were easy problems, they would have been solved by now. At present, there are no widely recognized and agreed-upon solutions, but there are some hints that solutions may be possible. One approach that may help is the enlisting of students as producers of OEC. Many variants are possible: Students can polish or refresh course contents for release as OEC as part of a class or independent project; students can collectively construct and refine curricular materials over multiple, sequential offerings of a class (in the way that many professors currently use classes to refine and polish book manuscripts); more-advanced students can construct lessons or exercises for credit for use by less-advanced students in the same curriculum; and so on. The students will gain status rewards for participation; some also gain more material benefits, such as course credit and the ability to show potential employers or graduate schools a published portfolio of their work. For example, Utah State University's OpenCourseWare site uses student "service learning" (independent study and senior thesis) projects as the foundation of its strategy and produces OEC, sustainably, at a small fraction of the unit-cost of the MIT and Open University initiatives.

Student-based approaches are CSS-style strategies. They share with CSS the critical virtue that they give participants (students) institutionally structured incentives to produce as well as consume; in other words, they cast students in the same role for OEC projects that software developers play in OSS projects. Enrolled students ordinarily cannot choose their curricula or rewards for themselves, and so they require the active involvement of at least the instructor and probably of the institution's governance structure in order to work out this alignment of benefits. Most such approaches will require incentives and infrastructure outside of any particular class or even department, such as academic credit for participation in OEC production and faculty review processes to vet the quality of the resulting content; consequently, integrating these approaches into the entire curriculum would require an adjustment to instructional and course-credit policies institution-wide.

Another option may be to structure incentives based on discipline rather than institution—a "best OEC" award to go alongside the disciplinary "best paper" and "best dissertation" awards, for example, and programs and awards for undergraduate OEC contributions as well. Discipline-based initiatives might become valuable complements to institution-based initiatives, but experience with discipline-based OEC initiatives is so limited that one can say little as yet about its prospects.

If an institution moves to adopt OEC production widely, student-centric strategies may be preferable to instructor-centric strategies at first. This is not because student-produced OEC would be better than faculty-produced content—even the best student-produced content will need to be vetted carefully by instructors—but rather because it may be easier, faster, and cheaper for institutions to create the necessary incentives among their students than among their faculty. As many OEC advocates have noted, faculty face powerful counterpressures from their institutions and disciplines against over-investing in the production of teaching content, and those pressures are difficult or impossible for any single institution to change. If OEC is to thrive, effective faculty involvement is eventually imperative; however, the most direct road to that change in faculty culture may not be the most successful. OEC advocates may be more successful in changing faculty culture by changing student culture and then waiting for those changes to trickle up.

Moreover, OEC production by students does not solve entirely the problem of incentive alignment. Faculty will most likely need to change teaching and other practices in order to support student-generated OEC activities, and such changes are unlikely to be costless; therefore, OEC initiatives would still need to offer benefits to faculty to compensate them for any extra effort involved. Most likely, incentives would need to be constructed and aligned to ensure ongoing institutional support as well. To repeat, these motivations need not be mercenary. One can hope for and work toward a future in which both individual faculty and institutional support for student-based OEC production is based in large part on philosophical commitments to student engagement and deeper learning. What matters is not the currency of the incentives; what matters is that all participants in the OEC production process, both individuals and institutions, believe that it is in their interest to participate.

Finally, one's choice of an OSS-like versus a CSS-like approach to OEC development should not blind one to the merits of the other approaches. There is room in the OEC community for both OSS-style and CSS-style projects, as well as faculty-centric, student-centric, staff-centric, and perhaps even other, as-yet-unknown approaches to content production and the alignment of interests. As with OSS and CSS, it may be that the right approach depends greatly on what sort of content one is trying to produce. At the same time, however, differences in approach should not be allowed to fragment the nascent OEC community. If OEC is to have the best chance to grow and thrive, every OEC advocate should become an advocate for all sorts of OEC projects, including those using approaches different from or even antithetical to one's own. There will be time enough for adjudicating the respective merits of the various approaches when OEC as a movement is tightly interwoven into the fabric of higher education worldwide.

Discussion

Perhaps the greatest frustration in writing this chapter is the inability to be more prescriptive about the path to success for open educational content production. Ideally, I would like to be able to say "here are the three (or five, or even twenty-five) steps to sustainable success with OEC"—but the present state of activity around OEC does not yet offer that clear a vision. OEC faces real sustainability challenges, for many of which there are as yet no satisfactory answers.

One reason that prescription is so difficult is that much of the plan for sustainability in OEC production relies on hope for a culture-change within higher education. Every credible vision of OEC sustainability that I have seen relies in some significant part on the hope or expectation that higher education institutions and their faculties will adopt OEC production as a core value. More specifically, the hope is that culture-change would create status and other incentives that would substitute for monetary incentives and thereby reduce the economic costs of OEC production to levels that institutions could justify long-term. Based on the (admittedly limited) data and procedures now available, the irreducible labor costs of OEC production appear to be high enough that a purely monetary compensation scheme would seem to be impossible for all but the wealthiest institutions, and difficult to justify even there. Providing non-monetary benefits via a changed faculty culture may be the only feasible path to affordable, hence sustainable, OEC production.

Planned, intentional culture change is incredibly difficult, especially in dispersed, interlocking, multi-stakeholder environments like higher education. However, the emergence of open culture in software development in higher education suggests that it may not be impossible. I would urge OEC advocates to learn from the rise of OSS culture in higher education, but not to confuse the two arenas. Different contexts require different incentive patterns, so one cannot assume that the simple-minded adoption of OSS cultural patterns into OEC production would necessarily succeed. It also seems only sensible for advocates to start with the aspects of higher education culture that are least entrenched and most malleable. This suggests to me that student-centric approaches may be a good starting point. It is easier to change a culture that turns over its membership entirely every few years; moreover, all campuses have a range and degree of authority over their students that many do not have over their faculty members. Finally, teachers learn from their students, too, so student-led pressure to open educational content could be transformative over time.

In closing, if I cannot offer much advice on exactly what to do to guarantee the sustainability of OEC production, let me at least reiterate some advice on what, beyond culture change, to think about. First, the alignment of incentives is key. If you are running an OEC project, how will you organize your project to provide all participants with the tangible and intangible rewards necessary to keep them involved? How will you ensure that everyone with some incentive to contribute gives everything that he or she can be motivated to give? Can you rethink the process to bring previously unconsidered incentives or participants into play?

Second, pending a culture change that replaces monetary compensation with other rewards, it is imperative that all costs associated with OEC production be kept down to their practical minima. How can the process of OEC production be made more efficient? How can it be integrated more closely into the production of "ordinary" educational content, to further reduce costs?

Third, and in the interests of supporting culture change, how can more people be drawn into the production of OEC? How can OEC projects, even if they cannot achieve full, independent sustainability today, lay the groundwork for a sustainable culture of openness tomorrow?

Finally, continue to learn from your peers in related endeavors. Openness begets openness; that is the hope. Participants in any successful culture of openness are likely to learn over time to value openness as a virtue, to overcome challenges to openness as they arise, and to discern when openness is, and is not, an appropriate strategy. Consequently, they should become more willing, perhaps even eager, to find ways to express the value of openness in other communities and cultures in which they participate. The shortest, surest path to the hope for open educational content lies through the creation of sustainable, inevitably imperfect, but fundamentally open software, content, and scholarly projects that grow the community of people who have participated firsthand in, and benefited firsthand from, a culture of openness.

Acknowledgments

Ira Fuchs provided information and counsel at many points before and during this project. I am also grateful to Don Waters, Bill Olivier, Randy Metcalfe, and Malcolm Read, each of whom also read one or more of the earlier drafts. Their comments and suggestions have substantially improved the work.

The section "OEC Differences from OSS, CSS" owes a particular debt to Prof. David Wiley and colleagues for insights into the daily practice of open content generation.

Section II

Open Educational Content

Open Educational Content: Transforming Access to Education

Flora McMartin

Today, people world-wide have access via the Internet to information and artifacts of knowledge—by which I mean the textual, visual, and audio works that embody knowledge. They access this widely available range of resources to learn, and in so learning, apply knowledge and thereby change some part of their lives. This is a perfectly reasonable example of open educational content, in that by accessing knowledge, an end-user accomplishes an educational goal.

But definitions are controlled by those who make them. UNESCO has defined open content as part of the broader conceptual movement of open educational resources (OER), where content is described as "digitized educational materials and tools freely offered for educators, students and self-learners to use and reuse for the purposes of teaching, learning, and research" (2002). Others have defined open content and open educational resources differently and more simply, emphasizing the practical perhaps more than the theoretical by describing open educational content and resources as digital learning objects, such as "small (relative to the size of an entire course) instructional components that can be reused a number of times in different learning contexts . . . deliverable over the Internet . . . any number of people can access and use them simultaneously (as opposed to traditional instructional media, such as an overhead or videotape, which can only exist in one place at a time)" (Wiley, 2000). Still others, especially members of the digital library world, view open content as being anything used for educational purposes, usually free, that someone has posted to a managed collection of learning materials and resources such as MERLOT or the National Science Digital Library (NSDL). For the purposes of this overview, I will use the term "open educational content" to describe actual contents as well as the projects that provide and support the generation and distribution of that content.

I have characterized these definitions with sweeping brush strokes to a) give you a flavor of what we mean by educational content in the context of this collection and b) to give you the lay of the land. As you engage with the authors of the following chapters, you will find that their definitions of open content, while generally consistent with the definitions above, contain nuances, caveats, and exceptions to these definitions. All agree, though, that open content relates to knowledge.

You will also find in their descriptions that content derives meaning only from within a context (formal or informal learning), community (target audience for the learning), and purpose (ranging from educational change in local settings to changing education world-wide). These later dimensions of the definitions are extremely important, for they represent the challenges that open content providers must meet in order for the OER movement to succeed.

If Content Is King, Then Why Are the Context, Community, and Purpose So Darn Important?

Content is King, or so Internet mythology supports. A simple Google search of "Content is King" results in a standard Google return of millions of hits. Yet, just as the first result (Callen, 2007) claims in its title that content is the most important aspect of a Web site, since the Internet is about searching for content, the very next hit, "Content is Not King" (2001), claims that content is a pretender and that the true king is interconnectivity. The hit list might be seen as rich discussion material in and of itself about the role of content in the Internet and how that role is changing.

The chapters within this section ground issues related to open content in the reality of what it takes to make it accessible in today's Web environments, then discuss how that reality may change in the future and internationally. Each chapter is written by authors who are intimately involved in providing access to open educational content, the creation of open educational content, or in the study of its use, albeit primarily from the perspectives of members of the U.S. and UK higher education community. Though each author has a different perspective, the chapters touch on three important themes related to: 1) the context for an open content project; 2) the community it engages as part of the project; and 3) how its purpose can affect its use and potential for sustainability. Underlying both use and sustainability are questions about intellectual property that impact both issues.

Use

Use is a particularly sticky problem, partly because we know so little about how learners use open educational content and partly because we know so little about what content is most useful to users and why. Open educational content digital libraries and repositories share the problem that once someone visits their site and downloads an item, they have no way of learning how that person has used the material, if at all. Yet this is a primary metric by which these providers judge use. To date, time spent at the site and the most popular items visited at the site are the primary ways that use is measured. These rather primitive measures provide only a snapshot of how the site itself is used, and do not explore other issues like what happens between access and the final outcome of learning. This is a large gap in our knowledge and one that is not easily filled.

Access to content is not enough, as Andy Lane (2008) of the Open-Learn project shows in the first chapter of this section. Lane draws the distinction between what is technologically possible—making materials available to people—and the more challenging part of the equation: ensuring that people can make use of the content and resources to further their learning. He challenges us to consider what it might mean for a university to become truly open: that is to remove cost and availability restrictions to educational resources as well as restrictions as to who can participate in higher education. Within this challenge, he asks us to consider the kind of support teachers would need in such an environment, as well as the social support necessary for learning. From the standpoint of an Open University educator, Lane concludes that the advent of Internet-based social networking will be the final link in an educational system that will change the market economy of higher education, expanding it to serve the many, rather than the few.

The challenges of involving a community of higher educators to create high quality open digital resources, which can be reused or remixed and maintain their quality for the learner, is taken on by Candice Thille (2008). In her chapter, Thille describes the challenges in scaling up a relatively small, campus-specific project (the Open Learning Initiative [OLI]) that has worked effectively with faculty members to create and assess the effectiveness of complete online courses to meet the needs of the growing OER movement. In Thille's view, content is not context-free; instead, it extends to the learning environments, incorporating research on effective pedagogical practice, resulting in open educational content that is a complete enactment of instruction. Essential to the mix is the development of learning support communities (both virtual and local) where faculty content experts, learning scientists, and software engineers collaborate to make and test these enactments. She believes this will lead the OER movement to reach its full revolutionary potential: that of improving teaching and learning, and at the same time making instruction, in the formal sense we usually associate with institutions, available to the widest possible audience.

At the core of their chapter, Tom Carey and Gerard Hanley of MERLOT (2008) make the argument for extending the definition of open educational content to include open pedagogical content. In their view, the OER movement can only reach its potential when faculty members participate in the development of open educational content by contributing their digital learning materials *and* their pedagogical expertise in using those materials. They highlight the paradox that the OER movement faces in the United States: that full participation by faculty members and instructors requires overcoming many barriers—time being a primary obstacle. This barrier is so significant that they believe the OER movement must employ a strategy of involving institutions of higher education in planning and creating incentives for the use, reuse, and adoption (in addition to the creation) of these resources by U.S. faculty members.

Sustainability

Sustainability issues that are associated with the continuation and growth of open educational content center not so much on the need for continual creation of new open educational content, tools, or services, but more around sustaining the organizations that support and promote the OER movement. Diane Harley's (2008) research links issues related to the need to know more about users and user demand for open educational content with those associated with the cost and sustainability of projects within the OER movement. Harley suggests there is a chasm that must be bridged between the hoped-for scale of the OER movement and what faculty and instructor users (or non-users) say they need to meet changing educational environments. While her research focuses only on one region within the U.S. system of higher education and the use of these resources only among faculty members to the exclusion of students and self-learners, she raises important questions about the barriers the use and reuse of open educational content that must be addressed if U.S. systems of higher education are to support or sustain the movement to open up higher education in the ways envisioned by the leaders of the OER movement.

MIT's OCW is the most mature of all OERs; as such, Steve Lerman, Shigeru Miyagawa and Anne Margulies (2008) reflect on their experiences in establishing the project and discuss the factors that led MIT to become the leading institution in making this educational transformation. In this look back at MIT OCW history, they uncover a unique and critical confluence of the scientific community's value of sharing ideas before publication with MIT's support for the open software movement along with their membership in the World Wide Web Consortium. From this background, the OCW was born and nurtured (with significant external funding) to the extent where it is becoming an integral part of MIT's culture. The authors also look ahead to their vision for a global community of higher learning beyond MIT. While wide adoption of OCW outside of MIT is necessary, they reflect on the need for an OCW Consortium to promote the OER movement and thus its sustainability.

Richard Baraniuk (2008), using Connexions as a case study, examines how this open educational content provider has envisioned its role in the OER movement and is building a sustainable organizational model taking advantage of technology tools to help people be authors by creating new materials from old, personalizing shareable materials, mixing materials together to create new collections, and publishing these new products in inexpensive, accessible ways. Acknowledging the problems associated with intellectual property and licenses, Baraniuk hypothesizes that today's version of open educational content is about remixing materials, whereas yesterday's model focused on providing access via a broadcast metaphor. Tomorrow's open educational content will bring broadcasting and remixing together with interactive tools to complete the feedback circle necessary to bring authors, instructors, and learners together in the creative process.

Science fiction has a way of coming true, as David Wiley's (2008) imaginative account of what a future history of the OER movement might look like demonstrates (including a set of outcomes intended and unintended by members of the OER movement). Wiley's fictional auto-biography lays out how, once started, such a movement might funda-mentally change higher education in the United States and by implication elsewhere. In this vision of the future, Wiley describes the impact that economic and political powers have on educational changes and how, by offering the same services as OCWs, commercial ventures such as Google and textbook publishers rapidly propelled the changes desired by the OER movement forward and out of control. This starts the reader on a ride involving intrigue, politics, court action, and finally, student rebellion. While fanciful in nature, this chapter challenges the future views of previous authors and cautions us with "sometimes you get what you wish for, and then some!"

Catherine Casserly and Marshall Smith (2008) bring us back to reality by describing the OER movement and the vast need for open knowledge worldwide. They refocus us on the purpose of providing open content, resources, and knowledge to transform teaching and learning. They chal-lenge us to look ahead and consider how the OER movement may transform our formal education systems by changing how we think about "going to school": for example changing from the printed text to online immersive environments or by simply changing the process from an instructor selecting a textbook to an instructor compiling a textbook. Perhaps their most challenging notion is that of what formal education looks like—will future education have the same definitions and boundar-ies as today's? Will, for example, there be a difference between "formal" and "informal" education?

The Future of Open Educational Content

Each author in this section illustrates the great potential that open educational content has for changing education through the (seemingly and relatively) simple act of making open to anyone for any purpose educational content, resources, and tools. Each author shares with us a vision for that change from his or her standpoint. In what follows, I raise for the reader questions I found myself asking after reading these chapters and considering the future of open educational resources.

So far the history of open educational resources has had a storyline, or plot if you will, driven by providers and creators of that content and knowledge, but little from its users has been added to round out the story. The question of how content and knowledge is controlled and shared is a risky one with regards to the OER movement, for it raises such questions as "What content? Which knowledge? How best is it shared and to what end? Whose content and knowledge?" These questions are and should be at the center of the discussion about the future of open educational content and resources.

If the shared content, and therefore knowledge, that is valued and promoted is only that from the existing providers who reflect mainly elite institutions of higher education or from those with the economic wherewithal to support, for example, an OCW, this seems to be the antithesis of the goals behind an "open" movement, for it continues to privilege the privileged, just as our current system of education has historically done. Even the growing numbers of members in the OCW Consortium represent only a small fraction of the potential open educational content available in the hidden or invisible Web (Barker, 2006). For example, consider the vast amount of course content and educational resources stored in course and learning management systems of the world's schools. At issue here is who decides which content is of value, what is shared with whom, and how it is shared? Is the model that of open submission of materials with a post-submission review process to insure quality, as with the MERLOT model, or as in the Connexions model, a post-publication model by third parties, or is it the careful construction of that knowledge per the OLI model? Or is quality a matter of institutional branding, such as the materials found at OCW sites?

It is telling to note who the leaders of the OER movement are in developing the online mechanisms for providing access and providing the content. Those providing access to these materials are a small, select group; primarily members of the developed world. What would happen if we stood the OER movement on its head, and the leaders, instead of being the "elite", were today's users: that is, those experiencing the "unfreedoms" described by Amartya Sen (1999). How might open educational content be different? How might content, open or closed, be described? How might use change? How might knowledge change? How might the developed learn from the developing? Are we members of the OER movement ready to embrace the unintended change we foment as well as the intended?

In the Web's market economy, the end-user is viewed as the arbiter of quality and value. Yet in education, that is rarely the case—it is in fact, the opposite. Placing the judgment of quality and value in the hands of the user implies that we trust an end-user, in this case the learner, to have the academic skills and ability to discern these characteristics. This is not the case, for as a profession, quality in higher education is discerned by the professoriate, the authorities who "make" the knowledge or content and then give permission to share it. (In the OCW movement we use the host institution as a proxy for quality.) The learner is rarely, except perhaps in graduate education or professional schools, deemed able to make these kinds of judgments without guidance by members of the academic profession.

Much of the educational materials available on the Web replicate the epistemological hegemony of higher education and the relationship between "developed" and "developing" nations, where knowledge (content) from the "developed" is privileged over the "developing." The hegemony reinforces a system where knowledge generation occurs within institutions of higher education, and use of that knowledge is seen as occurring outside of the "walls" of those institutions. With the current design for open educational content, do we replicate this hegemony by predefining quality or value based on the providers' credentials? For example, the quality associated with OCWs is that of brand—MIT being the ultimate example of quality defined by proxy. Already we know that the vision of improving the quality of open educational content through use, reuse, and revision is a huge challenge to overcome, given today's lack of involvement by faculty members and instructors in sharing open content. Do we reinforce "them" and "us" social practices (McNiff and Whitehead, 2005), however unintentionally, by relying too much on the existing "closed" system of education to define an "open" alternative? Are we creating a truly different alternative with open education?

Have our views of education changed to the point where our purpose as educators is to *work along with* learners as they acquire the tools and knowledge to *claim their education*? Here I use "work" and "claim" in the spirit of Adrienne Rich's 1977 essay, "Claiming an Education," in which she describes a radically different view of the educational experience where students take "as the rightful owner" responsibility for their education rather than "act as a receptacle or container" receiving education. She goes on to say that women need to own and use the tools to provide them with "a new intellectual grasp on their lives, new understanding of our history, a fresh vision of the human experience, and also a critical basis for evaluating what they hear and read" (p. 231).

It was only 30 years ago in the history of U.S. higher education that academe privileged only one part of the human experience—that of men. Women now make up over 50 percent of U.S. college and university students, and knowledge has indeed changed because of women's studies research and thinking on, about, and for women. In today's system of higher education in the United States, we have all but forgotten these struggles for recognition and acceptance. Is the story of opening higher education up to women and underrepresented minorities parallel to what we are trying to accomplish in the OER movement by opening up the contents of education to the broadest audience possible? How will making this content available affect our educational institutions as well as learning? Does simply making open educational content accessible lead to learning; that is, will and do students—formal and informal—claim this educational opportunity as intended?

Each author in this section has, in his or her own way, suggested that the real future of open educational content lies with the end-users and how they use that content to further their learning. Yet, this is the very group that we know so little about. Designers of open educational content and sites assume there are three categories of users: faculty members, students formally enrolled in higher education, and more informal learners—for example, the curious or those who are unable to participate in formal education for whatever reason. Are these our users, and are these sufficient descriptors of our audience? Knowing the audience for this service—for providing open education resources is a service—is essential for moving away from the simple act of providing access to resources to the more complex acts of creating the tools, situations, and environments necessary to support the educational experience most providers intend for their users.

Our current understanding of what our users do with these materials shows that, for example, almost a third of the MIT entering freshman used the MIT OCW site as a means for helping them decide to enroll in MIT. U.S. faculty are, as several studies have discovered (Harley, 2004; McMartin, 2007; Wolf, 2007), mainly using images to spice up lecture slides. Far less is known about informal learners. But, based on what we do know about the faculty users and student users, it is safe to say that these are not the uses providers and developers had hoped for. To which I borrow, again from the 1970s, a phrase coined by Planned Parenthood: "Hope is not a method." If we intend to change what and how people learn, then we must provide mechanisms, environments, and motivation to make that change. If access is not enough (some may say that it is— look at the unintended consequences of the opening of content via the invention of the printing press), then we must know what people need with regard to using open educational content to learn and how to best support those needs. Open educational content designers, providers, and those who are considering joining the movement need to ask: Who specifically is my audience? How do our services, tools, programs, and content meet their needs? As users become more sophisticated, will they need these same services, tools, programs, and content? Is there a lifespan for open educational content?

In these last few paragraphs, I end with perhaps the most frustrating and most intriguing questions: those related to learning, that have emerged along with the growth of open educational content. We claim that we make these resources available for the public good so that people can learn from and with them. Yet to date, we have no good way to assess that learning. This is, perhaps, in part because we are unsure or have not agreed on what users are to learn, and to what end. Open educational resources are resources with context, with purpose, with pedagogical frameworks. They are not stand-alone pieces of information.

How do people learn with them if they do not share the context, purpose, or pedagogical framework? To what end is this learning devoted? And from the standpoint of the provider, should, or do they wish to support, that end?

One sure way to demonstrate learning, but which is little discussed in this context, is how people reuse open educational content. The power of the Web and the power of making content available is that it can be changed. Yet our views around change, informed by intellectual property rights, prohibit free reuse. Yet reuse, as in the form of new or derivative artifacts formed from original artifacts, is one extremely effective way to demonstrate learning. This is how we measure students' learning—we often call this the essay test. Students put into their own words knowledge—make it their own, claim it. But what if there is no such artifact? What if a piece of open educational content has changed some opinion or understanding of how things work, or has instigated a creative thought or motivated a change in behavior? These are perhaps the prime outcomes we wish for in "educating" people. They are, however, the most difficult to measure. Perhaps we need not measure them, perhaps we should ask: Is it enough that we have provided access, we have provided tools to help contextualize knowledge, and we have opened up educational content with the sincere desire to change how, what, and perhaps why people learn? Perhaps we too must learn. We must learn to trust that users are learning in ways that are new to us, mostly unintended, and that they will demonstrate that learning by changing the way our societies view who should be educated and why.

References

Baraniuk, R. G. (2008). Challenges and opportunities for the open education movement: A Connexions case study. In T. Iiyoshi and M. S. V. Kumar (Eds.), *Opening Up Education: The Collective Advancement of Education through Open Technology, Open Content, and Open Knowledge* pp. 229–246. Cambridge, MA: MIT Press.

Barker, J. (2006). Invisible or deep web: What it is, why it exists, how to find it, and its inherent ambiguity. In UC Berkeley—Teaching Library Internet Workshops. Regents of the University of California. Retrieved April 17, 2007, from http://www.lib.berkeley.edu/TeachingLib/Guides/Internet/InivisibleWeb.html

Callan, D. (2007). Content is king. In Marketing.com. Retrieved April 17, 2007, from http://www.akamarketing.com/content-is-king.html

Carey, T., and Hanley, G. L. (2008). Extending the impact of open educational resources: Lessons learned from MERLOT. In T. Iiyoshi and M. S. V. Kumar (Eds.), *Opening Up Education: The Collective Advancement of Education through Open Technology, Open Content, and Open Knowledge* pp. 181–195. Cambridge, MA: MIT Press.

Casserly, C. M., and Smith, M. S. (2008). Revolutionizing education through innovation: Can openness transform teaching and learning? In T. Iiyoshi and M. S. V. Kumar (Eds.), *Opening Up Education: The Collective Advancement of Education through Open Technology, Open Content, and Open Knowledge* pp. 261–275. Cambridge, MA: MIT Press.

Harley, D. (2008). Why understanding the use and users of open matters. In T. Iiyoshi and M. S. V. Kumar (Eds.), *Opening Up Education: The Collective Advancement of Education through Open Technology, Open Content, and Open Knowledge* pp. 197–211. Cambridge, MA: MIT Press.

Lane, A. (2008). Widening participation in education through open educational resources. In T. Iiyoshi and M. S. V. Kumar (Eds.), *Opening Up Education: The Collective Advancement of Education through Open Technology, Open Content, and Open Knowledge* pp. 149–163. Cambridge, MA: MIT Press.

Lerman, S. R., Miyagawa, S., and Margulies, A. H. (2008). OpenCourseWare: Building a culture of sharing. In T. Iiyoshi and M. S. V. Kumar (Eds.), *Opening Up Education: The Collective Advancement of Education through Open Technology, Open Content, and Open Knowledge* pp. 213–227. Cambridge, MA: MIT Press.

McMartin, F., Wolf, A., Iverson, E., Manduca, C., Morgan, G., and Morrill, J. (2007). What do faculty need and want from digital libraries? Joint Conference on Digital Libraries, June 17–22, Vancouver, BC.

McNiff, J., and Whitehead, J. (2005). Teachers as educational theorists: Transforming epistemological hegemonies. A paper presented at the British Educational Research Association 2005 Annual Conference at the University of Glamorgan on September 16. Retrieved May 10, 2007, from http://www.jeanmcniff.com/Teachers%20as%20educational%20theorists.htm

Odlyzko, A. (2001, February). Content is not king. *First Monday*, 6(2). Retrieved April 17, 2007, from http://firstmonday.org/issues/issue6_2/odlyzko/index.html

Rich, A. (1977). "Claiming an education." In Rich, A. (1979). On lies, secrets and silence: Selected prose 1966–1978. New York: W.W. Norton & Co.

Sen, A. (1999). *Development as Freedom*. New York: Alfred A. Knopf, a division of Random House.

Thille, C. (2008). Building open learning as a community-based research activity. In T. Iiyoshi and M. S. V. Kumar (Eds.), *Opening Up Education: The Collective Advancement of Education through Open Technology, Open Content, and Open Knowledge* pp. 165–179. Cambridge, MA: MIT Press.

UNESCO. (2002). Forum on the impact of open courseware for higher education in developing countries. Final report (was this presented at a particular meeting?). Paris: UNESCO.

Wiley, D. (2008). 2005–2012: The OpenCourseWars. In T. Iiyoshi and M. S. V. Kumar (Eds.), *Opening Up Education: The Collective Advancement of Education through Open Technology, Open Content, and Open Knowledge*, pp. 247–259. Cambridge, MA: MIT Press.

Wiley, D. A. (2000). Connecting learning objects to instructional design theory: A definition, a metaphor, and a taxonomy. In D. A. Wiley (Ed.), *The Instructional Use of Learning Objects: Online version*. Retrieved April 14, 2007, from http://reusability.org/read/chapters/wiley.doc.

Willinsky, J. (2007). Sorting and classifying the open access issues for digital libraries: Issues technical, economic, philosophical, and principled. Joint Conference on Digital Libraries, June 17–22, Vancouver, BC.

Wolf, A., Iverson, E., Manduca, C., McMartin, F., Morgan, G., and Morrill, J. (2007). Use of online digital learning materials and digital libraries: Comparison by discipline. Joint Conference on Digital Libraries, June 17–22, Vancouver, BC.

10

Widening Participation in Education through Open Educational Resources

Andy Lane

A significant feature of most educational resources is that they are restricted to many and can cost a lot to gain access to. This is largely because of a market economy around educational resources. They are copyrighted and packaged up as objects—books, journals, videos—that have to be bought from a store or accessed through course fees or university repositories (libraries in most cases). Even if this copyrighted material is available in public libraries, it is then effectively rationed by the numbers of copies available and the costs and opportunity costs involved in people travelling to the library to use them (with that use being further restricted by the all rights reserved copyright applied to them).

The philosophy of open educational resources (OERs) is that of making educational materials a common or public good from which all, in theory, can benefit, but most especially those who receive the least benefit from current systems of educational provision, whether publicly or privately funded (see Geser, 2006 for a thorough review of open educational practices and resources). However, this noble philosophy is constrained in practice by two major overlapping dimensions: (1) the degrees of openness presented by OERs in relation to the context in which someone lives and works, and (2) the degrees of freedom presented to that person by the nature of the OERs, whatever that person's context.

The distinction I am making here is between the properties of the OER (both its technical format and, most particularly, the rights license the originator applies to it) and the properties of the people who may wish to use that OER, which, for these purposes are a product of the circumstances in which they find themselves.[1]

Looking at this distinction in terms of systems thinking (Checkland, 1999; Lane, 2002a, 2002b), we might contrast the availability of all types of educational resources in traditional universities and open universities. The limitations on access to educational resources are much greater in traditional universities, because there are various technological, regulatory, and participatory barriers.

Access to Educational Resources: Two Approaches

Consider how universities make educational resources available to learners. In a traditional, campus-based, "closed" university, the educational resources available to registered students are within the perceived boundary of the system, and most learners usually sit in the system's environment, which itself is not very open. Universities limit the number of students they enroll, and determine the students' entry through selection methods such as previous educational achievement. Students are largely registered in whole programs and not individual modules. Further, most universities serve full-time students. Part-time students must structure their time around the institution's schedule, which can be difficult for those who work or have family and other commitments. The students must come to the campus to participate in the educational experience. The methods of teaching used are also very limited (and limiting): Students attend professors' lectures, along with some seminars, workshops and laboratory, or other practical activities. Educational resources are housed in a physical library or bookstore. Moreover, learning is assessed primarily through examinations and similar means.

In short, the experience of a traditional university is an individualized process where individual professors devise, specify, and deliver the courses studied by individual students even though present as groups in a classroom. The students are therefore largely guided by the views of a single source even though they may read the views of others in assigned texts. Although universities are normally very open to ideas around their subjects and professors usually expect to be able to freely study, research, teach, speak about, and publish on intellectual and academic matters that they are interested in, it is not always so obvious that those professors are as open to new ideas around teaching and learning—ideas that may change the methods they have always employed.

This is, of course, a stark generalization. Many individual universities are much more open than my stereotype (the advent of open courseware and the extent of outreach programs is growing rapidly), and some countries have systems that are more open than others (and there are other forms of openness, such as time and cost, that I am not going to address here). But generally, most universities are still fairly closed in terms of accessibility to their educational resources and participation in their educational offerings.

Figure 10.1 illustrates the point. The top diagram represents the traditional university, with its limited access to educational resources. The second diagram describes a distance teaching university, such as the UK's Open University. Many more resources span or are found outside the boundary, and these resources both influence and are influenced by learners in the system's environment, as well as registered students within the boundary.

With a mission set by its founding chancellor, Lord Crowther, in 1969 "The Open University is open as to people, places, methods and ideas" (as cited in Daniel, 1999), the Open University has no entry qualifications to its modules or programs, is only limited in the number of students on a module by the availability of sufficient tutors (to date, the greatest number on any single presentation of a module has been 14,000), and allows students to register for one module at a time rather than requiring commitment to a complete degree program.

The Open University (OU) also invests in providing pedagogically robust, multiple-media educational materials produced by teams of academic and media experts. There is a high degree of coherence and congruence between the contributions of the team, and contrasting views can be expressed. The media are also chosen carefully to have the most impact for that area of learning.

A further layer of mediation is provided: The university employs tutors for set groups or batches of students working on an individual module. Recognizing that different students have different learning styles and approaches, the tutors help the students in their groups to navigate and approach the materials in ways that suit each student's individual needs. The tutor therefore facilitates the learning process as much as directly reinterpreting parts of the teaching embodied in the educational materials. This gives greater control of the learning process to the students

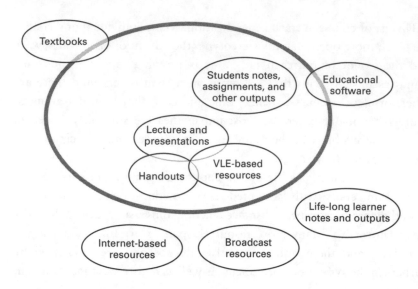

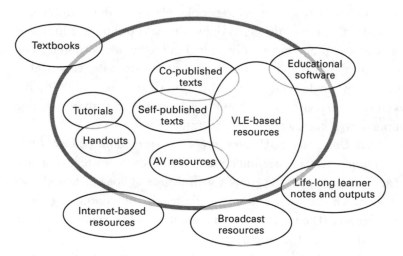

Figure 10.1

themselves and gives students much greater flexibility in how and when they study, allowing them to meet other commitments to family and work.

Furthermore, while individual modules are timetabled, students have more flexibility in the order and times they study them, even allowing for breaks in study. Thus, whereas most universities usually have cohorts of students studying together on the full course or program, the OU has a particular cohort on individual modules and not on full courses or programs. For some students, studying one module is enough. However, students may also complete programs over time.

The OU has an open access policy: No prior qualifications are needed to register for the courses, and there is no age restriction (generally students must be at least 18, but the OU does have special schemes allowing those under 18 to study modules alongside their school level qualifications). Over one third of those who enroll in the OU annually do not have the educational qualifications that would normally ensure their entry to other UK universities. Many of these "underqualified" people successfully complete all or part of a program; their success demonstrates the efficacy of the levels of support provided and suggests that good exit achievement is readily attainable without any entry selection.

Lastly, the OU recognizes and gives credit for certified study at other institutions. The OU also assesses prior experiential and work-based learning, enabling learners to access more learning opportunities. These services acknowledge and support the mobility of the learners: They can learn where they want, when they want, unrestricted by rigid schedules and specific locations.

Our model of supported open learning is rated highly by our students. The OU has consistently placed in the top ten UK universities for the quality of its teaching, as assessed by the UK's Quality Assurance Agency over a number of years, and topped the National Student Satisfaction Survey in 2005 and 2006 (BBC News, 2006; Teaching Quality Information, 2006), the first two years of this government-sponsored initiative.

From this comparison, I draw three themes: (1) the extent of *availability* of educational resources (how many of them in what forms, both formal and informal), (2) the degree of *accessibility* to those resources (where can they be found and by whom), both of which can contribute to (3) the *level* of use of those by learners (the degree of participation). Greater availability and accessibility are necessary, but not sufficient, pre-requisites for increasing participation in higher education per se.

Opening Up Higher Education

Higher education can, however, do better, and open up to yet more people. In a fully open, participatory university, the boundaries around learning would be wider still as the distinctions between teacher and learner and who produces the educational resources becomes even more blurred.

Wider Availability

The infrastructure of the Internet and its reliance on digital technologies has vastly increased the amount of available educational resources (of all types and qualities), even those under copyright, that can be accessed, or changed and shared around by anyone who has the means to access it. The mobility of content has never been faster or greater. The adoption of "some rights reserved" licensing regimes such as Creative Commons (See http://creativecommons.org/) and the decisions by many universities (For example see OpenCourseWare Consortium at http://ocwconsortium.org/index.html) to make some or all of their educational resources available under such licenses in digital form on Web sites, as well as open access publishing of research papers and reports is significantly widening the availability of OERs and so overcoming one of the barriers to use by learners and educators alike.

Wider Access

Wider availability of OERs is, however, of no benefit to those who have few or no means of accessing it. The challenge here is providing a public-wide infrastructure (whether publicly or privately funded) of information and communication networks that everyone can access and derive services from—if, of course, they can privately afford the PC or cell phone that can link to those networks. Although this is a significant barrier for disadvantaged groups or those suffering multiple deprivations within developed countries, and an even bigger barrier for the many more disadvantaged groups in developing countries, it can be partly surmounted by ever more affordable and accessible devices and investment in new infrastructure.

However, such a technological solution does not help with the greater issue of wider access to formal education programs, since at the basis of that issue are the social norms surrounding the value placed upon formal education as superior to nonformal, and the ways in which systems of education are organized. People may be able to access OERs on their own, outside of the constraints of a university, but what recognition and benefits do they gain from doing so if universities still require high prior achievement for entry, and employers recognize only those achievements made at universities? Further, if they are inexperienced and unconfident learners, without the types of support that university staff can provide for registered students they may not gain much learning benefit from OERs.

Wider Participation

Having an open door does not mean that new learners will pass through it or that they stay "inside" the system for very long. There are a number of differing social and cultural reasons that inhibit certain members of society from even thinking they could participate in higher education, let alone feel confident to start any form of formal program on offer. The social and cultural norms of their family, friends, or work colleagues can instill and reinforce personal views and attitudes that keep them from accessing what might be available: That they are not smart enough or suited to study at a higher education level (and often not even at lower education levels). To be able to engage in higher education programs and to find success of some form in that engagement usually requires active support and encouragement from someone in the family or peer groups, or active support and encouragement from professionals or para-professionals.

OpenLearn

Drawing on its long experience of innovating and delivering supported open learning to a mass market both in the United Kingdom and increasingly abroad, the university expects to make a significant impact on both the quality and reach of open content delivery at an international level, as well as a major contribution to the electronic delivery of learning resources worldwide. One of the primary aims in doing so is to meet the learning needs of a wide range of people with differing levels of educational achievement, skills, and confidence. And it sees the key to widening participation being the support of users of open educational resources through extensive networks of partners. The need is for a social economy, not a market economy, in education to empower all those involved, whether they are teachers, learners, or employers of educated people.

Toward this goal, the Open University has begun to make some of its educational materials freely accessible in a Web-based environment called OpenLearn (See http://www.open.ac.uk/openlearn/). In so doing, the OU is trying to advance open content delivery methods and technologies by

1. Deploying leading-edge learning management tools for learner support;
2. Encouraging the creation of nonformal collaborative learning communities; and
3. Enhancing international research-based knowledge about modern pedagogies for higher education.

The Open University describes what it offers to its student body as "Supported Open Learning," whereby it adds a wide range of support services (for example information, advice and guidance, tuition, assessment, credit rating, credit transfer, specialized hardware and software for disabled students) around the specially developed educational materials that students need to study. As many support staff are employed specifically to deliver these support services as there are academic staff designing and authoring the materials, programs, and assessing the students' achievements. In fact, there are four types of support which are built into all its programs in different mixes:

1. Pedagogic support built into the educational resources, such as exercises and activities that challenge students and enable them to assess for themselves the learning they are achieving (examples of these can be seen in OpenLearn units);
2. Personal support through encouraging self-reflection and guidance within some of the in-text activities, but also in formal assessments and underpinned by a broad range of guidance material on study skills and

the recording of learning and achievements in e-portfolios or learning journals (examples of which are also on OpenLearn);

3. Peer support providing mutual reflection and guidance created within tutorial groups that can meet physically or virtually (every taught module has associated electronic conferences run by tutors or specialized moderators, but the OU Students Association also runs separate conferences just for students for each module, for each program, and for other purposes—similarly each unit on OpenLearn has an associated forum);

4. Professional support, the expert reflection and guidance provided by subject tutors available through face-to-face meetings, telephone calls or an online conference, and the guidance provided by support specialists whether individually or collectively through comprehensive online systems. Indeed, new technologies have greatly facilitated the mobility of support so that the supporter and supported do not need to be in the same country or communicate at the same time.

For OpenLearn, the OU is using as much of the first three approaches as possible while for registered students it adds the fourth, often most important type of support for its current student body. Even so, there are still significant limits to what OU staff can achieve through information and communication technologies when students or potential students cover vast geographical areas. It does have regional centers, but staff based in these cannot always provide the very local or community-based support that many suffering from deprivation or disadvantage most need to get started.

For this reason, we have long recognized in our formal programs, and expect it to be the same for the nonformal OERs on OpenLearn, that local intermediaries are essential for ensuring successful participation. Such intermediaries can vary widely, ranging from employers and unions to local charities, nongovernmental organizations, and various professional and interest-led associations, all of whom provide different types of support and encouragement to their members or the groups they seek to serve. This means that, in nearly all cases, the potential higher education student is a member of, or receiving other forms of support from, that organization. In other words, the intermediaries are part of that person's broader peer network, and that person can find that they are not alone in their newly restored ambitions to study.

Opening Up Universities

As the design of OU's OpenLearn suggests, open educational resources are but a small part of open education. They truly are just resources for teachers and learners to use as suits their needs. Their fitness for that purpose will vary, dependent on the pedagogic nature of the resources and the learning styles of the users. Just producing or using OERs does not greatly open up a university. To do that requires attention to the teaching, learning, and support methods and systems that draw upon those resources. I have indicated above many of the factors that need to be addressed by universities, but a major significance of OERs is what it does for the role of learners within education—changing relationships between teachers and learners.

Lessons for the Teachers

There is enormous potential if the open education movement embraces the practices of open and distance learning (ODL), as well as the notion of free or open educational resources. I see four implications for teachers at both traditional and distance teaching universities.

Increased Volume   First, while teaching at traditional universities is more like a craft-based operation, ODL can be operated at an industrial scale so that thousands can study the same course at the same time, not just tens as is the case for campus and classroom-based teaching. But it does require much greater collaboration between people, dividing the labor between them rather than one teacher handling most of it alone. The downside is that it can cost a lot to develop and run an operation centered on ODL materials. However, the collective development and sharing of OERs could mean that the effort and cost to any one teacher or institution in using ODL may be lessened, assuming of course that they want to collaborate in such a way. An implication for distance teaching universities is that this might enable them to run modules for small numbers of students at a time, rather than having to rely on large numbers to help recoup the up-front investment and infrastructure costs.

Increased Access   The type of support models used in ODL can also enhance access to groups who would not previously have tried higher education, while new communication technologies enable distance teaching universities to provide more direct contact activities that are more usual in traditional universities. In other words, the wide availability of content that students can access requires a shift in the emphasis away from direct teaching of content through lectures to facilitating learning around resource-based individual and group activities and assignments.

Broader Recognition of Learning A third significant change is the greater recognition of nonformal and informal learning achieved through OERs that can replace or supplement the formal learning offered by existing higher education institutions. This is the lifelong learning agenda: Individuals approach postsecondary education as developing a personalized portfolio, picking up formal bits of education from different providers and mixing it with nonformal learning experiences, obtaining recognition of their achievements from trustworthy professional organizations such as universities, professional associations, or peer review, by a trustworthy community of people working or active in the same field. In other words, open education opens up not only who produces the content and controls the context in which the "content is learned", but also who validates that learning so that it has currency in the labor or interest markets.

Global Reach Lastly, the capabilities of Web 2.0 technologies mean that this lifelong learning can also be truly international or global in scope with the content and services to support learning coming from different countries, as well as the peer group an individual may be studying with.

Lessons from the Learners

Experience at the OU indicates that while learners like choice and flexibility, they also want structure and targeted support. The challenge is to provide the appropriate choice and structure to meet the differing needs of most people—without the educational experience becoming too messy or costly to provide.

Quality Educational Resources First, learners like good quality educational resources and many like them to be in small enough chunks to engage with. Good quality materials can be costly to develop as noted above, but now learners can access and see materials from many universities, not just those on offer at their own university. The OU generally offers large modules (100, 300, and 600 hours of study) because these offer economies of scale; through OpenLearn it offers them in much smaller sizes, 4 to 30 hours.

If the demand increases for smaller modules, then it may force the OU to return to the situation of a single lecturer developing a single module, which then affects the creativity of the shared group effort, unless that were to operate across institutions rather than within an institution, through OERs. Equally, if the demand for good quality resources by traditional students means they question the resources provided by their own university, that could lead to an OER "arms race" if people compete rather than collaborate to produce the best resources.

Learning with Peers   Learners generally like being part of a peer group that they can interact with, whether as an active participant or as a passive onlooker. That is why in OpenLearn the OU has added tools and technologies that encourage and enable sharing, collaboration, and knowledge generation between educators and educators, educators and learners, and learners and learners—as much as its own content and to have much of that interaction recorded for others to look at and review. The distinction between who is the generator of content, what is the nature of the knowledge embedded in that content, who is the mediator of the content and interprets it for others, who validates the value of the processes involved in generating that content, and how the achievements of the people involved are assessed will increasingly become less clear.

Learning for Life   Lastly, people are increasingly active lifelong learners, seeking or being expected to undertake learning for both personal and professional development throughout their lives. They also want to take those opportunities from a wide range of sources. This means that they want more than just degree programs. The OU is fairly flexible in this manner, but most universities are tied in to full degree programs because that is the traditional model and because it has become enshrined in national government policies.

A Social (and Market) Economy in Open Education

Up to now I have focused on what OERs might mean for individual universities. I now want to widen the system boundary to consider the collective marketplace for higher education. Most higher education students today have a relationship with just one university in their life. At that university they have any number of individual relationships with individual professors and fairly small groups of fellow learners. As my opening example suggests, many other potential students are denied access to this because of scarcities in prime resources—lecture rooms and professors. There are now more people than ever wishing to participate in higher education, and increasing numbers of them want that participation to be more flexible to meet their needs. They want to be able to combine modules from different universities. They want to get credit for other types of study and experiences. They want to be full-time at some points in their life and part-time at others. They want to stop and start up again when they can. They may still want to study when they are retired. They may want to be teachers, as well as be taught.

Publicly supported and funded open universities have been in the vanguard of opening up education for more people and giving them more flexibility in their studies. Some private online universities such as the University of Phoenix and corporate universities attached to multinational corporations are extending this social economy into a market-based economy (Paton, Peters, Storey, and Taylor, 2005). Open educational resources are working in the other direction, opening up previously closed resources. Closed resources, whether privately or publicly funded, have to be paid for either at, or close to, the point of need. Open resources will probably need to be funded by public or philanthropic monies and effort, but are then free thereafter to all who can reasonably access them. But the dominant market relationship is still the few producers serving up resources to the many consumers.

The really significant development for open education is the advent of Internet-based social networking and collaborative technologies. This enables far more people to be producers of resources and providers of particular services—such as tutoring a specific course for anyone, anywhere. The marketplace is global, not just local or even regional. So, in principle, all can become producers and consumers. However, such relationships can still be largely meeting market needs rather than social needs.

The Internet and OERs do not spell the end for traditional universities any more than open universities have done so, or any more than radio has replaced printed texts or television has replaced radio. They both expand the overall market and differentiate it into a greater number of sectors, including the social element of the economy. However, it may be that the Internet and open education, now the smallest sector in the market, will become the largest sector in the education market.

Although the shape of this market may be decided by the future users of open educational resources, not the current producers of closed educational resources, current producers have the opportunity to influence what happens and decide what role they wish to play in the new market. To that end, I close with the following observations:

• Making educational content freely available for people to use is easy to do, technically.
• Making educational resources available for reuse under a Creative Commons-style license is more difficult, because it works against the current culture and traditions of copyright and intellectual property rights that permeate the modern knowledge society.
• While making open educational resources accessible to the most disadvantaged groups in the world is also challenging, it is readily achievable as the digital technologies of all types being developed and refined by multinational companies offer different and more affordable routes to such content and resources. However, the difficulty comes in ensuring that people can make any significant use or reuse out of the content and resources that may be available to them.
• In terms of open educational resources, the question is who benefits and how do they benefit: What conditions are needed to convert the vast number of browsing consumers of a wealth of variable information to serve functional needs, into many communities of learners seeking to transform themselves though education?

Note

1. Before expanding on these themes, I want to comment on the issue of intellectual property rights. The debate around the rights licenses to use with OERs mostly revolves around issues of freedom of use by others against being free of direct cost to those users (there are other, less direct costs that the user still has

to bear, particularly their own time). I acknowledge that this is a significant real (or perceived) barrier to people engaging in the OER movement, but it is not one I address much more here, because I see it as but one component of a wider system.

References

BBC News. (2006). *Student Satisfaction Survey Results*. Retrieved March 4, 2007, from http://news.bbc.co.uk/1/hi/education/5277938.stm

Checkland, P. B. (1999). *Systems Thinking, Systems Practice*. Chichester, UK: John Wiley and Sons.

Daniel, J. (1999, May 8). *Preston Degree Ceremony*. Retrieved March 4, 2007, from http://www.open.ac.uk/johndanielspeeches/Prestonpm.htm

Geser, G. (Ed.). (2006). *Open Educational Practices and Resources: OLCOS Roadmap 2012*. Retrieved March 4, 2007, from http://www.olcos.org

Lane, A. B. (2002a). *Systems Thinking and Practice: A Primer* (2nd ed.). Milton Keynes, UK: The Open University. See also http://openlearn.open.ac.uk/course/view.php?id=1289

Lane, A. B. (2002b). *Systems Thinking and Practice: Diagramming* (2nd ed.). Milton Keynes, UK: The Open University. See also http://openlearn.open.ac.uk/course/view.php?id=1290

The Open University. (2007). *OpenLearn LearningSpace*. Retrieved March 4, 2007, from http://openlearn.open.ac.uk/

The Open University. (2007). *About the OU: How Studying Works at the OU*. Retrieved March 4, 2007, from http://www.open.ac.uk/about/ou/p5.shtml

Paton, R., Peters, G., Storey, J., and Taylor, S. (2005). Corporate universities as strategic learning initiatives. In R. Paton, G. Peters, J. Storey, and S. Taylor (Eds.), *Handbook of Corporate University Development: Managing Strategic Learning Initiatives in the Public and Private Domains* (pp. 5–16). London: Gower Publishing.

Teaching Quality Information. (2006). TQi: Teaching quality information. Retrieved March 4, 2007, from http://www1.tqi.ac.uk/sites/tqi/home/index.cfm.

11

Building Open Learning as a Community-Based Research Activity

Candace Thille

Improvement in postsecondary education will require converting teaching from a "solo sport" to a community-based research activity.
—Herbert Simon (1998)

The open educational resources (OER) movement has the potential to provide broader access to higher education and to markedly improve the quality of higher education for a diverse body of learners. Many OER projects to date have focused on making content that supports existing traditional forms of instruction openly and freely available. In these projects, the power of the Internet is used to overcome barriers to access by serving as a medium for freely distributing content. Making existing content available in this way is based on the revolutionary idea that education and discovery are best advanced when knowledge is shared openly. These OER projects have enabled a great leap forward in democratizing access to educational material. The next step in the *revolutionary* potential of the OER movement is in using technology to make *instruction*, as well as materials, accessible to the widest possible audience of learners and, at the same time, *improve* teaching and learning.

The Challenge of Meeting the Growing Demand for Quality Higher Education

Pressures of many kinds grow in both the developed and, especially, the developing world to provide more people with increased access to education (United Nations Educational, Scientific and Cultural Organization [UNESCO]-World Bank, 2000). At the same time, report after report announces that the quality of education, even in the developed world, is not keeping pace with the demands of what is now and what will be an increasingly knowledge-based economy (Desjardins, Rubenson, and Milana, 2006; The National Academy of Sciences, 2007; President's Information Technology Advisory Committee, 2005; President's Council of Advisors on Science and Technology, 2004).

Traditional forms of developing and delivering instruction do not scale well to meet the growing demand. Individual faculty members working as solo practitioners who are experts in a domain of knowledge are often ill-equipped to address this changing context. A long-standing concern of many who have worked in higher education is that most faculty members' knowledge of how students learn is not only insufficient but also largely intuitive (Smith and Thille, 2004). Most faculty members are dedicated instructors and spend much time and energy preparing for their course presentations. In traditional teaching this meant spending hours reading and rereading books and articles, writing and rewriting lecture notes, anticipating student questions and formulating answers.

Historically, one of the fundamental errors in this process has been that faculty members often equate their own learning processes with their students' learning processes. Unfortunately, research has shown that as teachers become more expert in any discipline, they are less capable of seeing and understanding the difficulties encountered by the novice learner. This well-documented phenomenon of the "expert's blind spot" tells us that instructional intuitions of experts can be faulty, because expertise in a domain can cloud judgment about what is difficult for novice learners in that domain (Nathan and Koedinger, 2000). In traditional small-scale, face-to-face instruction with a fairly homogeneous student population, the problem of the expert's blind spot is sufficiently mitigated by the dynamic feedback that the instructor receives from students through the instructor's observations in class and through student questions.

In an open online environment, the dynamic feedback loops that mitigate the problem of the expert's blind spot are no longer present. In developing instruction for a diverse population of novice learners in these environments, it becomes critical that content experts not rely exclusively on their individual experiences and intuitions about learning. These challenges led Open Learning Initiative (OLI) to undertake a community-based research approach to course development.

A Research-Based Approach to OER Development

The fundamental goal of OLI is to develop Web-based learning environments that are the *complete enactment* of instruction. Our focus on designing and evaluating the *enactment of instruction* elucidates some of the opportunities, challenges, and implications of open educational resources for transforming education.

Our research is part of an effort to (a) develop better resources and practices, (b) include cycles of evaluation and improvement of resources and practices that are developed, and (c) contribute to advancing fundamental understanding, in this case, of learning. We develop courses and conduct studies designed to provide feedback for improving the courses and also to develop and evaluate hypotheses about the kinds of learning that occur.

At the beginning of an OLI course design, we investigate the learning challenges particular to the domain through literature reviews, analysis of artifacts of learning, or observational studies. Our team of faculty content experts, learning scientists, and software engineers then explore how best to use the benefits of the technology and the research from the learning sciences to design an environment to address these challenges. The design is then tested and evaluated through actual student use. OLI courses are guided by principles from current cognitive and learning theory and each course attempts to reflect in honest and authentic ways the core epistemic structure of the domain it represents.

For example, a challenge in chemistry education is that students can be quite proficient at solving the mathematical problems in chemistry textbooks without being able to flexibly apply those tools to novel chemistry phenomena in which their application would be useful. Prior to designing our course, we observed that students typically solve traditional chemistry textbook problems via a shallow ends-means analysis, by matching the information given in the problem statement with the equations they can pull from the chapter text.

To address this and other issues in chemistry education, rather than the traditional approach of teaching the abstract mathematical skills of chemistry out of context, the OLI chemistry course situates the learning in an authentic investigation that addresses real-world applications and asks students to approach chemistry problems as a chemist would approach them (Evans, Karabinos, Leinhardt, and Yaron, 2006). The OLI chemistry unit on stoichiometry is situated in a real-world problem of arsenic contamination of the water supply in Bangladesh.

Many of the course activities take place in the virtual chemistry lab, which provides opportunities for students to interact with the environment by exploring and manipulating objects, grappling with questions and designing experiments. This approach promotes deeper learning and lets students solve problems in different ways.

An analysis of the data logs of student use from a study conducted on the OLI stoichiometry course revealed that the number of engaged actions with the virtual lab not only matters, it matters a lot, explaining about 48 percent of the variation observed in the post-test scores for students taking OLI. The number of interactions with the virtual lab outweighed all other factors including gender and SAT score as the predictor of positive learning outcome (Evans, Yaron, and Leinhardt, 2007). The virtual lab activities are connected to computer-based mini-tutors so that students may ask for hints as they design experiments and get immediate targeted feedback on the results.

The computer-based OLI mini-tutors are derivations of the extensive work on cognitive tutors that was conducted for more than a decade at Carnegie Mellon (Koedinger and Anderson, 1993; Anderson, Corbett, Koedinger, and Pelletier, 1995; Koedinger, Anderson, Hadley, and Mark, 1997). The OLI mini-tutors behave in a similar fashion to cognitive tutors and to human tutors: making comments when the student errs, answering questions about what to do next, and maintaining a low profile when the student is performing well. The mini-tutors are grounded in studies that have attributed sizeable learning gains that students achieve with tutors to the targeted and immediate feedback given by tutors in the problem-solving context (Butler and Winne, 1995; Corbett and Anderson, 2001; Bransford, Brown, and Cocking, 2004).

The project's research activity begins with the initial design of the course and continues through implementation. During the design process and during use, the courses are continually evaluated through studies of student use and learning. All student learning activities in OLI courses and labs are, with the student's permission, digitally recorded in considerable detail to monitor student activity and capture the data required by such studies. The results of this built-in research inform the next iteration of the course. The research results also contribute back to the underlying design principle or learning theory.

Quality Web-based open learning resources can do more to realize the use of effective strategies from the learning sciences than other methods of delivery. OER courses can instantiate effective designs without requiring the faculty who are using the courses to develop expertise in the learning sciences. The students using the materials benefit from applications of strategies about which the instructor might have no knowledge. The instructors using the materials to support their teaching benefit from the information the system can give them about which areas their students are mastering and in which areas their students need additional instruction and support.

Developing a Community of Practice

The community engaged in this OLI research activity was originally composed of cognitive scientists, learning scientists, experts in human computer interaction, software engineers, faculty content experts, and learners mostly in the Pittsburgh area. As the project has developed, the community has expanded to include learning scientists, technical experts, and content experts from different kinds of institutions in the United States and several other nations. This expansion facilitates the development of new courses and contributes to an understanding of how the course materials and course contexts need to be adapted to be effective in diverse settings. It also raises new challenges for developing the best processes for engaging a larger community of research, use, reuse, adaptation, creation, and practice.

Through the open education movement, we have the potential to create a community of instructors, learning scientists, instructional support specialists, and others who strive together to make open learning as effective as it can be by studying how people learn and by engaging in use-driven design processes. OLI exemplifies the creation of such a community on a small scale. OLI faculty members remain engaged in the project because they have the opportunity to redefine what to teach and how to teach their domain in light of the benefits of the technology and the information from the learning sciences. The effort has produced a community of scholars from diverse disciplines who are also committed to scientifically based, online teaching as a path to improving quality and access to instruction.

The process is intensely reflexive. Our challenge now lies in extending this enthusiasm and process to an even larger community. In spite of our lack of promotion of the approach, participating in such a community has already captured the imagination of faculty at institutions in several countries. Faculty from institutions in Chile, Columbia, India, Mexico, Qatar, and Taiwan are currently collaborating with us in using, evaluating, and extending OLI courses or in developing new OLI courses. The nature of the relationship varies by institution and course area. At Qatar University (QU), the statistics faculty is collaborating with OLI to develop alternative and additional data-analysis examples that are more culturally appropriate. The QU biology faculty members are using and evaluating the OLI biology course material and actively working with the Carnegie Mellon biology faculty members to extend the material. In Colombia, the department of psychology at Universidad de los Andes implemented and formally evaluated a blend of the material from the OLI statistics course and the OLI causal reasoning course. In Taiwan, faculty members and technical staff from National Chiao Tung University (NCTU) attended the OLI developers' workshop at Carnegie Mellon and have since installed an OLI appliance (a fully configured server with the OLI development and delivery environment and all the course content), hosted an OLI technical workshop at NCTU, and are actively developing a calculus course in Chinese. OLI is now collaborating with NCTU on development of the calculus course and will work with NCTU to translate the course into English rather than continuing development on our own calculus course.

The Challenge of Use and Reuse

Some of the OER's greatest challenges are in the area of use and reuse. The OER movement has successfully facilitated the production of a large amount of open content. Deliberate efforts to create diverse kinds of high quality open educational resources for different purposes and audiences have arisen in the last six or seven years. These efforts are changing the Internet as an educational resource in several ways and are increasing the amount and diversity of quality educational resources that can be found (Atkins, Brown, and Hammond, 2007).

In the OER movement, instructors have expressed the desire to create, reuse, and remix resources to better fit their teaching approaches and the needs of their students. Instructors who create, use, reuse, and remix OERs possess different levels of expertise, interest, time, and resources to select, organize, adapt, and create material. Some instructors have a clear idea of what material to include and how to organize it so they can create a flow that they believe will work best for their students. These instructors are more likely to want modular materials that they can adapt and fit into their own design. Other instructors seek a well-tested collection and organization of material that they can adopt and teach. The challenge in reuse and remix of OER courses and course components is in addressing these diverse needs and abilities of instructors while still maintaining the quality of the OER for the learner.

Some challenges to reuse and remix are technological. Standards bodies provide a forum for building agreement on standards of interoperability. For example, the International Organization for Standardization (ISO; See www.iso.org) is making Sharable Content Object Reference Model (SCORM) a standard. The Sakai organization (See http://sakaiproject .org) has participating members from many institutions. The IMS Global Learning Consortium (See www.imsglobal.org) has representatives from industry and educational institutions. OKI Open Service Interface Definitions (OSID; See www.okiproject.org) have gained considerable attention and compliance by a number of online educational tools, encouraging service-oriented architectures that promote interoperability. While many projects try to instantiate these standards, there are challenges. OERs are of different types, are intended to meet diverse needs, and are developed and used by audiences with varying levels of technical expertise and resources. This diversity accentuates some challenges of standardization, such as complexity of standards, cost and difficulty in implementing standards, grain-size issues with content aggregation, and less-than-perfect interoperability even when one adheres to standards. Developers often perceive adhering to a standard as both limiting what an individual can do and as imposing requirements that the individual does not perceive as related to his or her work.

The need for standardization and interoperability has become more critical as users with little technical expertise attempt to assemble components built from vastly different technologies. This is especially true when the goal is to physically move, assemble, and deliver diverse OERs from a single location or when the goal is to leverage common middle-ware and data stores. It is the right goal; it remains challenging to achieve.

An interim and low-cost approach might be to virtually assemble OERs through links on the Web. One can link to a resource on a remote server to include it in an educational intervention rather than actually having to move the resource into a local environment. If a sequence of diverse OERs that have been virtually assembled in this way are to be used for credit-granting purposes, then the areas in which interoperability are most critical are in areas of authentication and reporting. Shibboleth (See http://shibboleth.internet2.edu/) is designed to leverage each institution's authentication strategy to create a trust fabric. Using the trust fabric, an instructor could virtually assemble a sequence of OERs and direct his or her students to follow a sequence of links. The students would be able to seamlessly follow the sequence without having to authenticate at each server, and the students' work from the diverse servers would be reported back to the instructor.

The technological challenges may well be easier to overcome than the greater challenge of creating a self-sustaining ecology in which members are active participants not only in production, adaptation, and consumption of learning resources but also in reflection and evaluation. As described above, we have had successes in facilitating reuse and extensions to the OLI courses with our partners at other institutions both in the United States and abroad, but the efforts are time- and labor-intensive and do not scale easily.

Several projects in the OER movement have taken an alternate approach to supporting reuse and remix. The Connexions (See http://cnx.org/) project provides tools and environments that support teachers and others to author, share, select, remix, mash-up, and deliver OERs without the need for direct collaboration with the original authors. In addition to making some very good content available, Connexions has done excellent work in developing an environment and tools to support faculty to author, mash-up, and remix content to support their teaching. Faculty with little or no technical expertise can author original materials and courses and also modify and extend existing materials and courses that others have created. Connexions has also made it very easy for faculty to take the original material or the mashed-up and remixed material and deliver it as a textbook. In spite of this focus and the development of the easy-to-use tool set, there are still very few examples of faculty members who were not involved in the original development of the courses who have taken a course developed by someone else, made significant changes, adaptations, and/or extensions that they used in their teaching, and then contributed their adaptation back to the collection. A recent study has suggested that a key barrier to faculty adopting and adapting others' innovations into their teaching is the scant preparation, help, and reward that typical faculty receive for continually updating and improving their courses (Ehrmann, Gilbert, and McMartin, 2007).

The Knowledge Media Lab (KML) at The Carnegie Foundation for the Advancement of Teaching has been investigating how to support educators and students in documenting, sharing, and building knowledge of effective practices and successful educational resources to collectively advance teaching and learning for some time. OER projects are using the KEEP Toolkit developed by the KML to document and communicate both the original design rationale and the many variations on contextual use of the OER courses (Iiyoshi, Richardson, and McGrath, 2006). In the OLI project, course development teams complete the KEEP OLI author template to document and communicate the instructional goals and learning theory that guide course development. Instructors at a variety of institutions who are using OLI courses complete the KEEP OLI user template to document and communicate a description of the context in which the online courses are delivered and the impact of using the OLI course on teaching and learning. The combination of the KEEP OLI author document and the collection of the KEEP OLI user documents for each course provide potential users with an understanding of the logic and goals behind each course and with rich information about the institutional, sociocultural, and curricular contexts of teaching and learning.

In addition to the case study-type documentation that OLI and other projects are creating using the KEEP Toolkit, perhaps we need a schema by which authors and instructors can tag their resource, or their remix of another's resource, with references to the following: the context in which the resource has been used effectively, and either the learning principles that underlie its design or an evaluation validating the effectiveness of the resource or remix. At minimum, we need a common terminology that describes different types of OERs so that members can more easily find resources and audiences that meet their needs.

OERs Supporting Instructors to Improve Teaching and Learning

The initial motivation of the OLI was to develop exemplars of high quality, online courses that support individual learners in achieving the same learning goals as students enrolled in similar courses at Carnegie Mellon University. Although originally designed to support individual learners, OLI courses are increasingly used by instructors inside and outside of Carnegie Mellon as a complement to their instructor-led courses to address the challenges they confront due to the increasing variability in their students' background knowledge, relevant skills, and future goals.

Creating an effective feedback loop to instructors using the OLI courses is our current area of investigation. The process goes something like this: The instructor assigns students to work through a segment of the online instruction. The system collects data as the students work. The system automatically analyzes and organizes the data to present the instructor with the students' current "learning state." The instructor reviews the information and adapts instruction accordingly. The richness of the data we are collecting about student use and learning provides an unprecedented opportunity for keeping instructors in tune with the many aspects of students' learning.

An interesting result of the OLI involves the effects of this kind of effort on the community of faculty engaged in the project. While a high level of commitment existed from the beginning, the nature of the commitment changed over the course of the project. Initially, the participation of many faculty and departments was motivated by a desire to share expertise and knowledge with the world—much the same motivation of OpenCourseWare projects. Some faculty members were also motivated by a curiosity to explore how critical aspects of their domain could be taught effectively in an online medium. Most faculty and departments did not initially consider using the OLI courses at Carnegie Mellon. As the OLI courses were originally intended and developed to be generally used by a wide range of faculty and students at various institutions, as well as self-learners, some faculty members were concerned that OLI course materials might not be specialized enough to improve current instruction, especially given Carnegie Mellon's specific needs and high-level goals for teaching and learning. Many also held the belief that an online learning environment would always be inferior to a classroom with a human instructor.

It is now the case that almost all OLI courses, or major components of them, are used in Carnegie Mellon courses. We now receive requests from faculty and departments to "put their courses in OLI." Faculty members hear from their colleagues about the impact of OLI courses, and they contact us to explore how to create an OLI environment in their domain to address student learning challenges. Another unanticipated benefit is that faculty members involved in the project have improved the way they teach traditional courses based on what they learned in the OLI course development process. At the beginning of the process, we insist that faculty clearly articulate the learning objectives as observable student-centered measures and then work with the development teams to construct learning activities and assessment that align with the stated objectives. Articulating student-centered measurable learning objectives is often the hardest part of the process for faculty.

Evaluation of Open Educational Resources

Sustaining an open education movement requires a demonstration of effectiveness. More studies of impact of OERs are needed. Much of the data remains anecdotal. The careful studies have yielded hopeful results, but in the end, data about the value of the efforts is part of maintaining the current high level of enthusiasm.

A major goal of the OLI is to provide access to high quality postsecondary courses (similar to those taught at Carnegie Mellon) to learners who cannot attend such institutions. OLI course design has been guided by principles of learning theory that stress the importance of interactive environments, feedback on student understanding and performance, authentic problem solving, and efficient computer inter-faces. The expectation of high educational quality in these courses stems from close collaboration throughout the development of the OLI courses among cognitive scientists, experts in human-computer interaction, and experienced faculty who have both deep expertise in their respective fields and a strong commitment to excellence in teaching. Ensuring that these expectations are realized falls to the formative and summative evaluation strategies that are built into OLI course-creation methods.

Our summative evaluation efforts to date have studied the degree to which we have achieved our goal in developing online courses that enact instruction at least as effectively as existing instructor-led courses. We have collected empirical information about the instructional effectiveness of OLI courses as stand-alone courses and in blended modes (online instruction supplemented by faculty instruction or tutoring) in contrast to traditional instruction.

The OLI's overall evaluation plan/approach has included several important components. First, there have been several analyses of the cognitive and pedagogical features of curricula currently offered by others in an online model. These reports are typically generated at the beginning of a course development effort to guide the course design. Second, there have been a number of formative assessments and usability and design studies. These reports are generated throughout the design process and guide us in the revision and retooling of course components. Third, there have been a number of learning and effectiveness studies that use randomized controls or ABAB designs that have pointed to the comparability of OLI courses and face-to-face courses. The array of studies has produced an *Evaluative Portfolio* for OLI work that appears on the OLI Web site. We have discovered that our courses have the potential not only to do as well as traditional instruction in supporting students to achieve learning outcomes, but also to improve instruction and learning beyond traditional levels.

Our current studies focus on the *accelerated learning hypothesis*: that an individual can learn more material in a shorter amount of time with equal learning gains for each topic covered. We seek to demonstrate accelerated learning by showing that a learner can complete a semester-long course in significantly less than a semester and/or that a learner can complete significantly more than a semester's worth of material within a semester's time. In both cases, we are assessing students to ensure that the OLI and traditional groups demonstrate similar learning outcomes on the core material. The first accelerated learning study demonstrated that students using the OLI statistics course could complete the course in 8 weeks with two class meetings per week compared to the students in the traditional control condition who completed the same course in 15 weeks with four class meetings per week. Students in the accelerated OLI and traditional conditions spent the same amount of time in a given week on statistics outside of class. The OLI accelerated students demonstrated significantly greater learning gains than the traditional controls, and there was no significant difference in retention between the two groups in tests given 4 to 6 months later (Lovett and Thille, 2007).

Conclusion

Ultimately, it is not the technology itself but rather the new practices and communities that the technology enables that will revolutionize postsecondary education. In the case of OERs, the technology, the communities, and practices that develop around the OERs may ultimately allow us to close the feedback loop and support institutions of higher learning to become learning institutions.

References

Anderson, J. R., Corbett, A. T., Koedinger, K. R., and Pelletier, R. (1995). Cognitive tutors: Lessons learned. *Journal of the Learning Sciences*, 4(2), 167–207.

Atkins, D., Brown, J. S., and Hammond, L. (2007). *A Review of the Open Educational Resources (OER) Movement: Achievements, Challenges, and New Opportunities*. [A publication of The William and Flora Hewlett Foundation]. Retrieved March 23, 2007, from http://www.hewlett.org/Programs/Education/ OER/OpenContent/Hewlett+OER+Report.htm

Bransford, J. D., Brown, A. L., and Cocking, R. R. (Eds.). (2004). *How people learn: Brain, mind, experience, and school*. [Expanded edition]. Washington, DC: National Academy Press.

Butler, D. L., and Winne, P. H. (1995). Feedback and self-regulated learning: A theoretical synthesis. *Review of Educational Research*, 65, 245–281.

Corbett, A. T., and Anderson, J. R. (2001). Locus of feedback control in computer-based tutoring: Impact on learning rate, achievement and attitudes. Proceedings of the Association for Computing Machinery 2001 CHI conference, held in Seattle, WA, from March 31–April 5, 2001.

Desjardins, R., Rubenson, K., and Milana, M. (2006). Unequal chances to participate in adult learning: International perspectives. Paris: UNESCO International Institute for Educational Planning. *Fundamentals of Educational Planning*, 83.

Evans, K., Karabinos, M., Leinhardt, G., and Yaron, D. (2006, April). Chemistry in the field and chemistry in the classroom: A cognitive disconnect? *Journal of Chemical Education*, 83(4), 655.

Evans, K., Yaron, D., and Leinhardt, G. (in press). Learning stoichiometry: A comparison of text and multimedia formats. *Chemistry Education: Research Practice*. Mercyhurst College, Education Department; Carnegie Mellon University, Department of Chemistry: Pittsburgh, PA; University of Pittsburgh, Learning Research and Development Center, Pittsburgh, PA.

Ehrmann, S. C., Gilbert, S. W., and McMartin, F. (2007). *Factors Affecting the Adoption of Faculty-Developed Academic Software: A Study of Five iCampus Projects*. Takoma, MD: The TLT Group.

Iiyoshi, T., Richardson, C., and McGrath, O. (2006, October/November). Harnessing open technologies to promote open educational knowledge sharing. *Innovate*, 3(1). Retrieved May 15, 2007, from www.innovateonline.info.

Koedinger, K. R., and Anderson, J. R. (1993). Reifying implicit planning in geometry: Guidelines for model-based intelligent tutoring system design. In S. Lajoie and S. Derry (Eds.), *Computers as Cognitive Tools*. Hillsdale, NJ: Erlbaum.

Koedinger, K. R., Anderson, J. R., Hadley, W. H., and Mark, M. A. (1997). Intelligent tutoring goes to school in the big city. *International Journal of Artificial Intelligence in Education*, 8, 30–43.

Lovett, M., and Thille, C. (2007). Measuring the effectiveness of OLI statistics course in accelerating learning. Milton Keynes: Proceedings of OpenLearn2007.

Nathan, M. J., and Koedinger, K. R. (2000). Teachers' and researchers' beliefs of early algebra development. *Journal of Mathematics Education Research*, 31(2), 168–190.

National Academy of Sciences Committee on Science, Engineering and Public Policy. (2007). *Rising above the gathering storm: Energizing and employing America for a brighter economic future*. Washington, DC: The National Academies Press.

President's Information Technology Advisory Committee. (2005). *Computational science: Ensuring America's competitiveness*. Arlington, VA: National Coordination Office for Research and Development.

President's Council of Advisors on Science and Technology, Workforce/Education Subcommittee. (2004). *Sustaining the Nation's Innovation Ecosystems, Information Technology Manufacturing and Competitiveness*. [Report approved at full President's Council of Advisors on Science and Technology meeting on December 3, 2003.] Washington, DC.

Simon, Herbert. (1998). Teaching: Need it be a solo sport? Delivered at Last Lecture Series, Carnegie Mellon University, Pittsburgh, PA. [Videorecording].

Smith, J. M., and Thille, C. (2004). *The Open Learning Initiative: Cognitively Informed e-Learning*. London: The Observatory on Borderless Higher Education.

United Nations Educational, Scientific and Cultural Organization—World Bank. (2000). *Higher Education in Developing Countries: Peril or Promise*. Washington, DC: The Task Force on Higher Education and Society.

12

Extending the Impact of Open Educational Resources through Alignment with Pedagogical Content Knowledge and Institutional Strategy: Lessons Learned from the MERLOT Community Experience

Tom Carey and Gerard L. Hanley

Educational resource repositories are of growing importance in extending access and quality for higher education. New educational materials are now frequently made available through repositories for reuse and adaptation by faculty, with networks of repositories of varying scopes appearing at the national, regional, state, and discipline levels. However, educational resources can be more effective and more frequently reused when faculty have the motivation, time, and expertise to incorporate effective learning designs that meet the needs of their students.

The Challenges of Using Open Educational Resources

An emerging body of research results is helping to inform our thinking about the use of—and contributions to—repositories of learning resources and teaching expertise. Studies of digital resource reuse in single disciplines have illuminated the variety of ways that faculty search for learning resources to engage their students (Borgman and others, 2004), the challenges of evolving users of learning resources into contributors of feedback and teaching expertise (Yaron, Cuadros, Leinhardt, Rehm, Karabinos, and Palucka, 2005), and the importance of a sense of community beyond a traditional information needs framework (Marshall and Bly, 2004). The recent study on the use and users of educational resource repositories across multiple disciplines, described by Diane Harley in this volume, identified the key challenges that faculty cite as obstacles to application of open educational resources, including the following:

• *Impact on teaching practices*: "The foremost reason for *not* using digital resources was that they did not support faculty's teaching approaches."

• *Time to identify and adapt resources*: "Lack of time was a major constraint, regardless of institution."

• *Reusing resources in new contexts*: "Faculty, including those active and enthusiastic in their use of digital resources, identified many other obstacles to using these resources for teaching, including how to . . . reuse them in new contexts" (Harley, Henke, and Lawrence, 2006, p. 7).

Studies in specific content areas further define the nature of these challenges and describe their mutual dependence. For example, a recent project in physics demonstrated the need to rethink instructional designs when resources from a research-intensive institution are reused in the differing context of a four-year institution (Loverude, 2004). Another study, focused on geoscience faculty, noted that "While many faculty have a general knowledge of teaching methods, they are most interested in the application of these methods to the specific topics they teach, and they prefer to learn about teaching methods within such a context . . . This required a design . . . that would capitalize on faculty use of the web to find materials for class as a mechanism for bringing them into contact with materials that could be used later to support their redesign of a course" (Manduca, Iverson, Fox, and McMartin, 2005).

Based on our experience over the last several years with the MERLOT community, we offer two strategies to begin to address these challenges. One strategy supports faculty in reusing open educational resources in their local contexts through the incorporation of pedagogical content knowledge as part of open educational resources. The need for expertise in adapting resources to local contexts—and the time this requires—can be addressed in part by enhancing the pedagogical content knowledge available for reusers of open educational resources. The other strategy aligns the processes and services of open education repositories with the strategic priorities of partner academic institutions to insure their ongoing support for faculty involvement and for the underlying social and technical infrastructures. In this context, the challenge of creating faculty motivation to adapt teaching practices and make time for change can be addressed by aligning our provision and promotion of open educational resources with institutional priorities and initiatives that are already initiating changes in educational practice.

The Example of MERLOT

MERLOT is a network of 16 higher education systems and seven leading institutions collaborating on strategic directions in teaching and learning through the exchange, reuse, and adaptation of exemplary learning resources and shared teaching expertise. The MERLOT open repository, www.merlot.org, provides a portal to over 16,000 open educational resources and contains nearly 8,000 contributions of teaching expertise about those resources (these function as open educational resources in their own right). Use of this repository continues to experience dramatic growth: At the start of 2007, the 40,000 unique users per month seeking out shared learning resources represented a 50 percent increase from the previous year.

Behind this public face, MERLOT is also a leadership cooperative for faculty communities, sharing teaching knowledge and managing digital resources to enhance learning and student success in higher education. MERLOT has created 15 discipline communities that peer review the learning materials, as well as expand the shared teaching expertise available for reuse and adaptation. MERLOT programs enable faculty to provide exemplary learning experiences in their content areas through professional and scholarly collaborations with their disciplinary and institutional colleagues.

Enhancing Pedagogical Content Knowledge

The term *pedagogical content knowledge* was first used by Lee Shulman to characterize the knowledge needed to teach effectively in a discipline (Shulman, 1986). Including but not limited to the knowledge of the discipline content, this expertise is situated in specific disciplines and topics, and both supplements and instantiates more generic pedagogical knowledge (Bransford, Brown, and Cocking, 2000). Based on a combination of practical experience and scholarly research, this knowledge includes implicit and explicit elements across a range of learning issues:

• the various outcomes associated with particular topics and student cohorts;
• the challenges students and teachers experience in engaging with the topic;
• the teaching and learning approaches which are effective, and the contexts in which they work best;
• assessment of student accomplishment and support of their learning needs.

A Complementary Source of Open Educational Resources

Pedagogical content knowledge is an important component of open educational resources (OER). From that perspective, a number of additional collections or repositories come into view as potential sources of OER. Many institutional repositories showcase their exemplary teachers and share effective practices. Some repositories facilitate sharing of pedagogical content knowledge across institutions, including the KEEP Toolkit from the Carnegie Foundation, discussed in this volume, which has been used to document over 50,000 instances of exemplary teaching practices across K–12 and higher education settings (Iiyoshi, Richardson, and McGrath, 2006). However, most of the repositories do not highlight the discipline-specific contexts in which these approaches have been applied, and few of them complement the representations of teaching expertise with reusable learning materials that would accelerate the implementation of exemplary teaching approaches.

Through MERLOT, we have seen that it is possible to integrate learning materials and teaching expertise. Teaching strategies for the effective use of the resources are currently being shared and extended through evolving repository elements for pedagogical content knowledge. Below we describe some of our past experience and the new directions now being explored to make the process of using and reusing content and related resources more effective and sustainable.

"Segmenting" and "Capturing" Pedagogical Knowledge

Time, motivation, and expertise affect the likelihood of instructors contributing and reusing pedagogical content knowledge as well as disciplinary content. Therefore, a key principle of MERLOT's strategy is to segment pedagogical knowledge into units of work that can be produced by different instructors with different levels of expertise and in small enough units that the process can be integrated into the instructor's normal workflow. Also, most of the pedagogical expertise captured in MERLOT is produced in an open process by individuals using MERLOT's user-friendly tools freely.

Identifying Content   Finding and selecting prospective content to transform into curriculum is a significant challenge (Hanley, 2005). Since 2000, using pedagogical content knowledge as well as disciplinary content knowledge to facilitate finding and selecting OER has been MERLOT's key focus. Five of MERLOT's current open pedagogical resources, in particular, focus on enabling teachers and learners in discovering and researching the educational resources appropriate to their needs. Below, we summarize the lessons learned from deploying and supporting resources in this format (examples of all these formats for pedagogical content knowledge can be accessed at http://www.merlot .org/merlot/materials.htm).

• *Member comments* are personal reflections on the value of the MERLOT resource. This service was designed so that instructors who might consider using a MERLOT resource would have access to direct reflections of students, faculty, and staff. These reflections would provide valuable pedagogical context for their decision making. We have found that it is relatively easy to create and review member comments. About 140 new comments are being added to MERLOT per month. In April 2007, the MERLOT collection contained about 5,000 member comments on about 2,500 materials, with about half the people writing comments being students.

• *Personal collections* are individualized collections of MERLOT resources created and annotated by MERLOT members. These collections enable any user to leverage the search and review processes of their colleagues. The number of times a resource is placed in a personal collection also becomes a citation index and can be used as another indication of the resource's value. When annotations are added to a personal collection, other users can learn the member's pedagogical purpose(s) for organizing the collection. We have found that personal collections are also relatively easy to create and review. About 170 personal collections are being added to MERLOT per month. In April, 2007, the MERLOT collection contained about 8,800 personal collections created by about 4,800 members, about half created by faculty and a quarter by students.

• *Learning assignments* provide practical examples of how a specific OER can be used for a particular learning objective. The member contributing an assignment describes important pedagogical context, including the learning objectives, pre-requisite skills and knowledge for the assignment, and estimated time to complete the task. Assignments can aid other instructors in selecting resources, as they provide a lesson plan and considerations about how to use the content as curriculum. We have found that contributing an assignment is relatively easy but requires significantly more pedagogical expertise to create. About 15 assignments per month are being added to MERLOT. In April 2007, the MERLOT collection contained about 1,100 assignments on about 900 materials, about two thirds written by faculty and about one third written by students and student teachers.

• *Author snapshots* provide valuable insights into an author's rationale and design for the educational resource that can be very useful for instructors assessing if their own rationale and design aligns with the author's in the process of selecting materials. Author Snapshots were created in partnership with the Carnegie Foundation's Knowledge Media Lab. We have found that they require a comparatively significant effort and pedagogical expertise. In April 2006, MERLOT provided 16 author snapshots, all created by faculty. Without specific MERLOT interventions to invite, train, and manage the development of these snapshots, none have been generated in the last year.

• *Peer reviews* are structured evaluations of the MERLOT resources conducted by at least two trained experts in the discipline. The evaluations provide a structured report on the quality of content, pedagogical effectiveness, and usability of the resource. Other instructors considering using open resources can have some confidence in their selection of OER by reviewing the expert evaluations about its quality of content, pedagogical effectiveness, and usability. The work by peer reviewers requires significant time, motivation and expertise. The institutional support for the peer reviewers that augments the individual commitment of time, motivation, and expertise is essential to the sustainability of MERLOT's peer review process. This support can be provided through a variety of institutional reward and recognition strategies; but whatever strategy used, we have learned some strategy is essential. In April 2007, the MERLOT collection contained about 2,300 peer reviews produced by 15 editorial boards at a rate of about 25 per month.

Although there are many causes for the differences in contribution rates to Member Comment, Assignments, Personal Collections, Author Snapshots, and Peer Reviews, the differences illustrate the connection between the richness of pedagogical content knowledge and the challenges of generating the pedagogical content knowledge in a sustainable manner. It appears that Member Comments and Personal Collections are sustainable and are growing in an open community; MERLOT simply provides the access to tools to generate this pedagogical content knowledge, and instructors freely contribute. Generating Assignments is also sustainable for MERLOT (we simply provide access to the tools, and instructors freely generate them) but is less scaleable.

The Author Snapshots were not sustained within the current MERLOT context (although the use of the KEEP Toolkit is sustainable, based on other Carnegie Foundation projects). The Peer Reviews have been sustained, but MERLOT's challenge is scaling the peer review process to keep up with the rate of contributions of materials—about 200 materials per month in April 2007, for example.

Future Directions: Pedagogical Content Knowledge as an Open Educational Resource

The impact of the pedagogical knowledge represented to date has been promising, and these initiatives are being shared within the OER community. Other repositories are also extending their formats for pedagogical knowledge, including representations for community expertise through Expert Voices in next-generation prototypes of the National Science Digital Library (Lagoze, Krafft, Cornwell, Eckstrom, Jesuroga, and Wilper, 2006), and student skills, misconceptions and assessments in pilot studies for extensions of the Digital Library of Earth Science Education (Kastens, 2004; Holzman, Kastens, and Arko, 2006).

Designing for Specific Contexts   Most of these existing initiatives do not directly address the need to tailor learning designs to suit specific learning contexts, nor do they provide a link to research results and community scholarship. These are key elements in developing faculty expertise for more effective learning designs—and thereby to address the challenge of committing time and effort to adapt teaching approaches to take full advantage of open educational resources.

How might we move forward in new directions that would more directly address these needs? Within the MERLOT community, we are beginning to address these needs by experimenting with the following innovations for pedagogical content knowledge associated with open educational resources:

• *Analytic reviews* would extend existing peer review facilities by incorporating research results on learning in the subject area. Many disciplines have maturing collections of research results that could be made available to faculty accessing shared learning resources through online repositories. (See, for example, the repository maintained by the physics department of the University of Illinois at Urbana-Champaign, http:// research.physics.uiuc.edu/PER/.) As noted by Shavelson and Towne (2002), "We cannot expect reform efforts in science education to have significant effects without research-based knowledge to guide them" (p. 1).

• *Guides to best evidence for engaging learners* would build on existing approaches like the ERIC Digests (see http:// www.ericdigests.org) and syntheses of evidence for clinical practice in medicine (Grolo and Grimshaw, 2003). We are developing and testing new formats for community contributions of pedagogical knowledge from both practice-based and research-based sources. This process would follow the spirit of *How People Learn: Bridging Research and Practice* in seeking to "combine the expertise of researchers and the wisdom of practitioners" (Donovan, Bransford, and Pellegrino, 1999, p. 248). This approach also allows for multiple levels of scholarly activity to match with the contexts of application (compare the distinctions amongst personal, local, and public scholarship and faculty development in Ashwin and Trigwell, 2004), and provides a base for enriched formats with stronger support for social interactions (Sumner, 2002).

These future developments fit well with the growing movement to consider the scholarship of teaching and learning as part of faculty activities as scholars. As a consequence, these experiments with pedagogical content knowledge have the potential to align with institutional strategies for the development of teacher-scholar models for faculty.

Aligning Reuse with Institutional Strategies

MERLOT continues to work on the challenge of providing pedagogical content knowledge that can be produced in a sustainable manner. We know that it is important to increase the recognition resulting from these activities, both from the relevant teaching community and subsequently within the institutional reward systems. It is also important to increase the institutional support available for these activities, which means that MERLOT must continue to enhance the alignment between these activities and the institutional goals and initiatives which are (or will be) resourced within other plans of our sponsor academic institutions. These two efforts are synergistic. We envision that most of the faculty time required to exchange, reuse, and adapt pedagogical content knowledge will be supported as part of the ongoing strategic institutional initiatives, and that the additional effort required to share pedagogical content knowledge with the wider teaching community will be supported within the institutional recognition and reward systems for teacher-scholars.

Shared Expenses, Shared Governance

Other chapters in this book describe how institutional plans and strategic positioning have led to the creation and dissemination of open educational resources, through incentives to faculty and the provision of time, staff support, and the like. An ongoing challenge for OER communities is the development of sustainable programs which will continue this good work without the one-time external support that was pivotal to launching a critical mass of these creation and dissemination initiatives but is not available on an ongoing basis.

A related ongoing challenge for OER is the development of institutional plans and incentives for the reuse and adaptation of these resources. Indeed, any long-term value from creation and dissemination of resources derives from the benefits of their reuse and adaptation.

In this context, the way the MERLOT community has sustained its operations over the last seven years may be instructive for other OER initiatives. The costs of operating the Web site infrastructure and of the processes that support it are underwritten by MERLOT's sponsor academic institutions. The sponsoring institutions (currently 16 state or regional systems and seven individual universities and colleges) invest in supporting operations for the public Web site, and also provide faculty time to serve as members of the 15 MERLOT discipline-specific editorial boards to provide oversight, management, and quality control of the Teaching Commons content.

A critical investment these institutions make is supporting their leadership role in the MERLOT shared governance process. Each sponsor institution commits to support a MERLOT project director who participates in MERLOT's yearly cycle of strategic and operational planning processes and is the steward of MERLOT services in his or her institution. Through the project directors, MERLOT aligns its services to the needs of the institution's initiatives. The key to this continued engagement of sponsor academic institutions in MERLOT over the last seven years is to reduce the costs and risks of their own strategic initiatives, as well as increase their impact through the systematic exchange, reuse, and adaptation of resources, services, and tools provided through MERLOT.

Our sponsor academic institutions contribute financial support to MERLOT because that involvement augments and accelerates their own initiatives. They contribute faculty time to the MERLOT Teaching Commons for the representation and application of open pedagogical content knowledge because it supports their institutional plans. Our plan to sustain institutional support for the innovations described in the previous section also builds directly on the success of this MERLOT positioning for academic partnerships. Aligning OER activities with strategic institutional initiatives also has the synergistic effect of overcoming other barriers to use by increasing the value and visibility of benefits.

Below we offer some examples of the institutional strategic goals that MERLOT has been able to support, and the ways that reuse of OER and MERLOT services within these institutions has helped them to address these goals—and, as a consequence, has enabled the ongoing operations of the repository and the ongoing contributions of the faculty involved. Each of these brief examples involves an institutional initiative where OER-based collaboration furthered the institutional priorities and improved the return on investment of institutional funds in the initiative.

1. Accelerating Course Development with Online Learning Activities[1]

The Tennessee Board of Regents is a leader in engaging faculty with discipline colleagues using MERLOT. The board seeded this engagement by supporting leadership roles for key faculty as MERLOT discipline editors and coeditors, content reviewers, and so on. The contributions of these leaders are leveraged across the system, through seminars and workshops, and other faculty members who identify and submit ten exemplary learning objects that have been accepted by the peer review team have their work recognized at the system level through support for participation in MERLOT activities.

This investment has enabled the institutionalization of MERLOT use into development of the Regents Online Degree Program. As part of the quality assurance process, course designers are expected to document their use of exemplary learning resources with high quality reviews. Online mentors for the program find additional resources and submit 10 learning objects to MERLOT as part of their contract. MERLOT is posted in every online course and highlighted on course Web sites. Students have shared on their course evaluations that they have used MERLOT as a tutorial tool for their online courses. Faculty and staff report that they use MERLOT as a curriculum enhancer for course development of online materials and for their own professional development.

Similarly, the Oklahoma State Regents for Higher Education have initiated a project to help state residents complete a bachelor's degree through an innovative statewide approach involving public universities. Tens of thousands of Oklahomans have completed more than two years of college but have not finished a degree (P. Moss, personal communication, May 19, 2006). Collaborative curriculum development, learning materials, faculty development, and technology will be important components in this effort to help working adults complete a degree. The system office will be institutionalizing use of MERLOT as a key tool in advancing this project.

2. Integrating Institutional and Discipline-Oriented Faculty Development

Our sponsor academic institutions use MERLOT workshops and on-site presentations for faculty and professional development. The advantage that open educational resources offer in this context lies in the unique integration of expertise from multiple disciplines, across a range of teaching issues—all supported by exemplary online resources to give faculty a head start on the adoption of new methods.

In examining the cost-effectiveness of this strategy, the Office of Academic Affairs and Educational Technology of the Tennessee Board of Regents determined that the system investment for the resources provided by MERLOT, in terms of "24/7" professional development and accessibility to the learning objects, comes to around $3.00 for each faculty member using MERLOT. The system staff concluded that this return on the investment made a compelling argument to sustain support of faculty engagement with MERLOT (R. Melton, personal communication, May 2006).

Further developments are extending these system-wide faculty development activities with customized Teaching Commons that integrate the activities of the larger OER community with the institutional priorities and initiatives of a particular academic sponsor. For example, within the California State University, custom disciplinary Web spaces such as "Teaching Business in the CSU" (see http://teachingcommons.cdl.edu/business/) have been created as mini-MERLOT communities, which can provide a potential faculty development path from local disciplinary exchanges to more impact within a larger community of teaching practice.

3. Developing System-Wide Collaborations in Teaching and Learning

The previous example about institutional teaching commons sites demonstrates both immediate impacts in terms of faculty development and longer-term impacts in terms of fostering collaborations across a system. The OER community can provide additional benefits through focusing collaborations around specific resources and their use.

For example, K–20 MERLOT Triads program of the South Dakota Board of Regents supports faculty from public, private, and tribal colleges and universities in collaboration with K–12 teachers. Each triad within a discipline selects one MERLOT learning object, applies it in three different classrooms, and gathers student evaluations. This knowledge exchange has provided a direct return in terms of improved effectiveness in the learning process; it has also provided an indirect return in building stronger relationships across the sectors, which can support other goals like curriculum alignment and articulation across programs (Schamber, Turchen, and Sprung, 2006).

The Cooperative Learning Object Exchange (CLOE), the MERLOT sponsor academic institution in the Canadian province of Ontario, has adapted MERLOT's peer review processes as part of the collaborative development of learning resources across 25 university and college sites. Each CLOE learning resource was developed by a team representing several campuses, to insure reusability in multiple contexts. This intentional effort to build in collaborations in the early stages of OER development has led to increased re-usability of the resulting resources and the creation of several case stories of successful OER reuse (see, for example, http://cloe.on.ca).

The Challenges Ahead

These collaborative approaches to exchanging, reusing, and adapting resources show how the OER community can move beyond operating on the premise "build it and they will come" and start building so that users will be supported and resourced by their own institutions to come, and providing a return on the institutional investment in terms of the institution's strategic goals.

At the same time, pedagogical content knowledge is vital to insure an effective fit with student learning needs in the institutional context. Current efforts that focus on augmenting the learning materials in educational resource repositories with facilities for sharing (and developing) associated teaching expertise about the appropriate use and adaptation of the materials offer a way to "build it to provide more utility when they come—so they will come back."

Both approaches show promise to help us achieve the full potential for open educational resources. Insuring an effective alignment with student learning needs is essential for the effectiveness of open educational resources in enhancing learning outcomes, and insuring the institutions can generate additional value from those enhancements is vital to the continued sustainability of the open educational resource community.

Open educational resources hold much promise. Yet there are many questions about how OER will need to be designed and implemented to fulfill its promise. The OER community must shape a strategy for continuing success: Design effective learning experiences using open educational resources, and sustain openness in the community and collection of resources. Without adaptation and embedded effective learning designs, the OER community will not be able to transform the teaching and learning needed to achieve educational outcomes. Without collaboration to provide sustaining resources and support, the OER community will not be able to achieve the pervasive use of online educational resources needed to transform the education of the world's population.

Note

1. We appreciate the contributions of Dr. Robbie Melton and Dr. Phil Moss to the descriptions of the MERLOT benefits for the Tennessee Board of Regents and the Oklahoma State Regents for Higher Education.

References

Ashwin, P., and Trigwell, K. (2004). Investigating staff and educational development. In D. Baume and P. P. Kahn (Eds.). *Enhancing Staff and Educational Development* (pp. 117–131). London: RoutledgeFalmer.

Borgman, C., Leazer, G., Gilliland-Swetland, A., Millwood, K., Champeny, L., Finley, J., and Smart, L. (2004). How geography professors select materials for classroom lectures: Implications for the design of digital libraries. In *Proceedings of the 4th ACM/IEEE-CS Joint Conference on Digital Libraries* (pp. 179–185). Retrieved July 27, 2007, from http://portal.acm.org/

Bransford, J., Brown, A., and Cocking, R. (2000). *How People Learn: Brain, Mind, Experience, and School.* Commission on Behavioral and Social Sciences and Education. Committee on Developments in the Science of Learning. Washington, DC: National Academy Press.

Donovan, M. S., Bransford, J., and Pellegrino, J. (Eds.). (1999). *How People Learn: Bridging Research and Practice.* Committee on Learning Research and Educational Practice, National Research Council. Washington, DC: National Academy Press.

Grolo, R., and Grimshaw, J. (2003). From best evidence to best practice: effective implementation of change in patients' care. *Lancet*, 362(9391), 1225–1230.

Hanley, G. L. (2005, November). *MERLOT: Supporting Faculty Workflow in the Design and Delivery of Distance Education.* Paper presented at the University of Hawaii Distance Learning Conference, Waikiki, HI.

Harley, D., Henke, J., and Lawrence, S. (2006). *Use and Users of Digital Resources*, Center for Studies in Higher Education, U.C. Berkeley. Retrieved July 27, 2007, from http://cshe.berkeley.edu/research/digitalresourcestudy/report/

Holzman, N., Kastens, K., and Arko, R. (2006, October). *Adding Value to NSDL Resources through Pedagogical Content Knowledge Annotations.* Poster presented at the Annual Meeting of the National Science Digital Library, Washington, DC. Retrieved July 27, 2007, from http://www.ldgo.columbia.edu/edu/eesj/directors/kastens/talks_posters/posters/NSDL06.pdf

Iiyoshi, T., Richardson, C., and McGrath, O. Harnessing open technologies to promote open educational knowledge sharing, *Innovate Journal of Online*

Education, 3(1) 2006. Retrieved July 27, 2007, from http://innovateonline.info/index.php?view=article&id=339

Kastens, K. (2004). Making DLESE into *the* source for pedagogical content knowledge pertaining to the earth and environment. White paper for DLESE Quality Workshop. Retrieved July 27, 2007, from http://swiki.dlese.org/quality/uploads/1/Geo_PCK_source.pdf

Lagoze, C., Krafft, D., Cornwell, T., Eckstrom, D., Jesuroga, S., and Wilper, C. (2006). Representing contextualized information in the NSDL. In J. Gonzalo, C. Thanos, M. F. Verdejo, and R. C. Carrasco (Eds.), *2006, Research and Advanced Technology for Digital Libraries: 10th European Conference, EDCL 2006, Alicante Spain, September 17–22, Proceedings* (pp. 329–340). Heidelberg: Springer.

Loverude, M. (2004). Measuring the effectiveness of research-based curriculum at a university serving a diverse student population. In J. Marx, K. Cummings, and S. Franklin (Eds.), *2003 Physics Education Research Conference*. AIP Conference Proceedings 720 (pp. 7–10). Melville, NY: American Institute of Physics.

Manduca, C., Iverson, E., Fox, S., and McMartin, F. (2005). Influencing user behavior through digital library design. *D-Lib Magazine*, 11(5). Retrieved July 27, 2007, from http://www.dlib.org/dlib/may05/fox/05fox.html

Marshall, C., and Bly, S. (2004). Sharing encountered information: Digital libraries get a social life. In *Proceedings of the 4th ACM/IEEE-CS Joint Conference on Digital Libraries* (pp. 218–227). Retrieved July 27, 2007, from http://portal.acm.org/

Schamber, S., Turchen, L., and Sprung, R. (2006, August). *South Dakota K–20 MERLOT Triads: One Object—Three Different Applications*. Paper presented at MERLOT International Conference, Ottawa Canada.

Shavelson, R., and Towne, L. (Eds.). (2002). *Scientific Research in Education*. Committee on Scientific Principles for Education Research. Washington, DC: National Academy of Sciences Press.

Shulman, L. S. (1986). Those who understand: Knowledge growth in teaching. *Educational Researcher*, 15(2), 4–14.

Sumner, T. (2002). Promoting scholarship through design. In W. H. Dutton and B. D. Loader (Eds.), *Digital Academe: The New Media and Institutions of Higher Education and Learning* (pp. 135–151). London: Routledge, 2002.

Yaron, D., Cuadros, J., Leinhardt, G., Rehm, E., Karabinos, M., and Palucka, T. (2005). *The ChemCollective: Monitoring the Path from Seeing to Using to Contributing*. Internal project report. Retrieved July 27, 2007, from http://www.chemcollective.org/papers.php

13
Why Understanding the Use and Users of Open Education Matters

Diane Harley

My colleagues and cocontributors to this volume make eloquent arguments for the promise and potential of open educational resources (OER) to improve educational opportunities locally and globally.[1] Many also point to the importance of determining how the high quality use of their tools and content can be achieved in diverse educational communities and how demand for those resources can be increased and sustained. We all recognize that it is one thing to make high-quality content and tools widely available and another to identify the best strategies for integrating them into a critical mass of meaningful teaching and learning contexts. How (or if) materials are used and valued will vary by type of institution, the background and needs of faculty and students, the intellectual requirements of the discipline, and the characteristics of the open knowledge collections themselves. Beyond the largely anecdotal, however, what do we really know about how these important variables interact with open education content? And how might such knowledge allow the OER community to better assess user demand for open educational (as well as other) digital resources?

There is no dearth of prognostications about the needs and requirements of "millennials" and how faculty in higher education must adapt to their technology habits.[2] Yet faculty—not students, technology professionals, or librarians—are the arbiters of pedagogical quality in certificate and degree-granting contexts. Arguably, understanding the needs of faculty will be essential as we envision new technology-mediated academic environments. To that end, we conducted an empirical University of California, Berkeley-based study of faculty in specific U.S. tertiary education milieus. In doing so, we uncovered disconnects between what a potential pool of faculty users of digital resources say they need in undergraduate education and what those who produce those resources imagine as an ideal state. (I use the term "digital resources" because, as is described in more detail below, OER represent only one small galaxy in the total universe of digital tools and content available to faculty and others in tertiary education.)

Understanding the Context for the Research

The chasm between what many technological enthusiasts envision in terms of scale and quality of use on one hand, and what productive and creative academic scholars say they need on the other, is often manifested in the suggestion that "the lack of willingness of faculty to change" is a key barrier to wider adoption of and demand for a variety of technologies and digital content in scholarship. Faculty culture, individual pedagogical proclivities, time, budgets, and access to support structures are all major impediments to the use of digital resources in undergraduate education, and each of these factors will have an effect on the demand for resources by faculty.

The question of use and user demand is itself intimately tied to questions of cost and sustainability: There is no avoiding the fact that sustainability of open education resource initiatives will be determined ultimately by actual user demand. Although there is an implicit assumption that faculty at a variety of institutions import digital content to enhance their undergraduate teaching, we simply do not have much rigorously collected data that can tell us whether such importation occurs on a measurable scale or what the quality of integration might be. In an era of shrinking institutional budgets and deflated expectations of profitable consumer markets for digital curricular materials, such a lack of knowledge about user demand can make strategic investment decisions by institutions difficult (See, for example, Matkin, 2002). Even if we all agree that open content should be made freely available for the public good, some entity—be it federally, state, or privately funded—will ultimately need to pay for it. A demonstration of robust demand from a set of relevant constituents will be undoubtedly needed to justify such investment.

Methodology: The Challenges of Studying Users, Uses, and User Demand

Between 2003 and 2006, we gathered attitudinal data relatively quickly and systematically from an array of stakeholders in the humanities and social sciences (H/SS) undergraduate education community, and we attempted to triangulate those attitudes and perceptions. We employed a combination of surveys, discussion groups, and interviews to create our scan, with primary focus on faculty. In the interests of achieving rigor and depth versus breadth, we talked with educators in a subset of H/SS disciplines at three institution types in California only: public research universities, liberal arts colleges, and community colleges. Our faculty survey employed a carefully designed methodology that included random stratified sampling and non-response surveys. To provide important institutional context, we also spoke with digital resource providers and those who support faculty in digital resource use such as librarians and IT staff. The entire report that describes our results and the various research lenses we employed can be found online.[3] Recent publications resulting from the details of this research are also cited throughout where appropriate.

At the outset, we recognized that we needed to assiduously avoid judgments about the "value" of specific types of resources if we were to assess faculty demand for the vast array of available resources and to elicit responses as unbiased as possible. We also recognized that there are many types of resources proliferating in different environments, and that these resources are being created by different kinds of developers who have varying goals. Therefore, our definition of digital resources was intentionally broad and included rich media objects (for example, maps, video, and images) as well as text. These digital resources may reside in or outside of universities, digital libraries, and museums, may be "free" or proprietary, and can include those developed by individual scholars and non-academic entities such as commercial and non-commercial media outlets.

The challenges to rigorously measuring demand and uptake of material floating freely out on the Web should not be underestimated. Such measurement requires that researchers not be biased in favor of any one type of resource. It also demands complicated definitions about, and analyses of (1) the scope, variety, and origins of the available resources, tools, and services available to "users"; (2) how and why the resources are actually used (or not used); and (3) the variation that exists between and among a diverse group of "users" and "owners" (and a recognition that users and owners are often embodied in the same person).

In framing our research as questioning the value of studying users and attempting to measure actual demand for resources, we discovered an especially complex set of stakeholder interests and agendas. Beyond users, there are the interests of policy makers, funders, and administrators who oversee, and ultimately finance, educational reform efforts; developers who create resources; and technicians or designers who develop tools for the integration of resources into undergraduate settings. These stakeholder interests encompass a number of broad and overlapping expert domains in the humanities and social sciences—not just OER providers—and include digital libraries, cultural heritage institutions, educational and information technologists, higher education policy makers, and liberal arts education advocates, to name a few. We also found that, although digital resource providers may share a desire to measure how and for what purpose materials are being used once accessed, it is often difficult to ascertain what, if any, concrete plans are in place for undertaking this measurement in a systematic, replicable, and shareable way. This diversity of perspectives, motivations, and agendas results in few common terms, metrics, methods, or values for defining use, users, or value.

Results: Focusing on Faculty Cultures

From our conversations with humanities and social science faculty, we learned that they used almost every conceivable type of digital resource available, many of which fall outside of what are formally called "collections," "educational," or "courseware." Faculty from different disciplines often have different needs with regard to the types of resources they want and how they ultimately use resources in particular educational contexts. In addition to disciplinary differences, organizational culture, location, and an individual faculty's personal needs and experiences can influence specific choices and challenges. In the following, I summarize our findings.

User "Types," User Behavior

The humanities and social sciences are not a monolith, nor are user types. The degree to which personal teaching style and philosophy influence resource use was striking. There is a broad spectrum of user types, ranging from the nonuser, to the inexperienced-novice user, to the highly proficient and advanced user of digital resources. Nonusers were themselves diverse and included those who were passionately opposed to the use of technologies in their classroom for a variety of valid pedagogical reasons (for example, the technologies cannot substitute for a faculty member's preferred teaching approaches; they undermine learning). Nonusers also included self-described enthusiasts frustrated by technical and nontechnical barriers and those simply without time to think about, let alone use, technology in teaching.

What Digital Resources Faculty Use

Respondents used an exceptionally wide range of resource types for a variety of reasons.[4] Images and visual materials were the most frequently used resources and were often used for classroom presentation or posting on the Web. Similarly, high use of images was found by Green (2006). News and other media resources, video, and online reference sources were also heavily used. Google-type searches were the most frequent way in which faculty found resources. Many of the resources faculty use and value are proprietary; definitely not "open." Indeed, we found that many of these valued resources may be licensed by an institution, but faculty view them as free simply because they have access. Many may be derived from public media and other technically noneducational sources. A faculty member's own "collection" of digital resources, described more fully below, was the second- most frequent source of material after the Google-type search. Curricular materials were relatively low on the list of what faculty reported using, although community college faculty, perhaps predictably, were the heaviest users within that relatively small group. Among those who said they used curricular materials, instructors in foreign language, writing, and art and architecture were the heaviest users; instructors of anthropology, language and literature, history, and political science used these resources the least.

Why Faculty Use Digital Resources

Faculty respondents used digital resources to improve their students' learning, to integrate primary source materials into their teaching, to provide students with a context for a topic, to include materials or teaching methods that would otherwise be unavailable, and/or to integrate faculty research interests into a course. Some reported that they used digital resources to teach critical thinking because it increased convenience for themselves and/or students, and/or because it was expected by their students or their colleagues. Very few indicated that it would help their promotion and tenure prospects; indeed, in research university environments, too much time spent on integrating technology into teaching can have negative consequences on career advancement.

Why Faculty Do *Not* Use Digital Resources

The foremost reason for *not* using digital resources (~65–80 percent) was that they simply did not support faculty's teaching approaches. A number of faculty commented about the degree to which technology represents a distraction to students and may undermine, or at least compete with, other crucial skills: argumentative writing, careful and critical reading of long texts, and oral argument. Lack of time was a major constraint for faculty, regardless of institution. Nor was it easy for most of our respondents to use the plethora of digital resources available to them. Faculty—including those active and enthusiastic in their use of digital resources—identified many obstacles to using these resources for teaching, including how to find, manage, maintain, and reuse them in new contexts. One of the most-cited obstacles to the effective use of digital resources was the availability, reliability, and expense of the necessary equipment, both in the classroom and for personal use. Almost all faculty need support for a variety of tasks. Both novices and advanced users face challenges when integrating digital resources into their teaching, but they experience somewhat different needs and barriers; thus, support systems that are helpful to one group may not be for another.

Personal Collections

As noted above, responses also emphasized the importance of personal digital collections in faculty work practices. More than 70 percent of faculty said they maintain their own collections, although relatively few of them make their resources available to others on the Web. It was clear from our discussions and from comments on the surveys that many faculty want the ability to build their own collections, which are often composed of a variety of materials, including those that are copyright protected. How to manage this potpourri of resources and integrate them into teaching practice is the challenge. Although there may be an array of tools available to faculty for collecting, developing, and managing resourcas, the efficacy and interoperability of these tools for the immediate tasks that faculty need supported often fall short. We identified a number of challenges faced by those charged with building the future tools to reaggregate varied resources for easier use:

• The difficulty, if not current impossibility, of reaggregating objects that are bundled and "locked" into fixed, often proprietary resources.
• Managing and interpreting digital rights, which may include pulling data from one resource for integration into another.
• The unevenness of interface usability and aesthetics (in some disciplines, such as art history, faculty may care a lot about resolution quality while, in other disciplines, faculty may create "hodgepodge" resources, often not caring about varying resolution quality from one record to the next).
• The growing demand from users for granularity (for example, the ability to search and find the one particular image or piece of text they need within an entire resource and to do it quickly).
• The issue of knowing about and finding digital objects (many faculty have no idea about the existence of local and nonlocal resources, especially licensed resources, that may be available to them).

Discipline

An analysis by discipline revealed variation among scholarly fields. Faculty who use texts extensively depended on different kinds of digital resources (or none at all) for different pedagogical goals than did faculty who rely heavily on images, such as those in art, architecture, history, and anthropology. Faculty in political science were the heaviest users of datasets, and faculty who teach writing had special needs around information literacy and the use of reference materials. Not only do faculty in different disciplines require different types of resources, they use them in different ways and for different reasons.

Demographics

When the data were analyzed by age, the oldest instructors (age 62 and up) were the lightest users. A multiple regression analysis demonstrated for our sample, however, that age alone is a very weak predictor of a faculty member's overall level of digital resource use. Regression and path analysis further showed that individual opinions and attitudes have a greater effect on a person's total level of digital resource use than do institutional, disciplinary, or demographic characteristics.

Working within, or Changing, Faculty Culture?

It is worth noting that the most-cited reason for faculty *not* using digital resources was that these resources simply do not mesh with faculty members' pedagogies. This finding has implications for those who wish to increase technology adoption by faculty. It would be an over-simplification to assume that faculty simply need to change their approach to teaching (approaches that may, in fact, be exemplary, even if old-fashioned), or to dismiss nonadopters as aberrations, Luddites, and dinosaurs, without reflecting about the complex reasons why many scholars have not yet embraced new technologies. We encourage those charged with developing new tools and content not to expect faculty, whom we can assume know more about teaching their subject than nonspecialists, to shoehorn their approaches into a technical developer's ideas of what is valuable or the correct pedagogical approach. We also caution against relying too heavily on serving the technical proclivities of a new generation of "always on" kids if such a focus overshadows the needs of the disciplinary experts who will teach them. Such a one-sided approach could have a potentially negative impact on scholarly practice and the teaching mission of the academy in the long run.

Our work indicates that faculty who do find digital resources useful, even if only occasionally, use a variety of strategies for negotiating the digital morass. And a morass it is for the time-pressed. For most, the path of least resistance is the one usually taken—a Google search, a walk down the hall or an e-mail to a colleague, a visit to the Web site of a trusted archive, or often a personal and eclectic "collection" of digital stuff. What is deemed "good enough" for users will depend on the problem at hand; a single individual may have different standards and strategies that are determined by the immediate objective, time constraints, budgets, personal and institutional equipment, and support staff, among other variables. Given the importance of time as a limiting factor to technology adoption, it will be important to expand quality criteria beyond "enhanced learning." The quality of learning can be quite high without technology. What technology frequently adds is an opportunity to rethink time and space so that convenience and choice are enhanced for both faculty and students (without reducing the quality of education). The issue then is not only high quality content, but content married with the appropriate delivery and communication technologies that serve the needs of faculty and the students they teach.

A large number of faculty told us that they want to build their own reaggregated resources, using their own materials, and mix them with resources they have collected over time. They are concerned, however, about the significant inadequacy of the classroom and other technologies available to them for collecting, developing, managing, and actually using resources. A "personal digital library," as envisioned by Borgman (2003), would go a long way to addressing this problem. The ubiquity of personal digital "collections" for teaching, the uncommon practice among faculty of reusing someone else's curricular materials, and the relatively low number of faculty who use digital "curricular" materials begs questions of where this personal "stuff" originates, in what formats, and how it is stored and preserved. This wealth of material is off the radar of most institutional or commercial support providers, but it appears to represent a large percentage of what faculty value (see also Smith, 2003). If this is so, how can institutions support this element of current scholarly practice, and what are the implications for the reuse of digital resources, especially finely crafted curricular materials that are developed for specific pedagogical goals and carry the weight of the developers' preconceived ideas of value?

Based on our research, we predict that there will be an exceptional amount of variation among individuals, disciplines, and higher education sectors in the willingness to embrace "canned" and relatively fixed curricular resources. Our previous work suggests that faculty in research university environments simply do not reuse course materials created by others on any appreciable scale, even if they are willing to share the materials they create and collect (Harley, Henke, and Maher, 2004). Teaching, at least in these environments, is fundamentally a "roll your own" culture. Trow (1997) predicted that the willingness to reuse other's curricular materials will very likely map to institution type (and sectors within an institution), with faculty in extension divisions, community colleges, and high schools falling toward one end of the willingness-to-reuse spectrum. Faculty in liberal arts institutions and research universities (in those cases where large enrollment courses are not off-loaded to adjunct faculty) will likely fall at the other end of this spectrum. To our knowledge, whether these patterns typify non-U.S. tertiary education is not known, nor can we predict the degree to which such patterns will persist over time. The topic certainly warrants more systematic research.

Understanding Users and the Challenges of Assessing Value, Demand, and Sustainability in Context

How can self-reports from a pool of faculty users (*albeit* the limited sample of them described briefly in this study), be jibed with an ideal vision of sustainable use by those who provide resources and tools? We are confident that users, when compared to resource providers, often employ a different level of granularity in defining and valuing a resource (for example, whether they can find a format, a photo, a picture, or a passage on the Web). "Categories" of users and nonusers often comprise diverse individuals with varying and idiosyncratic needs, perceptions, and ways of finding and using digital resources. Whether the users are students, K–12 teachers, college faculty, or self-learners will certainly be important. Correspondingly, users will be differentiated by varying skill levels and learning objectives. Some may seek a particular digital object for a specific purpose, some seek a completely stand-alone course, some seek supplemental material for a research project or assignment, some seek to create their own online course or resource site, some may be in need of remedial education, and others may just be engaged in lifelong learning. An obvious question then is how developers of open educational content can afford to simultaneously meet the needs of formal and informal audiences that range from scholars to school children, both internationally and domestically.

The vast universe and diversity of available resources on the Web and personal hard drives, the great variety of users and their needs, and the ubiquity of faculty personal collections considerably complicate our thinking about the sustainability and economics of open educational resources. These factors compound the reality that determining the real costs to institutions to create and maintain their digital education assets is perhaps impossible, given the mosaic of development and funding models that exist for any one set of assets, and the imprecision of cost models. Funding sources are often cobbled together from a variety of institution and foundation budgets; there are the frequently unpredictable, ongoing costs of maintenance and updating, and the significant time faculty spend on development and adoption is rarely entered into the cost calculations.

Moreover, are there significant costs incurred to customize resources for nonpaying, nonaffiliated audiences, many of whom are simply impossible to study because of the informal way in which they access resources on the Web? It is not always so clear what tangible value informal users bring to an institution's investments if there is no obvious benefit to the institution's faculty and current or future matriculated students (for example, a pool of transfer students from community colleges). Indeed, how a site accommodates unintended use may require a complicated calculus that takes into account the site's mission, scope, financial model, desired impact, quality control, and targeted constituencies. To some, unintended and informal use may be an opportunity for creative reuse, while others believe a site should not or could not change course to serve an unintended audience. As illustrated by MIT OpenCourseWare's (OCW) evaluation work (2006), strong institutional leadership, high-quality, high-profile, and well-funded projects can bring advantages to the institution itself by serving its own students and faculty. This recognition of value by the sponsoring institution provides a potential route to long-term support and funding (including support for the subsidization of nonpaying informal users). "One size" approaches will not likely fit all, of course, and success of any one digital resource initiative will demand developing strategies of both the site and content design to initially meet the needs and desired outcomes of a clearly defined range of users.

For projects that make content freely available on the Web, clearly defining a target audience and measuring desired outcomes is a challenge. Studying unintended and informal users of Web site content is exceptionally difficult (Harley and Henke, 2007). User studies that measure the number of "hits" or page-views to a site, or report out on anecdotal and random responses to online Web site surveys, are ubiquitous and frequently used as evidence that a particular Web resource has "value." These measurements surely indicate a form of popularity, but they tell us only about relatively enthusiastic users of a particular brand of content. They reveal nothing about whether a brand may be valued or useable by a wider potential audience operating in complex formal educational institutions that confer degrees or certificates. We suggest that, in any study interested in assessing user demand, one key group to include is individuals who do *not* currently use digital resources, especially if the aim is to increase demand. If we better understood, through well-designed research, the myriad reasons for nonuse in specific educational contexts, including social and economic barriers, perhaps resources could be designed in ways that would be useful to targeted audiences (and that would potentially counteract existing disincentives and barriers).

Finally, the development of user communities around open digital resources, along the Wikipedia model, is much discussed, with many suggesting that sustainability *and* high quality can be approached when communities contribute to and organize content, primarily through new social software tools and associated practices. In the current "Web 2.0" climate, it might be a little too easy to dismiss valid questions about whether a "wisdom of crowds" vision can be realized while still ensuring high quality (see, for example, Duguid, 2006, among others). The costs to creating and sustaining high quality curricular resources are high. When coupled with the potential for rampant propagation of misinformation and poor quality educational materials on the Internet, tensions can be created for some developers of OER. Controlling quality by strictly enforcing pedagogical and production standards may make it more difficult for the material to be reused outside the educational context originally envisioned, but unbridled reuse of branded material introduces real concerns about user communities propagating misinformation and poor-quality educational materials.

Factors that will determine whether or not social computing models can actually create economies in OER production will depend on, first, serious users participating actively in these communities and, second, toppling the strong traditional role and value of peer review in the academy. Distributed processes of quality control where vaguely defined users, not faculty, are the primary arbiters, would likely create significant regulatory tensions because such a process is fundamentally antithetical to traditional concepts of higher education's purpose, in which credentials depend upon some modicum of quality assurance verifying that what has been achieved has met certain minimum standards. The strong central role (and interests) of faculty, formal institutions, scholarly societies, professional associations, and sometimes governments, in setting those standards cannot be dismissed lightly (Harley, 2007). Until overwhelming evidence arises to the contrary, we can assume the creation of high quality educational materials will be achieved only at considerable cost in time and resources to some relatively central, and expert, vetting agent(s), be they universities, individual scholars, or other entities.

In closing, it is worth recalling sociologist Martin Trow's (1997) prediction a decade ago that to understand the diffusion and uptake of educational technology resources in higher education, it will be crucial to understand how "the distinctions between elite, mass, and universal access to higher education point to different forms of teaching and learning, to differences in their contexts and uses." (p. 294) The OER community should be encouraged and supported in developing systematic research programs that target a clearer understanding of the differential needs and values of the particular educators and students they desire to serve.

Notes

1. This chapter was adapted from Diane Harley, 2007, Why study users? An environmental scan of use and users of digital resources in humanities and social sciences undergraduate education, *First Monday*, 12(1) (January 2007), http://firstmonday.org/issues/issue12_1/harley/index.html. This work was made possible by generous funding from the William and Flora Hewlett Foundation and the Andrew W. Mellon Foundation. Additional support was provided by the

Hewlett-Packard Company, the Center for Information Technology Research in the Interest of Society (CITRIS), the California Digital Library (CDL), and the Vice Chancellor of Research, UC Berkeley. Significant contributions were made by Jonathan Henke, Shannon Lawrence, and others. I am grateful to the many participants in formal and informal interviews, discussion groups, and those who contributed their valuable time and opinions to our survey.

2. See, for example, Kvavik and Caruso, 2005; Oblinger and Oblinger 2005 for some background definitions of millennials (also referred to as the "net generation," among other monikers).

3. The entire final report, a detailed description of our methods, survey instruments, and associated data sets are available online; Harley and others, 2006. The survey targeted 4,500 faculty from specific disciplines at a stratified random sample of community colleges, University of California campuses, and liberal arts colleges in California; the survey was administered both online and on paper. Surveys were conducted in 2004 and 2005. We received 831 valid responses (a response rate of 19 percent) to the large faculty survey. A follow-up telephone survey of selected non-responders found no convincing evidence of response bias in the survey. We also conducted a second, parallel survey of instructors from a broader range of institutions, disciplines, and geographic areas, recruited through online discussion groups; we received 452 responses. The results from this second survey corresponded closely with the main faculty survey on most dimensions. Discussion groups were conducted in fall 2003 and winter 2004, and are summarized in a separate publication that can be found at http://cshe .berkeley.edu/research/digitalresourcestudy/documents/faculty_discussion _group_june05.pdf

4. Preliminary results from McMartin and others, 2006 suggest a number of similarities to the general patterns reported here.

References

Borgman, C. L. (2003, 4 June). Personal Digital Libraries: Creating Individual Spaces for Innovation. Paper presented at National Science Foundation Workshop on Post-Digital Libraries Initiative Directions. Retrieved October 20, 2006, from http://www.sis.pitt.edu/~dlwkshop/paper_borgman.pdf

Duguid, P. (2006). Limits of Self–Organization: Peer Production and "Laws of Quality." *First Monday*, 11(10). Retrieved from http://firstmonday.org/issues/ issue11_10/duguid/index.html.

Green, D. (2006). Using Digital Images in Teaching and Learning: Perspectives from Liberal Arts Institutions. Retrieved November 7, 2006, from the Wabash College, Center of Inquiry in the Liberal Arts Academic Commons Web site: http://www.academiccommons.org/imagereport

Harley, D., Henke, J., and Maher, M. W. (2004). Rethinking Space and Time: The Role of Internet Technology in a Large Lecture Course. *Innovate*, 1(1). Retrieved from http://cshe.berkeley.edu/publications/publications.php?id=34

Harley, D., Henke, J., Lawrence, S., Miller, I., Perciali, I., Nasatir, D., et al. (2006). *Final Report: Use and Users of Digital Resources: A Focus on Undergraduate Education in the Humanities and Social Sciences.* Retrieved June 4, 2007, from University of California, Berkeley, Center for Studies in Higher Education Web site: http://cshe.berkeley.edu/research/digitalresourcestudy/report/

Harley, D. (September 2006). The Regulation of E-Learning: New National and International Perspectives. CSHE 1.07. Center for Studies in Higher Education. University of California, Berkeley. Retrieved from http://cshe.berkeley.edu/publications/publications.php?id=246

Harley, D., and Henke, J. (2007). Toward an Effective Understanding of Website Users. *D-Lib Magazine*, 13(3/4) March/April 2007. Retrieved from http://www.dlib.org/dlib/march07/harley/03harley.html

Kvavik, R. B., and Caruso, J. B. (2005). ECAR Study of Students and Information Technology, 2005: Convenience, Connection, Control, and Learning. Retrieved October 20, 2006, from the EDUCAUSE Center for Applied Research Web site: http://www.educause.edu/ir/library/pdf/ers0506/rs/ers0506w.pdf

Massachusetts Institute of Technology (2006). *MIT OpenCourseWare 2005 Program Evaluation Findings Report.* Retrieved from http://ocw.mit.edu/NR/rdonlyres/FA49E066-B838-4985-B548-F85C40B538B8/0/05_Prog_Eval_Report_Final.pdf

Matkin, G. (2002). *Learning Object Repositories: Problems and Promise.* Retrieved October 20, 2006, from The William and Flora Hewlett Foundation Web site: http://www.hewlett.org/NR/rdonlyres/18867B66-5E37-4626-A2CB-EF6544F608C7/0/LearningObject.pdf

McMartin, F., Iverson, E., Manduca, C., Wolf, A., and Morgan, G. (2006). Factors Motivating Use of Digital Libraries. *Joint Conference on Digital Libraries* (pp. 254–255). New York: ACM Press.

Oblinger, D. J., and Oblinger, J. L., Eds. (2005). *Educating the Net Generation.* Accessed October 20, 2006, from the EDUCAUSE Web site: http://www.educause.edu/educatingthenetgen

Smith, A. (2003). *New-Model Scholarship: How Will It Survive?* Retrieved October 20, 2006, from the Council on Library and Information Resources Web site: http://www.clir.org/pubs/reports/pub114/contents.html

Trow, M. (1997). The Development of Information Technology in American Higher Education. *Daedalus*, 26(4), 293–314.

14

OpenCourseWare: Building a Culture of Sharing

Steven R. Lerman, Shigeru Miyagawa, and Anne H. Margulies

Open sharing of knowledge is at the heart of the academic process. For many faculty, it is an intrinsic value, convincingly demonstrated in their teaching and research. OpenCourseWare (OCW), developed at MIT, is a structured, institutional manifestation of this personal and professional value. OCW is a free and open Web publication of course materials created by faculty to support teaching and learning.

OCW is consistent with the culture of MIT. The notion of open sharing is a long-standing academic tradition within many disciplines, as evidenced by open sharing of preprints of research work, the open source software movement, and the evolution of the World Wide Web—a facilitator of easy dissemination of materials. OCW was built on this culture of open sharing, and it has been further reinforced as faculty see the results and benefits of their contributions to OCW. Indeed, over 4,000 individuals, including nearly all of MIT's faculty, have voluntarily contributed original materials for publication on OCW.

The OCW idea is catching on. Currently, about 150 colleges and universities are operating or planning OCW Websites. As we describe in this chapter, many factors propel this trend, with many benefits that accrue to the institution, the faculty, and students. We believe that this increasing adoption of the OCW concept will promote an even more widely accepted culture of open sharing, which will become more and more mainstream and will eventually become customary practice in education at all levels.

As this culture takes root, it holds the promise of transforming education in two fundamental ways. First, it provides access to knowledge and educational resources for people around the world, including people who because of economic, political, or social disadvantages have never before had such opportunity. Second, it enhances the quality of education to levels never before imagined as educators share materials and feedback with each other. We have significant data demonstrating these phenomena.

We have all heard claims of educational transformation based on new technologies or new pedagogies. In many cases, although these new tools or approaches have made a difference, they have done so only incrementally. And, of course, in order to realize fundamental transformation many new ideas must come together: technology innovation, open licensing, communities of collaborating educators and learners, and new processes. But a culture of open sharing gives energy and purpose to the forces of change—the catalyst for transformation. We have learned that a culture of open sharing is a necessary condition for a successful OCW implementation, and successful implementation in turn reinforces that open culture in an upward spiral of educational innovation, reaching audiences around the world.

About OpenCourseWare

As figure 14.1 indicates, MIT launched the OCW pilot in 2002. In November 2007 OCW completed the "ramp-up" phase, resulting in a Web site offering 1,800 courses—virtually all graduate and undergraduate courses at MIT. This milestone also represents OCW's transition to "steady state" operation, an ongoing program of publishing new and updated courses at a rate of about 200 per year.

For any given course, the published materials should fully convey the parameters of the course's subject matter and include a substantially complete set of all the materials used in the course. Typical content may include:

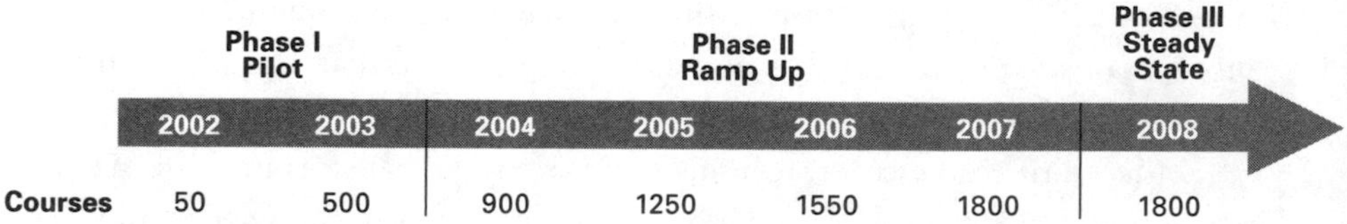

	Phase I Pilot		Phase II Ramp Up				Phase III Steady State
	2002	2003	2004	2005	2006	2007	2008
Courses	50	500	900	1250	1550	1800	1800

Figure 14.1
MIT OCW's history

• Planning materials: syllabus, calendar, pedagogical statement.
• Subject matter content: lecture notes, reading lists, full-text readings, video/audio lectures.
• Learning activities: problem sets, essay assignments, quizzes, exams, labs, projects.

OCW is decidedly not a distance education program or an online, mediated learning system. Rather, it is a publication. Target audiences are (a) educators, who may adopt or adapt the materials for their own teaching purposes; (b) students enrolled in educational programs, who may use the materials for reference, practice exercises, or mapping out their programs of study; and (c) self-learners, who may find the materials helpful for enhancing their personal knowledge.

A key feature of OCW is that the materials are IP-cleared, meaning that the institution has the rights, either through ownership or by license (permission), to make the materials available under open terms, and that nothing in the materials infringes the copyrights of others. MIT OCW is offered under a standard Creative Commons Attribution-NonCommercial-ShareAlike license, which:

• Grants users the right to use and distribute the materials either as-is, or in an adapted form.
• Allows users to create derivative works by editing, translating, adding to, or combining OCW materials with other materials from other sources.
• Obliges users to meet certain requirements as a condition of use:
  – Use is restricted to noncommercial purposes.[1]
  – Materials must be attributed to the institution and/or to the original author.
  – If original or derivative materials are subsequently republished or redistributed, they must be offered freely to others under compatible open terms ("share alike").

Who Uses MIT OpenCourseWare?
We are seeing about 2 million visits per month to MIT content (total for MIT OCW and translation affiliate sites). Since inception, over 25 million unique visitors have accessed MIT OCW, representing more than 1.5 billion hits on the Web site. In addition, there are over 100 mirror sites in Africa and Asia that deliver MIT content to users who have limited

Internet access. And users have downloaded complete course packages for off-line use over several million times.

From OCW's extensive, ongoing evaluation process, we have learned that about 16 percent of OCW visitors are educators, 32 percent students, and 49 percent self learners.[2] Some 96 percent of educators say OCW has helped them (or will) improve their teaching or their courses. Among all visitors, 98 percent say OCW has a positive impact. Thousands of users have expressed their appreciation for OCW and told us anecdotal stories about the impact it has had on their lives.

Foundations for Open Sharing at MIT

The idea of open sharing has deep roots in academia, but particularly at MIT, where sharing preprints, open source software, and the World Wide Web were quickly accepted ways of disseminating materials and bypassing cumbersome and expensive printing and distribution channels. This active engagement in increasing the flow of knowledge was a critical factor in the acceptance of OCW at both the institutional level and among large segments of the faculty.

For example, the widespread dissemination of preprints of to-be-published work as a means of making new research results known within particular research communities was well established by the time MIT faculty were asked to consider undertaking OCW. This practice of sharing new ideas before they became documented in the peer-reviewed literature was widespread in many of the scientific, engineering, and social science disciplines. Therefore, many of the faculty already were comfortable with sharing ideas prior to formal publication in journal articles and books. In many disciplines such as computer science, economics, and physics, it was well understood that no one could be up-to-date in the literature without being familiar with the preprint literature. The idea that one could widely circulate new research ideas and results freely and still retain credit for them had wide acceptance, which made the leap to sharing of educational materials far easier for most faculty.

Also laying the groundwork for acceptance of OCW was the open source software movement. Although this movement was already well underway before OCW was proposed, we believe that it had deeper roots at MIT than almost anywhere else. The GNU Project, announced by

Richard Stallman in 1983, fostered the creation of innovative software that is still distributed with its "copyleft" intellectual property conditions, was based at MIT. The Free Software Foundation, the GNU Project's primary sponsoring organization started in 1985, also has deep connections with the computer science community at MIT.

At a more institutional level, when MIT undertook Project Athena, a major research initiative sponsored by IBM and Digital Equipment Corporation from 1983 through 1991, it decided to release all the software that was developed in open source form (Champine, 1991). This software included major innovations such as the X Window System, the Kerberos authentication system, and Zephyr, a precursor to instant messaging systems now in widespread use.

Another antecedent to OpenCourseWare is the World Wide Web. Invented at CERN by Tim Berners-Lee in the 1980s, the Web had become the centerpiece of the "dot-com boom" of the late 1990s. By the time OCW was being considered, MIT was one of the headquarters for the World Wide Web Consortium. The universal acceptance of the Web as an inexpensive and ubiquitous means for low cost distribution of knowledge made it the natural medium for open sharing.

OCW: Institutional Manifestation of Open Sharing
OpenCourseWare was first proposed at a point in time when two forces were colliding: the technological developments that facilitated sharing information and the extraordinary economic growth of new ventures that were based on the Internet. At the same time that the MIT faculty were considering making their course materials freely available, many other leading universities were developing business plans to generate what they hoped would be major new revenue sources through various forms of Internet-based education and training. While hindsight tells us that many of these initiatives were ultimately economic failures, this outcome was by no means clear at the time MIT was considering OCW.

MIT's strong tradition of free and open sharing of various types of intellectual property exists in parallel with a tradition of licensing other types of intellectual property and the founding of companies to exploit these new inventions and ideas. MIT's Technology Licensing Office (TLO) is one of the most successful examples of universities commercializing inventions arising from faculty research. Given these two competing traditions and the seemingly unlimited promise of riches arising from Internet-based business ventures, what ultimately led MIT to choose the path of open sharing over the option of commercialization?

MIT's provost chartered the MIT Council on Educational Technology (MITCET) to make recommendations about how new computational and communications technologies could best be used by the university in support of its overall mission. This council undertook a series of studies to examine key choices facing MIT, including the future of Internet-based education.

A working group of the council, led by Dean Richard Yue, launched a study that looked at two fundamental questions. First, they explored what types and forms of distance education the faculty believed were consistent with the core values of the university. With the assistance of outside consultants from Booz Allen Hamilton, they interviewed faculty to find out whether they would be interested in spending time and energy on large scale distance education, and if so, under what terms.[3] Second, they built detailed economic models to analyze how much revenue these efforts might yield. The results of this work made it clear that the intersection between what faculty wanted (and were willing) to do and what might actually produce revenue to the university was almost negligible. There simply was no economically viable model for large scale, Internet-based distance learning that was consonant with the faculty's interests. Put another way, the council's analysis demonstrated that without fundamentally altering the institution's mission and core values, efforts at commercially successful Internet-based education from MIT were almost doomed to fail. The subsequent failure of commercial distance learning initiatives from other research universities suggests that MIT's economic analysis was correct.

Thus was planted the seed of the OCW concept. While the council saw no economic reason for offering educational materials on the Web, they also felt that given MIT's historical connection with the Internet and with the application of technology to educational innovation, why not consider exploiting the Internet for a higher goal: pursuit of MIT's mission "to advance knowledge and educate students in science, technology, and other areas of scholarship that will best serve the nation and the world in the 21st century"? (para.1, "MIT facts," n.d.).

OCW'S Launch: Reinforcing the Culture of Sharing

No one factor alone can explain MIT's commitment to OpenCourse-Ware. Rather, a confluence of external factors and institutional culture moved the institution to the decision. Once the decision was made, however, a series of carefully led processes ensured the successful launching of OpenCourseWare.

It was important that OCW originated from the grass roots, the faculty, rather than from the senior administration. The fact that a faculty-led council proposed OCW made it far more likely to be adopted. OCW would require a majority of faculty to be willing to donate their educational materials for noncommercial distribution. This virtual unanimous acceptance was likely only if the initiative resonated with faculty's core values.

Communication and Shared Decision-Making

MITCET undertook a careful process to understand how the rest of the faculty would respond to OCW. A team of council members met with every MIT academic department to discuss the idea before MIT would make a final commitment. This gave all faculty members time to hear about the idea and express their support or concerns.

By far the most common theme arising in these meetings was what might best be described as "conditional support." By and large, the MIT faculty expressed great enthusiasm for the idea of making their materials freely available. The guarantee that each faculty member was free to decide whether to contribute his or her course materials was important in getting such wide acceptance. Simultaneously, they also expressed their worry that participating in OCW would take too much of their already over-committed time. Their participation would largely depend on how much of the publication process could be offloaded to other staff; the plan for implementing OCW had to minimize faculty burden.

An Infrastructure for OCW

OpenCourseWare's designers needed to build an organization that could take on most of the work involved in creating course Web sites for publication. Another MITCET working group was created to develop options for organization structures that would balance staff costs against effectiveness in offloading course publication work from faculty. The chosen model was a hybrid between a centralized organization, where expertise about publication processes and management would reside, and a decentralized structure, where liaisons residing within the academic departments would be housed. The primary links between the OCW organization and individual faculty members are the departmental liaisons, whose jobs essentially are to handle preparation of materials for publication. This approach has kept the average time for a faculty member to get his or her course on OCW to five hours or less and has been an important element in the project's acceptance.

Some fraction of the MIT faculty worried that MIT was forgoing the possibility of major revenues by giving away its educational materials. The work done earlier by MITCET to model the economics of Internet-based distance education was crucial in addressing such concerns. The culture of data-based decision making is very strong at MIT, and the ability to provide reasonable evidence that we weren't "giving away the store" was essential.

Support from Senior Leadership

The scale of OCW required that the university itself be committed to the idea. This type of institutional commitment can only come through the leadership of the senior administration. MIT's then-president Charles Vest publicly supported the launch of OpenCourseWare in the most visible form possible. On April 4, 2001 the president held a press briefing at which he announced MIT's intention to make the educational materials from virtually all MIT courses freely and openly available. This announcement led to a front-page story in the *New York Times* and a flood of subsequent publicity. Notably, President Vest did not describe OCW as an experiment or even as an initiative. Rather, he described it as a permanent feature of the MIT academic program. He also made clear his confidence that OCW would not be competitive with MIT's enrollments for traditional education. In doing so, he clearly delineated the distinction between educational materials and the processes of teaching and learning.

A Firm Financial Foundation

The final factor important to OCW's adoption was financial support. Preliminary discussions with several foundations indicated that the OCW idea fit well with their visions of what they would be supporting in the coming years. This led to a more detailed dialog with the William and Flora Hewlett Foundation and Andrew W. Mellon Foundation, both leaders in educational innovation. The presidents of both these foundations were receptive to proposals for major support for OCW, and this satisfied MIT senior leadership that the required resources could be found. These two foundations initially committed $11 million for the pilot phase of OpenCourseWare and have since awarded an additional $15 million.

OCW: A Convergence of External and Internal Conditions
What if MIT had not traveled down this road? What if course materials continued to be locked up in internal course management systems? No doubt there would still be many heroic individual efforts at open sharing of course materials. Perhaps some other university might have hit on the OCW idea and started a similar trend. Maybe these efforts would eventually have led, through some other route, to the kind of increasingly broad-based culture of open sharing that we are now seeing. But perhaps not.

Impact at MIT: Realizing the Benefits of Sharing

OCW—and the open sharing that underlies it—has become well established as a part of the academic culture at MIT. With only a few exceptions, almost all faculty embrace the OCW concept. We attribute the widespread acceptance of OCW not only to its philosophical underpinnings, which resonate with the personal values held by many in our community, but also to the many tangible benefits that have accrued to MIT faculty, students, and the institution as a whole, all of which serve to reinforce the culture of open sharing.

Faculty Use of OCW
About 60 percent of MIT faculty use OCW materials in their teaching or advising at MIT. A third say publishing on OCW improves their materials. And OCW enables faculty to gain more detailed insight into what is taught in other courses. Some departmental curriculum committees have reported greater effectiveness in reviewing and

fine-tuning the offerings within their departments. Other faculty have used OCW to "flash students back" to earlier courses to help them better understand materials that should have prepared them for more advanced study.

Over 90 percent of users have told us that offering OCW as a free and open resource enhances MIT's reputation internationally both as a leader in improving education in less advantaged parts of the world and as a proponent of the open education movement. But beyond whatever prestige may accrue to the institution, some individual faculty also find that the added visibility OCW affords for their work not just as researchers but as teachers helps to enhance their professional reputations in their disciplines.

Alumni Use of OCW

The admiration that OCW elicits for MIT also generates considerable alumni and community pride. In a recent survey, we found that about 80 percent of MIT alumni are aware of OCW, and of these, 85 percent agree that it enhances MIT's reputation. An alumnus responded, "It's a wonderful gift to the world, and speaks to the nonproprietary and open nature of MIT: that the knowledge is there for the taking and is not hoarded. It's one among many things that has made me proud of the Institute over the years. . . . MIT is willing to stick its neck out and lead on many issues that are important to both science and society."

Alumni also access OCW in order to keep current in their fields, to review material from courses previously completed, and even to view materials from courses they did not take when they were here.

Student Use of OCW

Of greatest importance, of course, is how students use and benefit from OCW. Over 70 percent of current graduate and undergraduate students use OCW, and this percentage shows steady increase from year to year. As a student in electrical engineering/computer science explained, "OCW has given me countless materials that have inspired me for projects, helped me complete related projects, and helped me understand course material. My 6.111 report was posted on the OCW site. Since then, a student in Chile contacted me about it and we've been able to communicate across countries."

Students use OCW for their assigned course work, as a supplemental resource for study, or as a tool for planning programs and choosing courses. OCW has a positive impact on the student experience, say 96 percent of these students. About 35 percent of fall 2005 entering freshmen who were aware of MIT OCW say it significantly influenced their decision to attend MIT.

Looking Ahead

The original faculty discussions on OCW naturally centered on what MIT should do to contribute to the world of online education. A key part of the discussion was anticipation—speculation, really—about what impact OCW would have on education, both formal and informal, around the world. Many in the committee felt that MIT OCW, once brought to life, could represent a vital step toward fundamentally changing the culture of education—from the "dot-com" mentality of the late 1990s to a culture of sharing educational materials freely and openly.

Toward a Global Culture of Sharing

Article 26 of the United Nations Universal Declaration of Human Rights begins, "Everyone has the right to education."[4] Some on the committee felt that an important marker of true success would be the spreading of the OCW vision beyond MIT to the global community of higher learning. Would institutions around the world launch their own OCWs? The wide adoption of OCW outside MIT would suggest that the culture of open and free sharing had taken root. And once realized, we envisioned a world in which the combined strength of many institutions' OCWs would represent a virtual global knowledge base of high-quality educational materials, in many disciplines, in many languages, with many pedagogical approaches, interactively accessed. With this in mind, one of the stated goals of MIT OCW was—and continues to be—inspiring other institutions to offer their own OCWs.

Toward this vision, work to create a global OCW Consortium began in earnest in the spring of 2004, three years after MIT's OCW announcement and two years into the actual building of OCW at MIT. By this time, 500 courses had been published on OCW, and many of the issues in design, administration, intellectual property, and infrastructure had been identified and mostly resolved. The reputation of OCW had begun to spread around the world thanks to wide press coverage. No funding had been acquired specifically for the purpose of building the OCW Consortium, which made it impossible to undertake a major effort on a global scale. Instead, MIT convened small, informal meetings of representatives from schools that showed interest in OCW. These meetings included not only domestic schools but also those from our international translation partners, China Open Resource for Education and Universia (Spanish and Portuguese). These two consortia represent a large number of schools in China and in Portugal, Spain, and Latin America.

From those humble beginnings, the OCW Consortium grew rapidly. Today, in 2007, there are about 150 members worldwide, freely and openly offering the materials for nearly 5,000 distinct courses. This indicates to us that the concept translates well beyond MIT and across national borders. The culture of open and free sharing is indeed taking root.

Why do institutions embrace OCW? Though many anticipate the same kinds of benefits realized at MIT—accelerating the adoption of educational technology, improving the quality of teaching materials, gaining visibility, enhancing recruitment, and the like—we have seen first hand that the foremost motivating factor is a spirit of intellectual philanthropy that aligns closely with the mission of the institution. This spirit takes many forms, and it often finds its expression in the unique identity of a particular institution.

Of course, an institution needs more than just a spirit of open philanthropy to make progress on an OCW implementation. For example, we have observed that every OCW school has someone (or a small group) that has served as an inspirational advocate from the beginning. This champion might be a faculty member, department head, or school leader. But in every case, the advocate has had to generate buy-in and enthusiasm at multiple levels within the institution.

Once there is the will and commitment to move ahead with OCW, the implementation process itself can be fairly straightforward, depending on conditions at the school. For example, many schools already have much of their teaching materials in digital formats that can be published with relatively simple manipulations. Tools such as eduCommons[5] are already available to help transform materials from internal course management systems into publishable OCW courses. In 2004, MIT OCW published a comprehensive "how-to" manual covering topics such as making the case for OCW, organization and staffing, publishing process, intellectual property and licensing, user support, communications, technology, evaluation and measurement, and costs. The OCW Consortium plans to update this material and adapt it to reflect emerging best practices from all the consortium members.

The Next Horizon: Two-way Sharing through Communities of Practice

Many educators and learners who use OCW send feedback on published course materials, making suggestions or pointing out errors, and this feedback is passed on to the faculty who contributed the materials. But in the OCW community, we do not yet have formal mechanisms to facilitate collaboration or to manage "feedback loops" to promote continuous improvement of teaching materials, though we are aware of some experiments in this area and in formal collaboration in the development of educational materials. One example is the UK's Open University OpenLearn initiative, which postulates a set of tools, a virtual collaboration environment, and a "labspace" of learning objects that educators and course developers can use to create course materials (The Open University, n.d.).

Down the road, we envision a more organized effort to facilitate two-way interaction among suppliers and consumers of OCW materials, eventually leading to an "ecology of knowledge" in the educational context (Brown, 1999, Spring). This will be one more manifestation of the culture of open sharing, and, we believe, an important means of enhancing the quality of educational materials and ultimately raising the level of education around the world.

The future of OpenCourseWare seems rosy, but it is not without threats. Some in the OCW community are concerned about maintaining quality as more and more materials become available. Another worry is the possibility of disruptive forces—persons or organizations with different interests or motives (perhaps commercial publishers, those with political agendas, or who knows what) challenging or slowing the momentum of the OCW movement. And of course, there is the ever-present challenge of sustaining institutional will and financial support for the program. These are all subjects of active discussion among consortium members, and we remain optimistic that the power of the OCW concept will prevail.

We believe this because four years of evaluation research clearly demonstrate that the OCW concept and its implementation at MIT and other universities are having a profound impact. The many benefits may encourage institutions and their faculties to build OCWs and publish their materials. It affords access to high-quality teaching materials for millions of people, and it enhances the quality of education in many corners of the globe.

Notes

1. Not all OCW institutions impose a noncommercial use restriction. For MIT's interpretation of this restriction, see http://ocw.mit.edu/OcwWeb/Global/terms-of-use.htm#noncomm

2. Data in this chapter are from surveys of statistically significant numbers of OCW users and from ongoing tracking and web analytics. For the most recent evaluation report, which includes a detailed description of survey and tracking methodologies (and their limitations), see http://ocw.mit.edu/OcwWeb/Global/AboutOCW/evaluation.htm. Site traffic and usage data are current as of August 2007.

3. Booz Allen Hamilton did this work for MIT pro bono, in part because of strong ties several principals had with MIT, and also because management saw the entire area of Internet-based education as a promising field for future consulting work.

4. For the complete UN Universal Declaration of Rights, see http://www.un.org/Overview/rights.html

5. An open source tool, eduCommons is built around a workflow process that guides users through the process of publishing materials in an openly accessible format. This includes uploading materials into a repository, dealing with copyright, reassembling materials into courses, providing quality assurance, and publication of materials. It was developed by the Center for Open and Sustainable Learning (COSL), part of the Department of Instructional Technology at Utah State University.

References

Brown, J. S. (1999, Spring). Sustaining the ecology of knowledge. *Leader to Leader*, 12, 31–36. Retrieved May 23, 2007, from http://www.johnseelybrown .com/Sustaining_the_Ecology_of_Knowledge.pdf.

Champine, G. (1991). MIT Project Athena: A model for distributed campus computing. Bedford, MA: Digital Press.

MIT facts 2007: Facts and origins. (n.d.). Retrieved July 26, 2007, from http:// web.mit.edu/facts/mission.html

The Open University. (n.d.). Open Learn. Retrieved May 23, 2007, from http:// www.open.ac.uk/openlearn/home.php

15

Challenges and Opportunities for the Open Education Movement: A Connexions Case Study

Richard G. Baraniuk

A grassroots movement is on the verge of sweeping through the academic world. The open education (OE) movement is based on a set of intuitions shared by a remarkably wide range of academics: that knowledge should be free and open to use and reuse; that collaboration should be easier, not harder; that people should receive credit and kudos for contributing to education and research; and that concepts and ideas are linked in unusual and surprising ways and not in the simple linear forms that today's textbooks present. OE promises to fundamentally change the way that authors, instructors, and students interact worldwide. The OE movement takes the inspiration of the open source software movement (GNU Linux, for example, [Raymond, 2001]), mixes in the powerful communication abilities of the Internet and the World Wide Web, and applies the result to teaching and learning materials like course notes, curricula, and textbooks. Open educational resources (OERs) include text, images, audio, video, interactive simulations, problems and answers, and games that are free to use and also reuse in new ways by anyone around the world.

This chapter discusses some of the key opportunities and challenges of the OE movement using Connexions (See www.cnx.org) as a case study. It also points toward an as-yet-unrealized vision for OE that not only enables new ways to develop and share educational materials but also new ways to improve student learning by riding the wave of Web development from Web 1.0 to Web 2.0 and 3.0.

Open Education Opportunities

Participants in the OE movement are working toward a broad set of timely goals aimed at improving teaching and learning, including:

• bringing *people* back into the educational equation, particularly those who have been "shut out" of the traditional publishing world, like talented K-12 teachers, community college instructors, scientists and engineers out in industry, and the world majority who do not read and write English.

• reducing the *high cost of teaching materials*. The average community college student in America spends almost as much on textbooks as on tuition. Many schools in the United States get by with less than one textbook per child in many classes; the problem is far worse in the developing world.

• reducing the *time lag* between producing learning materials and getting them into students' hands. Many books are already out of date by the time they are printed. This is particularly problematic in fast-moving areas of science, technology, and medicine.

• enabling reuse, recontextualization, and customization such as *translation* and *localization* of course materials into myriad different languages and cultures. This is critical if we are to reach the entire world's population, where clearly "one size does not fit all" for education.

Several OE projects are already attracting millions of users per month (as of July 2007). Some, like the MIT OpenCourseWare project (See www.mit.edu/ocw) and its OCW consortium (See www.ocwconsortium. org), are top-down-organized institutional repositories that showcase their institutions' curricula. Others, like Connexions, are grassroots-organized and encourage contributions from all comers.

Open Education Challenges

While the OE movement is gaining speed rapidly, its current trajectory is taking it toward several roadblocks that will have to be carefully navigated for it to prosper.

The Challenge of Reuse
Unfortunately, widely used OER formats like PDF yield materials that are open in theory but closed in practice to editing and reuse, rendering

them often merely "reference" materials that are to be seen and not used. This stifles both innovation on the materials and also community participation.

Fragmentation

To date, many large OE projects have been institution-based repositories. However, intellectual ties are often much stronger between colleagues in the same discipline but at different institutions. Institutional repositories fragment a domain's knowledge base into distinct repositories and hinder interinstitutional collaborations.

Infrastructure Cost

Those who have put in the effort to develop new OERs or innovate on existing ones often have little opportunity to make the results accessible to a broader public. In the developing world, for example, it is a real challenge for many governments and institutions, let alone individual authors and instructors, to deploy and maintain indefinitely the hardware, software, and connectivity for their own OER repositories.

Intellectual Property

There is a debate in the OE world regarding whether open materials should or should not be commercially usable. Licensing that renders open materials only noncommercially usable promises to protect contributors from potentially unfair commercial exploitation. However, a noncommercial license not only limits the spread of knowledge by complicating the production of paper books, e-books, and CD-/DVD-ROMs, but also cuts off potential revenues that might sustain nonprofit OE enterprises into the future. Interestingly, an anticommercial stance is contrary to that of the more established open source software world (Linux, Apache, Firefox, and so on), which greatly benefits from commercial involvement. Where would Linux and Apache be without the value-adding contributions of for-profit companies like Red Hat and IBM, for instance?

Quality Control

Because of the sheer volume of the OE universe, OERs exist in various stages of development and, hence, at various quality levels. How do we ensure that high quality materials are easily accessible to users? This requires both a means to evaluate and credential OERs and a means to direct users to those deemed of high quality. Traditional publishers, as well as institution-based OE projects like MIT OpenCourseWare, employ a careful review process before their content is made publicly available. Such a prepublication review is necessary in situations where the publication medium is scarce—the paper making up books, for example. However, prereview does not scale to keep up with the fast pace of community-based OER development, where materials may change daily or even hourly. Moreover, the traditional binary decision to accept/reject a work is inappropriate when an OER can improve in an evolutionary fashion. Accept/reject decisions also create an exclusive rather than inclusive community culture. And finally, prereview does not support evaluation of modules and courses based on actual student learning outcomes.

Sustainability

A common and critical challenge facing all OE projects is planning for and ensuring their sustainability (long-term viability and stability). The complication is that the traditional revenue models employed as a matter of course in other educational settings (earning revenue from knowledge creation and dissemination such as enrollment fees, tuition, book sales, subscriptions, and so on) do not directly apply to OE projects, since their materials, and oftentimes their software platforms, are freely available on the Web.

Connexions as an Open Education Case Study

Connexions provides a useful case study in navigating the potential OE roadblocks.

Background

Connexions was launched at Rice University in 1999 to challenge current modes of teaching and learning, as well as how knowledge is developed and shared (Baraniuk and Cervenka, 2002). Befitting its name, Connexions has two primary goals: 1) to convey the *interconnected nature of knowledge* across disciplines, courses, and curricula; and 2) to move away from a solitary authoring, publishing, and learning process to one based on *connecting people into global learning communities that share knowledge*. By design and as a point of differentiation when compared with many other OE projects, Connexions is an interinstitutional and even noninstitutional endeavor.

Rather than the traditional content development model of one author to one textbook or course, Connexions invites and links worldwide communities of authors to collaboratively create, expand, revise, and maintain its OERs. In colloquial terms, borrowing from an Apple Computer slogan and a book by Lawrence Lessig (2001, p. 213), Connexions welcomes authors, teachers, and learners everywhere to "Create, Rip, Mix, and Burn" OERs. In particular, in Connexions, users are free to:

• **Create**: to author new educational materials and contribute them to a globally accessible OER repository (See the Connexions Content Commons at www.cnx.org/content);
• **Rip**: to customize, personalize, and localize the materials;
• **Mix**: to mix the materials together into new collections and courses; and
• **Burn**: to create finished products like Web courses, CD-/DVD-ROMs, and even printed books.

Reuse

Connexions employs a two-pronged approach to encourage OER reuse. First, rather than organizing materials at the "course" or "textbook" level, Connexions takes a modular, Lego™ approach similar to the concept of a learning object (Wikipedia, 2007b). Smallish, Lego-block *modules* communicate a concept, a procedure, a set of questions, and so on. Connecting several modules together into a *collection* creates a Web course, a textbook, or a curriculum that can be easily updated by adding, subtracting, or modifying modules. Breaking course materials into discrete modules drastically reduces the time commitment required of authors and instructors, who can now write a high quality module or weave a customized course in an evening or weekend. A vastly expanded and diverse community of authors has resulted. Furthermore, once contributed to the commons, a module can be reused in a myriad of different settings and rapidly adapted to new settings. For example, translation projects are currently active into Spanish, Portuguese, Japanese, Chinese, Vietnamese, and Thai; many of these OERs are Connexions' most popular.

Second, all Connexions materials are encoded in a common, open, and semantic XML format (XML, 2007). Since XML encodes what the content *means* rather than how it should be *presented* (displayed), modules are multipurpose and flexible. They can be displayed as an individual Web page, woven seamlessly into many different courses, converted to a PDF for printing, or even processed through a speech synthesizer to accurately read material to people who are visually impaired or unable to read. Mathematics encoded in content MathML can be copied and pasted into tools like Mathematica to experiment with formulas; similar XML markup languages exist for chemistry formulae, musical notation, and many other domains. The ultimate presentation of a module depends on a style sheet that can be customized by the end-user.

The Connexions commons is less a digital library or collection of courses than a dynamic *knowledge ecosystem* that is in a constant state of creation, (re)use, and improvement (Atkins, Brown, and Hammond, 2007). Since Connexions began long before the current XML boom, the cost for all of this flexibility has been the (fairly considerable) cost of developing a suite of open-source XML authoring, editing, and collec-tion-building tools. Examples include a Microsoft Word/Open Office to XML converter; a Web-based XML editing tool (Edit-in-Place); a Web-based CollectionComposer to weave modules into collections, courses, and textbooks; a print-on-demand pipeline that creates print-ready PDF files; and a version tracking system for all resources. Still in design and development are advanced and easier-to-use authoring and collection tools, advanced book formatting and printing, disciplinary community pages, import/export APIs for a variety of formats, translation and acces-sibility support, integration with learning and course-management systems, and a distributed repository infrastructure.

Fragmentation and Infrastructure Cost

The Connexions Content Commons houses works produced by authors from around the world in a single globally accessible repository. This obviates authors from developing, maintaining, and publicizing their own OER Web sites; all they need is a simple Internet connec-tion to upload their materials to make them globally available and reusable.

While a central repository of XML modules and collections goes a long way toward preventing content fragmentation, it also introduces several potential issues of its own. The first is the perception of Connexions as a kind of "Rice University OCW," when in fact most of its content has been contributed by authors from outside Rice University (fortunately, moving from the URL www.cnx.rice.edu to www.cnx.org has done a lot to change this perception). The second is the infrastructure that must be developed and maintained to deal with the large traffic loads (already several hundred thousand users per month and growing rapidly). The third is the pressure to ensure the sustainability of the infrastructure indefinitely to preserve the valuable OERs. A solution to these three issues is the planned development of a distributed repository infrastructure that will enable many different institutions to distribute the ownership, maintenance, and load of the Connexions Content Commons.

Intellectual Property

Connexions employs the Creative Commons "attribution" license ("CC-by"; See www.creativecommons.org) on all content to ensure attribution and academic credit for authors. The commercial usability of the Connexions OERs invites for-profit and nonprofit companies like publishers to become involved in the OE movement by adding value to the materials by enhancing them in some way (much as Red Hat and IBM enhance GNU Linux for their customers). For example, on-demand printer QOOP (See www.qoop.com) is producing print textbook versions of Connexions collections at very low cost (for example, a 300–page hardbound engineering textbook for only $25 rather than the more usual $125). Commercial competition resulting from the nonexclusivity of the Creative Commons license will work to keep print-book prices as low as possible so that everyone has inexpensive access and no one is exploited.

Connexions is collaborating with for-profit National Instruments (See www.ni.com) to build a free "LabVIEW player" specifically for use in Connexions that will enrich and enliven mathematics, science, and engineering content and promote active learning, exploration, and experimentation by users. This will allow an educator to provide an interactive visual simulation of a theoretical topic and enable a student to run and interact with the simulation virtually anytime and anywhere. National Instruments (NI) is adopting a model similar to that used by Adobe for its Acrobat PDF viewer, where any end-user (a student or instructor, for example) is able to make free use of the technology without purchasing the software necessary to run the simulations. The user merely downloads and installs a simple plug-in to activate the free technology on his or her computer.

The main challenge to Connexions' OER licensing strategy is, in fact, a challenge to the entire OE community: There are a multitude of different Creative Commons licenses (at least 12 at last count), which can confuse contributors and users. Unfortunately, when presented with such an extensive choice, contributors often default to the most restrictive, and hence least open, license. License incompatibility precludes some potentially innovative uses of OERs. The fact that mixes of materials from a project like Connexions with materials from a project like MIT OCW (which carry a "noncommercial" license) cannot be placed back into Connexions, contributes significantly to the fragmentation of the OE movement and unfortunately thwarts the primary aims of the OE movement (like enabling reuse and reducing time lags).

Quality Control via Lenses

Connexions recognized early on that a prepublication review process would not scale to the eventual large size and activity level of the Content Commons. So, rather than make a single prereview accept/reject decision regarding each module or collection, Connexions opens up the editorial process to third-party reviewers and editorial bodies for *postpublication review* (Baraniuk and Cervenka, 2002; Baraniuk, Burrus, Johnson, and Jones, 2004). While Connexions users have access to all modules and courses in the repository (whatever their quality), users also have the ability to preferentially locate and view modules and collections that have been endorsed by third parties using a range of different *lenses* (see figure 15.1).

Each lens has a different focus. Examples include lenses controlled by traditional editorial boards, professional societies, or informal groups of colleagues as well as automated lenses based on popularity, the amount of (re)use, the number of incoming links, or other metrics (See www.cnx.org/lenses). The National Council of Professors of Educational Administration (NCPEA) has launched a Connexions lens based on a rigorous peer review process involving both faculty

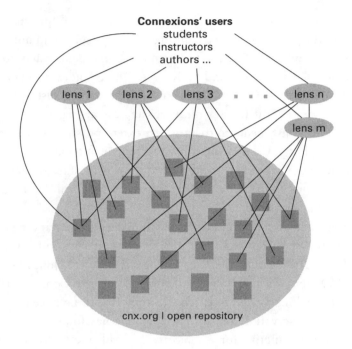

Figure 15.1
Connexions lenses for peer review and quality control

from educational leadership programs and practicing principals and superintendents. National Instruments has deployed a lens for engineering content using LabVIEW. Index-based and "referatory" educational resources such as MERLOT (See www.merlot.org) could also naturally serve as Connexions lenses.

While lenses were hypothesized from the inception of Connexions, the emergence of Web 2.0 "social software" has greatly simplified their implementation. Indeed, the prototype lens incarnation was based on the social tagging tool del.icio.us.

Sustainability

The crucial long-term sustainability question for OE projects appears to be "How do we acquire an adequate and ongoing stream of financial resources to keep our project running?". This leads immediately to considering various tactical programs to generate revenue; unfortunately, such programs often fail. The Connexions view is that a tactical approach is myopic because it focuses too much attention on the "product"—the features of the project and the technology underlying it—and not enough attention on understanding the users and working deliberately to grow their value (Dholakia, Roll, and McKeever, 2005; Bagozzi and Dholakia, 2006; Dholakia, 2006). The Connexions approach to sustainability is more "user-centric"; it focuses on increasing the aggregate value of the project for its constituents to the greatest extent possible. In its start-up and growth phases, Connexions aims first to gain and maintain a critical mass of active, engaged users and second to provide substantial and differentiated value to them; otherwise revenue models will be unlikely to succeed in the long run.

The important first step has been to gain a deep understanding of who Connexions' users are (and should be) and what constitutes value for them. Utpal Dholakia of the Rice University Jesse H. Jones Graduate School of Management has been studying the diverse Connexions users through formal marketing research, by attending to user feedback, and via informal observation and interactions. He has found, for example, that the primary motive for a majority of academic textbook authors who contribute their original content to Connexions is not to earn royalties; rather, it is to have the greatest possible impact on scholars, practitioners, and students within their disciplines through the widespread dissemination and use of their educational and scholarly materials. As a result, while authors may agree to forgo revenues from their contributions, it is important that they receive full credit for them; not surprisingly, this is often a prerequisite for them to participate. This points to the criticality of the "attribution" clause in the Creative Commons license and the noncriticality of the "noncommercial" clause.

The second step is to grow the value of Connexions for its users. Dholakia's research has generated four recommendations for how to provide significant value to Connexions' users:

1. Increase Connexions' *brand* equity by staying true to its values. This involves increasing awareness among Connexions' potential user base and creating a differentiated, consistent, and meaningful brand image where users associate the site with key elements or attributes that are important to them. The brand image must be aligned with the core values, principles, and purposes underlying the project, which include

freely sharing knowledge, building communities, collaboration, and so on.

2. Provide ample, high quality, useful *content*. Most users, particularly students, first find Connexions through a search engine like Google while looking for specific information on a particular topic. Research on virtual communities suggests that the initial motivations of most participants for joining a community are specific and purposive; that is, they join to solve a particular problem or to obtain a particular missing piece of information (Dholakia, Bagozzi, and Klein Pearo, 2004). It is therefore important for Connexions to provide high quality content across a wide spectrum of disciplines to attract new users and to encourage loyal users.

3. Foster an engaged and involved user *community*. One of the main objectives of Connexions is to foster collaboration among users. This follows from a vast literature in education research showing that collaboration and social interaction enhance students' learning experience as well as the quality and degree of learning (see, for example, Bowen, 1996, and Tinto, 1998). Research on virtual communities shows that with repeated participation, users form relationships with others, and this increases their engagement with the site (Dholakia, et al., 2004).

4. Improve the site *usability*. A key determinant of site adoption by authors and instructors is ease of use (Spool, Scanlon, Schroeder, Snyder, and DeAngelo, 1998; Wei, Maust, Barrick, Cuddihy, and Spyridaki, 2005). Authors and instructors will only be interested in Connexions if they can upload their content and modify it effortlessly in the format and layout of their choice (Dholakia, Roll, and McKeever, 2005; Bagozzi and Dholakia, 2006; Dholakia, 2006).

These four key recommendations are directly reflected in the Connexions tool, content, and community development plans.

Connexions is currently experimenting with a number of different sustainability models (Dholakia, 2006); space limitations prevent us from discussing all but two here. The first involves charging specific user segments for value-added services around Connexions' free and open Web content. In marketing terms, this is called versioning (Shapiro and Varian, 1998). Examples of specific services that could be offered include sales of paper copies of content organized around a particular topic, training and user support to institutional users for annual fees, housing and dissemination of copyrighted content within the Connexions site on a subscription basis, "ask-an-expert" services for a fee, and consulting services to provide custom education to corporate clients. To continue the example from above, the $25 final student price for the 300–page print-on-demand engineering textbook not only includes costs and profit for QOOP, but also a small (10%) "mission support fee" for Connexions and a small (10%) contribution to a fund that enables low-income students to obtain the printed book for free. This model naturally segments users at the individual level; they pay for a customized and value-added version of the content available freely within Connexions, yet end up paying a fraction of what they would pay if they purchased an equivalent traditional textbook.

The second sustainability model revolves around academic publishing. Connexions is the engine driving the Rice University Press (RUP), which reopened in early 2007 as an all-digital press after a decade-long hiatus (See www.ricepress.rice.edu). RUP operates just as a traditional academic press, up to a point. Book manuscripts are solicited, reviewed, edited, and submitted for final approval to an editorial board of prominent scholars. But rather than waiting for months for a printer to make an expensive paper book bound for a cavernous warehouse, RUP's digital files are instead modularized and input to Connexions for automatic formatting, indexing, and population with high-resolution multimedia and Web links. Users can view the monographs and books online for free (making RUP an "open access" publisher), or purchase a low-cost paper copy via print-on-demand. Unlike other presses, RUP's catalog will never go out of print and moreover will be continuously updated. The first RUP offering was the Mellon Foundation-supported report *Art History and Its Publications in the Electronic Age* (Ballon and Westermann, 2006). Fitly, the conclusion of the report is that academic disciplines such as art history are in jeopardy as more and more university presses shut their doors due to high operational costs. Connexions is currently building a consortium of presses that will adopt RUP's low-cost publishing model; in return, Connexions will charge a nominal sustaining consortium fee.

Fortunately, while building the infrastructure and tools to support the Content Commons has required a significant investment in the short- and medium-term, Connexions' long-term budget needs will be more modest as the effort transitions from building to maintaining software and communities.

A View toward the Future

If the OE movement is gaining momentum, can we predict in which direction(s) it is headed? A simple but reasonable prediction can be based on the evolution of the World Wide Web, whose free distribution and global communication forms the substrate of OE. In this case, the prediction problem can be rephrased as follows: As the Web evolves new capabilities, how will they impact the models of development, (re)use, and sustainability for the OE movement in general and Connexions in particular? Following the developments of O'Reilly (2005) and Markoff (2006), over the last two decades, two distinct sets of capabilities have emerged and dominated the Web (Web 1.0 and 2.0). A third (Web 3.0) is currently emerging and also holds great promise for OE.

Web 1.0—Broadcast, the first incarnation of the Web, emphasized building and deploying the basic infrastructure for broadcasting simple HTML Web pages from mainstream Web sites under the slogan "Content is King." The results have included millions of personal Web sites, publishing projects like Encyclopedia Britannica Online, music distribution projects like mp3.com, and so on. Correspondingly, **OE 1.0** projects have emphasized the open resources—the OERs—that broadcast freely to the world over the Web. The prototypical examples are MIT's OpenCourse-Ware, the members of its OCW Consortium, and EduCommons from Utah State University; these are top-down-organized institutional repositories that expose static HTML and PDF versions of course Web pages, syllabi, and other curricular materials prepared by their faculty. Outside-of-institution contributions are not accepted, and quality control is carefully performed prior to publication by a dedicated staff.

Web 2.0—Remix, which emerged around 2001, emphasizes participation and interaction under the slogan "Community is King" (O'Reilly, 2005). Using tools such as XML, wikis, tagging, and social networking, the results have included exponentially growing community Web sites like MySpace, the user-generated encyclopedia Wikipedia, hundreds of millions of user-generated YouTube videos, tens of millions of blogs, distributed file-sharing projects like Napster and BitTorent, and so on. These sites cater not to the mainstream content at the "head" of the demand curve, but rather to the niche content in the "long tail"

(Anderson, 2006). Correspondingly, **OE 2.0** projects have emphasized community building and participation on par with the open resources, and admit user-generated content that is continually remixed into new OERs. Examples include Connexions, the British Open University's OpenLearn LabSpace, ISKME's OER Commons, and Wikibooks and Wikiversity.

Web 3.0—Semantic Web, which is currently emerging, will add intelligence via natural language processing, data-mining, machine learning, and other artificial intelligence technologies (Berners-Lee, Hendler, and Lassila, 2001; Markoff, 2006; Jensen, 2007). The Web 3.0 will be attentive to and even predict user needs and behavior to provide richer and more meaningful and useful interactions. As such, it holds much promise for OE. **OE 3.0** projects will not just develop and deliver open content to students; they will also monitor student interactions with it, analyze those interactions, and then send *rich feedback* not only to the students about their learning, but also to the communities of curriculum builders, authors, and instructors to drive iterative improvement of the learning materials. To summarize in the language of control theory, while OE 1.0 dissemination projects run in a substantially "open loop" mode, by design OE 3.0 projects will "close the loop" and make educational material design, delivery, and redesign more interactive. An early example of OE 3.0 that currently focuses more on student feedback than continuous iterative content improvement is Carnegie Mellon University's Open Learning Initiative.

Connexions and Web 2.0/3.0

So what can Connexions in particular and OE projects in general do to more completely leverage the emerging capabilities of Web 2.0 and 3.0 in order to maximize student learning? Numerous opportunities exist (see figure 15.2):

• Connexions should enrich its current feedback loops from students and instructors back to its author communities in order to accelerate the continuous content improvement process. Since ultimately this will involve deploying learning assessments (problems and quizzes), an assessment system should either be constructed, integrated, or linked into the current Connexions architecture.

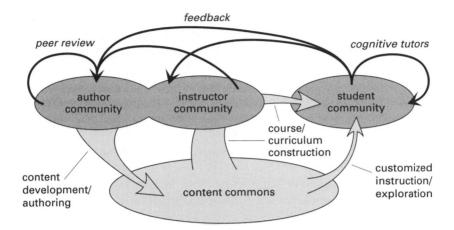

Figure 15.2
Connexions' architecture for OE 2.0 and 3.0 featuring enhanced feedback and Web 3.0 tools (from Baraniuk, Koedinger, Scheines, Smith, and Barnwell, 2003)

• Since many teachable moments arise when no instructor is present, Connexions should encourage student users to tutor each other. Interestingly, the recent finding that on average eldest children in families tend to have slightly higher IQs than their younger siblings (Kristensen and Bjekedal, 2007) has been hypothesized to be due to the fact that they spend more time tutoring and thus consolidating and integrating their knowledge base (Zajonc and Markus, 1975). To encourage student self-tutoring, Connexions should develop a dedicated tutoring community area.

• In addition to student-to-student tutoring, Connexions should provide spaces for students to collaborate on interactive, multimedia problems and projects—what John Seely Brown calls "thinkering," for thinking + tinkering (Atkins, Brown, and Hammond, 2007).

• As an adjunct to instructor-to-student and student-to-student interactions, Connexions should experiment with artificial intelligence tools such as cognitive tutors. These software systems provide direct, immediate, and individualized feedback and instruction to students as they work on problems based on a cognitive model of their understanding and potential misconceptions of the material (Wikipedia, 2007a; see also www.carnegielearning.com). While currently the design and implementation of realistic cognitive models is not scalable—they take Ph.D.-level cognitive scientists, working with domain experts, years to create—OE

2.0 projects like Connexions can harness the efforts of a large, global community of contributors to incrementally and iteratively generate the feedback, instruction, and cognitive frameworks required by these systems.

• As the Connexions repository grows in breadth across disciplines and depth within disciplines, Web 2.0 and 3.0 technologies can automate the process of discovering interconnections between ideas from even far-flung disciplines. This will provide educators and students with valuable context information to go along with the OER content and could even result in surprising new discoveries.

• As the Connexions repository grows in size and as content updates accelerate, the communities controlling quality control lenses will need help from emerging Web 3.0 technologies for automated content filtering based on both computed metrics and user preferences. This framework for quality control has recently been dubbed "Authority 3.0" (Jensen, 2007).

Conclusions

The OE movement has real potential to enable a revolutionary advance in the world's standard of education. Moreover, as it grows and spreads, the OE movement is likely to leave a large impact on the academic world itself. It promises to disintermediate the scholarly publishing industry, in the process rendering some current business models unviable and inventing new viable ones. It will also change the way that we conceive of and pursue authorship, teaching, peer review, and promotion and tenure. And by encouraging contributions from anyone, anywhere, Connexions in particular has the potential to aid in the democratization of the world of knowledge. While many challenges lie ahead on the road to these goals, with a concerted effort from the community of authors, instructors, students, and software developers, we can change the way the world develops, disseminates, and uses knowledge.

Acknowledgments

This chapter was greatly enriched by discussions with dozens of Connexions contributors and users worldwide, in addition to Sidney Burrus, Don Johnson, Douglas Jones, Christopher Kelty, Katie Cervenka, Paul Dholakia, Joey King, Joel Thierstein, Bob Maxfield, John Seely Brown,

Catherine Casserly, Marshall Smith, Toru Iiyoshi, Melissa Hagemann, Jimmy Wales, Tom Barnwell, Joel Smith, and Ken Koedinger. Connexions is supported by The William and Flora Hewlett Foundation, National Science Foundation grant PFI-0538934, and Rice University.

References

Anderson, C. (2006). *The Long Tail*. New York: Hyperion.

Atkins, D. E., Brown, J. S., and Hammond, A. L. (2007, February). A review of the open educational resources (OER) movement: Achievements, challenges, and new opportunities. Report to The William and Flora Hewlett Foundation.

Bagozzi, R. P., and Dholakia, U. M. (2006, July). Open source software user communities: A study of participation in Linux user groups. *Management Science*, 52(7), 1099–1115.

Ballon, H., and Westermann, M. (2006). *Art History and Its Publications in the Electronic Age*. Houston, TX: Rice University Press.

Baraniuk, R. G., Burrus, C. S., Johnson, D. H., and Jones, D. L. (2004, September). Connexions—Sharing knowledge and building communities in signal processing. *IEEE Signal Processing Magazine*, 21(5), 10–16.

Baraniuk, R. G., and Cervenka, K. (2002) *Connexions White Paper: Building Communities and Sharing Knowledge*. Houston, TX: Rice University.

Baraniuk, R. G., Koedinger, K., Scheines, R., Smith, J., and Barnwell, T. (2003). *Information Technology-Enabled Interactive Education (I3E)—Interactive Authoring, Interactive Teaching, and Interactive Learning*. Unpublished Information Technology Research proposal to the National Science Foundation.

Berners-Lee, T., Hendler, J., and Lassila, O. (2001, May). The semantic web. *Scientific American*.

Bowen, H.R. (1996). *Investment in Learning: The Individual and Social Value of Higher American Education*. Baltimore, MD: Johns Hopkins University Press.

Dholakia, U. M. (2006). *What Makes an OE Program Sustainable?* OECD papers on CERI—Open Educational Resources Program, Paris.

Dholakia, U. M., Bagozzi, R. P., and Klein Pearo, L. (2004). A social influence model of consumer participation in network- and small-group-based virtual communities. *International Journal of Research in Marketing*, 21(3), 241–263.

Dholakia, U. M., Roll, S., and McKeever, J. (2005, January). Building community in Connexions. *Market Research Report for Connexions Project*. Houston, TX: Rice University.

Jensen, M. (2007, June 15). The new metrics of scholarly authority. *Chronicle of Higher Education*, 53(41), B6.

Kristensen, P., and Bjerkedal, T. (2007, June 22). Explaining the relation between birth order and intelligence. *Science*, 316(5832), 1717.

Lessig, L. (2001). *The Future of Ideas: The Fate of the Commons in a Connected World*. New York: Random House.

Markoff, J. (2006, November 12). Entrepreneurs see a web guided by common sense. *New York Times*. Retrieved on July 7, 2007, from http://www.nytimes.com/2006/11/12/business/12web.html

O'Reilly, T. (2005, September 30). What is Web 2.0: Design patterns and business models for the next generation of software. Retrieved July 7, 2007, from http://www.oreillynet.com/pub/a/oreilly/tim/news/2005/09/30/what-is-Web-20.html

Raymond, E. S. (2001). *The Cathedral and the Bazaar: Musings on Linux and the Open Source by an Accidental Revolutionary*. Sebastopol, CA: O'Reilly Media.

Shapiro, C., and Varian, H. (1998, November). Versioning: The smart way to sell information. *Harvard Business Review*, 98610, 106–114.

Spool, J. M., Scanlon, T., Schroeder, W., Snyder, C., and DeAngelo, T. (1997). *Web Site Usability: A Designer's Guide*. North Andover, MD: User Interface Engineering.

Tinto, V. (1998). Colleges as communities: Taking research on student persistence seriously. *The Review of Higher Education*, 21(2), 167–177.

Wei, C., Maust, B., Barrick, J., Cuddihy, E., and Spyridaki, J. H. (2005). *Wikis for Supporting Distributed Collaborative Writing*. Proceedings of the Society for Technical Communication 52nd Annual Conference, Seattle, WA.

Wikipedia. (2007a, April). *Intelligent Tutoring System*. Retrieved July 7, 2007, from wikipedia.org/wiki/Intelligent_tutoring_system.

Wikipedia. (2007b, April). *Learning Objects*. Retrieved July 7, 2007, wikipedia.org/wiki/Learning_Object

XML. (2007). World Wide Web Consortium (W3C). Retrieved July 7, 2007, from www.w3.org/XML

Zajonc, R. B., and Markus, G. (1975). Birth order and intellectual development. *Psychological Review*, 82, 74–88.

16

2005–2012: The OpenCourseWars

David Wiley

Note to the reader: This is an excerpt from a longer chapter in my autobiography, written in 2045, about the history of open education. In the beginning of the chapter, which is not included in this excerpt, I remember the growth of the OpenCourseWare (OCW) movement within the United States and the passage of a Third Morrill Act that instituted OpenCourseWare initiatives at the majority of public universities in the United States. The complete version of the chapter from my autobiography is available online at http://opencontent.org/future/.

Courts, Clauses, and Campuses

The general excitement about opencourseware led two U.S. engineering firms to the federal government with accusations that Chinese companies were utilizing opencourseware materials from U.S. schools in training their employees. I had seen this coming. Since many people believed that the Creative Commons "Noncommercial" license used by most opencoursewares prevented U.S. corporations from using these materials, they expected the government to take some kind of legal or diplomatic action. The news rode a wave of Internet hype and was soon all over the technical sites like Slashdot and Digg. I was stunned to see it make its way to CNN and MSNBC. The Chinese admitted openly that they were not only using the materials, but relying on them heavily. They contended that they were exempt from the Noncommercial clause because they were state-owned companies—not private, for-profit companies—and, according to MIT OpenCourseWare's own "Terms of Use" Web page, using opencourseware materials for internal corporate training did not violate the Noncommercial license.

I believe it was Larry Lessig who coined the term "IP McCarthyism." Either way, a junior senator from California brought the argument to the floor of Congress in no uncertain terms: "These idiots like Byrd and others who supported the Third Morrill Act are traitors of the worst kind—traitors who believe they are patriots but who, through sheer stupidity, have sold out our country. We have now put in place federally funded machinery that makes the best of American teaching and learning available to the Communist competition but places it squarely out of the grasp of American companies." There it was—myself and all the other supporters of open education were communists and traitors. I was not surprised when this sound byte got its fifteen minutes on *all* the major networks. Public opinion toward OCW ranged from sour to hostile. Indignant citizens brought lawsuits against the Third Morrill Act and the Utah legislative funding (I had helped engineer) for opencoursewares. Organizers took steps to block the seven bills making their way through other state legislatures.

MIT OpenCourseWare tried in vain to redirect public opinion. Communism wasn't the issue; the companies could use the materials for internal training because that kind of use was specifically permitted by the Noncommercial clause. In fact, any corporation could use By-NC-SA licensed materials—but only internally. But, despite my hopes to the contrary, everyone immediately saw that this contradicted what Google representatives had been telling the media "Noncommercial" meant.

The Meaning of "Noncommercial"

It may be hard to believe that such different interpretations could be made of a document (unless the document is scripture), but there had long been significant confusion around the meaning of the Noncommercial clause. Creative Commons' own publicly posted discussion draft, "Proposed Best Practice Guidelines to Clarify the Meaning of *Noncommercial* in the Creative Commons Licenses," suggested we approach its meaning from the "nature of the user." To put it simply, the guidelines stated that use was legitimate if the would-be user was an individual or nonprofit institution. If not—if the would-be user was a for-profit company—then use of the materials was not permitted. Seemed very straightforward, right? MIT OpenCourseWare, however, saw things differently, providing its own definition of "noncommercial," which read "determination of commercial vs. noncommercial purpose is based on the use, not the user." As long as you were not trying to make money directly from MIT's materials, they were cool with whatever else you did.

So, on the one hand, Creative Commons was suggesting that "noncommercial" should be determined by the nature of the user, and on the other hand MIT was defining the very same clause of the very same license in the completely opposite way. I had known about this problem for years and had email discussions with a number of people at both Creative Commons and MIT, hoping to get it fixed. But the problem was extremely thorny politically.

The National Academies, long supporters of open resources in higher education, tried to reclaim the discussion by hurriedly issuing a joint report supporting opencourseware and openness generally, but condemning the Noncommercial clause specifically. They cited a number of blog posts, online discussions, and even transcripts of public addresses by people affiliated with Creative Commons that described the Noncommercial option as being so incredibly vague as to be nearly meaningless beyond its "common sense meaning." I wondered what would happen. . . . The Noncommercial clause was in trouble, and MIT had long said that without the Noncommercial clause their OpenCourseWare could never have happened. That sentiment was echoed by several other schools that had followed MIT's banner into the parade. (Fortunately, most of the courses in USU [Utah State University] OCW had dropped the Noncommercial clause by this point.)

This, it turned out, was what the publishers had been patiently and silently waiting for. A coalition of publishers worked behind the scenes to coordinate strategy on the existing lawsuits, combining them when possible, and bringing new suits as opportunity provided, dedicating an incredible amount of resources to the effort. It was all-out war on the Noncommercial clause.

The publishers' strategy was brilliant. Allow the opencourseware laws to pass, allow the universities to create tens of thousands of high-quality educational materials with funding from the government or private foundations, and allow these to be published under the Creative Commons By-NC-SA license. Then sue and wait. What no one but me and the publishers seemed to understand were the interactions of two key terms in all Creative Commons licenses. Term 7b of the Creative Commons license said that the licenses were "perpetual," and that once material had been licensed, that licensing could not be undone. Once a Creative Commons work, always a Creative Commons work (until copyright expired, of course). Term 8c of the license was a standard severability clause, which said that should a court void any portion of the license for any reason, the remainder of the license would remain in force.

In other words, the Creative Commons licenses were irrevocable and designed so that if any part was nullified, the remainder stood in tact. The publishers only had to wait until the Noncommercial clause was struck down in court, and there would be a world of free, high-quality content waiting to be leveraged in print and other media by the industry that already had the editorial machinery and the marketing know-how to do it. They didn't have to wait long. While the public was still angry over the whole IP McCarthyism, pro-Communist furor, the Noncommercial clause was struck down in New York and the ruling quickly upheld in the Supreme Court.

The end result: Tens of thousands of courses' worth of opencourseware that had been licensed exclusively for noncommercial use when we all went to bed were free to be used commercially when we woke up the next day, and there was nothing anyone could do about it. I didn't sleep at all that night.

Backlash and a Break

Faculty were furious. Lawsuits blossomed across the country as faculty sued their institutions for "knowingly stripping their faculty of commercial interest in their own intellectual property." But in a miraculous rash of right thinking by the courts, the first three suits failed. (Even today I still pull out these rulings and reread them when I need a pick me up.) The remaining suits were dropped. Faculty resigned themselves to a world of opencourseware in which commercial use rights were granted *carte blanche* to the world. Several bloggers wondered if the current state of things was not more communist than the previous. Others pointed out that since the Communists no longer had an advantage over U.S. companies, it couldn't be so.

As the original champion of opencourseware in Utah, I was the special target of criticism and frustration at USU and around the state. I tried to remind faculty and the media that USU had dropped the Noncommercial clause from most of our courses years before because the ShareAlike (By-SA) clause provided all the protection we really needed. Even if publishers derived all kinds of new commercial curriculum from our opencourseware, they were required by the remaining ShareAlike clause to share these new works with the academic community (and everyone else) for free. But nobody listened; nobody seemed to care. Lawsuits or not, the whole situation stank, and I was the stinkiest person in Utah. It was hard times for a while.

A colleague called one morning to tell me how wrong I was. The publishing companies had begun selling their first books derived from OCW content—he had received one from Amazon. And while they were attributing the materials' sources as required by the licenses, they did not relicense any of the materials By-SA, as required by the license. They built complete curricula around the materials and began selling the books, teacher's manuals, tests, and other accessories, with no mention of the Creative Commons license. I literally slapped myself for being so shortsighted. The publishers' end game included more than the Noncommercial clause: They were going after the ShareAlike clause as well. They were daring someone to sue them, with the goal of overturning the ShareAlike clause and reducing all of the opencourseware material in the world to no-investment, no-obligation fodder for their textbooks and other materials.

ShareAlike Goes to Court

Apparently the publishers were drunk with their first successes in court. Or they put too much faith in momentum. Stanford finally brought a suit against the publishers on behalf of its faculty, with Lessig arguing the case for Stanford. This court battle was uglier and much more protracted than the battle over the Noncommercial clause. Some questioned whether Lessig should have been involved at all after losing the Supreme Court fight over copyright extension and for having created the licenses that "started the whole mess." Of all the low blows thrown during what became known as "the opencoursewars," those thrown at Lessig during this time were the most despicable. First, he had consistently been one of the most vocal, hard working, and intelligent supporters of openness generally. And second, no one seemed to recall that Creative Commons had inherited the notion of options and specific options (relating to commercial use and derivative works) that we had put in the original Open Publication License back in the late 1990s. If retiring the Open Publication License in favor of the Creative Commons licenses had been one of the most difficult things I ever had to do professionally, hearing some of the things that were said about Lessig during this time were a close second.

I am very happy (and not at all surprised) to say, however, that Lessig turned out to be the right choice for the case, as the ShareAlike clause was upheld in the lower court and in every appeal at each level of the judicial system. And then the fun began. Publishers now found themselves in a bigger mess than even the universities had been in. You see, the universities could still charge tuition, even if their course materials were freely available online. The publishers would have a much harder time selling their textbooks for $100 a piece when the court had just relicensed the majority of their last eighteen months of work with a Creative Commons Attribution-ShareAlike license.

Students, Zealots, and Compatibility

Campuses went crazy. It turned out that students hated textbook publishers even more than they hated classes and exams. Even the least academically inclined fraternities and sororities held parties where textbooks went under the box cutter, the scanner, and the OCR software. My own Center for Open and Sustainable Learning at USU sponsored a "Textbook SCANdal Night" that was attended by over 50 students (and staff). Literally one week later, free electronic copies of the newest major textbooks were circulating on the Net. In a sick and twisted way, the commercial publishers became the biggest champions of open education in the United States.

The overnight availability of free digital textbooks catalyzed a number of unexpected developments. First, the decade-old struggling ebook hardware market suddenly came to life. For $100, students could buy a piece of hardware that let them read, annotate, print, and wirelessly trade all their textbooks at no additional cost. Sharing class notes came to mean something very different than it had just one semester before.

Second, Wikipedia's struggling textbook project came to life. People cut and pasted the textbooks into Wikibooks and began annotating them like crazy. Test questions that had been used on real tests began showing up as in-context chapter annotations. Phone photos of professors' classroom demonstrations began showing up. Clandestine mp3 recordings of lectures were uploaded. Student reexplanations of key topics, clothed in the language that only teens and young adults understand, made their ways into the books. Apparently when students feel like they're helping each other beat the system, they will go to great lengths to produce incredibly valuable educational materials.

Just when everything seemed to be going well for openness and higher education, the cyber-terrorists got involved. The "Libre License League" (LLL) had been a permanent fixture in the space for a number of years, hijacking every online discussion or conference presentation on any topic relating to open education and forcibly turning the discussion topic to licenses and why the nonfree Creative Commons licenses were inferior to the GNU Free Documentation License (GFDL).

Well, in an LLL-coordinated bot attack that lasted a full week, all the new textbooks, annotations, photos, and other contributions on Wikibooks were deleted and replaced with this message:

These stuffz originally uzed a ***NONFR33*** Creative Commons lisenz. Everything posted on wikipedia must uze the GFDL. RTFM you m0r0nz!!!! The CC lisenz don't work with the GFDL! Keep your ***NONFR33*** [expletive removed] off wikipedia!!!

The vast majority of students couldn't even interpret the message. Of course, I knew full well that all the material was preserved in the fully revisioned history of the wiki pages and had not been lost at all. But for the tens of thousands of students, who in a few weeks had come to rely heavily on the site, everything seemed to be gone permanently. The outrage was first directed at faculty, who the students were certain were behind the attack. The cyber-terrorists who had actually carried out the attack were designated the LLL at this time, and a translation of their message spread around the Net and the evening news: "These textbooks use a Creative Commons license. Materials posted on Wikibooks must use the GFDL (a different license). Because these licenses are incompatible, you can't post the books here."

Anger was quickly redirected toward the Free Software Foundation and Creative Commons for several years' worth of (what were characterized as) half-hearted, failed attempts to make the two most common open content licenses compatible with one another. The William and Flora Hewlett Foundation, which had funded MIT and several of the other early opencourseware initiatives during the 2000s, announced a $500,000 dollar bounty to be split evenly between the Free Software Foundation and Creative Commons the day the two organizations could make a joint announcement regarding license compatibility. It took them another *nine months* to reach an accord.

Reemergence, MetaU, and K–12

The Wikibooks content, complete with test questions, fifth-row photos of professors' slides, and other annotations, finally returned on a new wiki set up and run by students called MetaU.org (the MetaUniversity) and dually licensed under newly compatible Creative Commons and GFDL licenses. I started bypassing our opencourseware altogether, working instead with students to get material directly into the new MetaU site. Many other younger university faculty did the same. As an undergraduate said to me back around 2010, "Putting professors' lecture notes and things on a university Web site where students can't trib test questions and photos and things makes about as much sense as using email. It's for old people who just don't get it. I mean, even this ebook reader thing I just got from my sister—who finally graduated, by the way—is pointless. Why would anyone use a device that won't let you trib?" For readers too young to remember, "trib" is short for "contribute" (three syllables apparently being too many to say), and was slang for uploading user-contributed content, whether video, music, photo, or—and I can't believe I'm actually typing this—class notes.

My friend's attitude about trib'ing is indicative of the general feeling of the time. Although the individual opencoursewares were online all along, their "read-only" nature ("R/O" being about the rudest adjective one could use when speaking about a Web site) was anathema to then-current sensibilities. The feeling was so strong that when the Wikibooks site went down, you might have thought all the open educational resources in the world had been lost. (Even as I write decades later, R/O is still a derogatory term that embodies an entire generation's frustration with top-down, undemocratic, unparticipatory approaches generally.)

With the return of the MetaU content, the public once again had access to open textbooks, opencourseware, actual test questions, the phone photos and mp3 recordings of professors' classroom presentations, and other content all remixed and massively interlinked with itself and other online content from the BBC and Wikipedia, as well as open data streams coming out of places like NOAA and the International Linear Collider. Faculty began integrating links to open access journal articles into these mashups, but student wiki-gardeners consistently moved them to the bottom of the pages. I suppose they didn't permanently delete them out of respect for the lesson they learned from the LLL.

Opencourseware and K–12

The reemergence of MetaU made its way onto the television news and into the homes of several parents in North Carolina one evening in 2011. It seems the school board in their county had just adopted a very expensive commercial preengineering curriculum for the local high school. One of the parents, a professor at Duke University, had just completed an external review of an NSF-funded, CC/GFDL-licensed preengineering curriculum out of Purdue. Knowing it was as good or better than anything a commercial company could offer, he rallied dozens of other parents to hold their children from school until a public hearing could be held to discuss the decision to spend so much money on the commercial curriculum when a much less expensive alternative of equal or higher quality existed. The parents got their meeting, and before the 2011–2012 school year was over, the curriculum was in dozens of high schools around the country.

MetaU, WGU, and the EMOs

While it was a fight getting there, the situation at this point can only be described as a "learner utopia." It took less than fifteen years to get from the words "open content," to Creative Commons, to MIT OCW, to the Third Morrill Act or "Byrd Bill," to the MetaU. We had gone from a handful of pages on renegade faculty members' personal Web sites, to tens of thousands of courses from over seventy countries freely and openly accessible online, to student-driven mixing and remixing of resources in ways more innovative than any instructional designer could possibly imagine. But there were still a few big surprises left before 2012 was out.

At the time, the Western Governors University (WGU) was a fully accredited, completely online, *competency-based* university. Students were required to demonstrate their competencies through assessments, not suffer through classes whose content they may have already mastered. If you passed the tests, you got the degree. If students needed some refreshing or outright teaching, WGU would work with other universities to get students into online classes where they could gain the skills, knowledge, and confidence they needed to pass the WGU exams. Back in 2006 I had met with folks from WGU and recommended that they look at opencourseware content as a free, high-quality alternative to traditional online classes for their students. The timing was all wrong, though— everything was still R/O and there was little momentum in higher education generally. But during the summer of 2012, WGU announced a deal with MetaU.

It was a classic IBM/Linux-like arrangement between a business and an open source effort, and the first example of a successful partnership of its kind in the open content space. WGU agreed to pay two full-time wiki-gardeners to contribute to the care of the MetaU site and connect the WGU's existing competency standards with MetaU's content structure. This allowed WGU students to leverage the MetaU's open content *directly* as they prepared for their exams, without needing to wait for counselors to tell them what to study or help them find online classes at universities. The arrangement meant quicker service for the WGU students and cost savings for both students and the WGU organization. It was brilliant.

After years of waiting to be widely recognized as the leader in the innovative educational offerings, WGU finally made good by shedding its traditional, "R/O" reputation. Ten years before, WGU had plugged into the Internet technically; now it plugged in culturally. I actually heard WGU president Bob Mendenhall use the word "trib" (properly!) in a keynote at the 2012 Open Education Conference. A university president who really got it . . . you could have pushed me over with a feather.

LearnerSupport

The WGU—MetaU deal had two major repercussions. First, MetaU spun off a company called LearnerSupport. For MetaU users who couldn't afford to (or didn't want to) wait up to an hour to get a question answered in one of the site's self-organizing discussion forums, users could get live instructional support via Skype (which was then the dominant player in the VOIP space). A credentialed freelancer, a Neal Stephenson-style ractor in India, China, Hoboken, or who-knows-where, answered the phone and provided real-time help to students. Users paid LearnerSupport before they were helped and then rated the service they got after talking to the ractor. If the service was unsatisfactory, the learner got bounced to another ractor. The ractor who actually answered the user's question to their liking got a cut of the money the user had paid LearnerSupport up front. It was brilliant: a competitive market in actually helping people learn. When a ractor could not answer a question, he or she didn't bother trying. Those that could answer did the best job they could, since their pay depended on it. Students claimed to love the service because they knew that the vast majority of ractors were other students.

For-profit universities, like Walden and Capella, which had made extensive use of open content since the nullification of the Noncommercial clause, all made deals with LearnerSupport that gave each of their tuition-paying students all-you-can-eat access to the LearnerSupport service, effectively outsourcing two-thirds of their student support services. Advising and other services remained in-house for a while, until university advisors figured out that most of the advising calls had stopped coming because students were asking the ractors these questions too.

The University of Phoenix (UoP) spun off a LearnerSupport-copycat company, which also did very well. (In fact, it's all that remains of UoP as I write.) None of the traditional universities in the United States made the move, but several in Europe did, almost as quickly as the U.S. for-profits. The Open Universities of Catalonia and the Netherlands were the first in the chute.

The EMO

The second repercussion was the emergence of the much-predicted Education Maintenance Organization (EMO). Over night, a dozen companies sprang up, ready to provide corporations with "the ultimate lifelong learning/training solution" for their employees. These companies were also LearnerSupport knock-offs who relied primarily on the MetaU content, but their ractors used a more formal tone and business jargon that corporate executives found credible. By late 2013, Google and Microsoft were including EMO membership in their corporate benefits packages.

These were truly amazing times to be alive. U.S. higher education was changing before my very eyes. Not all of it, granted. Not even most of it. But some of it *was* changing. Of course, things were moving in the rest of the world as well. The Chinese and Indian MetaU's were both absolutely astounding. They would be, of course, with so many more students to trib and tend the wikis. (Some even claim that the Chinese MetaU was the final brick in the basket that tipped things in the direction of democracy in that country.)

In Hindsight

Critics may wonder why my discussion focuses on OpenCourseWare, and why a discussion of the broader open education resources movement is missing from this chapter. Those critics will have failed to see that MetaU was the quintessential open education resource. Generally speaking, opencourseware initiatives were difficult-to-sustain, R/O endeavors that relied on relatively small numbers of university employees and outside funding. As important as they were, most never got to scale and were unsustainable in the ways their original funders intended. On the other hand, open education resource projects were generally *democratic remix projects that lived and died on the quality of the trib'ing*. (Rice's Connexions was a great early example.) If the acronym OER or the phrase "open educational resources" is missing from my description of events, it is because the student trib'ers didn't use it. And this is a story about the students. Students associated every site that tried to promote either an "OCW brand" or an "OER brand" or any other brand with R/O thinking, whether the sites were open to trib'ing or not.

The editors of this excerpt (Toru, Vijay, and Flora) have asked me, "if you could travel back in time to 2005, knowing what you know now, what would you say to the OER field? How could we avert the crises that occurred with the Noncommercial clause, the Libre License League, and such?" We all tend to fight the fires that burn the hottest, and we all tend to pick the lowest hanging fruit. The Noncommercial clause had two things working against it in this regard. First, the problems with the clause were, to that point, purely hypothetical. Who wants to spend time on the hypothetical when there is "real" work to be done? So there was little incentive to fix the problem. And second, the Noncommercial problem was a *terribly* complex issue. Few people understood this well enough. Every group of Noncommercial clause users believed that "noncommercial" should mean something different, something specific to their space. How was Creative Commons supposed to choose to side with one group's interpretation and alienate all the others?

The only possible result would have been license proliferation on an unprecedented scale, with each community writing *boutique* licenses that defined "commercial use" just so. Dozens of them. It would have completely undercut the communicative simplicity that the Creative Commons licenses were designed to create. So in addition to having little incentive to work on a hypothetical problem, this particular hypothetical problem appeared intractable. While it caused upheaval, strife, persecution, and anger (some of it directed toward me personally, mind you), in the long run, a crisis resulting in a court ruling that invalidated the Noncommercial clause was actually the best possible outcome for teaching and learning worldwide.

We must also remember that at the beginning of the twenty-first century, U.S. college students had largely become self-absorbed and apathetic. The misbehavior of the publishing companies (a fuse that was just waiting to be lit anyway, thanks to the rising costs of turn of the century textbooks), and the crisis brought on by the LLL takedown of the Wikibooks site ignited the passion, energy, and effort that went into the initial trib'ing that gave MetaU the critical mass to become a success. Without the publishers' bad behavior, who knows how long the student body would have continued its collective nap?

But to answer the specific question, if I could go back in time and give one bit of specific advice to those early open education pioneers, it would be this: Embrace the trib culture. Embrace it as quickly and as fully as you can. Higher education does not have to remain an R/O endeavor. Open their eyes to what is happening all around you on YouTube, on Flickr, on Wikipedia, on Facebook, and evolve with the times rather than be left behind by them. The Industrial Age is over.

17

Revolutionizing Education through Innovation: Can Openness Transform Teaching and Learning?

Catherine M. Casserly and Marshall S. Smith

The need for educational access and greater effectiveness in teaching and learning is staggering. Today, there are over 30 million people qualified to enter university but denied access due to the restricted seat numbers and restricted finances. In the next 10 years, the number of potential students who will be denied access will grow to 100 million (Daniels, 2007). A major university would have to be created each week, starting now, to meet this overwhelming demand.

We need to rethink the traditional notions of where, when, and how people learn. Learning will continue within traditional structures, but it could also be more widely available through new emerging models. Can the simple but powerful notion of combining no cost high quality content with the reach of the Web fundamentally shape these emerging models and change teaching and learning? That transformation is possible, though yet untested.

Over the past five years, The Hewlett Foundation's Open Educational Resources (OER[1]) Initiative has worked to equalize access to education by sponsoring the development of high quality content made freely available on the Web, removing barriers to the use of the content and carrying out research to understand and stimulate use. Together with partners from universities, the private sector, governments and intergovernmental organizations, the foundation has helped nurture the field of open educational resources from an infancy of scattered, often low quality content across the Web to a robust early adolescence characterized by energy and idealism. Major accomplishments to date include shifting the culture in higher education universities and organizations to share content previously held private; helping to create a powerful portfolio of open, high quality education materials and tools that are used all over the world;

supporting the development of a more flexible copyright system; mobilizing a strong movement of individuals, institutions, and international agencies throughout the world; supporting the preservation and open access of books, moving images, audio and text; and demonstrating the capacity of freely available high quality online content to accelerate learning.

An evaluation of The Hewlett Foundation OER Initiative and two other recent reports (Atkins, Brown, and Hammond, 2007; OECD, 2007; Salzburg Research, 2007) argue that the field now needs to move from a culture of sharing to a culture of participation. The next phase of the work should focus on using the reach and power of OER to help meet the demands for high quality education experiences across the world. The potential for OER to transform teaching and learning exists, but is still essentially untested.

How Might OER Transform Teaching and Learning?

On first blush, the only distinctive feature of OER is that the materials and tools are free and available on the Web, "24/7," for everyone in the world. For many, this single feature, which potentially alters the balance of power around access to knowledge, is enough to justify the growth and importance of OER. Massachusetts Institute of Technology (MIT) OpenCourseWare (OCW) gives us a peek into a future where the student in East Los Angeles or Nairobi will have access to the same academic content as the student at MIT. We clearly acknowledge that the student at MIT has access to many resources that the Web users in Los Angeles and Nairobi do not, including MIT faculty, labs, and other students. The content is only part of the equation of learning—but, without question, it is an indispensable component.

However, open access is not the only feature of OER that distinguishes it from other content on the Web accessible by search engines or from behind a wall that requires status or permission or resources to penetrate. Fully open educational resources provide a license that grants permission to users not only to read the material but also to download, modify, and post it for reuse. Users are empowered to change the materials to meet their own needs. They can mix and remix. The capacity and right to reuse materials is an important step in providing users all over the world the opportunity to actively participate in the open education resources teaching and learning processes. It creates the opportunity for the localization of the materials, where users tailor materials according to their language and culture, and for personalization, where materials can be adapted and modified for individual learners. Reuse also makes possible continuous cycles of improvement of educational materials as users quickly provide critical reactions and evaluations to developers of the quality and effectiveness of the materials. These fast feedback loops of users and developers create an environment for the improvement of content similar to the environment of open source software.

To be sure, the private sector can do some of these things with proprietary data, such as asking for feedback, for example, and modifying a product on the basis of the feedback. We encourage this practice, but it is a pale imitation of the involvement a user could have by providing feedback information, modifying the materials, and reposting them on the Web for use by others. Moreover, the users who give feedback to a proprietary vendor are by definition only those with the privilege or resources to access the original material.

These two distinctive features of OER potentially have far-reaching consequences: They alter the balance of power around the accessibility to knowledge throughout the world, and they provide the opportunity for people to become empowered by taking control of their educational content and other materials.

A third, more controversial feature of OER requires attention. Over the past few years, we have observed that much of the better known OER material is of higher quality than even the best private sector or otherwise proprietary content. One reason for this may be that government or foundations fund much of the OER content and tend to value quality over cost. Quality is important since there is an abundance of Web-based content though much of questionable value. The Hewlett Foundation's OER strategy prioritizes exemplars to demonstrate the potential of Web-based materials for teaching and learning concurrent with the priority of accessibility.

Another reason may be that transparency creates implicit and explicit incentives to raise the standard of quality. By sharing content with the global community, the reputations of scholars, educators, and other creators of open education materials are exposed. When OER contributors know the world will scrutinize the accuracy and worth of shared content, increased levels of effort follow. A third reason may be that the private sector tends to be conservative in their approach to creating education materials in order to retain their market. For example, in the K–12 textbook space, curriculum developers do not want to get too far ahead of others for fear of being removed from approved textbook adoption lists. Mostly, curriculum developers compete on the margins with photos, engaging stories, and perhaps supplemental discs included in the book jacket. Whatever the reason, the virtual library of OER includes a variety of examples of exemplary materials which, over time, may create a positive influence over the private sector.

Finally, though no reminder is likely needed by readers of this chapter, the advent of Web 2.0 changes the face and character of the Web. The increased opportunity for serious and extended interactivity and communication and the use of software that enable three dimensional simulations and other immersive environments dramatically increase the possibilities for powerful educational experiences on the Web. These new dimensions of the Web are congruent with the OER spirit of the mix and remix culture which places the student in substantial control of her learning environment and in the role of creator as well as user.

Examples of Powerful Current OER Practice

We fully expect current innovative practices emerging from the availability of OER to evolve in ways we cannot even begin to imagine at this point. However, among the current open educational materials, some exemplify the features of OER and show promise of influencing teaching and learning across the world. Those that follow the OCW model will build on its path-breaking strengths, access to rich multi-media courses, and the influential dynamic of learning through creation.

OpenCourseWare and Open Courses

Perhaps the best known example of OER is the MIT OCW initiative. Described more fully in chapter 15, MIT OCW fits the profile for OER perfectly. Prior to OCW, MIT course materials were not accessible to the general public: Those not in the club were excluded. After 2002, the doors were opened to the world. And it is not only accessible but also downloadable and reusable, a characteristic that has been used by institutions and faculty all over the world. Further, it exemplifies quality.

Following MIT's lead, the acts of publishing the course materials by the many worldwide institutions participating in the OCW Consortium (See http://www.ocwconsortium.org) represent a significant shift within higher education in the traditional notion of how knowledge is controlled and shared. One of the recent members of the OCW Consortium, the Yale University Video Lecture Project (See http://open.yale.edu/), extends the concept of open courseware to include all of the actual lectures of the courses along with the variety of materials. Rather than attempt to cover the university's entire catalogue, Yale also has selected specific courses on the basis of their intrinsic interest to a large audience and quality of their instructional experience.

Yale is not the only institution that provides full courses. Full, high quality courses also are available on the Web through Carnegie Mellon's Open Learning Initiative (See chapter 12 in this volume and also http://www.cmu.edu/oli) and the Monterey Institute for Technology and Education (MITE; See http://www.montereyinstitute.org/nroc/nrocdemos.html). The MITE courses cover much of the subject matter of the early years of college (and for secondary school Advanced Placement courses) and use rich, engaging, media-based content. All three open learning initiatives allow students to pace their learning as appropriate and review conceptually difficult material as needed.

Learning through Creating

With the emergence of easy-to-use wiki environments and tools, anyone can now become a creator of online content. The most recognized example of this is Wikipedia (See http://www.wikipedia.org/), the largest free-content encyclopedia on the Internet. Translated in more than 200 languages, it is built on the contribution of many, though there is a core group of active Wikipedians.

The emergence of new resources such as Wikipedia generates new activities for learning. For example, the practice of using the Wikipedia Encyclopedia differs from the practice of using Encyclopedia Britannica in that users can review edits, contested points, and argument strings. The user has the opportunity to reflect on the provided information in a different way than with the traditional static encyclopedia. Learning "by doing," by actively engaging and editing content, being an "owner" of an entry, or by creating new entries are innovative activities enabled by the ability to use and reuse open content. WikiEducator (See http://www .WikiEducator.org/main_page), being built using collaborative development and open networks, also harnesses the participation of many.

A "participatory learning environment" is also encouraged through OER sites such as OpenLearn from the Open University of the United Kingdom (OU UK), Teachers' Domain, of the public television station WGBH, and Connexions (See http://www.open.ac.uk/openlearn/home. php; http://www.teachersdomain.org/; and http://cnx.org). The OU UK site allows learners to engage with content through their own learning path and to locate other users also exploring content through instant messaging. Other tools encourage online meeting spaces and mapping of knowledge paths that can be shared with others. The OU UK LabSpace (See http://labspace.open.ac.uk/) invites individuals to recontextualize content from their quality-vetted OpenLearn content, or add fresh content for others to build on. WGBH is opening its video collections for use by teachers all over the world. These rich video materials can be used and reused. The Web site Connexions provides tools for collaborative content building for faculty and students and the opportunity to bundle modules of content as desired. In particular, online sites such as Connexions enable the niche communities to gather, produce, and share content.

Open reusable content in settings such as the OU UK Lab Space or the WGBH site enables a particularly innovative development process. Part of the power of the Web is that its use makes possible the development of communities of people interested in the same sets of issues. Web-based communities interested in using and improving reusable education content are able to harness fast feedback loops, a form of continuous innovation, creativity, and social networking. Individuals in the community use, reuse, recreate and repost content; others do the same, and the original materials take on many different forms and modifications based on the diverse needs of the users.

Using the Web to create fast feedback loops, we can dramatically improve the quality and usefulness of educational materials by engaging faculty and students who are users. Continuous feedback and improvement can be applied to textbooks, lesson plans, workbooks, and professional development, to name a few. It also allows faculty to actively engage in the improvement of their field of practice by opening up the system to all.

Open Games, Simulations, and other Immersive Environments
Emerging forms of educational content that could powerfully impact teaching and learning include individual and multilayer games and simulations and other immersive environments. The potential power of the immersive environment is that the student is motivated to learn within a context that often requires them to engage in activities to continue. Players make choices, take actions, build, and often interact with other players to achieve their goals in the environment. The more complex environments often challenge learners to think in different ways to solve problems and provide rewards for success. Many environments have problems requiring the user to engage multiple times, to practice, learn, fail and retry. This sequence closely resembles the trials of real life. Embedded incentives and competition are key attributes of many immersive environments. Over time, a library of open, immersive educational environments that are explicitly educational will emerge. There are already a few examples. The game Discover Babylon teaches a user to be an archeologist with accurate historical and scientific information in three dimensional photorealistic simulations that allow open-ended exploration and discovery (See http://www.discoverbabylon.org). Surgery Simulator is a high fidelity laparoscopic environment that enables surgeons to practice complex operative tasks (See the ScienceDaily article at http://www.sciencedaily.com/releases/2005/06/050627062144.htm). The device emulates, with a high degree of accuracy, the anatomy of organs and tissues. Immune Attack teaches cell biology by placing the student into a warlike situation within a human circulatory system (See http://www.fas.org/immuneattack). The motivating characteristics of these games might be enough to convince students and faculty to make use of them.

Immersive environments such as these engage students in dynamic, rather than rote, learning and the opportunity to participate actively in scientific discovery. Students learn by doing rather than by simply knowing.

Looking Ahead

We imagine some powerful scenarios emerging in the years ahead, where combinations of open educational resources may be used to dramatically alter the opportunities for teaching and learning.

The three types of current OER content described in the section above are only a small part of a much larger virtual and somewhat inchoate Web library of free and reusable and, often, very high quality content and tools. The next few years promise amazing advances in the OER area.

The Open Content Alliance and Google Book Project will digitize a huge percentage of the books that intellectual property laws allow. Educational video archives will be at least partially open. Giant collections of original materials from government and university libraries will be open and more and more usable. New generations of teachers will be completely savvy with the Web. The technology that makes Moore's law continue to hold will drive down costs and speed up access. The telecommunications revolution will bring the Web to everyone in the world through hand-held computers, mobile phones, and other easily usable tools.

How can we capitalize on our current experiences with OER, the changes to come over the next few years, and the power of the communications and interactivity of Web 2.0 to transform teaching and learning? We do not pretend to have the answers. Transformation generally comes slowly but generally entails the changing of processes and opportunities. All we can do is to whet the readers' appetites, and stimulate their imagination with three possibilities.

Language Learning

Recently we have been involved with a very exciting example of the use of technology for learning. The Open Language Learning Initiative (OLLI), a highly innovative research and development project, will use online technology to teach foreign languages, 24/7, and be openly accessible around the world. The system is being designed to deliver a set of 24 basic English language units designed to bring 12- to 18-year-old students to the level of advanced novice proficiency by integrating the technologies of gaming, animation, and voice recognition via the Internet within a structured immersion pedagogy.

A user will also be able to communicate with others who are simultaneously using the program. This could build toward a community of learners. The initial two programs will teach English to Chinese native speakers and English to Spanish native language students. The design will then be applied to other languages. We fully expect OLLI to set the standard for a technology solution for oral language instruction and to be a motivating environment where students within schools and without can learn at their own pace. The timeline sets late spring of 2008 for a release of an open beta version of the program for Chinese speakers to learn English.

The programs will be fully open for use and reuse by others. The capacity to reuse will provide immense possibilities for tailoring the materials. Corporations, governments, and individual people will be able to adapt for their use. The demand for learning to speak English is world wide.

Secondary School and College Textbooks, Courses and Immersive Environments

In many countries, such as the United States, there is no method of validating the effectiveness of textbooks or other teaching materials. Textbooks are traditionally created by one or a few professors or teachers according to a set of publisher specifications that are selected to maximize sales rather than understanding and achievement. In some instances, such as Advanced Placement courses or freshman and sophomore college courses, the books weigh 5 to 8 pounds and, for college students, cost upwards of $100.00 each. In California, the textbooks for a community college student ordinarily cost more than the student's tuition and fees.

Imagine instead that there were a set of high quality text books open and reusable on the Web. Each open textbook has the conventional pages and figures as other textbooks but also has embedded laboratories, interactive simulations, video, and other supporting material. One powerful component of making this textbook freely available on the Web is that it could be continuously updated for new knowledge. A version of the textbook could also be available on a hand-held device. A low-cost, printable, on demand version of the textbook would be available. Though in the print form the book would lose its interactive characteristics, it would still be as useful as current textbooks.

The design would facilitate rapid improvement cycles. Faculty who use the textbook would be able to easily feed back information to the authors or publishers about its usefulness, highlight places and concepts where the presentation is not clear and their students did not understand the materials, and otherwise comment on the usefulness and effectiveness of the material. In the best of worlds, students also would feed back information. The original author could gather the information, and when it was clear from strong data that some area was problematic, she would improve the textbook to address the issues raised.

Or, perhaps, the local instructor might take on the challenge of making changes herself and then post the text that has been modified to adapt to the local environment. In either instance, the process would be a strong and rapid user-driven feedback loop that creates a cycle of continuous improvement.

A number of projects are already exploring the idea of open textbooks, particularly for community college courses. It is quite possible that three or four years from now we will have sets of community college textbooks that have actually been validated as effective by users.

Secondary School and College Courses
Textbooks are only a start. High quality full courses are openly available online. With the high quality courses from MIT, Yale, Carnegie Mellon, Monterey Institute, and others, we are tantalizingly close both to covering the academic track of a U.S. secondary school or the first two years of many colleges and universities. It would not be a great step to expand these materials to cover all of the key courses for secondary schools or colleges. As with textbooks, these materials could be used and reused to fit local and personal learning needs. The Carnegie Mellon and MITE courses are already highly interactive, and all of the courses could have the built-in communication devices so users could easily link to other users. And, the materials would be open to feedback from users so they could be continuously improved.

While open textbooks do not necessarily threaten the traditional ways of teaching, the existence of complete, very high quality, open, 24/7, Web-based instructional courses may. Why would an instructor lecture if similar, and sometimes more engaging, instruction, were available to students any time of the day or night? At a minimum, instructors might pause and reconsider their teaching styles, perhaps moving from a didactic to a coaching approach.

On the other hand, why would we need the technology materials at all since lecturers are doing just fine, thank you? We can think of three important reasons. One is simply that the materials supply a student with an alternative way of learning and reviewing the material of the course, just as enhanced textbooks would, or even as current textbooks lamely do now. A second is that it is possible that students might actually learn better or more or faster using the courses. And the third is that people outside of schools and colleges who do not have access to instructors may wish to learn the material on their own.

The first of these reasons will not be transformative. The second two might be. Indeed, regarding effectiveness, Carnegie Mellon has just completed the first in a series of evaluations of the OER programs. As with many technology-driven courses, a typical head-to-head evaluation of the effectiveness of the Carnegie Mellon cognitive tutor course with the effectiveness of the same course delivered by lecture ends in a draw: no difference. This, of course, is evidence of the effectiveness of the technology course and if the lecture course is effective, but it does not provide a strong argument for replacing the lecturer.

However, the fact that the technology course was available 24/7 for students and that lectures were at given times spaced across a semester suggested a different kind of evaluation, one that varied the time for learning, as well as the medium for learning. In this evaluation of an introductory statistics cognitive tutor course, one set of students took the cognitive tutor course with a meeting once or twice a week with the instructor but no lectures; a second set of students took the regular lecture course and had the technology-driven course available, but it was not required. All students carried a full load for the semester.

One other requirement, however, distinguishes this evaluation from other studies of course effectiveness. The students in the cognitive tutor course were given only one-half the semester in which to complete the course. The evaluation found that the students in the technology-driven course did slightly better in half the time than the students in the lecture course that took the entire semester. This is a very interesting finding, which Carnegie Mellon will need to replicate to see if it generalizes to other courses, and perhaps to explore whether a 50 percent reduction in time is the limit.

For many people in the field of education this is not a surprising finding. They point out that the lecture and semester structures have not changed over the past centuries and that many students attest that they learn little from lectures that they could not learn from textbooks and other students. Powerful and engaging instruction available 24/7 via laptop and, in the near future, cell phone would fit more naturally into the lives of students than do early morning lectures.

But while predictable, what are the implications for transforming the ways in which we traditionally think of learning academic materials? Perhaps college could be shortened to two or three years if students will learn just as much as before—or more. Perhaps instructors might only meet their students once a week to provide some emergency coaching. Instructors would be free to do more of their own research.

A third implication is for people who are not officially students in a college or university. The evaluation suggests that those prepared for college level courses could, with minimal support, learn the material at home or in a library on their own schedule. This is a great result in itself, and we can imagine corporations encouraging employees to engage themselves in relevant open learning courses.

In the long run, the possibilities for self-directed learning of this sort are wide open. There is, however, an important implication. If someone learns the material independently, why not get some credit or certification for the effort? Figuring this out might require that rigorous course final examinations be developed to determine if the person has actually achieved an adequate level of understanding of the material. Then an organization or organizations would have to be established to administer such an exam, and certify that the person has learned the material. The Western Governor's University, located in Utah, provides a service something like this.

Finally, the existence of a body of complete, free online courses suggests that it might be possible to populate courses that satisfy a full college major. These online courses would be made available to anyone and could carry credit for graduation without a residency. But, it also might be useful to create some new forms of institutions that would facilitate the self-directed learner both in obtaining the free, online learning materials and for providing opportunity for students to interact with other self-learners with like interests.

To extend this thought, it is now entirely within our technology capacity to create a virtual university in a simulated, interactive, three-dimensional setting like Second Life. Virtual student avatars guided by self-learners from all over the world would interact with each other, take rich media courses or cognitive tutor courses or lecture courses alone or with others, and participate in seminars that might be created by students or interested others (for example, professors who are taking a "busman's holiday," experts, practicing people in the field). Within the virtual university, music, performing arts, sports, clubs of all sorts could exist while cafés for conversation would spring up. Over time, perhaps a "silicon" league of universities would emerge.

Through our work with The Hewlett Foundation, we have talked with people all over the world about the possibilities for using OER to restructure teacher training, to provide medical practitioners with up-to-date information, to alter the opportunities for those millions of people who are now capable of attending university but do not have places in the conventional institutions. These three examples of how OER might influence teaching and learning only scratch the surface of possibilities.

Overcoming Obstacles

Not all is sanguine in the OER world. There are many possible impediments to bringing OER to the mainstream of education. Moreover, as progress is made from the perspective of an increasing use of OER in interesting ways, the more treacherous the landscape will become. There are obstacles to extending the use of OER to transform teaching and learning, but we believe they can be overcome.

As discussed throughout this volume, for example, intellectual property laws and customs are a very significant obstacle to the effective use of open educational content. Creative Commons and other organizations offer substantial help, but the basic structure of the laws tends to impede innovation in this area.

Sustainability is another major impediment. It is facile to argue that there is an inherent contradiction in the proposition that free content may be sustained through a business model. Yet a variety of models are springing up. In the most straightforward ones, the government or an institution such as MIT provides, updates, and otherwise maintains collections of materials; these entities do so because the content is either a public good or it is in the best interests of the institution to provide ongoing support. A second model comes from experience with open source software and may be called a "Red Hat" model. The content would be fully open, even to commercial use. Thus a company might take a set of fully open courses and provide a professional development service around the courses, and feed back a small percentage of the fees for the professional development service to the content developer to sustain and upgrade the content. A third sustainability model might arise from a group of volunteers who decide that they will maintain the integrity of a body of open content. The general area of models of sustainability is rapidly maturing.

A third obstacle is interoperability, as other discussions in this book have pointed out. The most important obstacles to rapid innovation, however, are not technical. They have to the do with the customs, standard practices, and vested interests of people in the universities and schools and within the markets, such as publishing, that may be forced to change as OER strategies gain more traction. Traditions have stood schooling well in the developed world and should not fall, unless there are overriding reasons of effectiveness, cost, and the public good. In the developing world, where the needs are far more dire and more urgent, the possibilities for major innovation may be better.

We have attempted to indicate that the criteria for change of effectiveness and cost might well be met by innovations in teaching and learning that stem from the use of open educational resources. On the matter of the public good, we argue from Amartya Sen's (1999) position that knowledge is an enabler of freedoms. Poor and oppressed peoples have an inherent right to the opportunity to better themselves, yet a lack of knowledge and information impedes that opportunity. And, in the long run, confining knowledge so that it benefits only those privileged and wealthy will limit the growth of knowledge for all.

Note

1. Open Educational Resources (OER) is a term fashioned in Paris in 2002 at a UNESCO Forum that engaged developing and developed world participants to envision the potential for digitized educational materials and tools freely offered for educators, students and self-learners to use and reuse for the purposes of teaching, learning and research. They envisioned OER content as knowledge, and argued that knowledge is not static but rather an ongoing dynamic process—interpretations, uses, and contexts vary—and the process of additions and modification advances the evolution of ideas.

Open Educational Resources includes high quality content, tools, and implementation resources. Educational content includes full courses, courseware, journals, data, modules and learning objects games, simulations, interactive instructional materials, journals, collections and data. Open search and management systems, easy to use content development systems, user-friendly repositories and portals and online resources that facilitate virtual learning communities are all part of the tools category. Implementation resources such as flexible intellectual property licenses and translation mechanisms are needed to ensure use, reuse and localization, and to facilitate dissemination.

References

Atkins, D. E., Brown, J. S., and Hammond, A. L. (2007). *A Review of the Open Educational Resources Movement: Achievement, Challenges and New Opportunities.* Retrieved July 2, 2007, from http://www.hewlett.org/Programs/Education/OER/OpenContent/Hewlett+OER+Report.htm)

Daniels, J. (2007, January). Commonwealth of Learning. Retrieved July 2, 2007, from http://www.col.org/colweb/site/pid/2833.

OECD. (2007). *Giving Knowledge for Free: The Emergence of Open Educational Resources* Retrieved July 2, 2007, from http://www.oecd.org/dataoecd/35/7/38654317.pdf.

Salzburg Research (2007). *Open Educational Practices and Resources. OLCOS Roadmap 2012.* Retrieved July 2, 2007, from http://www.olcos.org/cms/upload/docs/olcos_roadmap_summary.pdf.

Sen, A. (1999). *Development as Freedom.* New York: Knopf.

Section III
Open Educational Knowledge

Open Educational Knowledge: More than Opening the Classroom Door

Cheryl R. Richardson

Opening knowledge in education goes a step beyond opening our classroom doors to colleagues. It involves cocreating, experimenting, reflecting, sharing, and reusing accumulated ideas and knowledge about teaching and learning. It is active and welcomes the participation of everyone involved—student, instructor, researcher, policymaker, as well as faculty developer and administrator. We think of this genre as embracing the ideals of scholarship and the practices of our contemporary, digital-participatory culture.

Similar to knowledge generated within disciplinary circles, proponents of open knowledge see the field as gaining credibility from knowing which questions were asked and understanding how they were tested and examined, what results emerged, and how we can trust these results. More importantly, we want results measured in terms of better practice and improved student learning. We encourage contributions from all involved in education and advocate educational change that is driven from the ideas, practices, and reflection of all of these participants.

Opening knowledge harnesses the tenets of our current, digitized, and participatory culture. As described by Henry Jenkins in "Confronting the Challenges of Participatory Culture: Media Education for the 21st Century," this vibrant culture includes:

1. low barriers to expression and engagement;
2. strong support for creating and sharing;
3. informal mentorship;
4. an environment where members believe their contributions matter; and
5. connections to other people (2006, p. 7).

In other words, it is rich in particular practices of connecting, cocreating, and distributing teaching and learning. With the right kinds of support and development, this culture has the potential to quickly and broadly spread innovation and improved educational practices.

In the context of improving teaching and enhancing learning, authors examine different perspectives of open knowledge. Authors ask—and with theory, example, and description—answer questions about what opening knowledge about teaching and learning means, how it might be accomplished, the challenges of trying, and the various potential and realized benefits of doing so.

What Motivates Us

The motivation to harness the habits of our current, participatory culture to open knowledge in education resides in wanting to accelerate educational change. Authors variously acknowledge the need to provide universal access to education as well as to improve classroom practices, and they see the collaborative parameters of opening knowledge being an important part of quickly spreading and improving student learning.

Without doubt there is a dynamic and large educational research community that works to understand how people learn formally and informally, as well as the various impacts of personnel, classrooms, society, and development on learners. Likewise, there are teachers and innovators who expand their understanding of teaching and learning by trying new approaches, closely examining long-held practices, and/or by exchanging ideas with colleagues. Some of these changes in knowledge happen within schools, departments, communities, and projects, while others remain within the classroom walls of an educator. Open knowledge advocates insist that it is powerful, indeed necessary, to open these stores of knowledge—those that are generated by practitioners—and share them widely, to be reviewed, reused, and aggregated. As Gale (2008) explains in his chapter, a field of public inquiry and *utility* can be the ultimate result of private curiosity and investigation, if it is practiced in an open environment.

Can we adopt some of the practices of open education (for example, open source and open content principles of sharing) to work with reform communities to push toward opening practitioners' knowledge of teaching, learning, and innovation? Given a plethora of digital tools, what tools might support this kind of work?

Something Needs to Change

In the context of this volume, opening knowledge involves a set of ideas that includes inquiry, cocreation, connection, sharing, reuse, and reliability. Authors within this section emphasize these ideas in different ways, and offer practices from projects that move us closer to using participatory technologies to open knowledge in education. As they offer examples, they also describe key components of the culture of education that need to change to hasten the adoption of particular practices. Some of the ideas are individual (faculty members must change their focus), others are institutional (organizations must restructure), and others are all-encompassing (we must inculcate new values).

Key among these changes is a focus on student learning. Almost all of our authors remind us that student learning forms the foundation for knowledge building in education and that we must find ways to help faculty focus on this common goal and cultivate ways to pay attention to it. Oblinger and Lombardi (2008) encourage us to understand and apply contemporary learning strategies from students. Bass and Bernstein (2008) delve into this issue and share key strategies for helping faculty collaboratively make time and devote energy to focusing on student learning. Fong (2008) explains how faculty at her institution shifted to focus on student learning and argues that funding mechanisms must also follow suit, basing their budgets on student performance (and not seat time).

One complement of opening knowledge around student learning means changing how we develop teaching practice, be it face-to-face or not. Laurillard (2008), Gale, and Bass and Bernstein all talk of ways to use inquiry to open up the practice of teaching. Within networks, as individuals, and with various digital tools, they all consider the role of inquiry and the process of making one's practice useful to others. They also stress the need to build physical, digital, and social spaces in which faculty can engage in knowledge-building practices.

Authors in this section also describe knowledge generated in other areas of education and encourage us to change the way we think about merging all of these contributions. They think about and consider ways to extract and understand faculty and teacher knowledge of teaching practice, administrative knowledge of institutional support and reward, project leaders' knowledge of educational transformation and support, national leaders' knowledge of broad fields, as well as knowledge generated among these groups when they interact. How might tenets of community, participation, and knowledge building help aggregate all of this knowledge and make it useful?

Opening Knowledge Differs from Research

In some ways, opening knowledge in education follows a traditional research paradigm—it involves questioning, testing, reflecting, and disseminating findings. However, there are important distinctions that separate the two fields. First, Cambridge (2008) and Gale remind us that field building will happen through distributed leadership and among a broad base of contributors, and not among a limited circle of experts. Growth in this field will be collaborative and nonproprietary.

Second, collaboration is key. In "The Middle of Open Spaces" in this volume, Bass and Bernstein explain the unique and powerful role of faculty collaboration in opening knowledge in education. Not only are projects and work made more complex when many people contribute to it, they argue, "ideas and practices are more robust," and this activity helps local ideas take on larger forms of meaning.

Third, because leadership and knowledge will be distributed and cocreated, ideas around validating knowledge claims will need to change. Once educational knowledge sharing is truly open and collaborative, we can assume that dialogue and critique have occurred at all stages, that reviews of evidence among peers continuously happen, and that this process yields different, useful "results" for different collaborators. We therefore will need community-driven systems like those suggested by Iiyoshi and Richardson (2008), Laurillard, and Oblinger and Lombardi that help prioritize readings and synthesize contributions.

The potential for opening knowledge in education is immense. As our authors recognize, opening knowledge of teaching practice, educational transformation, and institutional change can help us reach our multiple goals for providing high quality education for all learners.

Challenged by Difference

As described above, opening educational knowledge cannot follow the rules of the research community—it's too different. Likewise, it cannot follow the precepts of the business community because, as Diana Laurillard reminds us, education is a political activity encasing the moral values of society. The clients here are youth, who often have no say in the products they "buy" from the educational market. And although we depend on technology to help us change, we cannot pace our change with technological development—changes in education happen much more slowly. We therefore must develop our own model for field development and growth, and develop the tools we need as we go.

We will need tools and resources to help teachers and lecturers develop, disseminate, and reuse pedagogies in generic forms. We also will need tools to help educators articulate and share their knowledge and be motivated to reuse and recontribute their knowledge. We will need ways to help the community find useful information. And we will need ways to sustain this field.

Generating and Extracting Knowledge

Tools for articulating and communicating our nascent and situational ideas about teaching and learning are important. Bass and Bernstein, Gale, and Laurillard all stress the importance of ease of use and guidance in using tools during this process. Dalziel (2008) and Iiyoshi and Richardson describe the development of particular tools that have helped ease the recording and retrieval of knowledge.

Some authors also look closely at the essential role of communities—open teaching and leadership communities—in generating knowledge. Laurillard outlines the components of this kind of community, and Bass and Bernstein specifically consider the role of faculty collaboration in generating, building, and validating knowledge claims. Others echo these emphases. But questions remain about how to develop tools that reflect the work of the community—to develop something more than a tool for commenting or critiquing.

Communicating Knowledge

Because the participants in this system all have different forms of situational knowledge, authors recognize numerous challenges to sharing what one person or group knows with another. Some of these challenges are technical (how might we develop fully interoperable systems for sharing), but most are ideological (how do we first capture what is known and then how does it move?).

While documentation is essential, authors variously refer to the role of intermediaries in synthesizing and disseminating what is known. Cambridge outlines the roles of intermediary groups in not only generating knowledge but in creating networks and in sustaining knowledge-building systems. She recognizes that intermediary people and projects hold a unique position for seeing and articulating accumulated knowledge. Other authors note that projects also have the benefit of creating safe middle spaces in which unlikely colleagues can convene and learn from each other. Issues around making the digital spaces that support convening fluid, easy to navigate, and responsive to change remain.

Sustaining Systems of Open Knowledge-Building Systems

Cambridge explains in her chapter that a knowledge-building society "presupposes open sharing of information and support of that sharing," and at various junctures our authors see a critical role for digital technologies to do this. They describe how digital tools have introduced new ways for us to access, deliver, share, and exchange knowledge with each other. But they also show that to deliver knowledge, to receive it, or to learn from others, stakeholders in education must create roles around exchange, methods, techniques, and strategies to foster interaction and collaboration.

Oblinger and Lombardi echo Jenkins's components of an emerging participatory culture that help us create these roles, which will be part of the basket of strategies we will need to sustain growth in knowledge of teaching and learning. Fong and Laurillard help us see which roles institutional administrators can play in sustaining a culture amenable to open educational change.

Huber and Hutchings (2008) speculate on future directions, conjecturing that both preserving and expanding openness about teaching and learning will remain central challenges for proponents of Open

Knowledge. Like other authors, they see key roles for experimentation, various forms of representation, policy makers, faculty, and technologists but they caution that increasing demands for "bottom-line forms of accountability" may decrease the current space we have for experimentation and exchange. Their view of the future reasserts the need for all of us to pay attention to and, if necessary, reshape our context.

Things to Think About

This section covers a wide range of territory. Authors discuss teaching and learning in U.S. community colleges, four-year colleges and universities, and higher education institutions in the UK. They also look at technology-enabled teaching as well as traditional classroom practices; propose new course redesign processes and ways that support of faculty teaching could change; and suggest how to drive educational innovation from the contributions of learners, teachers, lecturers, administrators, reformers, and policymakers.

Authors in this section therefore highlight a variety of concerns. As you read their chapters, you might ask:

• What role does opening knowledge play in promoting and sustaining systemic and systematic change? What are the various stages of change the authors describe—from the classroom to the institution—and the roles of various players, including faculty, external projects, and administrators?

• What are the implications for tools that may help capture and share knowledge?

• What is the role of intermediary projects, organizations, and people in sustaining movements and providing opportunities for shared thinking?

• How might the slow-to-change culture of education adapt elements inherent in a fast-paced technological world? When is it most appropriate to do so?

• What kinds of scaffolds and frameworks help introduce newcomers, carry novices further, and use the skills and attributes of "experts" to effectively nurture and encourage open knowledge?

Each of these chapters offers examples from various initiatives and makes different and overlapping proposals for effective ways to enhance student learning. Additionally, many initiatives and proposals in this section require the support of the open content and open technology described in sections one and two. All of these overlapping intentions and propositions show how it takes more than opening our classroom doors to keep up with the needs of education.

References

Bass, R., and Bernstein, D. (2008). The middle of open spaces: Generating knowledge about learning through multiple layers of open teaching communities. In T. Iiyoshi and M. S. V. Kumar (Eds.), *Opening Up Education: The Collective Advancement of Education through Open Technology, Open Content, and Open Knowledge*, pp. 303–317. Cambridge, MA: MIT Press.

Cambridge, B. (2008). Scaffolding for systemic change. In T. Iiyoshi and M. S. V. Kumar (Eds.), *Opening Up Education: The Collective Advancement of Education through Open Technology, Open Content, and Open Knowledge*, pp. 357–374. Cambridge, MA: MIT Press.

Dalziel, J. (2008). Learning Design: Sharing Pedagogical Know-How. In T. Iiyoshi and M. S. V. Kumar (Eds.), *Opening Up Education: The Collective Advancement of Education through Open Technology, Open Content, and Open Knowledge*, pp. 375–387. Cambridge, MA: MIT Press.

Fong, B. C. (2008). Community college perspective on open education. In T. Iiyoshi and M. S. V. Kumar (Eds.), *Opening Up Education: The Collective Advancement of Education through Open Technology, Open Content, and Open Knowledge*, pp. 401–415. Cambridge, MA: MIT Press.

Gale, R. A. (2008). Inquiry unplugged: A scholarship of teaching and learning for open understanding. In T. Iiyoshi and M. S. V. Kumar (Eds.), *Opening Up Education: The Collective Advancement of Education through Open Technology, Open Content, and Open Knowledge*, pp. 289–302. Cambridge, MA: MIT Press.

Huber, M. T., and Hutchings, P. (2008). What's next for open knowledge? In T. Iiyoshi and M. S. V. Kumar (Eds.), *Opening Up Education: The Collective Advancement of Education through Open Technology, Open Content, and Open Knowledge*, pp. 417–428. Cambridge, MA: MIT Press.

Iiyoshi, T., and Richardson, C. R. (2008). Promoting technology-enabled knowledge building and sharing for sustainable open educational innovations. In T. Iiyoshi and M. S. V. Kumar (Eds.), *Opening Up Education: The Collective Advancement of Education through Open Technology, Open Content, and Open Knowledge*, pp. 337–335. Cambridge, MA: MIT Press.

Jenkins, H. (2006, October 19). *Confronting the challenges of participatory culture: Media education for the 21st century*. Occasional paper for the MacArthur Foundation. Retrieved September 1, 2007, from http://digitallearning.macfound.org/atf/cf/{7E45C7E0-A3E0-4B89-AC9C-E807E1B0AE4E}/JENKINS_WHITE_PAPER.PDF

Laurillard, D. (2008). Open teaching: The key to sustainable and effective open education. In T. Iiyoshi and M. S. V. Kumar (Eds.), *Opening Up Education: The Collective Advancement of Education through Open Technology, Open Content, and Open Knowledge*, pp. 319–335. Cambridge, MA: MIT Press.

Oblinger, D. G., and Lombardi, M. M. (2008). Common knowledge: Openness in higher education. In T. Iiyoshi and M. S. V. Kumar (Eds.), *Opening Up Education: The Collective Advancement of Education through Open Technology, Open Content, and Open Knowledge*, pp. 389–400. Cambridge, MA: MIT Press.

19

Inquiry Unplugged: A Scholarship of Teaching and Learning for Open Understanding

Richard A. Gale

The heart of open education is the sharing of accumulated knowledge and developed resources that improve teaching, student learning, and research. The scholarship of teaching and learning thus is naturally committed to open education, for it has always supported and been sustained by open understanding of principles and practices, examples and exemplars, made available and usable to the broadest of publics. This commitment was reinforced in the closing plenary of the 2004 Colloquium on the Scholarship of Teaching and Learning, when Carnegie Foundation President Lee S. Shulman described "Scholarship as Community Property." In doing so, he directed attention from making teaching and learning a shared commodity and process, to making the scholarship of teaching and learning more than a private, isolated act (2004a). His charge, echoing that of open education, was to build knowledge that illuminates and improves student learning and faculty teaching, to encourage institutions to support and promote this form of scholarship, and to establish a field of endeavor and expertise that facilitates the sharing of what Shulman calls "the wisdom of practice." To achieve this, students and teachers, administrators and staff, policymakers and the public at large would need to view learning, teaching, and scholarship in new and more collaborative ways.

Recently, Carnegie Foundation Senior Scholar and Knowledge Media Laboratory Director Toru Iiyoshi echoed this viewpoint, writing that "a crucial task before us is to build intellectual and technical capacity for transforming 'tacit knowledge' into 'commonly usable knowledge'" and that "true success in open education requires a change in education culture and policy" (2006). What Iiyoshi suggests moves far beyond the scholarship of teaching and learning, but is very much in concert with the objectives, processes, and on-the-ground realities of what it means to observe, investigate, examine, and apply knowledge and evidence of student learning within a wider and more public arena. These challenges have always been central to the Carnegie Academy for the Scholarship of Teaching and Learning (CASTL) Higher Education Program and its mission to understand and encourage, defend and disseminate, champion and support a scholarship of teaching and learning by making it visible and developing leadership for the field.

Since 1998, CASTL has built on the work of the 1990 publication, *Scholarship Reconsidered*, and the 1997 follow-up, *Scholarship Assessed*, creating a multifaceted program to support the work of individual faculty, campuses, societies, and other organizations committed to research that expands understanding of student learning through inquiry, peer review, and public dissemination. On one level, CASTL has been an exemplar of open understanding, committed through its philosophy and practice to the sharing of information and the cocreation of knowledge in an atmosphere of nonproprietary collaboration and collective scholarship. Viewed another way, it has also been a remarkably successful structure for field building through distributed leadership. This decade of dedicated work has helped to accomplish a change in the way higher education thinks about and acts on the knowledge that has been (and still needs to be) gathered with regard to student learning and assessment, faculty work and success, institutional mission and the manifestation of shared commitments to the teaching and learning process.

In creating CASTL's signature approach, key features contribute to the formation of open knowledge. These include attention to and cultivation of faculty commitment to gathering evidence of student learning, building capacity for leadership on campuses and within disciplines, and scaffolding individual and institutional definitions and examples of teaching and learning scholarship. Another key feature has been the creation of a support system that has grown from a handful of individuals working on a project on the scholarship of teaching and learning at a think tank in California, into an international movement embracing change initiatives in multiple countries, on several continents.

Overview of Structures and Strategies

From the beginning, CASTL has been dedicated to open education in all its forms. It has embraced open technology and the use of straightforward and public tools to aid understanding, scaffold inquiry, collect evidence, and "go public" with results; open content in the form of scholarly questions, a transparent investigatory process, and venues for dissemination and discussion; and open knowledge that informs and influences individual teaching and learning processes, transforms teaching and learning wisdom of practice from a private or semiprivate knowledge set to a public form of "community property" available and usable by all.

Working at the level of individual faculty scholarship, the CASTL Scholars Program created a signature approach to the cultivation of exemplars who changed how student learning was observed and evidence was gathered in the college classroom. This was accomplished by selecting faculty already committed to improving student learning and well placed to become leaders within their disciplines or on their campuses, working with them to build a community of scholars conversant in the process of inquiry and the projects of their cohort, then charging them with the responsibility to engage others in the scholarship of teaching and learning after their year of residence. The program's mantra has always included the understanding that work of this sort only matters to students and faculty if it is "passed on" to others, often within a disciplinary context.

Disciplinary work has always been a central feature of the CASTL initiative, most significantly through the Scholarly and Professional Societies Program, which sought to embed the scholarship of teaching and learning into the home of so much significant faculty work. The premise: Since most teaching and learning occurs within a disciplinary context, and most disciplines (or professional societies) operate through guiding and defining organizations, it was important that scholarly and professional societies understood, embraced, and validated this vital form of research, helping to embed it into so much significant faculty work. Locating the scholarship of teaching and learning in the disciplines has implications not only for undergraduate teaching and learning in individual fields, but for the future of how each field is understood and promoted through graduate education (Gale and Golde, 2005).

CASTL also created a Campus Program to bring the scholarship of teaching and learning discussion to individual schools and collaborative systems at the regional, national, and international levels, organizing a process of institutionalization that has moved from issues of definition and support to processes of leadership development and sustainability. This initially took the form of "campus conversations," promoted through our longtime partner organization, the American Association for Higher Education (AAHE), and then expanded during my time as senior scholar to include the campus clusters. After the clusters completed their work in 2005, another structure was designed to strengthen the role of the scholarship of teaching and learning among campuses poised to become leaders for what was clearly a growing movement. The Institutional Leadership Program, begun in 2006 and running through 2009, involves nearly 100 campuses, societies, and educational organizations from seven countries in a commitment to engaging locally, expanding regionally and nationally, working thematically, and building collectively toward the future. Among the themes serving as organizing features of this program are the role of the scholarship of teaching and learning in accreditation and assessment, liberal education, graduate education, and undergraduate research.

Finally, and in some ways most significantly, CASTL has been instrumental in bringing students and administrative leaders into the equation. Students are now viewed not only as a source of data or investigation, but as coinvestigators and collaborative scholars interested in and committed to improving understanding of the complicated and often opaque world of student learning. Likewise, through leadership forums and dedicated events, CASTL has been working to build knowledge and understanding among the individuals best positioned to make change on campus and within academic associations, including administrators, center directors, faculty leaders, and others. This, in concert with the Institutional Leadership Program, promises to have the greatest impact on the acceptance and influence of the scholarship of teaching and learning internationally (Gale, 2005).

The Goal of the Goal

Behind the work of the scholarship of teaching and learning is a teeming landscape of thought and practice, understanding and action, belief and engagement. Because teaching and learning are so hard to see and know, they are even harder to systematically analyze and improve. One reason why policymakers have turned their attention to the clamor and cry for assessment and accountability is higher education's "black box" of classroom excellence and student success. If the so-called "best practices" of teaching and learning could be identified and articulated beyond local environs, shared in a transparent and transferable mode with an assurance of accomplishment at the end of the day, then educators the world over might be convinced to embrace change. But the current reality for most higher education institutions is that learning is contextual and unexamined, teaching is ephemeral and private, and scholarship on both is frequently limited in scope and impact by the restrictions of the academy and the lack of resources (variously defined from funding to reward structures).

An underlying tenet of the scholarship of teaching and learning is that an evidence-based approach to understanding and improving student learning and faculty teaching can create significant pedagogical change locally and beyond when experience and wisdom of teaching practice are transformed from a private knowledge set available to only a limited audience, into a public form of community property available to all. Transformation of knowledge occurs by applying disciplinary and transdisciplinary scholarly processes to the study of one's own teaching, gathering convincing artifacts and evidence of student learning, and sharing the results of inquiry with interested, appropriate, and often influential audiences. This process values scholarship that is made public and used beyond the classroom where it was developed. Programs seeking to achieve these goals must be motivated by the need to systemically improve teaching and learning in higher education. They should build on the realities of faculty work, and be based not in a speculative theory of action but on the experience of working teachers committed to improving their own practice and the growth of the field. At the core, the scholarship of teaching and learning is about improving student learning through a deeper understanding of what students do, how students learn, and what students experience in college and university classrooms.

CASTL has always focused on student needs, faculty strengths, and administrative commitments to cultivate scholars and scholarly leaders dedicated to learning from student learning and passing that learning on to larger constituents. Of late, motivation has also been provided by changes in funding and support, as well as by a shift in emphasis away from centralized organizational structures to a distributed model of leadership and impact. As such, the program embraces the premise that student learning, faculty teaching, reflective inquiry, and institutional assessment work together toward improvement of the educational enterprise only when all aspects of the process are open to review and revision, understanding and use. In some cases, this enterprise can be part of a culture of evidence and inquiry, scaffolded through new media and innovative technologies, integrated into a "braided practice" involving disciplinary expertise, pedagogical experience, and scholarly inquiry (Gale, 2007).

Thus far, CASTL has contributed to the growth of the field via many types of interventions. But with the advent of its Institutional Leadership Program, new partners have entered into the work and familiar friends have taken their efforts to a new level, often in connection with allied campus initiatives or new systemic mandates. Impact has included significant growth in the number of faculty involved and substantial commitment from teaching and learning centers, as well as an increasing number of campuses and scholarly societies taking this kind of work seriously and giving it prominence in conferences or publications, and considerable progress internationally. This last has been especially noteworthy in Canada, where organizations like the Council for Higher Education Research and Development (CHERD) and the Society for Teaching and Learning in Higher Education (STLHE), and regional consortia in the Atlantic Provinces and British Columbia have worked to build capacity for the scholarship of teaching and learning. Great progress has also been made in the UK and Australia, Europe and Asia, where the scholarship of teaching and learning appears under the rubric of educational or pedagogical research. But while the Carnegie Foundation's work certainly informs this activity, the movement in support of a scholarship of teaching and learning continues to grow independent of its influence, contributing to an ever-expanding community of scholars sharing practice, reviewing evidence, and creating an open marketplace for improvement. The sign of a healthy, thriving concept is often the extent to which it extends beyond a single source, a single perspective. Given the amount of work in the scholarship of teaching and learning happening worldwide, and the extent to which these efforts subscribe to the values of free and open access, Carnegie's program is just one model of engagement in a growing movement.

The Accretive Model of Knowledge Building

One of the most important aspects of open knowledge and open education is the extent to which good ideas (and in some cases unsuccessful attempts) are made available for others to examine, interrogate, and build on. The culture that surrounds and enacts the scholarship of teaching and learning relies on a cycle of inquiry that has the public sharing of evidence as its connective tissue, its foundational infrastructure. Like an oyster's pearl that grows from a grain of sand into a valued commodity, the open knowledge of the scholarship of teaching and learning builds from commonplace observation of student learning in a single class—accumulating evidence and example through investigation and inquiry, using additive elements like peer review and institutional validation—until it becomes an accretive whole with significance for all who encounter it.

This additive model of inquiry extends beyond the process of observation and investigation to how questions about student learning build upon the work of others and work yet to come. Here the premises of open knowledge become guiding practices—inquiry cannot exist without open access to work that came before, ongoing investigation cannot thrive without critical analysis provided through transparency, and evidentiary datasets cannot influence practice in the absence of wide dissemination to informed and interested audiences. As with any form of scholarship, the process of seeing and reflecting, thinking and knowing, necessitates scaffolding, support, and critical exchange from outside the sphere of inquiry. Ideally, such underpinning can occur organically within a supportive community, but often it requires a formal structure and a thoughtful plan.

Some of this scaffolding has been intentional, forging connections between individual scholars, campuses, and participants in programs through electronic and other means. The new media supporting this work are in some sense the Carnegie Foundation's most important contributions to open education. With its commitment to resources and knowledge sharing, Carnegie developed and made public a wide variety of tools and technologies that have proven successful at building capacity and sustainability, including the now ubiquitous KEEP Toolkit and Sakai-based Workspaces for Carnegie scholars and institutional representatives. Pedagogical approaches have been central to using these tools, the most successful being the nested snapshot approach to project development (pioneered between 2001 and 2006), which guides beginning scholars of teaching and learning through the process of identifying, narrowing, and investigating the questions that are the genesis of inquiry. The series of guided snapshots that led scholars from inquiry to evidence also shifted the emphasis of their own dissemination from reportage to reflection. So successful is this approach that it has been used in other Carnegie programs as well, from the Initiative on the Doctorate to the Integrative Learning Project.

Nesting and accretion have also been important in the development of organizational capacity, publication outlets, online community structures, convening venues, and other means for creating and sharing knowledge related to the scholarship of teaching and learning. Journals dedicated to this form of scholarship continue to appear, including *MountainRise* and the *International Journal for the Scholarship of Teaching and Learning*, while other established outlets for dissemination increasingly turn their attention to this work. In fact, the journal *Science* recently recognized the importance of educational research in an editorial by Editor-in-Chief Donald Kennedy and Thomas Cech (president of the Howard Hughes Medical Institute), which stated that "learning is not a spectator sport" and "science and the teaching of science are inseparable," affirming their commitment to explore how to connect research and teaching for the benefit of both student and professor (Cech and Kennedy, 2005). Within the last few years an International Society for the Scholarship of Teaching and Learning (ISSOTL) has grown out of this movement, its ranks swelling to nearly 1,000 members and conference attendees in 2006, with venues ranging from Bloomington, Indiana, to Sydney, New South Wales, to Edmonton, Alberta. Similar growth in commitment to the scholarship of teaching and learning is evident within established organizations ranging from the Professional and Organizational Development (POD) Network and the aforementioned Canadian STLHE, to the Council on Undergraduate Research (CUR) and the Association of American Geographers (AAG).

Coordinated Scholarship and the Development of Sustainable Leadership

As the examples above suggest, of all the mechanisms and approaches, strategies and structures, none has been more important to the success of open scholarship of teaching and learning initiatives than the building of supportive and critical connections, collaborations, communities, and collectives. From the local collaborations of individual faculty, to the coordinated initiatives of campuses and other institutional groups, to the collective and unified efforts of multi-institutional consortia, it is the shared nature of teaching and learning scholarship that is most likely to have sustained and significant impact. It is also in the arena of such connected inquiry that observation and investigation, review and dissemination, all become significantly improved (one might go so far as to say that they only become possible on a regional, systemic, or disciplinary scale) in an environment of open knowledge-building, open understanding, and open critique. Such cooperation has been the stock-in-trade of multiple regional, national, international, and theme-based initiatives.

Cooperation has also been the watchword for Carnegie's efforts to promote the scholarship of teaching and learning widely, and to cultivate leadership for such efforts. Even before the term existed, CASTL worked within the premises of open education, and its efforts have always been predicated on the idea that, as understanding about the scholarship of teaching and learning is made public, increased responsibility for growth and sustainability will transfer to a widening ring of organizations and institutions committed to the movement. To achieve this goal, however, more institutions need to take on the mantle of leadership, increase their level of association, and create collaborative groups that are self-sustaining. Through leadership development, the cultivation of individuals and institutional structures committed to the premises and practices of the scholarship of teaching and learning, and the incorporation of multiple partners into ongoing and new initiatives, CASTL contributes to the cause of open inquiry. It also facilitates the creation of an open environment for investigation and collaboration by establishing benchmarks and touchstones for those new to the work and still developing a common language, common goals, and common experiences linked through a common organizational structure.

For this environment to thrive, for the scholarship of teaching and learning to continue its influence on institutions and improvement of student learning, access is critical. But access is often a feature of shared operational features and common understandings. The challenge is the great variability of venues for use and expansion. This translates to open education more generally, because of the variety of initiatives, participants, and potential users. In a very real sense, the challenge of open understanding with regard to a scholarship of teaching and learning is in synchronizing (or at least providing opportunities for connection and comparison) what happens at home with what happens elsewhere. And for that to happen, there needs to be a new vision of leadership, at the local level and beyond. Throughout its decade of operation, CASTL has been committed to distributing authority and leadership, and developing the capacities of individuals, institutions, and coalitions.

By training exemplars, organizing consortia, encouraging venues for dissemination, and linking innovations (as a kind of intellectual yenta), CASTL and its operatives have helped to build a sustainable network of expertise and experience, vision and viability, built on a platform of transparency and open access. If other organizations and initiatives are to follow a similar path, they will need a multifaceted community of graduate students, faculty, campuses, scholarly societies, and other educational spokespeople and institutions with deep understanding and appreciation of the scholarship of teaching and learning within an open education context, as well as commitment to its use and adaptation as a shared endeavor not bounded by proprietary issues of ownership. This kind of community would have the strength and depth to allow new and ongoing initiatives to develop in creative ways, and would be supported by institutional structures and external organizations committed to advancement and excellence, sharing their local and transnational experience while maintaining the connections necessary to follow the unbroken line of influence from innovation back to innovator, working within current and familiar forums but also cultivating new venues for action and inquiry.

Expanding the scholarly community also requires changing the rhetoric of inquiry and the ways research is defined and discussed, offering alternative views of and access points to new knowledge and experience, and creating new opportunities for engagement between various (and often geographically distinct) individuals and institutions. It suggests the need to identify and share (or perhaps even create) scenarios with the potential for self-propagation, to encourage development of high-profile participants who can serve as exemplars, and to expand access in ways that will foster security through guidance and mentorship, providing models of engagement with the scholarship of teaching and learning as an open collaborative experience. In other words, seeing the work of classroom inquiry as a contribution to open understanding and open education requires a new vision of peer review.

Peer Review as the Dream of a Common Language

In most disciplines and interdisciplines, the sharing, validation, and ultimate acceptance of new knowledge falls under the purview of peer review. It is a way to communicate the processes and results of authentic inquiry, authorized as such by well-informed, unbiased colleagues. Peer review tends to be considered the final adjudication process for scholarship, a validation of findings. When viewed as an integral, indispensable part of an open approach to education and its improvement, however, where dialogue and critique occur at all stages, an informed and informative context is less the domain of expertise and more the province of ongoing experience, and continuing analysis and improvement is the goal rather than penultimate determination prior to public review, then peer review becomes another animal entirely. Indeed, when evidence and its review by knowledgeable peers becomes part of the process of inquiry (as it has been with many institutional manifestations of the scholarship of teaching and learning), improvement and accountability become part of the warp and weft of scholarly practice.

Imagine a process by which researchers engaged in an inquiry project, studying student learning and the teaching that makes it work, receive regular assistance and review from peers both local and remote. Consider the benefits to scholars and peers when knowledge is shared with a connected, collaborative community throughout the process of investigation. When researchers and peers engage in mutual review as an integral part of the inquiry process, they establish a rich assortment of experiences that illuminate the complexities of this burgeoning scholarship, and they develop a common language of analysis that certainly borrows from disciplinary nomenclature but often goes well beyond. Unlike purely disciplinary research, the scholarship of teaching and learning often relies on a mélange of interpretive methodologies and evidence-gathering strategies; therefore, the peers for this kind of scholarship may not be found within the discipline (even though that is usually the first place we look). CASTL frequently champions the idea of involving peers from dissimilar disciplines to serve as "critical friends" during the inquiry process, precisely because disciplinary predispositions often get in the way of thoughtful analysis. In sharing approaches and strategies, venues and vehicles, scholars of teaching and learning expand their knowledge base and cultivate a wider, more open and accessible community of reflective peers. This last is vital for the more formal review that occurs during prepublication, and is an integral part of including the scholarship of teaching and learning in the retention, tenure, and promotion process.

Opportunities for Educational Change

The crux of all efforts to broaden the influence of the scholarship of teaching and learning is the conscious development of a community of scholars. From faculty-in-residence, to campus representatives working in collaboration, to all stakeholders working in coordination, CASTL has sought transparency and transferability of its products and processes. Staging has been the key for development of familiarity, creativity, and expanded use of tools, techniques, knowledge, and understanding, with scaffolding being essential in the early stages. Through work with hundreds of scholars and institutions, we see how one series of open education projects working as a cohesive initiative can help change the definitions of scholarship and influence classroom teaching practices around the world. Openly sharing knowledge of teaching and learning dramatically increases the role of inquiry in open education, and has enormous potential for changing the way faculty observe, think about, talk about, and transform their teaching practices. Likewise, this work has brought about a change in the understanding of what it means to view, study, and learn from student learning.

This approach to open understanding, while valuable to all professional and scholarly development programs, could also be applied to other venues and vehicles. Indeed, any knowledge-building initiative dedicated to open access, use, and collaboration might learn from the CASTL example (which was itself created in part from lessons learned in the peer review of teaching, the portfolio movement, teacher training programs, and collaborative classroom practice). By cultivating commitment among already interested individuals, building in a support and communication system with a leadership component, and scaffolding both individual and institutional definition by example, any initiative might work toward growth and sustainability of open knowledge and practice. Such has been the case with many individual scholars, who have expanded their own experience into leadership roles on campus, within disciplinary societies, and in tandem with other international initiatives from undergraduate research and support of STEM teaching and learning to affective development and attention to the aesthetic in student work. Likewise, the open understanding process has been central to collaborative groups from campus clusters to system-wide development practices, building from the one to the many, from the many to (in some cases) the whole. As with all open education initiatives, the key is a commitment to scholarly practice that looks beyond the individual classroom, public critique that engages and informs, and dissemination that sparks further work and leads the way for future practitioners. The CASTL model is one of openness from beginning to end, from research to resources, from practice to leadership.

Open education offers the opportunity to expand impact through access to individual faculty work, collaborative inquiry at individual institutions, and collective scholarship across multiple stakeholder environments. As the premises of CASTL and the scholarship of teaching and learning have always been directed to the sharing of information and the cocreation of knowledge, open education provides an important avenue for change and growth. Perhaps the best way to imagine the future of open understanding through open education, and the role of inquiry in this process, again comes from Lee S. Shulman's 2004 address on scholarship as community property, subtitled "From knowledge building, to field building . . . and back again." If anything encapsulates the work and development of the scholarship of teaching and learning, it is the ways in which knowledge is created in an open environment as a precursor to building a field of inquiry and investigation available to all, and the ways in which *that inquiry itself* builds new knowledge sets for future use and revision. This cycle of teaching and learning scholarship, this vision of public inquiry and utility resulting from private curiosity and investigation, is the key to open knowledge, open learning, and open understanding.

References

Carnegie Foundation for the Advancement of Teaching. See http://www .carnegiefoundation.org/programs/CASTL

Cech, T., and Kennedy, D. (2005, December 16). Doing more for Kate. *Science*, 310, 1741.

Gale, R. (2005, Fall). Leading from your strengths: Institutional identity and the scholarship of teaching and learning. *UTS Newsletter* [The University of Manitoba], 14(1), 1–3.

Gale, R. (2007). Braided practice: The place of scholarly inquiry in teaching excellence. In A. Skelton (Ed.), *International Perspectives on Teaching Excellence in Higher Education*. Oxford, UK: Routledge.

Gale, R., and Babb, M. (2004). Learning along the way. In B. Cambridge (Ed.), *Campus Progress: Supporting the Scholarship of Teaching and Learning*. Washington, DC: AAHE.

Gale, R., and Golde, C. (2004, Spring). Doctoral education and the scholarship of teaching and learning. *Peer Review*, 6(3).

Huber, M. T., and Hutchings, P. (2005). *The Advancement of Learning: Building the Teaching Commons*. San Francisco, CA: Jossey-Bass.

Hutchings, P. (Ed.). (2000). *Opening Lines: Approaches to the Scholarship of Teaching and Learning*. Menlo Park, CA: The Carnegie Foundation for the Advancement of Teaching.

Iiyoshi, T. (2006, April). Opportunity is knocking: Will education open the door? *Carnegie Perspectives*. The Carnegie Foundation for the Advancement of Teaching. Retrieved from http://www.carnegiefoundation.org/perspectives/sub .asp?key=245&subkey=1151

Shulman, L. S. (2004a, April 1). Scholarship as community property: From knowledge building to field building . . . and back again. Closing plenary for the CASTL Colloquium on the Scholarship of Teaching and Learning, San Diego, CA.

Shulman, L. S. (2004b). *Teaching as Community Property: Essays on Higher Education*. San Francisco, CA: Jossey-Bass.

Shulman, L. S. (2004c). *The Wisdom of Practice: Essays on Teaching, Learning, and Learning to Teach*. San Francisco, CA: Jossey-Bass.

The Middle of Open Spaces: Generating Knowledge about Learning through Multiple Layers of Open Teaching Communities

Randall Bass and Dan Bernstein

What is the role of faculty collaboration around teaching and learning in open education? Given the complexity of teaching and learning, and the shared nature of the responsibility for the curriculum, what is the role of individuals, their pedagogical knowledge, and reflection? When faculty look closely at the complexities of teaching and learning, they confront how much of their students' learning is out of their control, outside the boundaries of the semester or the individual course. This is one of the ironic dimensions of the *learning paradigm*: A more systematic focus on learning drives faculty into their own practice; yet, taking the complexity and fluidity of learning seriously diminishes the importance of any one course experience. In essence, the very learning paradigm that asks us to look more closely at teaching and learning demands that the turn to learning be about more than individual teaching practice. This is simultaneously generative and disruptive. If the characteristics of open education include open sharing of knowledge in various types of communities of practice, then a key challenge for open education's intersection with the scholarship of teaching and learning is finding ways to translate this generative disruption arising from faculty inquiry learning into a textured dialogue about meaningful knowledge-building practices that can be integrated into the professional lives of faculty and students.

While we recognize the limits of the knowledge generated by inquiry into individual faculty practice, this does not imply that the only valid studies are large-scale research projects undertaken across large populations. A challenge for the scholarship of teaching and learning movement in open education contexts is to find ways to combine, aggregate, and synthesize insights from local and individual practice into larger forms of meaning. And it is a challenge for open education systems to make this community and collaboration-based inquiry accessible, fluid, and rhythmic within the professional practices of education.

We propose that a key location for the scholarship of teaching and learning is in a middle ground between what we might call the "individual" and the "cosmopolitan." These two ends of a spectrum are often the focus of scholarly teaching and the scholarship of teaching: the individual engaging in reflection for the improvement of his or her own practice and the individual published work available for others more generally. There is a loop between them in that many individuals draw on cosmopolitan resources while some individuals aspire to produce written or digital work that contributes to a general body of literature. Thus, by "middle ground" we mean work that falls between individual practice and the world of generalized knowledge about teaching and learning. In some ways, this is related to the middle level of Keith Trigwell's three-tiered definition of the scholarship of teaching and learning, in which work is undertaken "by and for a community" (Trigwell, Martin, Benjamin, and Prosser, 2000, p. 159). Our sense of this middle space—what often will be local but could be virtually achieved communities of practice—is not merely one version of the scholarship of teaching and learning, but an essential link between individual practice and the eventual construction of knowledge in open systems. Perhaps this middle level is *the* critical bridge between the logic of the learning paradigm that turns us inward and the implications of a broader notion of learning that draws us outward.

So what would these middle spaces look like? We propose that they would typically involve collaborations by groups of individuals. They might have the shape of faculty inquiry groups or research collaboratives. They might have more or less formal structure; they might be tied to innovations (for example online learning or the use of new tools for learning), or tied to curricular reforms (a new general education program), or to dimensions of learning (for example writing across the curriculum). Regardless of their nature and how they are deployed, these middle spaces for inquiry into teaching and learning are an essential component for the success of open education.

There is well-established literature in feminist and cultural studies related to middle spaces or third spaces. These safe, hybrid spaces are conceptualized as separate from formal structures and boundaries. The middle ground of open education probably depends on very similar kinds of spaces and networks, but they are safe not just because they are informal and not tied to high stakes processes (like promotion and tenure). These middles spaces are also safe potentially because they offer collaborative interdisciplinary expertise that provides some rigor for looking at learning in its fuller complexity.

In these middle spaces, learning should be seen through the lens of a shared responsibility for the curriculum, and this ultimately defines how faculty in this middle space might function as communities of practice. First and foremost, they share questions that arise from shared curricular responsibility or from shared intellectual interests around "problems" belonging to the pedagogies of the disciplines or professions. These can be both faculty inquiry groups (locally convened) or broader social networks developed around common practices—disciplinary or interdisciplinary connections.

Potentially, this ripples out in concentric ways: Faculty in an institution grapple with a shared responsibility for learning, higher education links with K-12 education, and faculty across disciplines and professions should share and build knowledge about optimal education for a given field or practice. Open education and knowledge sharing is a way to address a growing divide between the integrative logic of the learning paradigm and the particularized dis-integrated nature of higher education, where knowledge—and by extension matters of teaching, learning, and the curriculum—are increasingly rationalized in terms of disciplines and subdisciplines.

We will now look at two examples of multi-institutional projects that connected scholars beyond individual work but in different ways. We will look at how each of these two "middle space" communities functioned, as well as what is instructive about their differences from each other. We will conclude with implications for where these projects might go next and for open education in general.

Prototype Communities of Collaborative Practice

Like many others in higher education, we aim to maximize the success of students enrolled in our institutions. This means that students reach a very rich and deep level of understanding and that a broad sample of students succeed in attaining those course goals. Attaining that goal promotes an additional motivation for teachers, namely that they want to answer questions about the best ways to teach and to share with colleagues new ways to encourage learning.

Peer Review of Teaching

Faculty members are accustomed to peers examining and commenting on their scholarly work, and we brought this same social context to reviewing students' understanding of the intellectual goals of a course. We invited faculty members to treat teaching as serious intellectual work, with products that merit the same careful consideration and review as other faculty activities. Based on the notion of making teaching "community property" (Hutchings, 1996; Shulman, 2004), faculty members met in face-to-face groups and read about teaching, shared their own work, and provided largely formative commentary for each other. As the supportive collaboration evolved, faculty members constructed course portfolios (Cerbin, 1994) that were literally collections of paper produced by students (for example exams, term projects, other assignments). A conventional linear essay accompanied the portfolio, reflected on how well the student work achieved the goals of the course, and identified the next steps in delivering the course to further students' success.

The first versions of these portfolios represented a benchmark of the current level of learning demonstrated by students and the learning faculty members derived from teaching and writing about their courses. As these portfolios were shared and read, some faculty members followed their own reflective conclusions and enacted the changes in course design they proposed. The existence of the open community of scholars provided a context that supported development beyond a benchmark of learning. These faculty members entered a culture of inquiry into learning, and later versions of portfolios show a trajectory of course development and change.

Faculty members were very engaged by the community of collaborative inquiry, and a consortium of similar universities emerged to share the work in a broader context. Participating faculty members met in brief conferences to share the best examples of their local collaborative work to identify the best ways to sustain the interactions at each university.

With many examples of individual course portfolios ready, we asked for an arm's length of commentary that would remain constructively helpful, but take a turn toward being evaluative as well. The prospect of passing around bulky paper portfolios inspired the creation of better ways to support the intellectual exchange.

The first change was our use of threaded discussions in a course management tool, allowing asynchronous work by faculty members. The exchange of comments was easier, and they could continue their interactions in the month-long intervals between meetings. Although the exchanges were organized in pairs, the discussions were visible to other group members, greatly increasing the potential value of each commentary. The second change emerged from observation of electronic representations of teaching artifacts and reflection in the Visible Knowledge Project (VKP). We hired a Web developer to adapt our course portfolio structure to a Web-based format, and we began sharing course portfolios through a Web site dedicated to the peer review of teaching. This format was ideal for quick navigation among descriptions and reflections and gave access to examples of digitized student work.

At this point we had three levels of making the work public. Each faculty member began by posting individual pieces of the work within a threaded discussion, receiving comments used to refine the work. The Web staff gathered the pieces together with student work samples and created an organized course portfolio, reviewed and revised by the author. Only then would the faculty participants from the consortium have access to the course portfolio to offer comments, and the author could revise again before the course portfolio was made public. That site now has over 200 course portfolios, with a searchable index that allows visitors to find work that matches their interests (for a full description, please see Bernstein, Burnett, Goodburn, and Savory, 2006).

The primary success from the Peer Review of Teaching Project (PRTP) has been the development of an open community of university teachers who present and reflect on the success of their intellectual work as teachers. Many faculty members use what they read in the work of other teachers, but fewer experience critical review and redirection of the kind they receive in other areas of scholarly work. There are some examples of promotion or tenure influenced by serious peer review of teaching and learning, but there is not yet a consensual conceptual map of the criteria for reviewing teaching and learning. The development of such a shared vision would greatly enhance the use of the open access to student and faculty work.

By using clear benchmarks of quality, we can use the evaluation work teachers routinely do to sustain a community of evidence-based teaching and estimate the trajectory of teaching and learning success over time. The primary question being asked is "Do these courses generate learning valued by students and programs?" Archives of student work also make it possible to track the complexity of the goals achieved by students. With this foundation, we look for insights about how practice has impact across courses, institutions, and fields. While deeply respecting, and drawing from, the cosmopolitan world of educational research, this community inhabits a middle space in which informal individual inquiry into learning is shared as a community resource. The middle space supports innovation and collaboration, but at a level of engagement commensurate with the realities of a teaching professor's professional life.

The Visible Knowledge Project

The Visible Knowledge Project was designed as a multiyear scholarship of teaching and learning project exploring the impact of technology on learning, primarily in the humanities (English, History, American Studies, Cultural Studies, Visual Art, and other fields). The project created a community of 60 to 70 scholars from 21 institutions who interacted over a period of years around shared questions. On core campuses, faculty participated in local research groups of four to six people that supported individual inquiries and developed shared, emergent findings. Faculty across institutions at the national level formed affinity groups along issues of teaching practice and learning themes. These cross-project themes complemented the individual practice and local faculty inquiry groups creating a scholarly discourse community built out of emergent and cross-connecting threads.

The focus of the VKP was on what faculty can learn about their students' learning by examining it in new and closer ways. We wanted to understand better what a group or community of teachers could learn if they looked at their own practice together over time. In contrast to the PRTP, we did have a specific change agenda: We wanted to investigate "constructivist pedagogies," inquiry-based approaches that begin with student knowledge and experience, and to investigate "cognitive apprenticeship," a theory of pedagogy that asks students to make their mental processes visible.

The VKP embodied characteristics of open education systems from the beginning, in exploring the knowledge that could be produced by a community of scholars asking a related set of questions, together, over time, and openly sharing insights, feedback, and mutual influence at every stage of the process. As we often asked at our gatherings: *What work can we do together that we cannot do as effectively as individuals?* We asked faculty to ask themselves the most important questions they could about student learning in their courses. How did they know that their students were learning? Did the students' learning promise to last? What did teachers really know about the processes of their students' learning, especially what we called "intermediate processes," or the processes that experienced or expert learners employ habitually in their work but that are often tacit or absent in instruction? By asking these questions, many faculty members discovered early on that what most interested—or eluded—them about their students' learning could not be answered simply by looking at regularly assigned course work. Put another way, examining the graded work that was part of a course raised questions that the work alone could not answer.

This individual insight also had a transformative impact as a result of the open collaborative atmosphere of the project. Something happens to the quality and nature of questions when faculty start asking them together and considering issues about learning that emerge from multiple projects. When dealing with matters of innovation alone for example, faculty tend to ask questions such as: Is this working? Can I do this better? Can students perform better this way? How do I assess this work? What kinds of learning do I see? In groups or collaborations, through interaction, discussion and critique that supports each other's work, faculty start to ask broader questions that could not be answered by looking at just a single course: What are the underlying competencies of this work? How does this work reveal developing expertise in new and expanded ways? What are the implications for the development of certain literacies or competencies over time? How would this learning fit into a course of study? How would these skills fit into a curriculum?

This broadening of questions opens up possibilities for the nature and value of knowledge that can be generated from any one faculty member's practice-focused inquiry. Two brief examples from the VKP will help illustrate the point. One collaborative emerged within the project around a specific pedagogical practice known as "digital stories," which are compact multimedia narratives created by students in a variety of course contexts. Implemented across a range of course contexts such as cultural history, ethnic literature, African American and other areas of US history, and others, digital stories raise compelling questions about assignment structure, modeling, scaffolding, and assessment. While each individual course context offers potential best practices, there is also cross-fertilization among participating faculty around issues of multimedia literacy, intersections of creativity and complexity, and challenges of assessing for the full range of learning. Similarly, another group within the discipline of history found commonality around using visual materials in teaching history (typically a text-based discipline), and through sharing their pedagogical rationale and examples of their students' work there emerged a cluster of essays around the "problem of the visual" in the teaching of history (Coventry, et al., 2006).

While individual projects yielded interesting stories of classroom practice, in the open context of the project there emerged across projects such shared products as rubrics for assessing new forms of student work and models for understanding novice-expert development in these new, complex, and hybrid forms of learning. The faculty engaged in open and communal inquiry underwent a powerful shift in their vision of the ways their teaching practice had an impact on student learning and the complexity of that exchange. Collaboration and open sharing became a key means for mediating the disruptive discovery of the complexity of teaching and learning into a dialogue and process that could easily document and translate certain insights into representations that others could build on.

Within the VKP, we saw this phenomenon on two levels. At the level of stories of teaching practice informed by student learning, the faculty cases were more complete. They represented thoughtful enterprises (like the PRTP inquiry portfolios): Faculty make observations about their teaching and their students' learning; they make an inquiry (which might include an innovation) into some dimension or question emerging from those observations; they then collect and analyze new evidence, and arrive at insights for further revision in practice.

At the same time, what emerges from every story of teaching practice is what we might think of as "fragments of insight" about learning in a particular field and context. The VKP conceptualized representation of its more summative and collective findings through syntheses of these fragments that effectively build knowledge for others. This is the challenge, and opportunity, for open education. But the key lesson from the VKP is that unlike closed and more competitive systems of publishing and scholarship, knowledge building in open systems is characterized by filtering and dialogue that leads to synthesis as or more often than selection.

All this also suggests a *developmental* model potentially different from or complementary to traditional scholarship. What if we strove to introduce faculty to the scholarship of teaching and learning initially as a foundational professional practice to improve their own teaching, but secondarily to cultivate a faculty motivated to join collaborative efforts around important local teaching and learning problems? How might that change the ways faculty think about the scholarship of teaching and learning as an intellectual and professional activity? How might institutions support this work, providing support and recognition for contributions to collaborative efforts to improve the local conditions of successful student learning? Collaborative faculty work on local issues might lead to publishing, although in forms that might be more varied than the individually authored article.

Within the VKP, we present the relationship between individual and collective work through what we call the "VKP Galleries," (See http://crossroads.georgetown.edu/vkp/) in which we represent clusters of individual work on key questions. Individual contributions are important, but it is the collection that aspires to the level of findings (see the VKP Project Galleries). We experimented with a variety of tools for sharing and building knowledge: We used a digital poster tool (based on the Carnegie Foundation's Knowledge Media Lab's KEEP Toolkit; See http://www.cfkeep.org/static/index.html) as a primary means of creating representations of projects and insights. We used a combination of the posters and online discussion spaces to launch *triads*, in which three faculty members would have rotating discussions about each other's evidence of student learning. In some cases, faculty made the outputs of these sessions public on their digital posters, bringing together the three critical elements of building knowledge: faculty analysis, student work, and peer critique and dialogue. (See, for example, O'Connor, 2004.) Finally, we started to experiment with collaborative portfolios (See for example Ugoretz and Theilheimer's "Looking at Learning Together" at http://crossroads.georgetown.edu/vkp/dportfolio/) where collaborative critique and analysis of particular pedagogies and student work can be made visible and usable by others.

Next Steps in Development Communities

Alignment among Teaching Conversations

Course portfolios and open reflection and review of learning generate excellent conversation, professional growth, and improved work by students and faculty members. To have any broad impact, however, they need to be integrated into all the conversations about teaching on a campus, including annual review of faculty members, tenure and promotion decisions, teaching awards, academic program review, and institutional accreditation. A vertically integrated and interlinked set of digital repositories from student portfolios to institutional reports could be the basis for an open structure that would both save enormous time and effort and make learning a visible and important mission of an institution.

For example, currently at the University of Kansas (KU), participation in face-to-face seminars and institutes on teaching produces good conversation and innovative instructional design; we use the KEEP Toolkit to represent and preserve those ideas in an open forum. With this open virtual community, faculty members follow each other's progress in implementing and learning from their innovative plans. Graduate student writing partners facilitate organization of faculty work into the components of scholarship explored by Glassick, Huber, and Maeroff (1997), and hypertext portfolios make their results and evidence-based conclusions visible to the whole campus.

After five years of developing faculty community around open representations, KU uses the open source KEEP Toolkit to engage individual students and programs in representing their own inquiries into learning. Students construct an intentional understanding of their education by connecting the learning across individual courses or projects. Departments and interdisciplinary programs identify locations in their curriculum in which students already demonstrate their understanding, knowledge, and skills related to key goals. Those units link to student and faculty portfolios for examples and evidence of their strengths and weaknesses in achieving those goals.

The emerging awareness of a shared model of inquiry is changing the local understanding of excellence in teaching and learning. Open communities organized around effective teaching demonstrate that faculty members can represent learning in an efficient and responsible way, allowing peers to use this work as one piece of evidence in any context that calls for evaluation of teaching. In a similar way, an institution could represent its teaching effectiveness by organizing a guided tour of its program, faculty, and student representations of learning. Once the work becomes visible, there is no limit to how it can be organized and viewed for different purposes.

Organizing for Collaboration
The fusion of the scholarship of teaching and learning movement with open education can be a powerful one if we see an increase in experimental models for organizing around these kinds of middle spaces for knowledge building. Faculty can contribute through their traditional identifications (disciplines, departments, institutions), as well as find new affinities based on other layers of commitment and interest (for example writing across the curriculum, inquiry-based learning in biology, ethics in professional studies, etcetera). Key challenges associated with creating such spaces include: How to integrate these spaces with the lives of faculty? Where does the work sit with institutional and professional rewards? Will faculty feel comfortable claiming ownership of their ideas while offering them freely into "the Teaching Commons" (Hutchings and Huber, 2005)? Some of the answers to these challenges have to be found in the social and professional structures intrinsic in different models for these spaces, whether "institutional," "cross-institutional," or "disciplinary," such as the newly created History Scholarship of

Teaching and Learning organization intended to create and form international research teams around shared research questions in the teaching of the field.

In part, the capacity of these new spaces depends on the tools and digital environments that enable them. We need to continue to refine our vision of learning, yet this refinement should be fluid and dynamic, not hyper-specialized. It would be good to be able to "search the literature" across the diverse kinds of documentation being produced through the use of some common vocabulary around kinds of work, genres, and learning problems. We also should expedite collaboration between local networks and scholarly subcommunities across boundaries. For example, at the annual meeting of the International Society for the Scholarship of Teaching and Learning (ISSOTL), 50 or so different local faculty programs are being discussed as models and experiments of involvement. How can we connect faculty across these local efforts and with other open projects? What metadata will make their cross-connections possible, and with what tools?

Open communities generate a large collection of learning objects, including practices, examples, conceptual schemes, artifacts, and reflections that tie them together and connect them with other work. Users can be overwhelmed partly because of sheer volume and partly because of no filtering of the materials. The democratization of knowledge has been a good development, but those people who previously limited the channels of print distribution also made it possible for readers to contact a representative sample of mainstream work. Perhaps some peer review will appear in open systems, less to exclude material and more to organize and synthesize the contributions and to suggest priorities for reading within the large pool of available work.

Community "publication" can address larger issues in teaching. It is one thing to say "my students have learned X, and X is an instance of deep understanding." It is another to say that a group of students in a program have achieved some overarching goal not found exclusively in one course. It is more generative to say that several courses used an approach that emerged from sharing prior work, and all of them demonstrated enhanced integration by learners. Work can be more complex when several people take on individual aspects of it, and ideas and practices are more robust when they can be implemented in many different contexts by instructors with different perspectives. Tools that support this work must enable the flow of knowledge in both directions: to make it relatively easy to find available insights to apply to one's own work (both individual and local communities), and to make it possible for representations of that work to be available for others. It is also critical that scholars and practitioners be able to share insights along the path of discovery. If all shared insight has to rise to the level of published articles, then this will become merely another subfield within fields.

In writing about teachers' ability to develop knowledge about effective classroom practice, Thomas Hatch suggests four critical influences: ". . . the prior knowledge and experience that teachers bring into the classroom, the interactions they have, the representations of thinking and practice that they develop and have access to, and the contexts that shape their opportunities to draw on their prior knowledge, interact with others, and develop and access representations" (Hatch, 2006, p.39). And as we saw in the two examples of such communities, the Peer Review of Teaching Project and the Visible Knowledge Project, all four of these elements were essential.

Both the PRTP and the VKP include conventional face-to-face meetings, and the constraint of scheduled gatherings provides an occasion for participants to be prepared. Whether it is gathering examples of student work, writing about a course, or making comments on colleagues' work, participants get work done to contribute to the scheduled meetings. The advantages of asynchronous programs are clear, but there are also advantages to having an identified window for the completion of work or the posting of commentary. Work is more likely to occur, and the engagement and dialogue are better when the substance of the conversation is fresh.

Without ties to a fixed timeline and process, highly motivated independent learners use whatever time is available for the flexible learning opportunities open courses offer. In practice, however, some people interested in open education opportunities have complex lives that do not support ideal priorities, and the structures built into the PRTP and VKP programs provide nonintrusive ways to guide participation without stripping the process of its fundamental independence. The VKP Crossroads Online Institute, for example, generated good interaction, but progress on writing and scholarship lagged. In its second semisynchronous iteration, specific dates indicated accountability for completion of critical steps, with moments of common work at a common time separated by larger periods of very independent work. With these changes, participants completed more work, and several met for the first time when they presented their work jointly at an international conference.

Three kinds of tools or spaces are essential to support these middle space faculty collaborations: (1) The tools and means to create digital exemplars of student work and faculty analysis; (2) Tools for robust search, retrieval, and indexing so scholars can locate each other through their work and identify cosmopolitan resources; and (3) Social networking tools that enable collaboration to build and share knowledge. As documentation and representations of teaching and learning proliferate, we will need the ability to search, sort, and remix our collective work.

If traditional scholarship, as it emerged in all its modern forms in the late nineteenth century, belonged paradigmatically to the twentieth century, then the scholarship of teaching and learning and the forms of knowledge building we have been discussing belong to the twenty-first century. These scholarly practices share certain qualities with other forms of knowledge circulation and community building in the digital era, including more porous boundaries between the individual and the collaborative. These practices will be readily and transparently interconnected, supporting both easy reader-directed navigation and straightforward creation of intellectual structures that reveal relations among components available in the network of learning objects. An open electronic space will provide a flexible and dynamic home for both ongoing collaboration as well as *post hoc* identification of common themes and coherent results. To maximize the potential of open education, we need to learn how to link local and cosmopolitan work with vibrant and visible practice, and to find a middle space between isolation and full participation in a research community.

References

Bernstein, D., and Bass. R. (2005). The scholarship of teaching and learning. *Academe*, 91(4), 37–43.

Bernstein, D., Burnett, A. N., Goodburn, A., and Savory, P. (2006). *Making Teaching and Learning Visible: Course Portfolios and the Peer Review of Teaching*. Bolton, MA: Anker.

Cerbin, W. (1994). The course portfolio as a tool for continuous improvement of teaching and learning. *Journal on Excellence in College Teaching*, 5(1), 95–105.

Chism, N. (1999). *Peer Review of Teaching: A Sourcebook*. Bolton, MA: Anker.

Chism, N. (2007) *Peer Review of Teaching: A Sourcebook* (2nd ed.). Bolton, MA: Anker.

Coventry, M., Felten, P., Jaffee, D., O'Leary, C., Weis, T., and McGowan, S. (2006). Ways of Seeing: Evidence of Learning in the History Classroom. *Journal of American History*, 92(4).

Glassick, C. E., Huber, M. T., and Maeroff, G. I. (1997). *Scholarship Assessed: Evaluation of the professoriate*. San Francisco, CA: Jossey-Bass.

Hatch, T. (2006). *Into the Classroom: Developing the Scholarship of Teaching and Learning*. San Francisco, CA: Jossey-Bass.

Hutchings, P. (Ed.). (1996). *Making Teaching Community Property: A Menu for Peer Collaboration and Peer Review*. Alexandria, VA: Stylus.

Hutchings, P., and Huber, M. T. (2005). *The Advancement of Learning: Building the Teaching Commons*. San Francisco, CA: Jossey-Bass.

Shulman, L. (2004). *Teaching as Community Property: Essays on Higher Education*. San Francisco, CA: Jossey-Bass.

Trigwell, K., Martin, E., Benjamin, J., and Prosser, M. (2000). Scholarship of Teaching: A Model. *Higher Education Research and Development*, 19(2), 155–168.

21

Open Teaching: The Key to Sustainable and Effective Open Education

Diana Laurillard

Why Do We Need Learning Technologies?

If the current plans for education are fulfilled, then the twenty-first century will become the century in which we transform the quality and reach of education. There are some impressive ambitions to be found in educational strategy documents, both national and international. The United States has the "No Child Left Behind" campaign. The United Kingdom has "Every Child Matters" as the vision for a national strategy to join up all the public sector agencies responsible for the well-being and education of children. The European Union's Lisbon Agreement requires every country to build its workforce skills to a much higher level. The United Nations' millennium goal for education is one that every nation inherits, and it provides the ultimate challenge for education: to achieve universal primary education by 2015.

We are now several years into the millennium, but scarcely nearer to achieving this goal. It would require a teaching community capable of building its expertise and multiplying its numbers at a fantastic growth rate, even within the original 15 years. Similarly, the worldwide demand for higher education continues to grow. Estimates from The Observatory on Borderless Higher Education (OBHE) suggest that worldwide higher education places will rise to 125 million in 2020; demand for international education places are predicted to be 5.8 million by 2020; and the age participation rate is 40 percent to 50 percent in the "north," but less than 5 percent in many developing and emerging economies (2003).

Wherever we look, around the globe or in our own backyards, we can see that more and better education is needed. But the scale of the problem cannot be tackled through our traditional technologies for teaching. When you measure student numbers in billions, staff-student ratios of 1:30 make no impact at all. So the problem of scale is challenging.

Traditional education fails millions of students across even the highly developed countries: An average of 6.5 percent of 15-year-olds fail to achieve Level 1 literacy (Organisation for Economic Co-operation and Development-Centre for Educational Research and Innovation [OECD-CERI], 2006). We have not yet discovered how to achieve more effective education for those excluded or disaffected by our current system. The ambition to bring education to the world is laudable, but we have only a partially successful system to offer. The problem of quality is just as challenging as the problem of scale.

So we have to ask: How could such a transformation be contemplated without recourse to a technological solution?

Technology is never the whole solution. The recent history of technology in education always tells us that however good it is, it achieves little without the complementary human and organizational changes needed, and these are always more difficult. Using technology to improve education is not rocket science. It's much, much harder than that. Change in education is not a matter of a small number of extremely highly educated people moving a collection of obedient atoms from one place to another. It is about large numbers of partially trained people moving minds; millions of them. That is why we look to interactive communications technologies for help. They are capable of emulating the best-quality teaching, but on a larger scale and with wider reach.

The focus of this chapter is to work out how to achieve that. The argument is that we need technology to achieve the educational reform we dream of, but that we have to do it through the teaching community. An essential part of the open education movement will be "open teaching." The teaching community will need learning design tools and environments that will enable them to develop the new pedagogies afforded by digital technologies, use the open education resources becoming available, and achieve high quality teaching on the large scale.

What Is the Evidence That Learning Technologies Can Help?

The two educational challenges to technology posed in the previous section are the problem of quality (how do we ensure the quality of the learning experience and learning outcomes?) and the problem of scale (how do we provide for all the education needed?).

We know that technology offers the greater flexibility of education provision that enables more people to take part. The UK Open University (OU) has more than 200,000 students in over 70 countries, studying through a blend of online and printed materials, and online and face-to-face tutorials, provided locally. And technology-based methods work just as well for school-level study where, for example, online courses enabled learners at work to achieve the school qualifications they missed; a "virtual school" for children excluded for behavioral reasons gave them a combination of remote access and one-to-one teaching that brought 90 percent of them back into mainstream study or work-based learning (Department for Children, Schools and Families [DCSF], 2005). The feasibility and value of this flexible provision has been demonstrated in many such cases. Success depends upon the quality of learner support, and flexibility fails when this is not provided. The success of the OU model, for example, was demonstrated when the University came top of all UK universities in the survey of "quality of student support." Distance learning need not mean isolation. With these models of successful flexible online provision, we can see that it becomes possible to extend education well beyond the confines of the physical place to a much wider group studying online and attending only occasionally.

We only meet the challenge of scale, however, if we can make this kind of provision at a lower unit cost as numbers rise. There is a myth abroad in the minds of policymakers that online provision is cheap—that the same material can be provided to much larger student numbers than in a physical environment, and therefore, with much lower variable costs, educational provision can be expanded without a commensurate increase in cost. The cost/quality relation is not so simple, however. The UK OU has been more successful than any other distance-learning university in terms of retention, attainment, and expansion, because it provides excellent learner support, but has not significantly reduced its unit costs. In general, the bill for the introduction of ICT into education has been high (currently close to £1 bn per year if both government and institution costs are included across all education sectors in the UK), so the unit cost of education is increasing. The return is hard to measure, but is certainly not sufficient to make a dramatic difference in overall attainment measures. That should not surprise us because the major investment in schools, for example, began only 5 years ago and took time to put in place. The same is true in the commercial world; it can take many years to show a profit from a major IT-based reconfiguration of a company. As we learned in the latter decades of the twentieth century, "computer hardware's contribution to overall economic growth is limited. . . . To get a big pick-up, the return earned by computer hardware and software must surge in coming years" (Sichel, 1997, 10–11).

Transformational change cannot happen overnight. However, unless every education institution is focused on how to use technology to improve the value of education—a "benefits-oriented cost model"—costs will continue to rise without the return (Laurillard, 2006a). The model shows that technology only achieves improved value for money when an institution plans in *both* improved quality and improved scale. Critical to this approach is ensuring that the institution exploits the reuse and sharing of open education content and design tools, as we see below. There are few such examples on either side of the Atlantic, and they tend to be small scale. But when the management of innovation focuses on both quality and scale, as in the Pew program on learning technology, then the twin benefits are achievable (Twigg, 2002; Twigg, 2003). We return to the management issue later.

There is one sense in which education can expect new technology to improve the cost equation. As the ICT infrastructure in a country gradually expands for business and domestic reasons, its education systems can exploit this without always paying for it. Home access to computers and the Internet is already over 75 percent for schoolchildren in the UK, and higher education students studying online typically provide their own access at home and sometimes at work. This amounts to massive private investment in digital technology for education and means that it becomes feasible for public funding to provide access for the relatively small tail of the population who cannot provide for themselves. So the access problem is not insoluble; in time it lessens. The greatest problem is always to ensure that our human and organizational systems are capable of the change they need to embrace.

We need technology to address the scale of the educational challenges we face within developed countries, to raise the level of skill and understanding within the workforce needed for a knowledge society, and to achieve adequate levels of primary through higher education across the developing world. We have seen many case examples of improved quality through technology: teaching programs that motivate learners, offer higher levels of engagement and practice with difficult concepts and skills, and provide personalized and adaptive feedback to assist mastery learning (Becta, 2006). Such programs can be used to extend what an individual teacher can offer, making it possible to improve quality without expanding the number of teachers at the same rate as the number of learners (affordable improvements in quality are possible, for example, if we simultaneously achieve improvements in scale).

We know that technology can offer radically more flexible ways of learning, enabling people who otherwise would not be able to access education to do so. And we know that through careful planning of online communities and information systems, it is possible to achieve high quality student support for remote students. We have the technology. We do not yet have the quality of change management within our education systems that would enable us to exploit it.

If we are seriously to address our ambitions for education, we need to understand how to exploit learning technologies and the idea of open education to the limit.

Why Has There Been So Little Innovation and No Change of Model?

Digital technology has captured the imagination of many and enjoys constant invention of new forms of exploitation in business, domestic, and leisure contexts, resulting in radical changes in some cases. In the education systems of developed economies, digital technology has been available for experimentation for many decades and has now become ubiquitous in many educational contexts. It has not yet achieved significant improvement in the quality and scale of education, however, nor any radical change in the model of education.

Why so little progress? Here are five plausible explanations:

1. The education system is a complex system of powerful drivers—assessment, curriculum, inspection/quality requirements, funding flows, promotion criteria—none of which have changed significantly in recognition of what technology offers. These drivers determine the ways in which teachers and learners orient their energies and are judged by others. Unless the drivers of the education system change, the behavior of its members will not change.

2. Technological change is very rapid. We have seen the digital equivalent of many key technologies for education in the space of half a century—the equivalent of writing, the pamphlet, the book, publishing, photography, film, broadcasting, the telephone, the printing press, the postal system. While it took many centuries to develop our education systems through these old technologies, we have not yet had time to make the radical changes afforded by digital technologies (Laurillard, 2005).

3. The education system is run by leaders who are not comfortable with either the detail or the implications of the technology potential, and those who are, are not powerful enough within the system. There has been radical change in some institutions, demonstrating the importance of leadership. Institution leaders need the direction to be set at the national level, and they need more support for the changes they must direct within their own institutions (DCSF, 2005).

4. Education is essentially a political activity and a national enterprise, embodying the moral values of a country, so it does not easily become commercialized or globalised, and therefore avoids being subject to the innovation that market forces encourage (Readings, 1996).

5. Education systems change slowly because they tend to be hierarchical command-control systems, rather than devolved-power adaptive systems. Teachers and lecturers are given neither the power nor the means to improve the nature and quality of the teaching-learning process through technology (Elton, 1999).

On that analysis, our education systems are doomed to irrelevance and inefficiency, unable to even begin to meet the challenges of the twenty-first century, because they cannot rethink themselves fast enough.

One possible future is that the commercial world will eventually understand the nature of education as a business. Most commercial online education enterprises have so far failed (Garrett and MacLean, 2004), primarily because they have failed to understand the nature of education: that they are not selling a product, but a long-term personal service. The point is well understood by the most successful recent example, the University of Phoenix, which has used technology to tackle only reach, not scale. In 2003 its 72,000 students totaled a fraction of the UK Open University enrollments of 200,000. To minimize attrition, it maintains small classes for its online version (Symonds, 2003). This approach remains successful by maintaining the business models of traditional universities, not by developing new forms of education as the OU did.

The failure of private enterprise to reconfigure education through technology demonstrates how important it is to be clear about the fundamental and unchanging values of education. These constitute the fulcrum about which we move the world of education to a system fit for the twenty-first century. We make radical change through technology best if we understand what must remain constant.

Education is not like a normal commercial enterprise because the transaction between the individual and the provider is a very personal contract. There are no customers, and they are certainly not always right. It is a delicate relationship of mutual trust and nurturing, more akin to parenthood than commerce; it is selling the potential, and only the potential, for people to change and develop, more akin to a gym than a supermarket. Learners enter into an unequal relationship with the provider that helps them develop as individuals in ways they cannot yet specify, judges the extent to which they have developed, and accredits them on its terms, not theirs. The contract gives them no redress if they do not get what they hoped for—if they fail it is their loss. To achieve this, the education system has to be capable of great trust and authority. It is essentially unequal, with the formal system taking the responsibility of providing access to the key ideas of the culture, which enable individuals to take their place as citizens, and to use their understanding of the world and society in their community and in their work. This is true for every level of education. And formal education, in this contractual sense, is fundamentally different from informal education.

Similarly, the contract between the state and the education system is one of trust: that the education system will prepare the nation's citizens for what the nation needs. The state will pay for formal education, or subsidize it, while it appears to succeed in doing that. In 1997, the UK's National Committee of Inquiry into Higher Education made the definitive statement that "the aim of higher education is to enable society to make progress through an understanding of itself and its world; in short, to sustain a learning society" (National Committee of Inquiry into Higher Education [NCIHE], 1997).

Technology may change much about education, but the nature of its contract with individuals and the state is fundamental. Perhaps that will also change, eventually, but we are considering here what education "as we know it" could become.

How Do We Move Forward Faster?

If we accept that the future of education would benefit from appropriate exploitation of digital technologies, then we have to consider how our education systems are to make the shift to a trajectory of progressive, holistic innovation, a step change from the fragmented incremental innovation we have at present.

From the previous analysis it is clear that we have to address the powerful drivers that define education. Educational leaders have a responsibility to drive a strategic approach to the reform of education that fully exploits what technology can offer. This top-down, holistic approach to technology-based change has not yet been undertaken in any country. It would require a government to embed in every part of its educational strategic thinking the consideration of what digital technologies could contribute to what they are trying to achieve, and to coordinate those efforts across all the sectors of education. In an ideal educational system, an individual learner would move through seamlessly from primary to secondary to further and higher education and would be able, as a lifelong learner, to move between work-based, home-based, and formal learning as he or she wished. Digital technologies have the capacity to support the learner through the information and guidance needed in making those critical transitions. In practice, in many countries, the responsibility for the different educational sectors rests with different parts of government, making top-down coordination of the learner's experience almost impossible.

The UK has the first government e-learning strategy to embrace the whole education system in a drive to improve the use of technology (Department for Children, Schools, and Families [DCSF], 2005). However, responsibility for its implementation has been handed to external public sector agencies, divorcing it from mainstream educational policy. While educational reform is driven top-down, exploitation of technology in service of reform should be closely linked to it, remodeling educational drivers as appropriate. A good example is evaluation/assessment of students, one of the most important "drivers" of the behavior of both teachers and learners in all parts of education. Twenty-first-century students equip themselves with valuable skills for the acquisition and processing of information and ideas, and assessment of their learning could be carried out in very different ways from the suboptimal examinations and multiple-choice-question techniques of previous centuries that still dominate. Reform could be radical and highly productive if it were led in part by the new opportunities offered by technology.

Large-scale reform of education is risky for democratic governments; when linked to large-scale use of technology, the risk escalates. So why risk the top-down approach? The education systems in many countries have already effected very large-scale implementation of technology by providing targeted funding for hardware, software, and networking. In the UK, for example, this has not been run as a top-down project but has devolved the funding to local decision-makers, enabling local ownership of the acquisition and innovation that follows. This marks a success for top-down government intervention, essentially by enabling bottom-up change through targeted funding. The value of the approach is that it is low-risk—there is now widespread access and use, and no prospect of a big technology failure, because it is all so fragmented. That is also the problem. It is fragmented and nonstrategic. Such a change process cannot achieve radical system reform because the top-down drivers of the educational system remain unaffected. While technology is still just an interesting sideshow, unrelated to the strategic drivers of curriculum development, assessment, qualifications, accreditation, inspection, teacher pay, and promotion, it cannot deliver radical change.

Suppose we make the assumption that governments will not easily achieve holistic, system-wide, technology-aware reform of education. It could still be possible to work towards radical reform through the open education approach. Open education has the great advantage that it can support directly the people within the system whose practice will be changed most by the proper integration of technology: teachers and lecturers. It therefore has the potential to mitigate the characteristics of education that constrain its ability to innovate.

Many teachers and lecturers have embraced technology to assist their own pedagogic ambitions for their students, but most have not. The powerful drivers of their behavior as professionals do not drive them towards use of technology—assessment methods, inspection criteria, promotion criteria, and funding flows continue to be directed towards traditional teaching—and yet these are the determinants of classroom practice. Inevitably, with little system support around them, any teaching innovator will expend much energy in working against the grain of the existing system. To counter these endemic constraints on innovation, we need education leaders to create the "learning organizations" that are "capable of adaptive learning" (Laurillard, 2002), in which professionals can work together to experiment and build a better system. But it cannot all be "top-down." We also have to prepare for what this means for teachers and lecturers, and how they could drive system change "bottom-up."

The idea of a learning system capable of adapting itself to new environmental conditions is applicable also to the teaching community itself. Our knowledge and understanding of "technology-enhanced learning" will accelerate faster in a teaching community that acts like a learning system—one that makes knowledge of *what it takes to learn* explicit, adapts it, tests it, refines practice, reflects, rearticulates, and shares that new knowledge. Teaching must become problematized, innovative, and professional, taking research as its model. If lecturers were to conduct the process of teaching as rigorously as they conduct their research, then they would expect 1) support for some personal development in how to teach; 2) the means to build on the work of others to design their approach; 3) the means to experiment and reflect on what the results imply for their design and their understanding; and 4) the means to articulate and disseminate their contribution. Those four characteristics together define the essentials of what we might call "open teaching"—what James Dalziel has called "open source teaching"—such as an environment in which "educators can freely and openly share best practice teaching" (Dalziel, 2005). This communitarian approach reflects the ideals of the research community in general, and the scholarship of teaching in particular (Kreber and Cranton, 2000). It would enable the teaching community, throughout the education system, to learn how to adapt to the new challenges for education and to exploit technology in the process.

The idea of "open education" makes this possible. "Open technology" means that the documentation of our findings transfers as easily across departments and institutions as paper does. "Open content" means we can adopt and adapt each others' technology-based teaching innovations as easily as we can build on research findings. "Open knowledge" means we have the means to capture and disseminate our pedagogic ideas as easily as we can write and publish papers.

The key to change and progress within the education sector is to use open education to create the innovative forces throughout the whole system that will help to drive it forward. Education leaders have not used the opportunity of digital technologies to transform education top-down—could it now begin to happen bottom-up?

What Will It Look Like?

Part of the point of a bottom-up approach to reform is that we cannot know exactly where it will go. It will be up to all of us to shape it. That would make it a much more dynamic system, where learning is a joy and teaching is fun because learners are enjoying the struggle it undoubtedly is to grapple with difficult ideas and high-level skills.

The promise of fun lies in the creative opportunities provided by open education tools and resources, which offer a kind of toy box for teachers. The digital world frequently achieves an epidemic of interest because the technology being offered provides opportunities for individuals to communicate or be creative, or both; email, PowerPoint, online games, blogs, wikis, social software education could do the same by providing the tools and resources for teachers to make their own pedagogy.

At the Open University a few years ago, we attempted to build the means for lecturers to capture and disseminate their best pedagogical ideas. The research project SoURCE (Software, Use, Reuse and Customisation in Education) identified proven interactive learning products, turned them into a generic form, and then transferred them to a different department. For example, a learning design on eliciting and comparing learners' personal constructs of historic paintings was adapted to the generic form of an "elicitation engine," and then customized to chemical reactions, enabling chemistry students to generate and compare their constructs of different chemicals. In both cases it was a valuable initiation into thinking about new ideas. The project took as its basic methodology the following stages:

Stage 1:　Identify a learning design for a specific objective which has been proven as valuable for students (such as an art history program).

Stage 2:　Adapt this learning design to its generic form (replace the links to files showing paintings with requests to the teacher for links to content files; replace the links to expert definitions and their links to the exemplars with requests to the teacher to insert such links; leave all the interactive pedagogic functionality that directs students to select three items and think of how two are similar and different *from the other*, etc.).

Stage 3:   Customize this form to a new context with a similar objective, inserting new content as appropriate (insert the links to video clips of chemical explosions; insert the links to expert descriptors and associated chemicals).

Stage 4:   Implement and test the new combination in its new context.

The whole process was evaluated, and generated as final products: (a) two interactive learning designs for similar objectives, but applied in different content areas; (b) two sets of content objects; and (c) one generic learning design. The project concluded that the process was feasible but that significant effort was required to ensure dissemination and reuse of the learning activities, which could only work in a system that supported "the exchange of learning objects" (Laurillard and McAndrew, 2003).

Learning object repositories are now being established in the form of both content "assets" (such as digital libraries of photos, sound archives, and video footage) and in the form of learning activities that present and test content (such as a heart simulation or a game to balance equations). The former are usually managed by libraries, whereas the latter are found in academic repositories such as MERLOT (See www.merlot.org), OpenLearn (See www.openlearn.open.ac.uk), and JORUM (See www.jorum.ac.uk). These are good initial approaches but do not constitute the means by which we can capture and disseminate pedagogic innovation for others to build on. The pedagogic basis of the art history project was attractive to the chemists but without the extraction of the generic form they could not use it. Learning objects typically bind together the pedagogic form and the specific content. Learning object repositories are beginning to provide valuable digital assets for insertion into generic pedagogic forms but we do not yet have many examples of the latter.

If the teaching community could cultivate an "open teaching" approach, making use of the opportunities digital technologies offer, then we would have the means to build and develop this kind of knowledge: a collective understanding of what kinds of pedagogies, or learning designs, are capable of achieving a specific learning outcome. As an

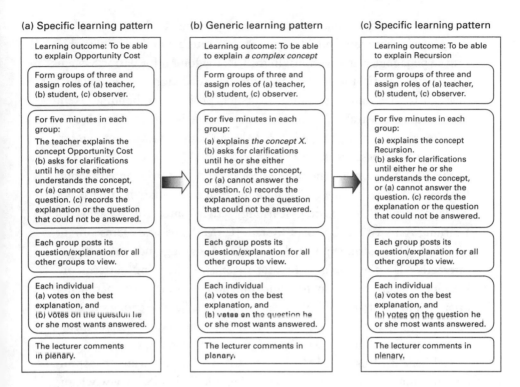

(a) Specific learning pattern

Learning outcome: To be able to explain Opportunity Cost

Form groups of three and assign roles of (a) teacher, (b) student, (c) observer.

For five minutes in each group:
The teacher explains the concept Opportunity Cost (b) asks for clarifications until he or she either understands the concept, or (a) cannot answer the question. (c) records the explanation or the question that could not be answered.

Each group posts its question/explanation for all other groups to view.

Each individual
(a) votes on the best explanation, and
(b) votes on the question he or she most wants answered.

The lecturer comments in plenary.

(b) Generic learning pattern

Learning outcome: To be able to explain *a complex concept*

Form groups of three and assign roles of (a) teacher, (b) student, (c) observer.

For five minutes in each group:
(a) explains *the concept X.* (b) asks for clarifications until he or she either understands the concept, or (a) cannot answer the question. (c) records the explanation or the question that could not be answered.

Each group posts its question/explanation for all other groups to view.

Each individual
(a) votes on the best explanation, and
(b) votes on the question he or she most wants answered.

The lecturer comments in plenary.

(c) Specific learning pattern

Learning outcome: To be able to explain Recursion

Form groups of three and assign roles of (a) teacher, (b) student, (c) observer.

For five minutes in each group:
(a) explains the concept Recursion. (b) asks for clarifications until either he or she understands the concept, or (a) cannot answer the question. (c) records the explanation or the question that could not be answered.

Each group posts its question/explanation for all other groups to view.

Each individual
(a) votes on the best explanation, and
(b) votes on the question he or she most wants answered.

The lecturer comments in plenary.

Figure 21.1
Generalization and migration of a learning pattern
(a) A specific learning pattern is designed for a topic-specific learning outcome, with topic-specific details in bold; (b) This is generalized to a generic form for this learning pattern by generalizing the topic-specific detail as a place-marker; this is a form that can migrate across subject disciplines, but still carries its pedagogic design; (c) The generic form is then customized to a new topic by inserting it in the place-marker for topic-specific detail, creating a new specific learning pattern.

illustration, figure 21.1 shows an example of how a specific simple learning design can be generalized to capture the pedagogic design and enable this to migrate across discipline areas.

The process will not work for all types of learning patterns, but many pedagogic forms are capable of being adapted in this way (the lecture is one obvious example from traditional teaching methods). As the teaching community explores the new pedagogies available through digital technologies, we will need tools capable of assisting this process and, happily, the technology can provide them (Laurillard, 2006b).

A new research project is attempting to build the kind of learning design tools that would enable lecturers to capture and disseminate their proven pedagogical innovations. In the UK, the Joint Information Systems Committee (JISC) for higher and further education has launched a "Design for Learning" program, in which projects are building exemplars and demonstrators to test the idea that it is feasible for lecturers to take more control of pedagogic design and development, and to exchange their best ideas, so that they can build on each others' work as they do in research. One of the projects, the "User-Oriented Planner for Learning Activity Design," is building pedagogic analysis, advice, and guidance around an existing learning activity authoring system (the Learning Activity Management System [LAMS]; See www.lamscommunity.org). The system supports lecturers in designing and building good interactive learning designs, linking to existing learning patterns and learning objects for them to build on, and eliciting an experimental approach to the design of learning activities. It is flexible enough to cover sequences of activities that enable their students to communicate, collaborate, and consult existing materials and learning objects.

The benefit of using LAMS is that it provides the means to capture and disseminate a lecturer's proven pedagogic design (See www.wle.org.uk/d4l). The approach would therefore contribute to all four conditions of building a more communitarian approach to teaching: 1) some personal development in how to teach, through advice and guidance; 2) the means to build on the work of others through links to existing learning designs, learning objects, and content assets; 3) the means to experiment and reflect on what the results imply for their design and their understanding, through a simple learning activity authoring system; and 4) the means to articulate and disseminate their contribution, through the pedagogic design captured and customizable in the form of a LAMS activity, and to disseminate it through the LAMS community Web site. The project is carrying out a needs analysis with faculty from different disciplines, designing and testing a succession of prototypes of how the tool might work to assist them. We have a long way to go, but if we can make this kind of design support tool work for faculty, we would then have a robust and sustainable means to accelerate wider engagement with the scholarship of teaching. It would complete the vision of open education with a new kind of activity: open teaching.

Conclusions

To summarize, the micro factors that will do most to accelerate the growth of this new kind of teaching community are both "bottom-up" and "top-down":

• professional training for teachers at all levels of education, including higher education, to acknowledge that it is needed for teaching as much as for research;
• support for strategic leadership in e-learning at institutional and national levels of education, to ensure a "learning institution" environment for innovators;
• R&D on technology-enhanced learning, carried out through partnerships between research labs, publishers, software houses, and teachers to build the tools, resources, and learning design environments necessary for open education; and
• a common systems architecture for learning and teaching, and common open standards for digital tools and resources to ensure exchange across institutions and disciplines.

Technology is innovative, complex, and expensive but can deliver our highest ambitions for education. If it does not achieve improved quality of the learning experience, at least in terms of the level of outcome, and does not operate at scale, in terms of improved reach to those currently unable or unwilling to participate, then we have failed to exploit its potential. Reaching out to new learners or reengaging learners throughout life exploits the large-scale capability of digital technologies, and needs top-down, strategic leadership to make the most of what they offer. On the other hand, the quality of the learning experience is highly dependent on the teacher and how the learning process is conducted. That has been the focus of this chapter—to use technology to transform education bottom-up through enabling the teaching community to act in the most scholarly and professional way possible. But even this is only feasible if education leaders act to provide the infrastructure and reform education drivers to promote the changes that open education offers.

How will we know when we have succeeded in transforming education through the use of technology to build "open education"? What are the key indicators?

For really difficult questions about new technology, it is often valuable to go back to old technology and ask the same question: What would have been the right indicators by which to judge the major educational innovations of earlier times? The invention of the printing press was important because it gave more people access to knowledge; perhaps the great political revolutions were a natural consequence, so the right indicator would be "does it trigger change in the structure of society?" Universal schooling was certainly designed to create a different structure in society. But what is the right indicator for its success? More people with a sense of responsibility for what they know? Yes, there has certainly been a shift from an agricultural workforce to the knowledge workforce we have now. The educational innovations of old provided both a different quality of engagement with ideas (not just sitting at the foot of the master, but having direct access to the ideas) and a wider reach (through universal access). What will happen when we have a new level of engagement, offered by user-controlled interactive programs, together with even wider access through digital presence: a worldwide sustainable learning society, capable of understanding itself and its world? Educational aims should be ambitious and should set out to challenge the technology that is so often in the driving seat of change. The idea of open education is to wrest the reins from technology and harness it to a higher cause.

References

Becta. (2006). *The Becta Review 2006: Evidence on the Progress of ICT in Education.* Coventry, UK: British Educational Communications and Technology Agency. Retrieved October 16, 2007, from http://www.becta.org

Dalziel, J. (2005). LAMS community launch [electronic version]. *LAMS Foundation News, 6.* Retrieved October 16, 2007, from http://www.lamsfoundation.org/news/#6

Department for Children, Schools and Families. (2005). *Harnessing Technology: Transforming Learning and Children's Services.* Retrieved October 16, 2007, from http://www.dfes.gov.uk/publications/e-strategy/links.shtml

Elton, L. (1999). New ways of learning in higher education: Managing the change. *Tertiary Education and Management, 5,* 207–225.

Garrett, R., and MacLean, D. (2004). *Pricing Online Learning: Practice, Rationale and Transparency.* [Briefing note]. London: The Observatory on Borderless Higher Education. Retrieved October 16, 2007, from www.obhe.ac.uk

Kreber, C., and Cranton, P. A. (2000). Exploring the scholarship of teaching. *The Journal of Higher Education*, 71(4), 476–495.

Laurillard, D. (2002). *Rethinking University Teaching: A Conversational Framework for the Effective Use of Learning Technologies* (2nd ed.). London: RoutledgeFalmer.

Laurillard, D. (2005). E-learning in higher education. In P. Ashwin (Ed.), *Changing Higher Education: The Development of Learning and Teaching*. London: RoutledgeFalmer.

Laurillard, D. (2006a). Modelling benefits-oriented costs for technology enhanced learning. *Higher Education*, 54, 21–39.

Laurillard, D. (2006b). *The Teacher as Action Researcher in Open Digital Environments*. [Invited keynote]. Paper presented at the International Society for the Scholarship of Teaching and Learning (ISSOTL), Washington, DC.

Laurillard, D., and McAndrew, P. (2003). Reusable educational software: A basis for generic learning activities. In A. Littlejohn (Ed.), *Reusing Online Resources: A Sustainable Approach to e-Learning*. London: Kogan Page.

National Committee of Inquiry into Higher Education. (1997). *Higher Education in the Learning Society*. No. NCIHE/97/850. London: HMSO.

The Observatory on Borderless Higher Education. (2003). *Redesigning Reaching and Learning in Higher Education Using ICT: Balancing Quality, Access and Cost—A Study of the U.S. Pew Grant Program in Course Redesign and Its Potential for UK Higher Education. A Report to the Department for Education and Skills.* London: University of Surrey and the Observatory on Borderless Higher Education. Retrieved October 16, 2007, from www.obhe.ac.uk/resources/.

Organisation for Economic Co-operation and Development—Centre for Educational Research and Innovation. (2006, December 21). PISA 2003 Country Profiles. Retrieved October 16, 2007, from http://www.pisa.oecd.org

Readings, B. (1996). *The University in Ruins*. Cambridge, MA: Harvard University Press.

Sichel, D. E. (1997). *The Computer Revolution: An Economic Perspective*. Washington, DC: The Brookings Institution.

Symonds, W. (2003, June 23). University of Phoenix online: Swift rise. *Business Week*. Retrieved October 16, 2007, from http://www.businessweek.com/magazine/content/03_25/b3838628.htm

Twigg, C. (2002). *Improving Quality and Reducing Costs: Designs for Effective Learning Using ICT*. London: The Observatory on Borderless Higher Education. Retrieved October 16, 2007, from www.obhe.ac.uk

Twigg, C. A. (2003, September/October). Improving learning and reducing costs: New models for online learning. *Educause Review*, 28–38.

22

Promoting Technology-enabled Knowledge Building and Sharing for Sustainable Open Educational Innovations

Toru Iiyoshi and Cheryl R. Richardson

The pursuit of more effective teaching and greater student learning is a lifelong journey—or so it should be. Many educators make this journey solo, but it could be more rewarding and fruitful for them, their students, and their institutions if they did so collectively, sharing experience, skill, and innovation. The more "open" intellectual eyes and minds we have investigating various pedagogical issues and challenges, the more educational innovations are encouraged.

Pooling intellectual resources about pedagogical practice is also becoming a necessity in a world where domains of knowledge are fluid, continuously changing, and expanding. The local and global issues of education in the twenty-first century are such that we have to harness the "wisdom of crowds" (Surowiecki, 2005) to keep building on each other's best practice. As Lee S. Shulman has observed, we "can treat our courses and classrooms as laboratories or field sites in the best sense of the term, and can contribute through our scholarship to the improvement and understanding of learning and teaching in our field . . . the professional imperative [to engage in this act] is both individual and communal." (Shulman, 2004a, p.158).

The "professional imperative" extends beyond solely disseminating content or domain knowledge, as disseminating only content does not always result in educational improvement and transformation. It is necessary to share both the tacit and explicit knowledge that informs pedagogical action as well as the creation and use of resources, tools, and curricula (Iiyoshi, Richardson, and McGrath, 2006; Iiyoshi, 2006).

While ever-evolving information and communication technology and an increasing number of educational resources enable us to continuously move education forward in various ways, it is important to keep in mind that improving teaching and learning does not necessarily require "cutting-edge" tools. Indeed, as is often the case in the field of educational technology research and in many efforts to adapt new technologies and new pedagogical methods, the impulse is to keep moving to newer and niftier "gadgets" without learning thoroughly from what worked and what did not. In many cases, familiar educational tools and resources could be more effective if educators, in partnership with students, would simply try to devise ways of using them to deepen learners' understanding.

All this, of course, sounds easier than it is to practice. Meeting the challenges of knowledge sharing also takes committed effort on the part of individuals, institutions, and the organizations that support educational improvement, although a passion for and mindful engagement with improving day-to-day practice and a willingness to share openly and learn from each other can be the drivers for acting on the "professional imperative" for individual and collective attention to teaching and learning.

So how best can we learn from each other's successes and challenges in teaching and learning? How can we promote successful educational knowledge building and sharing by harnessing technology and open practice? How can we connect people, tools, resources, and knowledge across disciplines, institutions, and projects? What cultural and institutional change is required to promote this organic and systemic effort in a sustainable way? We explore these questions in this chapter.

Challenges in Knowledge Building and Sharing

We see three primary challenges to building and sharing knowledge of practice: understanding the sources of local knowledge, extracting it, and representing it in a way it can be used by others.

Understanding Local Knowledge

Educators—alone and in groups within institutions and across communities of practice—have vast amounts of knowledge about how to improve particular aspects of student learning, and although they make use of that knowledge daily, much of it remains in their local realm. Howard Gardner explains that this kind of local knowledge is acquired in specific contexts and, while difficult to capture, is "essential to productive work in any domain" (Gardner, 1999, p.98).

Further, local knowledge of teaching and learning is acquired, over time, in particular environments and activities: collaborating with colleagues, instructing, evaluating or building new tools, curricula, and environments. Knowledge about teaching and learning thus is situated in practice and often is tacitly held by the knower. As is all tacit knowledge, knowledge of teaching and learning is hard to formalize, difficult to communicate to others, deeply rooted in action and in one's commitment to a specific context; it consists partly of technical skills and has an important cognitive dimension (Nonaka, 1991, pp. 26–29).

Consider the practice of teachers. As Shulman explains, knowledge about teaching and learning can be classified as content knowledge; pedagogical knowledge; curriculum knowledge; and knowledge of learners, educational contexts, and educational ends. In putting their knowledge to use, teachers exercise pedagogical reasoning to guide their actions (Shulman, 2004b, pp. 227–228). How, then, might a teacher understand, capture and exchange this knowledge? Linda Darling-Hammond and colleagues identify reflection as key in bringing this tacit knowledge to the surface so that others can use it (2005, p.424).

However, capturing and sharing knowledge of teaching and learning does not stop with reflection and exchange of teachers' particular knowledge and skills. Teaching and learning also involves the tools and resources of curriculum delivery and learner acquisition, and the motivations of learners themselves. How these parts of the educational ecosystem interact depends on the context. Moreover, each participant in the process has particular pieces of knowledge and experiences. Thus, improvement of the system of teaching and learning involves exchange of knowledge among the various stakeholders.

Capturing Knowledge

As suggested by figure 22.1, the personal, contextual, and accretive nature of knowledge of teaching and learning, with its complex interaction of people, tools, and resources, makes it difficult and time-consuming to capture and examine, either in verbal or other modes.

As Richard Gale describes in "Inquiry Unplugged," in this volume, careful prodding, probing, and support from the Carnegie Academy for

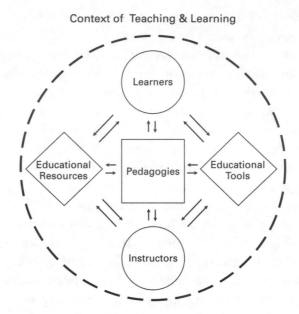

Context of Teaching & Learning

Figure 22.1
Knowledge of Teaching and Learning

the Scholarship of Teaching and Learning (CASTL) program has helped faculty articulate their knowledge (2008). CASTL has created environments for collaboration and provided prompts and instructions for faculty to reflect on and articulate what they know about their teaching. They also have provided environments for representing what is known. As one can see from this careful work, the formula for extracting knowledge is difficult to duplicate, scale up, and apply to all fields with a stake in educational transformation.

Making Knowledge Portable
John Seely Brown and Paul Duguid explain that knowledge is something digested rather than merely held. A knower understands what it is known and is committed to it (2000, pp.119–120). How, then, can this assimilated knowledge be represented to others? More specifically, can knowledge of teaching and learning be represented in a way that is portable, and that others can readily acquire, learn from, and build upon? And, given the multi-dimensional nature of teaching and learning, what forms might it take?

Other Obstacles

Through our experience at the Carnegie Foundation, we have also found knowledge sharing to be complicated further by the culture of educational institutions, which often value individual expertise and particular kinds of research over the kind of collaboration and inquiry necessary to advance teaching and learning.

Faculty, administrators, supporters of improved student learning, and even students are often frustrated by lack of incentives, time, return on investment, support, and guidance (especially for the process of reflection and rewards and recognition). They are stymied by technical challenges, literacy issues involved in such activities as reflective writing and multimedia composition, and sustainability.

Technology-enabled Knowledge Building and Sharing

The Knowledge Media Laboratory (KML) of The Carnegie Foundation has been inspired by both the challenges and potential rewards of capturing, documenting, and sharing knowledge of teaching and learning. In partnership with CASTL and other partners, the KML has been devising ways to take advantage of emerging technologies and new media to design Web-based portfolios that demonstrate how teaching practice and student learning can be documented with multimedia and then shared on the Internet.

Support Tools for Knowledge Representation: The KEEP Toolkit

Our initial efforts at multimedia documents to capture and share pedagogical knowledge were handcrafted. They were time-consuming to create, and publishing them online required both technical and intellectual expertise. Over time, interest in developing and using these portfolios to make visible the experiences of teaching and learning increased among educators, programs, and institutions. However, they told us, the process needed to be engaging, efficient, and simple. Most educators do not have the time to create novel versions of their work and sometimes do not have the language for expressing what they know (Iiyoshi, Richardson, and McGrath, 2006).

In response, the KML developed a set of tools that instructors and students could use to represent and share knowledge about the experiences that permeate instructional settings every day. Our underlying design philosophy was that while creating engaging online multimedia representations of teaching and learning and sharing them effectively will always be intellectually challenging, it need not be technically challenging, and technology must cognitively support users in the process of this work. The resulting KEEP Toolkit (See http://www.cfkeep.org) has become an economical and accessible means of achieving this goal, making it possible for users to take advantage of Web technology in order to share their work and reflections on their work.

The primary functions of the KEEP Toolkit provide educators with the ability to create "snapshots," succinct online overviews of teaching and learning experiences, along with reflections, supplements, and related resources. To create snapshots, users work through a set of Web-based tools that allow them to organize and present artifacts and evidence of teaching and learning such as classroom videos, student work examples, audio recordings of student interviews, and reflective notes; employ either preestablished or personally created snapshot templates that quickly organize those materials; and share the snapshots with others in visually appealing and intellectually engaging formats. Snapshots are delivered primarily online as Web sites, but they also can be distributed as local electronic files or in printed form as handouts and posters.

Making Tacit Knowledge of Practice Travel Across Boundaries
While the KEEP Toolkit enables educators to document and share knowledge, making this work understandable to others often requires additional support and scaffolding. The process of knowledge sharing can seem a little easier when working in a closed community (such as a department or academic discipline) in which all the members speak a similar language. Directions, goals, and activities can be directly explained and tweaked using terms known within the community. The process of finding suitable language that transcends disciplinary boundaries, as well as encourages users to understand and capture their deeply held implicit knowledge, is not as simple but can certainly bear rich results. The experience of the Carnegie Initiative on the Doctorate (CID) project sheds some light on these issues.

The CID worked with leadership teams from over 80 departments to promote reform of doctoral education in six disciplines. One of the goals of the project was to encourage teams from different disciplines to learn from each other about the core concern of preparing students to profess their disciplines as researchers, teachers, and members of a profession. Thus, the project needed rich descriptions of collective work. However, the language, methods, and benchmarks of one discipline, for example neuroscience, were vastly different from another, like English or mathematics.

Together, the CID and KML teams developed a set of prompts and guidelines to elicit descriptions of curriculum reform. We worked iteratively until we had four thought-provoking templates to elicit descriptions about the work of doctoral curriculum reform. The prompts used language that transcended disciplines, encouraged reflection on concerns of educational transformation, and did so in a format that displayed clearly on a Web-based platform. Every section on each template provided clear, specific instructions on how to respond to each question as well as the kinds of support materials to attach or to link to.

The CID directors sent the templates to participant teams, asking them to respond to each prompt and to supply unique supportive evidence of reform. Each team created snapshots of their varied efforts—all within the same framework. The standard presentation ensured that all teams knew where to find particular information and, because it was based on common language, they knew what it meant.

In this case, snapshot templates were built to help share knowledge, to nurture nascent ideas, and to support efforts to improve teaching and curriculum. By asking project participants to include common elements, meaningful reflections, and supported assertions about better curriculum models, project leaders helped make knowledge portable. This work has helped to build sustainable, collegial networks that will continue to contribute knowledge of teaching and learning long after the project's close.

Knowledge Building and Sharing in Action: Three Cases in Open Education

One of the major impediments in promoting educational innovations is the lack of a support structure for sharing ideas and experiences and building collective knowledge around effective use of openly available educational tools and resources. This kind of global knowledge of practice, if successfully represented and accumulated, can help improve local practices in various contexts.

The following three cases provide examples of how technology like the KEEP Toolkit enables effective knowledge building and sharing to advance open education. Expanded versions of these cases and other cases are available online at: http://gallery.carnegiefoundation.org/gallery_of_tl/keep_toolkit.html

Case 1: Sharing Course Transformation Experience to Promote Instructional Innovations   While converting an ineffective course into an effective one is a complex and daunting task, sharing the knowledge and experience gained from such an effort is even more challenging.

John Belcher, a physics professor at the Massachusetts Institute of Technology, and his colleagues in the Department of Physics, successfully changed a large introductory physics course from a traditional lecture format to a student-centered active learning arrangement. The overhaul resulted in substantial increases in student conceptual understanding and decreases in failure rates.

Belcher and his colleagues captured their efforts and the knowledge they gained and shared it in two KEEP Toolkit snapshots. The first snapshot, *Transforming Introductory Physics Courses: From a Large Lecture Classroom to a Student-Centered Active Learning Space*, provides a succinct overview of the transformation.

Although the effort and its results have been widely recognized by the MIT community and beyond through various articles and publications, as Belcher noted, "Changing institutional teaching practices is enormously hard, especially in research universities. Even though scientific studies repeatedly show that the 'transmission of knowledge' model is not particularly effective, there is a real inertia in moving away from this model, because it has been common practice for centuries. The way to facilitate even tentative moves toward scientific teaching is to hold up best practices for faculty to see, and to publicize them widely using tools like the KEEP Toolkit" (2005).

The second snapshot, *Technology Enabled Active Learning (TEAL): Studio Physics at MIT*, offers a compelling model for sharing pedagogical knowledge and associated resources. It was created specifically to advance two major MIT initiatives—OpenCourseWare (OCW) and the D'Arbeloff Fund for Excellence in MIT Education—using a set of framing questions developed in collaboration with MIT's Teaching and Learning Laboratory. The snapshot is intended to promote understanding of pedagogical decisions and design for faculty and students who use the OCW materials.

Case 2: Promoting Effective Use of Open Educational Resources by Sharing Pedagogical Experience Two challenges for MERLOT community members, specifically users wishing to use available educational materials, are (1) to gain access to the author's knowledge and experience in designing and using the materials; and (2) to share their challenges and successes in using them. With the ability to do these two things, MERLOT community members would be better equipped to learn from each other's work, continue improving these educational materials, and build on each other's pedagogical innovations.

In response to these challenges, MERLOT embarked on a pilot project. Selected winners of MERLOT Classics and Editors' Choice Awards and other highly rated authors of educational materials used the KEEP Toolkit to tell their "stories" about developing and refining these materials (for more information on these awards, see http://taste.merlot.org/awardsoverview.html). The author snapshots were created from a template that was designed with specific guiding questions in order to communicate why the learning objects were developed, how they were used in teaching, and what the impact of their use had on student learning or their own teaching. These authors also reflected on what they learned through using these educational materials and provided potential users with guidance on how they might adopt the materials. With their rich contextual descriptions of ways to use a resource in developing a course or curriculum and learning activities, the snapshots equip users with valuable information, including specific pitfalls to avoid.

Furthermore, a similar snapshot template for the users of these materials has been developed. Sharing their pedagogical experiences and offering valuable suggestions for materials contributes to creating a community of users and authors that will collectively improve both the quality of MERLOT resources and teaching and learning worldwide.

Case 3: Enabling Cross-Institutional Learning about Effective Use of Open Educational Technology In 2005, Indiana University-Purdue University Indianapolis, Portland State University, University of California Berkeley, University of Minnesota, and Virginia Tech University, all participants in a cross-institutional project to develop open source educational technology, wanted to pool their knowledge about using Open Source Portfolio (OSP) software. A snapshot template was developed to help each of these institutions succinctly document its local OSP implementation. The template prompted reflections on why the institution wanted to use the OSP; the background and context for the work; the goals, processes, and activities; the impact using OSP; the challenges, issues, and innovations; the institution's recommendations; and technical information.

Each institution then created a case study snapshot. In order to exhibit these case studies, an online gallery was created. Documenting, reflecting, and disseminating the products of documentation helps both community-source and open-source development of educational software by enabling participating institutions to learn from each other's implementation effort—what worked and what did not—as well as how the software effectively supported teaching and learning.

Environments for Nurturing Open Knowledge

As we described in the previous section, technological tools can enable educators to represent their knowledge, take advantage of multimedia, and make it portable. In this section, we discuss three different kinds of technology-supported environments that make the process of educational knowledge building and sharing more productive, engaging, and sustainable both individually and collectively.

The first space, the Carnegie Workspace, is a place for incubating ideas and sharing ongoing work for peer-review. The second space, the Gallery of Teaching and Learning, provides educators a rich source of inspiration for improving practice and educational transformation. The third space, the Teaching and Learning Commons, allows communities of practice and reflection to grow and develop around open exchange of knowledge and building on each other's work.

A Space for Incubation: The Carnegie Workspace

The Carnegie Workspace, an open-source Sakai-based online community environment, provides a "local" space for the development of representations for Carnegie Foundation programs and their participants. The Workspace supplies meeting places, resource repositories, and information portals to support projects' efforts. It is used for communication, collaboration, and documentation of the work completed during the course of the program, allowing for tentative ideas, successes, and challenges to be shared along every step of the process. By taking advantage of the KEEP Toolkit and other features of the Workspace, like Wiki and discussion forums, program participants can efficiently document, share, comment upon, and further develop their inquiries into teaching and student learning.

This incubation space is relatively private and secure—only program participants and invited guests have access—which help program participants freely discuss possibilities and dilemmas as well as processes and methods. Offering such a space can give participants a chance to explore, improve, and build on each other's knowledge of and experience in successful educational transformation efforts. It also allows risks to be taken, design principles developed, and lessons learned and recorded without penalty.

A Space for Inspiration: The Gallery of Teaching and Learning

Originally created in 2000, the Gallery of Teaching and Learning houses premier multimedia representations carefully chosen to encourage knowledge sharing of particular kinds. The work, created by participants of the Carnegie Foundation's programs and partners in educational transformation, focuses variously on the scholarship of teaching and learning and teacher and faculty development. The examples come from the classrooms of K–12 schools and undergraduate programs, doctoral programs, community colleges, and open education efforts.

As previously mentioned, these select public examples in the Gallery are the end products of more private, scaffolded processes of investigation, data collection, analysis, and reflection. Many of the representations were cultivated and articulated through idea sharing and peer-review in a local context like that offered by the Carnegie Workspace.

Meticulously vetted, these examples in the Gallery—individual exemplary work, carefully arranged collections and exhibitions and descriptive case studies—are meant to inspire new forms of practice and encourage more educators to learn about how they can improve teaching and student learning.

New Questions Triggered by a Burgeoning Interest

As the Gallery's collections increased and reached into different areas of education, we noticed increasing numbers of visitors and page views. At the same time, popular use and creation of snapshots by the KEEP Toolkit has also increased dramatically: Since we made the KEEP Toolkit publicly available in 2004, over 30,000 educators and students from all over the world have created over 100,000 online representations and collections (as of December 2007).

This burgeoning interest in the Toolkit implied that increasing numbers of people want to share their knowledge of teaching and learning. The increase of visitors to the Gallery suggested to us an even more distinctive role for the representations than simply as inspiration. We see that as efforts to build and share their educational knowledge and experience advances and expands, it can become more collective and collaborative. We see a need to offer a new space for users and creators of these representations to exchange and build upon each other's ideas and efforts.

Because of this dramatic growth in interest and use of these tools and spaces, we found ourselves wondering how we might develop ways for these representations of educational knowledge to be found and used so that greater numbers of educators and students can build, share, use, and reuse knowledge of effective practice: What environment could we create to provide necessary support in sustaining and further advancing this effort and reflection through peer-review and peer-learning? As more knowledge is represented and shared, how might we create a "bootstrap mechanism" that helps a community of practice surface useful, high quality knowledge and make it easily findable?

A Space for Interaction: The Teaching and Learning Commons

Building on Shulman's view of "teaching as community property" (1993), Mary Taylor Huber and Pat Hutchings (2005) have described the need to create a conceptual space, a "teaching commons," in which communities of educators can exchange ideas, inquiries, and innovations about teaching and learning to meet the challenges of helping students better learn. While we can imagine the teaching commons as a "knowledge trading zone," we wondered if it could be built at many levels, in various ways. It seemed critical that we try to theorize how we could continuously develop and sustain an educational knowledge economy in such a trading zone.

Daniel E. Atkins, John Seely Brown, and Allen L. Hammons (2006) also suggested the need for constructing an open participatory learning infrastructure/environment as "a shared, distributed, reflective practicum where experiences are being collected, vetted, clustered, commented on, tried out in new contexts, and so on." They assert that "we want to create a space where the teacher as entrepreneur—whether a certified schoolteacher, a home schooling parent, a librarian, a community center leader, or a retired professional can share and learn-share material, exercises for students, experiments, projects, portfolios of examples, etc." (p.61).

In response to these challenges and visions, we have started building a technology-enabled open knowledge forum, called the Teaching and Learning Commons, which is designed to enrich and encourage exchange of knowledge about teaching and learning (See http://commons .carnegiefoundation.org). The Teaching and Learning Commons is an open forum where educators from all over the world can create and share their own representations of practices and participate in an ongoing conversation about improving teaching and student learning. It also allows them to build on the work of other community members; and, based on what is learned, recreate new representations to further contribute to the Commons.

Toward Building Sustainable Knowledge Networks

The vision of the Teaching and Learning Commons is to harness the power of sophisticated knowledge management and community support technologies (such as tagging, commenting, rating tools, recommendation engines, and social bookmarking and networking tools) to help educators find, peer-review, and use a growing number of collections of documented educational knowledge and experience.

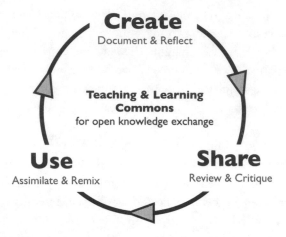

Figure 22.2
A Circle of Knowledge Building and Sharing

As shown in figure 22.2, the Teaching and Learning Commons is a means of supporting a circle of knowledge building and sharing.

As the figure suggests, the process of knowledge building and sharing is collective and recursive. It begins with an experience that is recorded, tested, and shared. The interpreted experience becomes more reliable as others examine, review and critique the first assertion. Knowledge then builds as it is assimilated and adapted by others, creating new experiences, interpretations, and assertions. Our work with educators has shown that technology can support this process, but not without challenges that include issues around finding appropriate representations and being able to build and share collectively.

Because we cannot predict where a user may enter this circle of knowledge building and sharing, we should provide various support features they may need accessible at any point. Elements of search, inspiration, creation, guidance, harvesting, and commenting are imminently important. Users also need different ways to locate useful representations of knowledge to improve their own practice. Using disciplinary categories and level of schooling offers a familiar and comfortable means to find work. However, as proven at Amazon.com and other commercial and social networking service Web sites, tracking behaviors of users, such as common search terms, number of page views, and bookmark activities, can also provide helpful recommendations to users of this kind of community space.

This space should also include a means for harvesting and reflecting on what is found and created. Users need different kinds of "annotated lists of favorites," "private bookshelves," or "personally created galleries of representations" that can be organized in multiple ways and differ based on authorship and levels of privacy. For example, some originally created pieces may need to be private while authors percolate ideas. Other collections of found items could be private for the same reason. Yet in time, both kinds of collections could be made semiprivate, allowing knowledge to be built within a group. And, should it be appropriate, the collection can be made public to build collective meaning or to assert a claim.

But first, the urge to create individual representations of knowledge has to be met. In this era of open authorship, users must have an efficient way to create relevant representations for this space. They need not only authorship tools, but also conceptual templates, direction, and guidance so that their representations are as reflective, evidenced-based, and rooted in the practice of teaching and learning as other pieces contributed to the space. Making connections between one's own work and others' works or within one's own private space must be made easily. Tagging offers one way for users to develop such a structure for naming what they see, as well as for various communities to develop their own folksonomies.

Participants in this community must also be able to submit their thoughts and connections in the form of essays and comments. The ability to blog, rate, and comment should be a part of the space. In this way, conversations and synergies among various kinds of locally produced work and the world of teachers and learners can begin. Finally, participation in this space must grow organically and be sustained by the deepening knowledge of users. It also should be engaging and rewarding.

Building the Teaching and Learning Commons is, in one sense, like building a global "knowledge banking network" system. We hope a community support system like this enables practitioners to flexibly deposit, withdraw, and transfer useful knowledge from one local context to another just like one can wire-transfer money in a local currency to someone's account overseas to be withdrawn in another currency.

Looking Ahead with Lessons Learned

The KML has worked extensively with various partners to understand more deeply how knowledge sharing around teaching and learning innovations can be facilitated by technology. In the process, we have learned various ways, large and small, to sustain knowledge building toward educational change.

One set of lessons concerns relationships. As a broker between technology and teachers, we have found it essential to provide guidance to interested users. It has been important not to manage, but to facilitate change by steering users toward new processes and allowing them to flourish and experiment on their own. We think it is important to allow stakeholders' strengths and conditions of work to influence their practice as well as inform ours. Communities of practice form around shared ideas and needs. It is imperative to keep this concept in the mind's eye as their processes are documented and shared.

A second set of lessons revolves around the specific kinds of practices that enable the relationships to yield positive results. While we need to pay heed to the needs of users, it is also important to challenge current practices by presenting new processes; to inspire shared vision by providing concrete examples; to enable others to act by giving effective mechanisms for inquiry and reflection; and to encourage the heart. We found that it is crucial to support participants in creating multidimensional packages of knowledge so that with each piece of knowledge, participants must share their context, their reflections, as well as their experience with various tools. Similarly, as new tools are developed, users' knowledge of how, why, and impact of the tools must travel with these resources.

The third set of lessons involves issues of tool development and promotion. We shifted from supplying tools and trying to get others to use them to responding to their demands. This was key. We thus sought forms of technology that make mechanisms for inquiry and reflection work, as well as those that make knowledge representations findable, useable, and reusable. In addition, we found it is essential to use a common platform for all tools and forms of communication.

Guiding Questions for Future Work

Practical knowledge gained through teaching, educational transformation, and the creation and use of educational tools and resources can be captured as engaging and useful representations in particular contexts. Although these representations can then be used for many purposes, one of the most promising is to use them to encourage similar efforts in different contexts. Harnessing open source technologies and ideas may help develop and connect similar ideas over space and time.

As our work continues to evolve, naturally, new questions and issues emerge. We can easily become focused on addressing issues, providing new tools, prompts and engaging activities. However, we try to keep in front of us these core questions, which we leave with the reader:

• How can educators, students, and educational institutions harness a growing number of open technologies, resources, and knowledge representations to effectively improve education quality and accessibility? What help or guidance is needed?

• How can we take full advantage of a wide range of technologies and the latest research findings to make invisible aspects of teaching and learning even more visible and shareable?

• How can we know when someone tracks down other people's resources and knowledge of practice, and build on them? How do people and niche communities see each other's work? What can Web 2.0 do to turn these pieces of knowledge created by niche communities into knowledge that is broadly available?

• How can we drive more participation and engage more people in reviewing and critiquing each other's work in a rewarding and meaningful way (for example, reviewing others' work in a way that would help advance their own work)?

• What does it take to build and support networks of educational projects, organizations, schools, and centers of teaching and learning in order to enable them to share their local knowledge and experience globally in a way that it becomes practical and useful in a local context?

References

Atkins, D. E., Brown, J. S., and Hammons, A. L. (2007). *A Review of the Open Educational Resources (OER) Movement: Achievement, Challenges, and New Opportunities*, The William and Flora Hewlett Foundation.

Belcher, J. (2005). Transferring knowledge and experience in innovative educational transformation, *KEEP Toolkit Case Studies*. Retrieved March 15, 2007, from http://gallery.carnegiefoundation.org/gallery_of_tl/transferring_knowledge_and_experience_in_innovative_educational_transformation.html.

Brown, J. S., and Duguid, P. (2000). *The Social Life of Information*. Boston, MA: Harvard Business School Press.

Cerbin, B., and Kopp, B. (2006). College lesson study project, *KEEP Toolkit Case Studies*. Retrieved March 15, 2007, from http://gallery.carnegiefoundation.org/gallery_of_tl/college_lesson_study_project.html.

Darling-Hammond, L., and Hammerness, K., with Grossman, P., Rust, F. and Shulman, L. (2005). The design of teacher education programs, in L. Darling-Hammond and J. Bransford (Eds.). *Preparing Teachers for a Changing World: What Teachers Should Learn and Be Able to Do*. San Francisco: Jossey-Bass.

Facilitating conversation between disciplines (2005). *KEEP Toolkit Case Studies*. Retrieved March 15, 2007, from http://gallery.carnegiefoundation.org/gallery_of_tl/facilitating_conversation_between_disciplines.html.

Gale, R. A. (2008). Inquiry unplugged: A scholarship of teaching and learning for open understanding. In T. Iiyoshi and M. S. V. Kumar (Eds.), *Opening Up Education: The Collective Advancement of Education through Open Technology, Open Content, and Open Knowledge*, pp. 289–302. Cambridge, MA: MIT Press.

Gardner, H. (1999). *The Disciplined Mind: What All Students Should Understand*. New York: Simon & Schuster.

Huber, M. T., and Hutchings, P. (2005). *The Advancement of Learning: Building the Teaching Commons*. San Francisco: Jossey-Bass.

Iiyoshi, T. (2006). Opportunity is knocking: Will education open the door? *Carnegie Perspectives*. Retrieved April 1, 2007, from http://www.carnegiefoundation.org/perspectives/sub.asp?key=245&subkey=1151

Iiyoshi, T., Richardson, C., and McGrath, O. (2006). Harnessing open technologies to promote open educational knowledge sharing, *Innovate Journal of Online Education*, October/November Issue, 3(1). Retrieved April 1, 2007, from http://innovateonline.info/index.php?view=article&id=339&action=article

Nonaka, I. (1991). The Knowledge-Creating Company. *Harvard Business Review*, 26–29.

Promoting effective use of open educational technology (2006). *KEEP Toolkit Case Studies*. Retrieved March 15, 2007, from http://gallery.carnegiefoundation.org/gallery_of_tl/promoting_effective_use_of_open_educational_technology.html.

Sharing effective pedagogical innovations (2005). *KEEP Toolkit Case Studies*. Retrieved March 15, 2007, from http://gallery.carnegiefoundation.org/gallery_of_tl/sharing_effective_pedagogical_innovations.html.

Shulman, L. S. (1983). Teaching as community property: Putting an end to pedagogical solitude. *Change*, Nov.–Dec. 1993, 25(6), 6–7.

Shulman, L. S. (1986). Those who understand: Knowledge growth in teaching. *Educational Researcher*, 15(2), 4–14.

Shulman, L. S. (2004a). From Minsk to Pinsk: Why a scholarship of teaching and learning? *The Wisdom of Practice: Essays on Teaching, Learning, and Learning to Teach*. Jossey-Bass: San Francisco, pp. 156–162.

Shulman, L. S. (2004b). Knowledge and teaching: Foundations of the new reform (originally published 1987). *The Wisdom of Practice: Essays on Teaching, Learning, and Learning to Teach*. Jossey-Bass: San Francisco, pp. 217–248.

Surowiecki, J. (2005). *The Wisdom of Crowds: Why the Many Are Smarter Than the Few and How Collective Wisdom Shapes Business, Economies, Societies and Nations*. Anchor Books: New York.

23

Scaffolding for Systemic Change

Barbara Cambridge

Thinkers about the open source movement in software development can teach educators about critical elements of systemic change. Two thinkers point, for example, to the centrality of system development in promoting change. John Seely Brown contends that open source is an institutional innovation, not just a technological one. He calls for an "ecology of experiments and systems for the learning landscape." These systems can provide incentive systems, constitutions, governance, and practices that embody a "coevolution between technology and society" (2004). Another thinker and writer, Steven Weber, describes a set of organizing principles undergirding the open source community: "criteria for entering (and leaving), leadership roles, power relations, distributional issues, education and socialization paths, and all the other characteristics that describe a nascent culture and community structure" (2004, p. 15). Building communities marked by collaborative interchange around visible educational assets requires planned systems.

Seely Brown's use of the word *landscape*, however, is not coincidental. While making claims about institutions, Seely Brown places them within an ecological model. Such a model requires building social networks, developing ways to accelerate capabilities, and assuring staying power. Three large-scale projects illustrate practices that serve these three ends. The Urban Universities Portfolio Project (UUPP) fostered institutional linkages, courage to change rapidly, and interplay of ideas and practices (See http://www.imir.iupui.edu/portfolio/). The Carnegie Academy for the Scholarship of Teaching and Learning (CASTL [See http://www.carnegiefoundation.org/programs/index.asp?key=21]), which gave birth to the International Society for the Scholarship of Teaching and Learning

(ISSOTL [See http://www.issotl.org/]), exemplifies a design that fosters continued invitation for involvement while cultivating emergent leadership, encouraging change through national endorsement, and providing interchange among individuals, campuses, and associations, first nationally and then internationally). The Inter/National Coalition for Electronic Portfolio Research (Inter/National Coalition) links researchers across institutions and countries, insures rapid sharing about process and of findings, and provides a framework for interaction and dissemination (See http://www.ncepr.org/ncepr/drupal/). Each project offers evidence of what it takes for campuses and coalitions to share learning leading to systemic change.

Building Social Networks

Open education presumes that knowledge is socially constructed. Through reflection and interaction with others, people turn information into knowledge. In *The Social Life of Information*, John Seely Brown and Paul Duguid contend that knowledge, unlike information, involves a knower, knowledge is not separable from that knower, and people become knowers by integrating new information with their own prior knowledge through application in the world with other people (2000, pp. 119–120).

The scale of a social network that fosters knowledge-building can be as small as a classroom and as large as a network of networks. Knowledge-building may begin with a group of students doing service learning who discover a new way to communicate with service providers for the mentally ill; it may continue with a university that modifies another institution's tenure guidelines to increase the value of scholarship of teaching and learning; it may involve a state that builds a repository of lesson plans gleaned from schools throughout the state and vetted for quality based on rubrics; and it may even become "a network of networks." Marlene Scardamalia and Carl Bereiter have imagined "a network of networks—people from schools, universities, cultural institutions, service organizations, businesses—simultaneously building knowledge within their primary groups while advancing the knowledge of others. We might call such a community network a knowledge-building society" (2000, p. 312).

Intermediaries

A knowledge-building society presupposes open sharing of information and support of that sharing. In *Reconnecting Education and Foundations*, Ray Bacchetti and Tom Ehrlich advocate for educational capital, which they define as "the progressive accumulation, in forms useable by educators, of validated experience and knowledge about successful educational ideas and strategies" (2007, p. 23). In other words, "validated experience and knowledge" are shared as the means to effective change. Bacchetti and Ehrlich advocate for a category of knowledge-builders that they deem essential for a social network involving education: these knowledge-builders are intermediaries. Often organizations, these intermediaries "can offer the stability, expert depth, and field-wide reach to make assembling and circulating elements of educational capital a signal contribution to their constituents" (2007, p. 43). Open education is supported by intermediaries that provide the environment necessary for wide-scale knowledge-building. Each of the national projects used as primary examples in this chapter has thrived because of effective intermediaries. The Urban University Portfolio Project (UUPP) had collaborating intermediaries: an association (the American Association for Higher Education) and an institution (Indiana University Purdue University Indianapolis). The Carnegie Academy for the Scholarship of Teaching and Learning (CASTL) had The Carnegie Foundation for the Advancement of Teaching; the International Society for the Scholarship of Teaching and Learning (ISSOTL) has become the next-generation intermediary. The Inter/National Coalition has a set of directors with partners for various cohorts, like the Centre for Recording Achievement supported by the Higher Education Academy in the United Kingdom and the National Association for School Personnel Administrators in the United States. In each case, funders have channeled resources through the intermediaries, and the intermediaries have provided the "stability, expert depth, and field-wide reach" advocated by Bacchetti and Ehrlich.

Intermediaries can serve various purposes. For example, in the Peer Review of Teaching Project analyzed in *Reconnecting Education and Foundations*, Pat Hutchings notes the duties of the American Association for Higher Education, which coordinated the participating campuses. "Project central" would "articulate the central ideas and vision of the project, organize meetings, broker communication across sites, solve problems, share successes, and inspire" (2007, p.314). When certain campuses faltered in their progress, project central provided ideas about how to negotiate the bumps; when a campus stalled because of entrenched practices, project central linked that campus with one that had released energy for change in the practice; and when campuses developed innovative ideas and practices, project central helped broadcast the successes throughout the project and beyond.

Another illustrative example of intermediary function emerges from collaborative research in the Inter/National Coalition. To answer the question "How do electronic portfolios generate and promote reflection that supports student learning?" each campus in the first two cohorts examined artifacts from student eportfolios for evidence of the influence of reflection on learning. The Coalition directors then derived a taxonomy of reflective practices particular to learning in electronic portfolios, practices reintroduced into individual campus research as a next step of investigation. No single campus or even the collected campuses were as well-positioned as the project-central directors to develop the taxonomy, but the network was essential for field-based examples and reapplication of learning.

Continued Invitation to Involvement and Cultivation of Emergent Leadership

A second element in the building of social networks is continued invitation to involvement and cultivation of emergent leadership. Change initiatives often choose or invite a set of players willing to work toward mutual educational objectives but also structure future entry points into the project.

One model for involvement in a national project is the Campus Program of CASTL. This model might be labeled the hourglass. During the first two years of CASTL, an open invitation drew over 200 campuses that participated in the first phase of the project, defining the scholarship of teaching and learning for their campus and examining the supports and barriers for its health on their campus. All kinds of participating institutions throughout the United States were at varying stages of support for this kind of scholarly work.

The next phase narrowed the hourglass to focus on continued learning: through an application process, 12 campuses were selected to lead clusters focusing on topics selected through analysis of past work as essential for the next phase of work. Then campuses chose the cluster in which they wanted to participate. At the same time that campuses long in the project were focusing on collaborative goals; however, new campuses were welcomed into an affiliate group that also met to share information about their individual efforts. At the end of the clusters' three years of work, the hourglass expanded again. Certain campuses applied to lead the ensuing leadership groups, but any campus, whether veteran in the project through being in a cluster or the affiliate group or novice with no prior affiliation, was invited to join one of 12 leadership groups. The international scope of the work also expanded as more campuses outside the United States joined in. This model honors campuses with significant successes by placing them in leadership positions but also honors institutions doing continuing work or newly entering the scholarship of teaching and learning.

Other models of social networking also foster continuing inclusion and foster emergent leadership as campuses and individuals demonstrate abilities for coordinating others. In *Stewardship: Choosing Service Over Self-Interest*, Peter Block writes: "stewardship begins with the willingness to be accountable for some larger body than ourselves—an organization, a community" (1993, p. 6). The UUPP project demonstrates this aspect of social networking on two levels. First, project campuses became accountable to one another as the range of challenges in building an institutional electronic portfolio became more and more evident. Campuses increasingly reached out to share knowledge as they sensed a roadblock of a member institution. For example, when the University of Massachusetts Boston lost its leading supportive administrator, other campuses offered the local project leader strategies for enlisting the endorsement of the new administrator. In the social network needed for building an institutional electronic portfolio, as in most large projects, the advocacy of a key senior administrator is essential. Second, each UUPP campus served as host for project meetings so that the strengths of each campus could be highlighted and used to advantage. Sometimes pairs of institutions found common cause through their growing knowledge of the educational environment on one or the other campus. For example, California State University Sacramento began its electronic portfolio work at the department level, the process explained by department chairs at a UUPP national meeting. Georgia State, which had focused on campus strategic development as its nexus for the institutional portfolio, decided through interaction with Sacramento faculty and administrators that moving to the department level was a crucial next move.

Individuals, as well as campuses, emerge as important leaders within a social network. The American Council on Education (ACE) study of institutional change recognized that "change leaders develop connections among different initiatives and individuals across campus that create synergy and provide momentum for the initiative" (1999, p. 4) and that "collaborative leadership identifies and empowers talent across campus and at a variety of levels" (1999, p. 6). In other words, leadership development helps to sustain initiatives and continue progress during the extended time often necessary for institutionalizing change.

Interaction of Individuals, Campuses, and Organizations, Both Nationally and Internationally

Sometimes the nature of the work itself elicits interaction. For example, in chaos theory, randomness coalesces at different times because of a certain attractor. In a dynamic time of specific or potential change, electronic portfolios in the UUPP project and in the Inter/National Coalition have served as attractors. They have allowed change to be discussed, provided a vehicle for required accountability, operated as a mechanism for improvement, provided occasions for discussion that give practice with new language and concepts, served as a source of curiosity, and connected core attributes of learning with other parts of the educational system.

Even if the work serves as an attractor, projects need to intentionally set up interaction. The CASTL project design, discussed in depth in this book's chapter by Richard Gale (2008), epitomizes that careful intentionality with its three-part structure encouraging individuals in scholarly work on teaching and learning, bringing together campuses for mutual exploration and support, and aiding disciplinary organizations in sharing experience and ideas. The Inter/National Coalition carefully designs cohorts for diversity of institutional type, geographical location, and kind of work proposed. During meetings, however, campuses with similar problems or questions are paired, cohorts meet together at times and singularly at others, and members are encouraged to do professional writing and presenting in different groupings.

According to Etienne Wenger and his colleagues, "communities of practice are groups of people who share a concern, a set of problems, or a passion about a topic, and who deepen their knowledge and expertise in this area by interacting on an ongoing basis" (Wenger, McDermott, and Snyder, p. 4). Wenger and colleagues have identified five stages in a community of practice: potential, coalescing, maturing, stewardship, and transformation. Through participation in the CASTL Campus Program, institutions moved from *potential* exhibited by developing common language across campus, through *coalescing* of definition and goals by a combination of local and synthetic national definitions, into *maturing* and *stewardship* marked by building infrastructures and expanding collaborations, and on to *transformation* characterized by instituting policies and assessing impact.

Both CASTL and the Inter/National Coalition expanded interaction from a start in the United States to current work across national boundaries. ISSOTL now attracts members from around the globe and conference participants from a growing number of countries each year. In addition to U.S. participants, the Inter/National Coalition's third cohort includes member campuses from Canada and England; its fourth cohort comprises members from Scotland, England, and the Netherlands. As participants interact, they discover elements of cultural diversity and of commonalities that create understanding and deepen the complexity of scholarship of teaching and learning and electronic portfolio practice and research.

Accelerating Capabilities

John Henry Newman once said that "growth is the only evidence of life." In an educational ecology, vitality is evident in a system that, as ACE puts it, "is an act to be managed, not a happenstance to be endured" (1999, p. 11). Although change can occur naturally, often those involved need encouragement and capacity-building to accelerate important change. Although faculty and administrators often complain about the glacial pace of change in colleges and universities, the three example projects in this chapter illustrate ways to accelerate capabilities of individuals and of campuses.

Courage to Change

First, both individuals and campuses need the courage to change. The label of "learned helplessness" coined by Watkins and Marsick applies to those whose efforts have consistently met with resistance so that they become helpless or passive. According to Watkins and Marsick, after being rule-bound for a long period of time, people will not be creative even when strictures are lifted. Also if goals are unachievable, people learn to underachieve. "Learned helplessness dulls awareness and innovation because people respond to a new situation with the assumption that they are incapable of doing anything to change events" (1993, p. 17). The CASTL Campus Program and the UUPP offer two cases in point. Overture about the scholarship of teaching and learning with some faculty members yielded an immediate throwing up of hands because of tenure strictures. Research universities claimed that scholarship of teaching and learning would never be valued because of rigorous criteria for scholarship. At an early Campus Program gathering of research institutions, however, the provost of the University of Michigan built a strong argument for the scholarship of teaching and learning as essential scholarly work at all research universities and affirmed both available and new dollars for innovative scholarship at Michigan. In addition, Mary Huber's research at four prestigious universities yielded examples of faculty members who had achieved promotion and tenure based on the scholarship of teaching and learning (2004). Visible administrative support and successful examples promote courage.

In the UUPP, a new genre was being developed. Representing the institution through an electronic institutional portfolio presented challenges: public expression of shortcoming might negatively affect funding, demonstrating student learning online could violate student privacy, and campuses needed common goals and assessment strategies for scaling portfolios. After trust-building during the first year of the project, campuses felt free to share such apprehensions, to admit failed attempts, and to put out for the use of others their discoveries and successes. At a meeting of the campuses with stakeholders from multiple sectors, the head commissioner of a state's commission on higher education asserted that campuses who claimed success on all counts were suspect; it was better to show challenges and how they were being addressed. Campuses that saw others taking that advice gained courage to do the same. Indiana University Purdue University Indianapolis (IUPUI) and Portland State University each subsequently broke new ground by using their institutional e-portfolios successfully for regional accreditation.

The Value of a National Context

In describing the Peer Review of Teaching Project, Pat Hutchings suggests that the national project provided a "demilitarized zone." She states that "the single most important condition in allowing the campuses to continue their work was the presence of one another working under a national project umbrella. Hard work needs good company" (2007, p. 317).

Another virtue of a national context is that disparate achievements can become more than the sum of the parts. On the campus level, Deryl Smith, a prominent researcher of higher education, analyzed the Mapping Project progress reports done by over 50 campuses in the fourth year of the CASTL Campus Program. Each campus examined key dimensions of change regarding the scholarship of teaching and learning, such as centrality, leadership, integration, resources, signs of success, reflection, and strategy. Smith writes: "The mapping process creates the possibility of bringing coherence to what could otherwise be isolated pieces, intentionality to what might otherwise seem random, collaboration and community without requiring everyone to occupy the same space and time, and a sense of importance to an effort that otherwise might be seen as just one more initiative" (2004, p. 149).

The effort of a national project to map progress across its constituent groups offers the same benefits. For example, CASTL's analysis of 58 Mapping Project reports yielded impressive statistics about the impact of systematic attention to the scholarship of teaching and learning: 95 percent of campuses had sponsored conferences, workshops, or retreats for faculty interested in the scholarship of teaching and learning; 72 percent reported grants, stipends, or released time for faculty or departments doing the scholarship of teaching and learning; and 60 percent of campuses had included the scholarship of teaching and learning in some form in promotion and tenure systems. These statistics from such an array of campuses were persuasive to institutions still altering their own terrains.

A national effort, of course, must recognize the individuality of each campus. Smith, however, asks the right question: "What are the core characteristics of change that will lead to the likelihood of sustainable and manageable efforts?" (2004, p. 147). Bacchetti and Ehrlich maintain that any project must identify its "non-negotiable core" (2007, p. 26). Although implementation may be varied, there must be identifiable features that warrant the spotlight of a national effort and of funding and support.

The Inter/National Coalition is attempting through research to locate the core kinds of learning that are supported by e-portfolios. In a forthcoming book, Coalition members present evidence that demonstrates the electronic portfolio as contributing in foundational ways to developmental learning, integrative learning, social learning, lifelong and life-wide learning, and organizational learning. Because the technology for electronic portfolios is relatively new, few programs yet have all these elements in equally robust form; yet an international project has been able to identify the core elements as signals of reason for investment at the local, state, national, and international levels. Open sharing of emergent practices and research findings speeds up the ability to learn and emphasizes the benefits of national and international collaborations.

Sharing and Assessing Process and Findings

"Build in assessment at every stage" is one of five criteria that Bacchetti and Ehrlich stipulate for building educational capital (2007, p. 27). They are not alone in emphasizing that formative assessment enables a project to learn during its implementation and to adjust from lessons learned. The ACE praises institutions that learn from their actions and adjust their plans accordingly (Eckel et al, p. 12). The Urban Universities Portfolio Project serves as a case in point. When the project was conceived, portfolios were envisioned as the vehicle for presenting evidence of each university's progress toward its goals, but the electronic element was only one option. Quite soon, as the six universities assessed one another's early efforts, the universities realized that the *only* way to represent the ever-changing landscape of their work was through a dynamic Web presence. Although many had had the obligatory Web site to provide information, this electronic portfolio would provide evidence of learning, including how the university was learning from its unsuccessful and successful efforts at providing excellent education, research, and service. The portfolio was not a PR effort, but a living representation of a learning organization that, through assessing its progress, adjusted its work and, thus, changed its educational outcomes.

Formative assessment was also important in the CASTL Campus Program. A single example is illustrative. When a sacrificial definition of the scholarship of *teaching* was offered to campuses to redefine according to their own context, an immediate lesson was that *learning* needed to be added to the term. Although project leaders had assumed teaching did not exist without learning, early analysis of definitions revealed that that assumption was not widely held by some faculty members. The revised key term became the *scholarship of teaching and learning*.

The pacing of interactions between Coalition leaders and participating campus teams changed in the Inter/National Coalition during the life of the first cohort due to assessment of projects' progress. Meeting twice a year, face-to-face, some project teams accelerated their work only during the month or two before the semiannual gatherings of teams. Assessing the negative effect of this pacing on project progress, Coalition leaders added an individual phone call with each team between meetings. With discussion questions for the calls distributed ahead of time, teams received added impetus for continual progress on their work. Openly discussing what was going well and what had stalled, teams gained new incentive to move forward.

Eckel, Green, and Hill remind us that change can look "like a failure from the middle. The work not yet accomplished is more visible than the changes made. Taking stock is helpful not only because it provides useful feedback for mid-course corrections, but because it also affirms accomplishment and nourishes future work" (2001, p. 27).

Ensuring Staying Power

Affirming accomplishment; embedding effective practices in institutional policies, infrastructures, and practices; and nourishing future work are essential in the course of a project. "Incorporate the means for ensuring staying power," advise Bacchetti and Ehrlich (2007, p. 27). Some national and international projects produce significant outcomes which die on the vine because enthusiasm and/or funding dries up before the projects can take root. From lack of nourishment and continued tending, the fruits of the project disappear, with later projects having to begin anew, wasting resources. Watkins and Marsick call this phenomenon "truncated learning" in which "Learning efforts don't take root because they are interrupted or partially implemented" (1993, p. 68).

Technological Support for Communication and Dissemination

One means for ensuring staying power is technological support for communication and dissemination of ideas and findings. Because intellectual work spawns tentative and not-yet-fully formed questions and thoughts, attention must first be given to safe space for exploring nascent ideas. In the Web Center that supported early work in the Campus Program, Darren Cambridge encouraged inclusion of "protopublic spaces in which to hatch and mature ideas, strategies, and representations in dialogue with like-minded others" (2004, p. 94). This notion is incorporated in the Knowledge Media Lab (KML) of the Carnegie Foundation (See http://www.carnegiefoundation.org/programs/index .asp?key=38) that now supports the thinking and doing of CASTL campus constituents in protected online workspaces that enable emerging ideas and practices to mature before they go public. UUPP and the Inter/ National Coalition have also offered protopublic spaces. Closed face-to-face meetings of the UUPP participants offered safe spaces to talk about unsuccessful portfolio structures, difficult campus discussions, and fears about media use of portfolio materials. Campuses grew to trust one another enough to admit failure, to solicit advice, and to offer hard critique, both in person and online. As campuses from three countries have interacted in Cohort III of the Inter/National Coalition, both in person and online, issues of cultural norms and contexts have necessitated clarifying conversations. When creating something new that has high stakes, people need conditions that shelter the creation until it is strong enough for the winds of sometimes uninformed public attention.

On the other hand, projects need to listen to Gerald Graff, who advocates strongly for transparency, a word heard often in discussions about accountability. Graff claims that "academia reinforces cluelessness by making its ideas, problems, and ways of thinking *look* more opaque, narrowly specialized, and beyond normal learning capacities than they are or need to be" (2003, p. 1). The UUPP discovered that the electronic portfolio genre and medium offered a way to communicate within and outside academia. For example, Portland State University and IUPUI both revamped their sites several times to provide paths for people in different roles, such as business people, families of students, and other educational groups. Online artifacts could be viewed in different order with different explanatory language dependent on the audience. Even emergent knowledge may be made public if made understandable. IUPUI chose to include lower-than-desired retention rates, for example, but provided the numerous ways in which it was working to raise the rates with the degrees of success of those strategies.

Whether a site is protopublic or public, project central can be responsible for knowledge managers to facilitate online communication and preliminary project findings. Literature about communities of practice accentuates the need for synthesizers who follow a threaded discussion to occasionally summarize main points or catalog central questions. Resource managers may take the role of supplying references to literature and experience when online conversations reveal such a need. In the CASTL Campus Program, the project central Web site was connected to those individual campuses with periodic mining of the individual sites for information potentially useful to all participating campuses. The online newsletter of the Inter/National Coalition provides a venue for dissemination of summaries from chats among members and of findings from research conducted by member institutions. Recognizing buds of ideas and fully formed fruits of work both are important in helping a line of work bloom over time.

Building on the Shoulders of Giants

Editors of educational journals know that faculty members get excited when they discover a new pedagogy that works in their classroom. Before writing up their discovery for publication, however, they forget to check the pedagogical literature to put their own application in the context of other versions of the teaching and learning strategy. They skip the important scholarly step of building on what is already extant. Effective national projects must build on what is already known, an admonition that seems obvious but is sometimes ignored. Avoiding tunnel vision that isolates a project from the national context, project leaders need to recognize and benefit from what other projects have learned. On the other hand, one mark of an effective project is that it spawns new work that builds on it. CASTL is a parent of ISSOTL; and the UUPP, a predecessor of the Inter/National Coalition. Huber and Hutchings note the offspring of the Peer Review project in their chapter in this book (2008). Building on the shoulders of giants entails benefiting from ancestors but also contributing to the next generation.

Publications are one way to contribute to that next generation. Leaders of projects highlighted in this chapter, for example, have generated books that describe processes and outcomes of the scholarship of teaching and learning and of learning supported by e-portfolios. For example, I have coedited *Campus Progress: Supporting the Scholarship of Teaching and Learning* based on Campus Program work; *Electronic Portfolios: Emerging Practices in Student, Faculty, and Institutional Learning* with a section featuring UUPP work; and *Electronic Portfolios: Emergent Findings and Shared Questions* based on research from the Inter/National Coalition.

Equally important are the numerous publications and presentations generated by project participants. CASTL and the Inter/National Coalition keep records of the many ways that project participants disseminate outcomes of their work. Having visible assets that can spark further research questions and additional scholarship is an important part of using the past to inform the future.

Part of the drive to take a project international emanates from the recognition that important work on significant topics is currently being done around the world. Both CASTL and the Inter/National Coalition began in one country but realized that staying there would be a mistake. The National Coalition, originally based in the United States, added *Inter* to its name to welcome into its third cohort member campuses from Canada and England and into its fourth cohort, administered in England, teams from Scotland and the Netherlands. The efficacy of including campuses from Ireland, Australia, and Hong Kong in the CASTL Institutional Leadership Program overrode logistical issues that had been anticipated by the Campus Program because international collaborative work so forcefully increases the pace of field-building. Using what has already been learned and collaborating to provide new shoulders for others means that the whole is stronger than the sum of the parts.

The Marriage of Patience and Impatience

Analyzing policy change, Duane Roen of Arizona State University notes that "institutional initiatives have resulted from wide-ranging, prolonged conversations" (2004, p. 6). Campus Conversations at the beginning of the Campus Program structurally supported discussion that contributed to sustainable change. CASTL has continuously collected successful promotion and tenure cases based on the scholarship of teaching and learning to demonstrate slow but steady progress in changing promotion and tenure requirements. In the UUPP, campuses developed incremental strategies for engaging more and more constituent groups as the electronic portfolios needed their input or offered them support for their work. Eager to be widely international, ISSOTL is cultivating faculty members from more and more countries each year. Because deep-rooted change takes time, patience is, as they say, a virtue.

But impatience is also necessary. The core values and commitments mentioned earlier in this chapter must propel a project to apply pressure when necessary to expedite progress through such means as reasonable deadlines, gentle prompts to action, and supportive peer pressure. Calls between face-to-face meetings in the Inter/National Coalition sometimes start with a litany of reasons for inaction, all understandable but few acceptable. Although crises and new circumstances can intervene, the campus needs to be proactive in adjusting to unexpected constraints, including altering the project scope or timeline. Prompts to action are often appreciated. In the Campus Program, deadlines for publishing about progress moved campuses to put in writing accomplishments and next steps. In the Inter/National Coalition, doing joint presentations at national conferences provides a built-in need for completion of work. UUPP meetings with external stakeholders provided input from those stakeholders but also instigated careful preparation by project participants.

Stimuli that prompt progress on project goals are beneficial for individual campuses and for the project. At every UUPP meeting each campus presented its electronic institutional portfolio with specific reference to changes from the last meeting. When a campus repeated itself from meeting to meeting, project colleagues called for expectations of greater progress. At each Inter/National Coalition meeting, mutual critiquing of project work provides written responses for sharing with campus colleagues. CASTL colloquia offer sessions for presenting progress and receiving response from colleagues on other campuses. ISSOTL's developing signature conference pedagogies provide reflection session presenters with feedback that sets high expectations but also offers helpful suggestions. Faculty members and administrators care what their colleagues think, so peer feedback can be an effective way to signal patience, impatience, or a mixture of both.

Learning theory and practice confirm that scaffolding supports learning in an open-education environment in important ways. Scaffolding can involve social networks, ways to accelerate change, and modes of staying power that are needed as an idea or project grows strong enough to endure, always open to change as the ecology of the environment develops but stable enough to find its place in the culture. The ACE contends that "institutional change leaders work within a culture while challenging its comfort zone to change the culture" (1999, p. 7). National and international projects can scaffold ideas and practices that productively challenge higher education and positively change systems. The three projects in this chapter and other initiatives in this book can rightfully claim progress toward desired changes in higher education through open education.

References

Bacchetti, R., and Ehrlich, T. (2007). Recommendations: Building educational capital. In R. Bacchetti and T. Ehrlich (Eds.), *Reconnecting Education and Foundations: Turning Good Intentions into Educational Capital*. San Francisco: Jossey-Bass.

Block, P. (1993). *Stewardship: Choosing Service over Self-interest*. San Francisco: Berrett-Koehler.

Brown, J. S. (2004, December 2). *The Changing Landscape of Higher Education: IT Infrastructure and Beyond*. Presentation at the Open Source Summit, Scottsdale, AZ.

Brown, J. S., and Duguid, P. (2000). *The Social Life of Information*. Boston: Harvard Business School Press.

Cambridge, B. L. (2004). Transforming campus cultures through the scholarship of teaching and learning. In B. L. Cambridge (Ed.), *Campus Progress: Supporting the Scholarship of Teaching and Learning.* Washington, DC: American Association for Higher Education. Stylus Publishing.

Cambridge, D. (2004). Technology as collaborative practice: Protopublicity, multivocality, and knowledge brokering. In B. L. Cambridge (Ed.), *Campus Progress: Supporting the Scholarship of Teaching and Learning.* Washington, DC: American Association for Higher Education. Stylus Publishing.

Cambridge, D., Cambridge, B., and Yancey, K. (Eds.). (in press). *Electronic Portfolios: Emergent Findings and Shared Questions.* Sterling, VA: Stylus Publishing.

Eckel, P., Green, M., and Hill, B. (2001). *On Change: Riding the Waves of Change—Insights from Transforming Institutions.* Washington, DC: American Council on Education.

Eckel, P., Hill, B., Green, M., and Mallon, B. (1999). *On Change: Reports from the Road—Insights in Institutional Change.* Washington, DC: American Council on Education.

Gale, R. A. (2008). Inquiry unplugged: A scholarship of teaching and learning for open understanding. In T. Iiyoshi and M. S. V. Kumar (Eds.), *Opening Up Education: The Collective Advancement of Education through Open Technology, Open Content, and Open Knowledge,* pp. 289–302. Cambridge, MA: MIT Press.

Graff, G. (2003). *Clueless in Academe: How Schooling Obscures the Life of the Mind.* New Haven, CT: Yale University Press.

Huber, M. (2004). *Balancing Acts: The Scholarship of Teaching and Learning in Academic Careers.* Washington, DC: American Association for Higher Education. Stylus Publishing.

Huber, M., and Hutchings, P. (2005). *The Advancement of Learning: Building the Teaching Commons.* Stanford, CA: The Carnegie Foundation for the Advancement of Teaching.

Huber, M. T., and Hutchings, P. (2008). What's next for open knowledge? In T. Iiyoshi and M. S. V. Kumar (Eds.), *Opening Up Education: The Collective Advancement of Education through Open Technology, Open Content, and Open Knowledge,* pp. 417–428. Cambridge, MA: MIT Press

Huber, M., and Morreale, S. P. (2002). *Disciplinary Styles in the Scholarship of Teaching and Learning.* Washington, DC: American Association for Higher Education. Stylus Publishing.

Hutchings, P. (2002). *Ethics of Inquiry: Issues in the Scholarship of Teaching and Learning.* Stanford, CA: Carnegie Foundation for the Advancement of Teaching.

Hutchings, P. (2000). *Opening Lines: Approaches to the Scholarship of Teaching and Learning.* Stanford, CA: The Carnegie Foundation for the Advancement of Teaching.

Hutchings, P. (2007). From idea to prototype: The peer review of teaching. In R. Bacchetti and T. Ehrlich (Eds.), *Reconnecting Education and Foundations: Turning Good Intentions into Educational Capital.* San Francisco: Jossey-Bass.

Roen, D. (2004). Instituting policies. In B. L. Cambridge (Ed.), *Campus Progress: Supporting the Scholarship of Teaching and Learning*. Washington, DC: American Association for Higher Education. Stylus Publishing.

Scardamalia, M., and Bereiter, C. (2000). Engaging students in a knowledge society. In *The Jossey-Bass Reader on Technology and Learning*. San Francisco, CA: Jossey-Bass.

Smith, D. G. (2004). Mapping progress. In B. L. Cambridge (Ed.), *Campus Progress: Supporting the Scholarship of Teaching and Learning*. Washington, DC: American Association for Higher Education. Stylus Publishing.

Watkins, K., and Marsick, V. (1993). Overcoming barriers to change. In *Sculpting the Learning Organization*. San Francisco: Jossey-Bass.

Weber, S. (2004). *The Success of Open Source*. Cambridge, MA: Harvard University Press.

Wenger, E., McDermott, R., and Snyder, W. (2002). *Cultivating Communities of Practice*. Boston: Harvard University Business School Press.

24

Learning Design: Sharing Pedagogical Know-How

James Dalziel

Open education has had two great successes and one significant failure to date. The first success is the development and adoption of open source course management systems. Moodle, Sakai, LRN, ATutor, and other systems demonstrate that open source development processes can create excellent course management systems that can readily be adopted by educational institutions throughout the world. The second success is the open sharing of educational content. OpenCourseWare, MERLOT, ARIADNE, and other initiatives illustrate how educators and students throughout the world can benefit from freely shared educational content.

The failure is harder to put into words. It could be described as our lack of progress on sharing "pedagogical know-how" among educators. We have systems to run e-learning courses and content to view, but we have not captured the teaching processes that expert educators use to bring learning alive in their e-learning courses. If an educator creates a great sequence of learning activities that leads to a rich learning experience for students in an e-learning class, how does this educator share the activity sequence with colleagues so that they can automatically run the same activities or adapt them to suit local conditions? How does the educator share the thought processes that led to the design of the activity sequence?

Related to this, e-learning's concept of education is often quite narrow. It is almost all "single-learner" content, rather than a mixture of content and collaborative learning tasks. This failure to capture the collaborative dimension of teaching and learning impoverishes the pedagogy of open education. Too much e-learning to date is analogous to the content stored in a library, not the collaborative learning experience of the classroom. Put another way, if good teaching can be like following a great recipe then we have lots of ingredients (content) but no instructions.

Of course, these problems are not unique to e-learning—they apply to all of education. Whether a class discussion is conducted face-to-face or in an online forum, we lack a shared descriptive framework for articulating how this discussion activity relates to prior activities (such as reading an article or listening to a speaker) and future activities (such as a team-based investigation of different topics arising from the class discussion, followed by teams reporting back to the whole class).

Put simply, what we lack is an agreed way to describe and share the teaching process, regardless of whether the activities are conducted online or face-to-face. As a result, individual educators spend heroic amounts of time on planning and preparation, but with enormous duplication of effort and no economies of scale. Apart from the lack of efficiency in preparation, educational quality also suffers: While some educators regularly create outstanding learning experiences for their students, some do not. How could the best teaching processes be shared among the widest number of educators?

Most importantly, if we could share descriptions of educational processes together with advice on the reasons for their design, then not only could a novice educator benefit from the work of experts, but all educators could collectively adapt and improve each others' work, leading to improved quality overall.

This suggests a fascinating question. Could the collaborative development processes of open source software be applied to open teaching? Harnessing the collective expertise of the world's educators to achieve greater efficiency and improved quality would transform education as we know it.

Recent innovations could make this a reality. The field of learning design seeks to describe educational processes in a standardized way that can be shared, and hence adapted and improved. Learning design systems provide educators with tools to describe and capture a structured flow of content and collaborative activities that can create rich learning experiences for students. They also provide a framework for describing the learning objectives that drive any given set of activities. Learning design systems can run some or all of the activities online, or instead, provide printed support material to facilitate face-to-face teaching. In either case, the teaching and learning process becomes explicit, and hence can be shared, adapted, and improved.

Overview of Learning Design

The field of learning design is based on the concept of a standardized "language" or framework to describe educational activities. In particular, it has a special focus on processes that involve group tasks, not merely individual students interacting with content on a screen. Students interact with each other—and their teacher—over a structured series of activities. Learning design is a superset of instructional design, as it incorporates the application of instructional design principles to single-learner contexts. But it extends these principles to collaborative learning activities and teacher-led environments as additional components of a broader model of education.

In one sense, the concept of structured descriptions of educational processes has a long history in the creation and use of lesson plans in K–12 school contexts. However, recent interest in a formal descriptive framework for educational activities arose primarily from the work of Rob Koper and colleagues at the Open University of the Netherlands in the late 1990s with their development of Educational Modelling Language (EML; See Koper, 2001). EML became the primary input to the creation of the IMS Learning Design specification (IMS, 2003), which is one of the main reference points for this field.

To understand how typical learning designs are different from other e-learning approaches, consider this generic example: An educator decides to break a seminar/tutorial class into small groups to debate an idea, with each group reporting back to the whole class. Next, the whole class debates the different groups' ideas. Then the educator presents an article from the literature with a new perspective, and the whole class discusses how its initial debate compares to the article. Students next choose one of three extension topics for further investigation and debate, and subsequently each student submits an essay on the topic.

This generic learning design could be applied to many different disciplines. It exemplifies current understanding of good pedagogy: fostering active consideration of the topic by students (rather than passively listening to an expert); encouraging students to construct their own understanding of the issues (as a conversation with the educators and peers); providing student choice within the relevant content. (There are, of course, other possible pedagogical principles that could be considered here, such as authentic assessment, negotiation of learning pathways, but the above is sufficient for this discussion. Further discussion of good pedagogical principles can be found in the higher education teaching and learning literature, such as in the work of David Kolb, Paul Ramsden, Diana Laurillard, Graham Gibbs, John Biggs, David Boud, Gilly Salmon, and many others.)

A learning design can be thought of as having a number of activities, and for each activity, it is necessary to specify *who* is involved, *what* they are doing, and *how* the task is conducted. These individual activities are then combined to create a sequence of activities (or "method" in IMS Learning Design), which may incorporate "stop" points that allow the educator (or the system) to control the progress of students through the activities. A learning design may also have one or more learning objectives, which can be considered the *why* dimension. As noted above, the concept of learning design is not just applicable to e-learning; rather, it can be used to describe both online and face-to-face contexts. And so the generic example described above is illustrated from a learning design perspective in table 24.1 (based on a class of 20 students), including examples of both face-to-face and online activities.

Most recent learning design work focuses on describing educational processes with sufficient detail so that a computer could "run" the series of activities described. This requires the computer to have clearly speci-fied information about the flow of activities, the relevant users and their roles, the activity tools required (for example, a tool to run a forum, present an article, receive an essay), the configuration of activity tools (such as instructions to students, content resources, tool behavior proper-ties) and other system information necessary to instantiate and run the relevant learning design.

One way to think of a learning design system is as a workflow engine for collaborative activities. For although learning designs can be linear and tightly structured, they can also be more flexible, allowing students to choose their own approaches to learning. The fact that an educator structures a series of learning tasks for a group of students need not

Table 24.1
A generic learning design
Learning Objectives/Why? [General learning objectives for this example could include skills such as working in small groups, debating concepts, evaluating different perspectives, and expressing ideas in writing. Specific learning objectives would be related to content in the discipline area.]

Sequence/ When?	What?	Who?	How?
Step 1	Break class into small groups	4 × group of 5 students	Teacher chooses; or system randomly selects
Step 2	Small groups debate idea	4 × group of 5 students	4 corners of classroom; or system provides 4 × online chat/ forum areas
Step 3 (stop)	Each group reports back to whole class	4 × designated group reporter	Presentation to class; or whole class online forum to post reports
Step 4	Whole class debates group reports	1 × 20 students (+ teacher facilitated)	Class debate facilitated by teacher; or whole class online forum
Step 5	Article from literature	Each student (20 × 1) reads article, or listens to teacher presentation	Teacher presents article ideas to class; or system provides article to read (could also include audio recording of teacher presentation)
Step 6 (stop)	Whole class debates article compared to earlier ideas	1 × 20 students (+ teacher facilitated)	Class debate facilitated by teacher; or whole class online forum (could be new forum, or new thread in an existing forum)
Step 7	Students choose one of three extension topics	Each student chooses 1 of 3 topics, results in 3 uneven groups	3 areas of room (or could arrange later meeting place) + topic resources; or system could provide 3 chat/forum areas + topic resources—students select relevant area
Step 8	Each student submits an essay	Each student (20 × 1) submits essay	Handwritten essay given to teacher; or system provides area to upload essay (and potentially could provide marking tools for teacher)

result in a teacher-centered "instructivist" learning experience. Instead, the educator, using a student-centered pedagogical approach, might give considerable freedom to the students' group to choose how and when they will achieve the relevant learning outcomes. An educator may appropriately provide considerable structure or freedom—or both—to students according to the educational context and learning objectives.

An example of a learning design system is the Learning Activity Management System (LAMS; Dalziel, 2003). Since 2002, I have a led a team of educators and programmers who have developed LAMS to illustrate the authoring, running, and monitoring of learning designs, including a suite of "learning design–aware," or, workflow-enabled, activity tools. Figure 24.1 provides a screen shot of the LAMS Version 2 Authoring environment for the example given in table 24.1. Additional authoring pages (not shown) are provided for the configuration of each activity tool. (To explore LAMS further, see the demonstration site at http://demo.lamscommunity.org/)

One of the key distinguishing features between a learning design system like LAMS and traditional course management systems is the

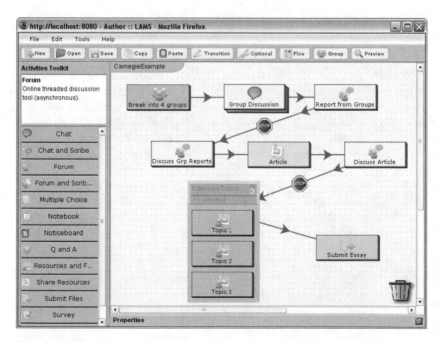

Figure 24.1
LAMS V2 Authoring environment for table 24.1 example

relationship between authoring and running activities. In a traditional course management system, if educators wish to add a forum on a particular topic to their course, they do this "live" into the relevant course (although they may not make the forum viewable by students until a later time, nonetheless, the live forum is created when it is authored). In LAMS, educators create a forum on a particular topic as an abstract design that is independent of any "run-time" implementation in a course.

At the heart of this separation of authoring and running activities in LAMS is the concept that when an educator decides to run a previously authored activity, it is only then that the relevant tool (for example, a forum) is created. The outcome of the authoring process is not a live running course, but rather a set of XML descriptions of how the activity is to be run when it is launched at a later time. This means that the authored set of activities can be exported and shared with others, who can in turn run them with students, or adapt or improve the design, and share it back. This authoring and sharing is independent of any specific course "instance." As far as I am aware, the seemingly simple concept of reusable sequences of collaborative student activities is absent from all known course management systems as of mid 2007.

The potential for sharing learning designs independent of the course in which they are implemented is central to the potential benefits of learning design for open education. Just as open educational content such as text, graphics, simulations, and other resources can be shared through learning object repositories to allow for reuse by other educators, learning designs can be shared in the same way.

A Case Study in Sharing Learning Designs: The LAMS Community

The vision of how learning design could contribute to improving education was, for me, best articulated by Diana Laurillard in the UK government e-learning strategy in 2005. Point 89 says:

"We want to stimulate greater innovation in e-learning design to accelerate the development of the next generation of e-learning. The focus should be on design flexibility for teachers and engaging activity for learners. Flexible learning design packages would enable teachers in all sectors to build their own individual and collaborative learning activities around digital resources. This would help them engage in designing and discussing new kinds of pedagogy, which is essential if we are to succeed in innovating and transforming teaching and learning" (Laurillard, 2005).

The LAMS Community (See www.lamscommunity.org) is an example of a Web site dedicated to sharing learning designs under open education licenses (generally Creative Commons BY-SA-NC). It provides a repository for sharing LAMS Learning Designs, including (brief) metadata and social software tools (such as download tracking, user ratings, and comments). To complement the repository, the Web site supports a range of community areas, such as K-12, higher education, healthcare, and technical, that provide forums for discussion of learning design ideas and experiences.

At the end of May 2007, the LAMS Community had 2,266 members, 191 shared sequences which had been downloaded 5,382 times, and 2,912 forum postings. In addition, the LAMS Version 2 software had been translated into 23 languages by community members. While these statistics are modest compared to other e-learning initiatives such as Moodle or OpenCourseWare, they provide a first glimpse of the potential for sharing learning designs.

Lessons Learned

What lessons can be learned from the experiences of the LAMS Community to date? As I have recently described (in Dalziel, 2006), these are some challenges for open education:

Examples of Sharing   Although there are now a reasonable number of shared sequences, there are as yet few examples of sharing back of improved versions of existing sequences. This suggests that the vision of increased quality and improved efficiency arising from collective development and improvement by the world's educators is yet to be realized.

"Real" Designs   While generic learning designs (or "templates") might appear to be more useful for widespread reuse and adaptation, anecdotal reports to date suggest that generic designs often appear "lifeless" to members of the LAMS Community. There is a preference for "real" (that is, discipline-specific) sequences that illustrate educational processes in relation to actual teaching content, not just an abstract activity design.

This suggests that further work on the creation and use of learning design templates is needed.

Engagement with Educators   Educational discussion of learning design issues remains patchy, whereas by comparison, technical discussion of the software is rich and sustained. While this pattern has been mirrored in the Sakai community (Masson, 2006), successful implementation of the learning design vision requires rich educational discussions of implementation and experiences with students. This suggests the importance of critical mass and active engagement by educators.

Selecting and Using Learning Design Templates

A new area of work involves creating generic learning design templates that include a selection process that provides advice to educators on issues to consider in their teaching, and hence which templates might best suit their teaching context. Template selection processes could take many different forms. They could be comprehensive, considering all aspects of a course, such as student needs and learning difficulties, topic challenges, and teaching context. Or they could be relatively brief: a small selection of activity templates that would suit a one-hour computer lab-based class.

In either case, the key concept is that an educator is guided to reflect on one or more issues relevant to their teaching, and this reflection can provide a basis for selecting an existing learning design template that can then be adapted to the relevant discipline context. In a typical course, there may be many learning designs for different topics and learning objectives.

Early examples of this approach include the "Pedagogic Planner" projects of Diana Laurillard and colleagues at the University of London, and Liz Masterman and colleagues at Oxford University. Both of these projects focus on fairly comprehensive reflection processes to identify issues in teaching the relevant course, and hence provide foundations for selecting possible templates. In related work, the LAMS team at Macquarie University is focusing on the creation and easy editing of "runnable" learning design templates that could be offered as suggestions to educators who complete the reflections required in a pedagogic planner. The

Macquarie work also includes consideration of much simpler selection processes, for example, choosing an appropriate template for a specific teaching context, such as a one-hour lab or a one-week online session.

Potential Advantages

The combination of pedagogic planners and learning design templates has two potential advantages. First, by providing educators with (mostly) prestructured learning design templates, educators can adopt existing good practice designs, with their only tasks being to select an appropriate template and apply relevant discipline-specific content to the template. (For the example in figure 25.1, this involved choosing and writing the relevant discussion questions, article, extension topics, and essay question.) This approach captures the educational processes used by expert educators, and it makes these processes available to and easily reused by all educators.

Second, the guided reflective process of a pedagogic planner can help educators to consider issues with their teaching that they may not have thought about before, and through this process the pedagogic planner could provide both theoretical and practical advice. The combination of reflective advice on teaching with recommended good practice templates could prove an important step forward in achieving the open education learning design vision. The creation of software to facilitate this reflection and selection process means the potential of widespread adoption without necessarily requiring hands-on assistance from expert support staff, such as an educational designer.

Iterative Planning   In practice, I suspect some additional factors will be relevant to this approach. The reflection and template selection approach is likely to be more iterative than linear: Educators will choose templates that appear promising, add content to these, and then, before running them in a "live" course, preview them from the student's perspective. From experience with LAMS users, we know that when educators see the student view of the activities, they often reconsider their choice of template ("Oh, that's not what I had in mind . . ."). The educator iteratively tries and reflects on templates until satisfied that the activities are appropriate for the live course. It is also likely that educators will return to the reflection and selection process after using a template in a live course, as additional issues or ideas may arise from implementation with students that did not arise at the time of initial planning.

Expert Support Staff   Another factor is the role of expert support staff such as educational designers (also called instructional designers). While the reflection and selection systems outlined above could be built to be used "stand alone," I suspect that in many cases, the greatest benefits will arise from the combination of these systems with advice from hands-on educational designers. In these cases, the reflection and selection software acts as a kind of decision support tool that complements the human advice of an educational designer working with the relevant educator. The combination of human and system advice could lead to improved educational outcomes with less relative time demands on expert support staff.

Often there are few educational designers available to assist educators, so only a small percentage of educators benefit from their assistance in creating pedagogically rich and engaging teaching and learning experiences. This problem exists not only at the level of educational institutions, but even at the level of whole country education systems where there is a recognized need to adopt pedagogically richer teaching and learning approaches, but relatively few expert educational designs who can assist the huge educator workforce towards new approaches.

In these cases, software to support pedagogic reflection and template selection may be a useful step towards addressing this skills challenge. In addition, a country (or an educational institution) could create its own pedagogic reflection and selection software packages based on an understanding on current educator practice and local culture. Rather than immediately introducing complex and advanced pedagogical structures (such as role plays), the reflective questions and template libraries could be configured to support incremental advances from current practices and culture. In this way, the introduction of new pedagogical approaches could be carefully staged relative to existing and evolving practice within the educator workforce.

Redefining the Pedagogical Task
When I initially began planning development of systems of this kind, I thought that the task was to create a single "best" pedagogical planner

and template library. I now see this problem differently. I believe the task is to build many different kinds of pedagogic planners and template libraries to suit different educational contexts, and then to investigate the benefits (and problems) of these as they are applied. For this reason, our recent development work in this area is attempting to create software toolkits to allow others to create their own selection processes and template libraries, rather than simply providing the "one" answer to this challenge. In time, I hope that perhaps even whole reflection and template library packages may become shared, reused, and adapted in the same way that individual learning designs are being shared today.

Meeting the Challenges

I opened this chapter by describing a dream in which pedagogical know-how was made explicit and shareable, and through collective effort, educators around the world could improve teaching processes to the ultimate improvement of global education. The new field of learning design provides the foundations for this vision to be achieved, and software like LAMS and Websites like the LAMS Community illustrate the first glimpses of progress towards this goal.

There are many technical and educational challenges yet to be solved, but the success of open education in other areas (open source course management systems and open content) provides hope for finding a solution to the challenge of sharing "open teaching."

If we can combine the great ideas and reflections of educators with exemplars of good practice in the form of "runnable" learning designs, and share these in a way that they can be easily adopted and adapted by any educator, then we will make new progress towards the goal of transforming education through the dissemination of pedagogical know-how.

References

Dalziel, J. R. (2003). Implementing learning design: The learning activity management system (LAMS). In G. Crisp, D. Thiele, I. Scholten, S. Barker, and J. Baron (Eds.), *Interact, Integrate, Impact: Proceedings of the 20th Annual Conference of the Australasian Society for Computers in Learning in Tertiary Education*, (pp. 593–596). Retrieved June 10, 2007, from http://www.ascilite.org.au/conferences/adelaide03/docs/pdf/593.pdf.

Dalziel, J. R. (2006). The design and development of the LAMS Community. Retrieved June 10, 2007, from http://www.lamscommunity.org/dotlrn/clubs/educationalcommunity/lamsresearchdevelopment/forums/attach/go-toattachment?object_id=311748&attachment_id=311750.

IMS (2003). Learning Design Specification. Retrieved June 10, 2007, from http://www.imsglobal.org/learningdesign/.

Koper, R. (2001). Modeling units of study from a pedagogical perspective: the pedagogical meta-model behind EML. Retrieved June 10, 2007, from http://dspace.ou.nl/handle/1820/36.

Laurillard, D. (2005). Harnessing Technology: Transforming Learning and Children's Services. Retrieved August 6, 2007, from http://www.dfes.gov.uk/publications/e-strategy/docs/e-strategy.pdf.

Masson, P. (2006). "Who are we?" Posting to internal Sakai mailing list, July 5th, 2006. Percentages retrieved June 10, 2007, from http://collab.sakaiproject.org/access/content/attachment/f767a7de-0f13-436c-80a6-440490560a73/SakaiDiscussionsPie.jpg.

25

Common Knowledge: Openness in Higher Education

Diana G. Oblinger and Marilyn M. Lombardi

Openness to new ways of knowing is the hallmark of the successful lifelong learner. Openness and adaptability in the face of changing circumstances are the traits of a resilient institution. Openness to new educational models is a prerequisite to remaining relevant in a global, networked world.

Technology has altered the way learners see themselves and their futures. Students face a job market defined by unprecedented change, ambiguity, and global competition. Technology has not simply allowed us to cross the once insurmountable barriers of time and space; it is also blurring the distinction between expert and amateur. In the era of search engines and common knowledge, where remote archives are a keystroke away, a new generation of learners has emerged. They regard visual media as their vernacular, multitasking as their modus operandi, and collaboration as their preferred mode of learning. What can we learn from them that should shape our educational practice?

Today's global economy is also driving a reexamination of educational practice. Developing countries are pinning their hopes for economic advancement on building a skilled workforce, which means that postsecondary education is fast becoming an imperative for vast segments of the world's population. For these areas of the world, where the existing infrastructure cannot keep up with exploding demand, the open access to educational resources made possible by online technologies may provide a solution. Nevertheless, the notion of universal access to freely available educational resources faces inherent tensions from within the academy, where the barriers to adoption have more to do with tradition and attitude than technology. Institutional reward systems and intellectual property alone pose significant challenges to the resource sharing principles that underlie open education (McSherry, 2001).

This chapter describes the emergence of a participatory culture supported by online technologies and marked by openness—to abundant choices, to cocreation, to art, to information—and insight that is freely shared for the common good. As this culture of free exchange continues to grow, educators must ask whether its participatory dynamics can be applied to meet the global demand for education. Typified by this ethos of sharing, the "open educational resources" (OER) movement may very well give rise to a worldwide learning community accessible to all.

The Participatory Culture

According to a 2005 study conducted by the Pew Internet & American Life Project, more than one-half of all American teens—and 57 percent of teens worldwide who use the Internet—could be considered media creators, producing blogs and Web pages, posting original artwork, stories, or videos online, or remixing the online content of others to construct their own creative pastiche. But this trend goes beyond teens; adults are participating in greater numbers than ever. This participatory culture is open to new information and new forms of expression, blending our traditional needs for information, expression, and socialization with new online tools and communities—bringing with it the potential to transform teaching and learning. Is higher education open to the changes this participatory culture might catalyze in our traditions?

Cocreation

In the participatory culture, there are relatively low barriers to expression and engagement. People can create, remix, repurpose, and pass along content with unprecedented ease. Anyone with a network connection can become an author, editor, movie distributor, recommender, or critic (Lorenzo, Oblinger, and Dziuban, 2006, pp. 5–6). Blogs have changed the very nature of journalism and politics by eroding the power of major media organizations, which have lost their exclusive right to comment on trends, file reports, or provide editorials. Would students learn more if asked to create and critique rather than to listen and absorb? If so, what does this mean for educational practice?

Multimodal Interaction

In a world where text, images, video, audio, and geolocation are all potential forms of communication, "conversations" are becoming multimodal. Mobile phones, for example, aren't just for talking; they are also for texting, sending photos, accessing the Web, and occasionally for watching video. New modes of interaction including videoconferencing, asynchronous threaded discussions, synchronous virtual interactions, networking, and small group collaboration using groupware, are able to support the kinds of learning activities (for example, brainstorming, concept-building, collaboration, and so on) that build skills twenty-first-century students need (Dede, 2006). We will advance learning for students and ourselves by opening scholarly dialogue to new media and new audiences.

Distributed Cognition

Network technologies make it possible to marshal the collective intelligence of many, irrespective of time or place. This dispersal of control away from the center and toward the periphery is perhaps best epitomized by the success of Wikipedia, where scholars and amateurs, professionals and hobbyists, use a highly generative online atmosphere to negotiate knowledge. Although Wikipedia may exemplify the trend, it is far from the only example. Students engaged in collaborative editing use their individual skills to create a document where the whole is greater than the sum of the parts (EDUCAUSE Learning Initiative, 2005). Professional scientists and amateur enthusiasts form virtual research communities to advance the study of astronomy, ornithology, and other fields that rely on the collection of large data sets. No longer the exclusive purview of credentialed scientists, data collection and analysis is open to all interested parties. With distributed cognition, contributors come from all walks of life, information flows in multiple directions, and a bottom-up energy drives discovery. Are we willing to open our scholarly circles to amateurs and interested parties who may be on the periphery? Would we gain from their contributions and questions? Would they gain from becoming members of the community?

In spite of the potential, a backlash against grassroots efforts to construct knowledge without centralized editorial control may be developing. For example, *The Chronicle of Higher Education* recently reported on an effort by Middlebury College's history department to dissuade students from citing Wikipedia because of the open-source encyclopedia's perceived inaccuracies (Read, 2007). A response indicating the original story had been exaggerated followed. In fact, the department was merely reacting to a single error in Wikipedia, an error that was amended in a matter of hours, demonstrating precisely what sets the online encyclopedia apart from its printed predecessors. More a community than "encyclopedia" in any conventional sense, Wikipedia rapidly corrected itself. The *Chronicle* coverage "echoed the most Luddite reactions to Wikipedia and other ventures in creating knowledge in a collaborative, digital environment" under the guise of maintaining scholarly standards: "Several comparative studies have shown that errors in Wikipedia are not more frequent than in comparable print sources [such as the *Encyclopedia Britannica*]. More to the point, the digital encyclopedia is superior to its printed counterparts in terms of *timeliness*: after all, the entire Middlebury debate already has its own place on Wikipedia" (Davidson, 2007).

Affinity-based Self-Organization

Wikipedia is not the only digital outlet for people who hope to shape collective understanding. People are committing more and more of their leisure hours to social networking Web sites, fan-fiction communities, multiuser online gaming environments, and other immersive online experiences where sociability is placed in service of a common creative enterprise. In effect, they are carving out their own informal learning circles infused with the activity and intellectual engagement one would want in an ideal educational environment (Gee, 2004). Self-organizing environments of this kind—called "affinity spaces" by educational researchers—capture key aspects of active learning environments, including abundant cooperation, self-expression, and collaborative problem solving.

Skills that emerge from these affinity spaces will likely be necessary for success in a global and unpredictable job market. Such skills include the capacity to:

1.) pool knowledge and compare notes with others in achieving a common goal;

2.) solve problems "on the fly";

3.) simulate real-world processes for experimental purposes;

4.) shift focus among multiple tasks undertaken simultaneously; and

5.) sample and remix media content (Jenkins, Clinton, Purushotma, Robinson, and Weigel, 2006, 3).

How do we capture the energy and enthusiasm of learners outside formal educational settings? Do we encourage learning that happens outside the classroom?

Virtual communities of practice are already beginning to play major roles in "authentic" learning activities that engage students in the type of disciplinary challenges that working practitioners encounter in the real world. Authentic learning immerses students in the complexities and ambiguities of real-world practice, asking them to participate in projects with the potential to impact actual stakeholders. Virtual organizations of scientists, engineers, historians, and so on provide students with a wealth of expertise to draw on as they begin to construct their professional identities (Lombardi, 2007).

Connections

Even more than a shift in communications, the cocreativity and self-organizing energies of the emerging participatory culture represent a significant shift in expectation. Users expect choice, control, and the opportunity to contribute to an environment that is open to their ideas and their ways of working.

Making connections, both intellectual and professional, is as vital to personal and professional success as the memorization of formulae and facts. When exposed to the discipline as it is practiced (rather than being told about it) learners can become practitioners much earlier, replicating the good practice that their professors model for them, as well as reflecting and refining their new skills with the guidance of mentors and more experienced peers (Siemens, 2005).

If higher education is open to these new ways of educating (such as legitimate peripheral participation), we can help students cultivate the skills learners have the most difficulty attaining on their own:

1) *judgment,* or the ability to distinguish the reliable from the unreliable information source;

2) *synthesis*, or the capacity to follow the longer argument or narrative across multiple modalities;

3) *research*, or the activity of searching, discovering, and disseminating salient information in a credible manner;

4) *practice*, or the opportunity to learn by doing within authentic disciplinary communities; and

5) *negotiation*, or the flexibility to work across disciplinary and cultural boundaries to generate innovative, alternative solutions (Jenkins et al., 2006, p.4).

We have the opportunity to help students acquire "portable skills." Allowing them to see patterns where others see only chaos, to distinguish between reliable and unreliable sources, and to forge interpersonal relations helps ensure they continue to learn and grow over a lifetime. Are we open to new ways of educating? Can we unlearn the habits of centuries?

The Economic Imperative

A participatory culture of unprecedented openness—to ideas, to people, to community—is also a culture of unprecedented flux and insecurity. Youngsters are driven by circumstance to adopt a new attitude toward job security and become far more receptive to change than their parents had been. Given the global job market that awaits them, today's college students are likely to switch jobs, even entire careers, several times over the course of their professional lives.

Acknowledging this reality, the U.S. Department of Education has declared the transformation of higher education "an economic imperative" for the country:

Much of U.S. education is still based on the premise that economic processes and institutions will mirror those in the 20th century. Students are prepared to be future employees of business organizations now rapidly becoming obsolete. Current trends suggest that more students will run their own businesses rather than work for others and as adults must constantly, quickly, and efficiently learn new skills and information to be effective entrepreneurs. To succeed in life and to keep our country strong and prosperous, all of today's students must graduate able to deal with ambiguity and capable of higher order analysis and complex communication. (Dede, Korte, Nelson, Valdez, and Ward, 2005, p. 3)

To succeed in life, then, today's students need more than access to higher education. After all, despite a continual rise in the number of college-bound students, the success rates of various ethnic and economic groups in the United States remain uneven. Increased delivery of educational materials via the Internet will only help students to a point. As John Seely Brown and Paul Duguid cautioned a decade ago, the Internet may "allow students to tap into community objects, but not into the community itself. They may find access to a text, but not to the [degree-granting] communities that give that text significance" (1996). Participatory forms of learning, those that are experiential, collaborative, and situated within a vital community of practice, will be more likely to ensure achievement on the part of all learners (Dede, 2007).

The Global Society

In a global knowledge economy, a skilled workforce has become essential to national prosperity. Even in the developed world, where 40–60 percent of young people take advantage of tertiary education, there is concern that the critical infrastructure will not be there to support the numbers of students who will seek postsecondary education in the future. In the United States alone, 75 percent of students who complete high school expect to go on to some form of postsecondary education (Association of American Colleges and Universities [AAC&U], 2002). Estimates are that an additional 1 to 2 million U.S. students will seek access to higher education by 2015, many from low-income or minority families (AAC&U, 2002).

Worldwide, the demand for postsecondary education will be nothing short of staggering. At the beginning of the new millennium, over 90 million students were already enrolled in some form of higher education worldwide. By 2025, estimates are that the number of enrolled students is likely to reach 160 million (Perkinson, 2005). At this point, the less-developed countries manage to provide postsecondary education for only 4 percent of their young people, yet they hold the vast majority of the world's prospective students. Nearly half the world's population (almost 3 billion people) is under the age of 25, and 85 percent of the world's youth live in developing countries (World Population Foundation, n.d.).

The possibility of financing enough buildings, books, technologies, and educators to serve millions of additional learners is close to unthinkable in less-developed countries where qualified instructors and critical resources are often lacking altogether (Larson, 2001, viii). To compensate for this lack of critical infrastructure, developing countries have relied on cross-border education as a way of fostering a skilled workforce. Unfortunately, programs that export learners do not always strengthen the local economy. After graduating with their degrees, an estimated one-third of students sent to the United States do not return to their home country (Futures Project, 2000, p. 9).

The Open Educational Resources (OER) movement has emerged against this global backdrop of unmet demand and uneven access to necessary resources. The phrase "open educational resources," first heard at a 2002 UNESCO forum, is commonly used to describe a strategy for sharing timely teaching materials (content modules, courseware, learning objects, online learning communities) that would otherwise not be available to instructors in less-developed countries (Johnstone, 2005). Open access to educational resources is expected to speed research progress and knowledge building, much as open access to scholarly journals is expected to fuel faster discoveries that benefit everyone.

To date, the OER movement has been associated with large-scale programs such as the China Open Resources for Education initiative involving over 150 universities in China or open education initiatives in the United States that have generated more than 2,000 freely available online university courses to date (Hylén, 2006, pp. 2–3). However, despite these early successes, the open education movement must evolve in order to meet global demand. Will the open education model remain wedded to twentieth-century assumptions and habits, or embrace the full implications of a participatory culture? The success and sustainability of the entire movement are at stake.

Some would argue that learning resources, while "open" in the sense of being freely available, should nevertheless be centrally developed, "fixed" in form and closed to modification in order to preserve their integrity as learning experiences. Yet such a strategy, essentially a top-down approach to content creation, cannot scale. It places an undue burden on the content creator and limits the material's usability for those who hope to add it to their curriculum. By contrast, the participatory culture associated with today's Web 2.0 world encourages others to author, sample, repurpose, and share content in ways that distribute the creative burden across a wide social network. In effect, the pool of common knowledge only grows more various and valuable the larger that social network grows. But how does the community judge the quality of its collective output? Here, too, the burden can be distributed across the community by providing support for user reviews and recommendations. To confront the implications of such a strategy, the open education movement will have to come to grips with the nature of valuation itself. Is the quality of a course something inherent within the learning resource itself or is it something that emerges only in use, judged by how it affects its users in a specific learning context (Hylén, 2006, p. 8)? If so, will we blend peer review with rating systems like Digg to determine the quality of a resource?

Several programs in the United States and the United Kingdom are pushing the concept of Open Education beyond the courseware model in order to build a sustainable practice capable of scaling broadly. Examples include the Connexions project at Rice University, the National Science Digital Library project, the Open University's OpenLearn pilot project, and Carnegie Mellon University's Open Learning Initiative (OLI), which is marked by its unique interdisciplinary course development process. Launched in the fall of 2002, OLI is dedicated to the development of freely available "stand-alone" college-level online courses informed by research from the cognitive and learning sciences. The OLI course design process is unique in its dedication to teaming faculty content experts with cognitive scientists, learning scientists, human-computer interaction specialists, formative assessment specialists, and programmers, along with ongoing course evaluation and iterative improvement. Ultimately, the collaborative nature of the OLI course design process has had an additional, unanticipated effect: inspiring participating faculty members to rethink their approach to teaching. Although OLI courses are designed as "stand-alone" online experiences, Carnegie Mellon faculty are successfully integrating OLI's Web-based instruction modules into their traditional instructor-led courses (Lombardi, 2006).

In light of these and other emerging initiatives, a more far-reaching vision of open education is beginning to coalesce: "A global networked community of tutor and student volunteers would produce a large pool of collectively developed resources (1) evaluated and ranked by the community as a whole, (2) distributed across the globe to be sampled, mashed up, remixed, and recontextualized for effective local use, and

(3) oriented to serving the emergent needs of ad-hoc learning communities in real time. In such a world, the university becomes a platform for collaborative, supported learning, and an arbiter of quality through research, learning design, and assessment" (Cole, 2006, p. 25).

This vision of a worldwide educational commons challenges traditional assumptions about knowledge, originality, and ownership. Are we open to facing these challenges if worldwide access to postsecondary education is at stake?

Conclusion

Due to changes in technology, a participatory culture is emerging with a new openness to sharing, collaboration, and learning by doing. As higher education and society work to address local, national, and global educational needs, we ignore the lessons of this participatory culture at our own peril. Sharing content is a first step in meeting the challenges of global education. But we can do more. Adopting the principles of connections, cocreation, and distributed cognition will allow us to move beyond learning-as-assimilation to a model that encourages engagement and the development of the complex skills our world needs.

References

Association of American Colleges and Universities. (2002). *Greater Expectations: A New Vision for Learning as a Nation Goes to College.* Retrieved February 3, 2007, from http://www.greaterexpectations.org.

Brown, J. S., and Duguid, P. (1996, July/August). Universities in the digital age. *Change: The Magazine of Higher Learning,* 28(4), 10–19. Retrieved February 2, 2007, from http://www.findarticles.com/p/articles/mi_m1254/is_n4 _v28/ai_18603192/pg_1.

Cole, J. (2006). Remixing higher education—the open content university. In *Open Education 2006: Community, Culture and Content: Proceedings,* 25. Retrieved June 2, 2007, from http://cosl.usu.edu/conferences/opened2006/docs/ opened2006–proceedings.pdf.

Davidson, C. (2007, March 23). We can't ignore the influence of digital technologies. *Chronicle Review,* 53(29), B20. Retrieved March 30, 2007, from http://chronicle.com/free/v53/i29/29b02001.htm.

Dede, C., Korte, S., Nelson, R., Valdez, G., and Ward, D. J. (2005, September). *Transforming Learning for the 21st Century: An Economic Imperative.*

Naperville, IL: Learning Point Associates. Retrieved February 2, 2007, from http://www.learningpt.org/tech/transforming.pdf.

Dede, C. (2006, November). *Teaching and Learning via Cyberinfrastructure*. Presented at the EDUCAUSE Learning Initiative (ELI) Web Seminar. Retrieved February 2, 2007, from http://www.educause.edu/ELIWEB0611.

Dede, C. (2007, January 23). *Emerging Educational Technologies and the Neomillennial Learning Styles*. Presented at the EDUCAUSE Learning Initiative (ELI) Annual Meeting, Atlanta, GA.

EDUCAUSE Learning Initiative. (2005, December). *7 Things You Should Know about Collaborative Editing*. Retrieved February 8, 2007, from http://www.educause.edu/ir/library/pdf/ELI7009.pdf.

Futures Project. (2000, October). *The Universal Impact of Competition and Globalization in Higher Education*. Retrieved February 2, 2007, from http://www.futuresproject.org/publications/universal_impact.pdf.

Gee, J. P. (2004). *Situated Language and Learning: A Critique of Traditional Schooling*. New York: Routledge.

Hylén, J. (2006). Open educational resources: Opportunities and challenges. In *Open Education 2006: Community, Culture and Content*: Proceedings 49–63. Retrieved June 2, 2007, from http://cosl.usu.edu/conferences/opened2006/docs/opened2006–proceedings.pdf.

Jenkins, H., Clinton, K., Purushotma, R., Robinson, A. J., and Weigel, M. (2006). *Confronting the Challenge of Participatory Culture: Media Education for the 21st Century*. Chicago: The MacArthur Foundation. Retrieved from http://www.digitallearning.macfound.org/atf/cf/%7B7E45C7E0-A3E0-4B89-AC9C-E807E1B0AE4E%7D/JENKINS_WHITE_PAPER.PDF.

Johnstone, S. (2005). Open educational resources serve the world. *EDUCAUSE Quarterly*, 3, 15–18.

Larson, R. C. (2001). *The Future of Global Learning Networks*. Boulder, CO: EDUCAUSE. Retrieved June 1, 2007, from http://www.educause.edu/ir/library/pdf/ffpiu011.pdf.

Lombardi, M. M. (2006). *ELI Innovations and Implementations: The Open Learning Initiative*. Boulder, CO: EDUCAUSE. Retrieved March 30, 2007, from http://www.educause.edu/ir/library/pdf/ELI5013.pdf.

Lombardi, M. M. (2007). *Authentic Learning for the 21st Century: An Overview*. Boulder, CO: EDUCAUSE. Retrieved June 1, 2007, from http://www.educause.edu/ir/library/pdf/ELI3009.pdf.

Lorenzo, G., Oblinger, D., and Dziuban, C. (2006, October). *How Choice, Cocreation, and Culture Are Changing What It Means to Be Net Savvy*. Retrieved February 2, 2007, from http://www.educause.edu/ir/library/pdf/ELI3008.pdf.

McSherry, C. (2001). *Who Owns Academic Work?: Battling for Control of Intellectual Property*. Cambridge, MA: Harvard University Press.

Perkinson, R. (2005, October). *Alternative and Innovative Financing for Nonstate Education*. Presented at The Organisation for Economic Co-operation and

Development (OECD) Global Forum on Education. Retrieved June 1, 2007, from http://biblioteca.mineduc.cl/documento/200601231127560.Ronald Perkinson, International Finance Corporation.ppt.

Read, B. (2007, February 16). Middlebury College history department limits students' use of Wikipedia. *Chronicle of Higher Education.* Retrieved March 30, 2007, from http://chronicle.com/weekly/v53/i24/24a03901.htm.

Siemens, G. (2005). *Connectivism: A Learning Theory for the Digital Age.* Retrieved June 1, 2007, from http://www.elearnspace.org/Articles/connectivism.htm.

World Population Foundation. (n.d.). Reproductive rights: Facts. Retrieved February 3, 2007, from http://www.wpf.org/reproductive_rights_article/facts.

26

Open for What? A Case Study of Institutional Leadership and Transformation

Bernadine Chuck Fong

In 1995, Barr and Tagg made the argument that a paradigm shift from teaching to learning was needed to increase student-learning outcomes in higher education (Barr and Tagg, 1995). Such a shift in emphasis, from teacher to student, entails changes in focus, mission, and locus of control—institutional transformation and academic and financial restructuring of seismic proportions. Open education, in every sense of the term, could provide the opportunity and momentum for such a major paradigm shift to take place.

Open education has two arenas: the academic and the technological. In the academic, policies and practices provide open enrollment and access—at a low cost for students. Open source, open availability (also called access), and nonproprietary technology solutions can support an institution's mission of open academic access. The technology offers not just the opportunity for education, in terms of availability, access, and low cost, but also the opportunity for realizing the *benefits* of education. Access to higher education can be barrier-free: readily available in terms of time, and accessible in terms of affordability and admissions requirements.

Further, open technology has the potential to address the important corollary of access: student success. A major challenge facing higher education, particularly community colleges is access without success, the student's successful completion of a course of study resulting in a degree, certificate or some type of credential. Mounting data report the low numbers of students who actually attain their objective (Bailey, Jenkins, and Leinbach, 2005/2006; Shulock and Moore, 2007). The lack of success in open access institutions seriously challenges the basic tenets of open admissions policies and practices. Open for what?

I came to fully appreciate the potential of open education technology to reinforce and enhance the open access mission of community colleges while serving as president of Foothill College, in California. "It's not so important what I teach as what it is my students are learning," said one of my most effective faculty members. Community colleges represent nearly half of the entire undergraduate population in the United States, a population widely diverse in, among other things, educational preparation and cultural and individual learning styles. That diversity alone would suggest an urgent need to shift our focus to how students learn rather than just what we teach. To truly support student success, it would be in the best interest of community colleges to shift the focus of education from the teacher and teaching to the student and learning: a shift in focus from information dissemination to learner engagement. This is what open education technology can support.

A Case in Point: Foothill College

To truly make learning student-centric, the learning and the opportunity for learning needs to be in the hands of the student. However, community college student lives are often more complex than those of the traditional college student. Many are working while going to school (or going to school while working), and may have families: about 80 percent of community college students work full- or part-time (American Association of Community Colleges, 2007); about 33 percent of community college students have children (U.S. Department of Education, National Postsecondary Student Aid Study 2003–2004, 2004). If we put education into the hands of our students, could we make that paradigm shift and increase student performance? Could we accommodate our students' schedules rather than having our students try to squeeze their learning into the teaching schedules convenient for faculty or the institution?

For Foothill, the prospect of an online course seemed to have several advantages. We would have the opportunity to increase access to students who might not be able to come to campus or align their work and daycare schedules with campus class schedules. We initiated our online effort with an open invitation to all faculty members to learn about the use of technology for the classroom. As president, I had made it clear that our college, located in the heart of the Silicon Valley, was uniquely positioned to be an educational leader in e-learning. The faculty was encouraged, though not coerced, into participating in this new endeavor. The process became faculty driven, beginning with the faculty author of our course management system. In 1995, a Foothill faculty member designed an online delivery system for the college. Interest in using our software, Easy To Use Distance Education Software (ETUDES, from the French *etudier*, to study), grew. The only incentive we offered faculty was a computer and free dial-up access from faculty members' homes so that they could teach online courses "anytime, anywhere." (This was quite a tantalizing offer in 1995!)

The only requirement for our faculty to teach online was participation in a workshop to learn the ETUDES system and how to tailor courses to best utilize the system. Our faculty author was clear from the beginning that online presentations were not merely a matter of cutting and pasting lecture notes into a software program. Thus, faculty members had to literally rethink and redesign their courses. Little did we know in 1995 that we were ahead of our time in course redesign.

Through Technology, Making a Greater Paradigm Shift

Foothill College's eagerness to become an educational technology leader created an unforeseen but most welcome by-product. A faculty member was struggling to identify what she really wanted her students to learn in her online classes now that she was working without the traditional milestones dictated by chapters in the book, the number of units and the hours of seat time. Yet this was the first step in making the shift from teaching to learning: focusing on what and how students are learning. She and other faculty members found that a virtual classroom had no structure at all beyond the content and pedagogy. As faculty teaching these courses began to focus on what students were learning, this became the catalyst of our college's paradigm shift.

Through Technology, Meeting the State Mandate for Open Academic Access

Our online program was such a success that it caught the eye of the state legislature. The chair of the higher education committee for the state assembly became concerned that we were able to offer classes accessible to anyone, anywhere, and that we were collecting funding for classes for which we did not offer the ancillary support, such as counseling and library services, for which state funding was also intended. As I sat in the hearing at the state capitol, that interchange told me that we needed to go back to the campus and put as many of these services online as possible, so that students, for which the college was receiving full state funding, had online access to a comprehensive set of support services.

Thus, our expansion to a virtual college accelerated. By 2001, we had four degrees offered totally online. We now have 12 such degrees and close to 20 certificates. We also have fully articulated online programs that transfer seamlessly to baccalaureate online degree programs, all of which are fully accredited.

Through Technology, Teaching Becomes Public

As faculty members from various disciplines began to tailor ETUDES for their own courses, the author of ETUDES either did it for them or gave them the source code; he was sharing the code with anyone who wanted use it. That was our first introduction to open source. Since some faculty users did not have the technical skills to manipulate the software, the faculty began to develop their own work groups and began sharing their issues in using technology. We also began hosting a series of workshops to address these issues.

At first, the focus of the workshops was on the technical issues. However, in time, the conversations evolved into discussions about pedagogy, collaborative course redesign, and what were the truly salient subject matter elements for students to learn. The shift in faculty focus to student learning led to a shared understanding of teaching as a public act toward a collective responsibility—a most desirable by-product of our entire online effort.

Faculty collaboration is one of the hallmarks of successful pedagogy but is not a natural occurrence. Teaching is normally a very private endeavor (Shulman, 2004). However, sharing ideas, resources, and experiences can foster collectively new ideas and approaches. The focus is on reception, not output. When a faculty member is released from the confines of a course that is structured by time and physical space, focus is redirected to the content and student. What needs to happen is to engage in course redesign that results in laser-like focus on how students learn effectively, greater student engagement, and improved student performance. Bransford and colleagues (2002) note that online courses need to be conceptualized differently from face-to-face courses. Course redesign is not simply transferring a lecture course online; it is "redesigning a course by starting from the learning goals and integrating various forms of knowledge and expertise to build a course that realizes these goals" (Cox, 2005, p. 1780).

At Foothill, across disciplines, faculty members began sharing other common issues they were experiencing with their students' learning. Concerns about students' performance became a focal point. For example, student retention in online classes tended to be lower than in traditionally offered classes. The faculty users created a questionnaire for students to complete before enrolling in an online course. It helps the student understand that "online" without scheduled class time did not mean that the class did not take any time. The student had to determine, given work hours and other hours in classes, whether he or she had enough time to also work online. The faculty users also designed some online tools that helped them detect when, how often, and how long students signed into the online class and other metrics that could be used to track student behavior. Furthermore, with the online tools, student participation rates and other characteristics were tracked and could be correlated with whether they were factors related to student success.

While individual faculty members have certainly created innovations and improvements for their courses, the common interest of improving the course management system they all shared prompted faculty members to pool their best thinking. They not only improved the tool they all shared, but improved student performance. This type of collaboration does not ordinarily occur when teaching is done in individual courses in the traditional classroom

Through Technology, A Shared Engagement in Learning

While these technology "developments" are not new today, they were groundbreaking in the 1990s and would not have been possible if we did not have open source and the resulting faculty collaboration. Faculty behaved as if they "owned" the software and therefore tweaked it and their courses as they saw fit. Formerly "out-of-class" exercises or assignments could be done online and easily shared with the class. Faculty-developed simulations and access to archival material can be easily shared with students. Consequently, faculty members have engaged students in different ways and students are in greater control of their own learning. Research for course assignments, group discussions, and contact between student and faculty member are all in the hands of students digitally.

From cognitive science, Driscoll (2002) suggests that learning occurs when it is in context, is active, is social, and is reflective. Similarly, Bransford and colleagues (2000) suggest that learning occurs when it is interactive, an exchange between new information and what is already known. These conditions are present in an open education environment.

Cognitive science and learning theory also tell us that learning occurs the most effectively when the learner is most engaged to learn, such as seeking an answer to a question. When this happens, at the moment students' curiosity is piqued and can be satisfied, learning takes place. Curiosity has long been understood as a corollary to learning (Arnone, 2003). Kearsley and Shneiderman (1999) propose engagement theory as the framework for technology-based teaching and learning. Because technology can provide easy access to information, learning, whether formal or informal, can take place any time, any place. The Pew Internet & American Life Project found "nearly 75% of college students use the Internet more than the library as an information and research resource." (Pew Internet & American Life Project, 2002). Furthermore, 70 percent of American adults use the Internet and 91 percent of those use a search engine to find information (Pew Internet & American Life, 2007).

The provost of the Western Governors University cites the ongoing learning that takes place from online use and the importance of mastering readily available digital resources for success in our global environment (Swenson, 2007). Whether this ultimately improves student academic success is still unanswered, but all the signs of student participation in an online open environment have been in the direction of the desired paradigm shift.

Open Source: Nonproprietary and Resource-Sharing

When Foothill College started down this path in 1995, there were no commercial online course management products on the market. We created ETUDES out of necessity and to precisely serve our need and desire to offer courses via the Internet. Furthermore, we knew that we would be investing a great deal of time and energy in faculty development as faculty members redesigned their courses and learned to teach through ETUDES. This faculty development represented a tremendous investment of time, knowledge making ETUDES literally a teachers' tool. This was an investment that we needed to protect. We needed to control ownership of the software product and not be held hostage by any commercial product that needed to meet a bottom line for investors and whose prices were therefore out of our control. Our financial autonomy was important to protect our academic autonomy.

ETUDES, in its second generation (ETUDES-Next Generation, ETUDES-NG), also reflects the input and collaboration of hundreds of faculty members from many different disciplines, from many different institutions, with different needs, and yet, with the same needs. This rich input is what drives the software produced. With open source in the education sector, the software objective is educational rather than financial as evidenced by the ETUDES Consortium. This consortium was established in 2002 and is open to all educational institutions. Currently, it has over 50 member colleges and other institutions, all of whom who pay a very modest membership fee to participate in the overall development and utilization of ETUDES-NG. A primary factor is that the consortium is made up of colleges and individuals who want to "influence the effort," which is not possible in commercial products.

Open Content

Open content is sharing among faculty, similar to open source among developers as both emphasize information exchange and active collaboration. Again, this is a "violation" of the faculty members' traditional classroom "privacy." Faculty members are sharing of not only how they approach various classroom issues but also the very content they have developed for their course. As they engage in collaboration within and across institutions, as faculty members make their curriculum available and access others', they advance the paradigm shift from teaching to learning. They engage in self-reflection in evaluating what works and what does not, enter into conversations with content authors of their discipline, and communicate with other faculty members beyond the boundaries of their campus.

Foothill's SOFIA project, Sharing of Free Intellectual Assets, has been my firsthand experience with open content and how it can be made available broadly and how faculty of similar disciplines can be motivated to collaborate with one another. Open tools and resources have allowed faculty and students to literally and figuratively think outside of both the box and the classroom. With the removal of artificial and physical barriers, such as walls, time, and conventional resources, we can focus on pedagogy, content, and learning outcomes.

Foothill is, of course just one example. MIT's OpenCourseWare initiative began in 2002, with the goal of putting MIT courses online, available to anyone for free (see, in this volume, the chapter by Lerman, Miyagawa, and Margulies). This project has provided an invaluable resource to faculty and students and was the first major attempt at viewing curriculum as open source, removing the privacy boundaries that might have existed for each class.

Rice University's Connexions Project, which is addressing the issue of common curriculum and publishing learning modules, is fostering online faculty collaboration. The Rice project provides an online platform for faculty to author, review, share, and mix content modules. Through the Connexions' "Content Commons," faculty can build, modify, and update course materials. Furthermore, materials can be constructed into learning modules, each equivalent to several pages in a textbook.

All the "Opens" = Open Education

Open source and access have spawned an open education movement, but are these yet passing educational trends? Sustainability is anchored in the users, faculty, and students. At Foothill College, open education is more than a passing trend: it has reached the core of what we do. More than 200 faculty members are using ETUDES, and it is used for totally online courses as well as a support system for hybrid or face-to-face classes. Our consortium supports over 70,000 students. With ETUDES, our faculty maintains the *academic locus of control* over their courses, curriculum, and pedagogy. An open source community is inherently synergistic with an academic community, and therefore, a highly compatible and self-sustaining relationship. Just as faculty members are forever engaged in discussions of their respective disciplines, ETUDES faculty extend those discussions to improvements in the course management system and how it facilitates the learning process. At this writing, the ETUDES consortium at Foothill College leads the development of open-source Web-based tools for teaching and learning in strategic alliance with McGraw-Hill Higher Education. "Working closely with ETUDES, McGraw-Hill Higher Education's instructional designers will create authoritative, thoroughly reviewed content and complete online courses, which can easily be deployed and accessed by instructors and students through ETUDES-NG open source software" (McGraw-Hill). An interesting open source and sustainability model is emerging. For example, college "adoptions of McGraw-Hill Higher Education's online courses developed through this alliance will fund additional research and development within the ETUDES Consortium community. And McGraw-Hill Higher Education's Learning Solutions team will gain insights into how instructors and students use Sakai-supported online course content in both distance and hybrid (online and traditional) learning environments." This type of alliance could signal another level of institutionalizing open source initiatives. Similarly, California community colleges, under the leadership of the Foothill-De Anza Community College District, have established the Community College Consortium for Open Educational Resources. This consortium encourages the establishment of college policies on public domain and the creation and use of open educational resources in the classroom. "The faculty is encouraged to develop and use public domain and open content materials . . . to provide high quality alternatives to traditional textbooks" (Advisory Committee on Student Financial Assistance, 2007, p. 22).

While we know open education can enhance access and collaboration, can it enhance the even more critical issue of success? When we put all the "opens" together, open source, accessibility, modality, content, and open enrollment, we have a form of open education that has enormous potential to truly make learning available to anyone at any time and anywhere a reality. We also have enormous potential for advancing the shift to learning and success.

A New Understanding of Learning
Through technology, a vast range of unique faculty applications is being shared among faculty and with students, facilitating an open education

environment. Furthermore, as the use of online technology becomes more integrated into a course, and particularly in its content delivery and dialogue between faculty member and students, an interesting shift emerges. That is the real shift from teaching to learning and, ultimately, deep learning. The issue of access and success could take on new and more important meaning as the unit of measurement of student work is increasingly more focused on *what* the student is learning rather than how much *time* is spent in a course.

The real educational issues, as articulated by some, are the importance of deep learning, and a better understanding of how and what students truly learn and, therefore, attain their educational goals. When teaching is no longer mere knowledge dissemination but facilitation of students' thinking, knowing, and understanding, the challenge for faculty is to think differently about what students are expected to know and how to perform and to develop new measurement and assessment tools that address the core of what learning means. The paths of collaboration and innovation have already been charted through OpenCourseWare and the like. Could the same be done with assessment?

Implications Beyond the Classroom, Beyond the Institution

To increase the complexity of this picture, we should also think of the implications for public institutions that receive their funding based on seat time; for example, on weekly student contact hours. Is this seat time relevant to the educational activities of the course? And if the answer is no, then what is it, or how is it, that schools and colleges should be funded? A recent study in the state of California notes, meticulously, all of the state's educational funding mechanisms, most of which are *not* related to the education mission (Shulock and Moore, 2007). When will legislators understand that seat time is not related to learning? Open education might push the issue.

The open education movement should stimulate policy makers to develop more meaningful accountability measures, measures that focus on student performance and institutional mission and effort. This is long overdue, particularly at community colleges. Open education, by definition, gives the power to the students to identify how they best learn and to take responsibility for their learning. Thus, the focus is on the student's performance and commitment. Likewise, institutional effort that contributes to enhancing student performance should be the account-ability measure that funders use.

However, *educational* governance is a new construct that needs to be developed. Policies, practices, and funding mechanisms need to be rede-signed to address and be aligned with, not only the educational mission, but also student performance. For example, Shulock and Moore (2007) note that all 109 community colleges in California are funded through enrollment and recommends that policy makers consider funding these colleges through course or program completions.

In a perfect world, open education should come to mean reduction in segmentation and territoriality. Policies should stem from student performance and all institutional factors that could affect that perfor-mance. Student-centrism should be paramount. Unfortunately, more often than not, college presidents tell one another, truthfully, that we would more likely lose our jobs over mismanagement of money rather than mismanagement of student performance. So the focus is on finances not education. And ironically, in this particular scenario, the assumption is that the *student* is responsible and we are not, and therefore, we are not held accountable for student performance. However, in every other aspect of education, we treat the student as the receptacle of our actions, without gauging whether the receptacle is half-full or half empty! Governance policies are focused on enrollment, not retention or student performance. For the last decade, accrediting agencies have become increasingly concerned with student outcomes (CHEA Institute, 2006). Even greater pressure has come from the recent report from the Commission on the Future of Higher Education (U.S. Depart-ment of Education, 2006). As colleges focus on student performance, so must legislative and governance bodies responsible for funding do the same.

An entrepreneurial and innovative climate is necessary, first and fore-most, to support and enhance open education and open educational tools development. Old frameworks of teaching and learning are changing, though slowly. The roots of education as a privilege reserved for the elite are deep roots to cut. An open educational environment, whether in terms of tools or students, is diametrically opposed to the elitism bred in the selectivity of the college admissions process. These tenets need to be challenged if open education and its tools are to survive.

One Last "Open": Leadership

Open education is clearly subject to great variety in quality and effectiveness. However, if we stay focused on how the student learns, and if we are able to effectively assess that learning, then the quality of open or any other educational tool or delivery method should be evident. Shulman (1999, 2004) comments that learning is least useful when it is private and hidden and is most powerful when it is public and communal (2004, p. 36). He says that learning is most effective when it is community property, to be shared, tested, examined, and challenged.

In an open enrollment setting, such as in community colleges, this need for sharing is even more critical because of the diversity of our students, not just cultural and ethnic diversity, but the academic diversity open enrollment brings to an institution. The best practices movement has taken hold because there are not singular solutions to learning challenges and the greater the variety of proven options, the better. Effective teaching and learning strategies are probably as varied as we have students, so the challenges, and the solutions, are boundless.

Therefore, we need educational governance and funding models to support educational entrepreneurship. We need *open* leadership. Currently, educational innovations wither within the educational system we live in. Educators have not been without innovative approaches to pedagogy, nor have interventions been ineffective, but best practices seem to have a shelf life, and lack sustainability. Many of these innovations cannot regenerate within an environment whose policies are not focused on the educational mission.

Foothill College was able to build its own form of open education without systemic changes at the state level. We could do this because we took the initiative from within the institution and manipulated the system to work for us, rather than the other way around. However, this took a different mindset, and a paradigm shift, if you will, centering on the student's perspective. The development of ETUDES and SOFIA would not have occurred had it not been for a culture that fosters innovation, allowed for missteps, and encourages entrepreneurship.

Such a culture was not created overnight. It evolved under institutional leadership that identified a set of core values for the college that were critical to creating an innovative culture. Values, such as openness, honesty, trust, integrity, and forgiveness, translate into an environment where all opinions are valued; people can be open and honest, where there is mutual trust and respect, and where people are forgiven for their mistakes. The senior vice president was famous for saying to new faculty members, "The president would rather see you try and not succeed than not try at all."

With open education, we have the opportunity to view education not from 30,000 feet above, but from the window of the space station. We are in a global society that is already connected, with access around the world. Open education is not a classroom without walls. It is education that encompasses the entire world we live in, connecting us through modalities that we have come to know and like best. Open education should be a cognitive/information/social entrepreneur's dream come true.

If I were to resume my presidential career, based on what I have learned from experience, I would develop an institution grounded in open education. As a leader, I would take the following 10 steps:

1. Build a culture of evidence with core values that include openness, trust, forgiveness: Openness requires trust and forgiveness if true innovation and resource sharing is to take place.

2. Create a climate of collaboration at all levels: everyone at the institution needs to be responsible for student learning: the students, the faculty, and the staff; for example, parking lot attendants should remind students of add and drop dates for classes.

3. Establish mission-based governance and decision-making: focus is on the performance of students; every decision about resource allocation to programs should be start with the question, "Will this result in a positive student performance outcome?"

4. Create expectations for innovation: everyone should be free to be innovative in an environment that is nonthreatening, built on trust, openness and forgiveness.

5. Build trust by allocating resources that support the mission.

6. Invite elementary school students (as early as the first grade) to demonstrate what they already do with technology at a faculty convocation.

7. Invite teens for a panel presentation on how they use technology for social networking and why.

8. Engage consulting firms like IDEO, which helps organizations innovate through design to think about course redesign with faculty.

9. Academically restructure the organization so that innovations are sustainable.

10. Invite Steve Jobs to be president for a day to help us "think different."

References

Advisory Committee on Student Financial Assistance. (May 2007). *Turn the Page: Making College Textbooks More Affordable*. Washington, DC.

American Association of Community Colleges (2007). *Fast Facts*. Washington, DC.

Arnone, M. P. (2003). *Using Instructional Design Strategies to Foster Curiosity*. Syracuse, NY: ERIC Clearinghouse on Information and Technology. (ERIC Document Reproduction Service No. ED479842)

Barr, R., and Tagg, J. (1995, November/December). From Teaching to Learning. *Change*, 27(6), 13–25.

Berkner, L., and Wei, C. C. (2006). *National Postsecondary Student Aid Study 2003–2004*, (NPSAS-04): Undergraduate Financial Aid Estimates for 12 States: 2003–2004 (NCES 2006–158). U.S. Department of Education. Washington, DC: National Center for Education Statistics (Data Analysis System). Retrieved from http://nces.ed.gov/das/.

Bransford, J., Brown, A., and Cocking, R. (Eds.). (2000). *How People Learn: Brain, Mind, Experience, and School*. Washington, DC: National Academy Press.

Bransford, J., Vye, N., and Bateman, H. (2002). Creating High-Quality Learning Environments: Guidelines from Research on How People Learn. In P. A. Gram and N. Stacey (Eds.), *The Knowledge Economy and Postsecondary Education: Report of Workshop* (pp.159–198). Washington, DC: National Academy Press.

CHEA Institute for Research and Study of Accreditation and Quality Assurance (2006, December). *Accreditation and Accountablity: A CHEA Special Report*. Washington, DC: Council for Higher Education Accreditation.

Community College Research Center [Teacher's College, Columbia University] (2005, updated 2006). *Is Student Success Labeled Institutional Failure? Student Goals and Graduation Rates in the Accountability Debate at Community Colleges*. New York: Bailey, T. R., Jenkins, D., and Leinbach, D. T.

Cox, R. D. (August 2005). Online Education as Institutional Myth: Rituals and Realities at Community Colleges. Community College Research Center, *Teachers College Record*, 107(8): 1754–1787.

Driscoll, M. P. (2002). *How People Learn (And What Technology Might Have to Do with It)*. Syracuse, NY: ERIC Clearinghouse on Information and Technology. (ERIC Document Reproduction Service No. ED470032)

Jones, S., et al (2002).The Internet Goes to College. *Pew Internet & American Life Project.* Retrieved from http://www.pewinternet.org/pdfs/PIP_College _Report.pdf.

Kearsley, G., and Shneiderman, B. (1999). *Engagement Theory: A Framework for Technology-Based Teaching and Learning*, Instructional Science and Development, Inc. http://home.sprynet.com/~gkearsley/engage.htm.

McGraw-Hill Higher Education (October 17, 2007). *McGraw-Hill Higher Education and ETUDES form Alliance to Expand Delivery on Online Solutions* [Press release].

Pew Internet and American Life Project. (2007, January). Tracking Surveys March 2000—December 2006, Washington, DC. Retrieved from http://www .pewinternet.org/trends/Internet_Activities_1.11.07.htm.

Shulman, L. S. (1999, July/August). Taking Learning Seriously. *Change*, 31(4), 10–17.

Shulman, L. S. (2004). *Teaching as Community Property: Essays in Higher Education*, San Francisco, CA: Jossey-Bass.

Shulock, N., and Moore, C. (2007). *Rules of the Game: How State Policy Creates Barriers to Degree Completion and Impedes Student Success in the California Community Colleges*, Institute for Higher Education Leadership and Policy, California State University, Sacramento.

Swenson, C. (2007). The Digital Divide: 19th Century Classrooms, 21st Century Careers. *Distance Learning Today*, 1(2), 6.

U.S. Department of Education (2006). *A Test of Leadership: Charting the Future of U.S. Higher Education: Final Report of the Secretary's Commission on the Future of Higher Education*, Washington, DC: U.S. Department of Education.

27

What's Next for Open Knowledge?

Mary Taylor Huber and Pat Hutchings

The transformations evoked by the name "open education" reflect prodigious ambitions. Our fellow authors in this volume describe changes aimed at dramatically expanded educational access, more widely effective teaching models and materials, and ongoing, systematic improvement in teaching and learning as educators generate and share new pedagogical knowledge and know-how. It's an impressive if daunting vision.

And it's more than a vision. Many relevant shifts and developments are already in evidence. Campuses, organizations, and individuals embracing open education now make course materials and "learning objects" freely available on the Web. Connexions, MERLOT, and Massachusetts Institute of Technology's (MIT) OpenCourseWare are among the most visible of these efforts, but there are many others in the United States and beyond with diverse approaches and patrons. Numerous national and international projects have developed online representations of classroom practice, tools and materials, and scholarship of teaching and learning projects. Some 17,000 teachers and students, for instance, are now using the Carnegie Foundation's KEEP Toolkit to make their work visible and available for others to build on—and the circle of users grows by the day.

Technology is not, of course, the only route to openness. Over the last decade, the number and vitality of face-to-face and more traditional publication-based forums, outlets, and occasions for serious exchange around matters pedagogical has shot ahead, helping to create a *teaching commons*: "an emergent conceptual space for exchange and community among faculty, students, administrators, and all others committed to learning as an essential activity of life in contemporary democratic society" (Huber and Hutchings, 2005, p. 1). In this commons, one can find a growing set of resources for and about teaching and learning, produced not only by pedagogical specialists, but by teachers and learners of all kinds.

Looking ahead, the questions that stand out most for us are how to expand and preserve the openness about teaching and learning that is increasingly in place and how to ensure that the new (or newly available) resources in the teaching commons are actually useful to those who can benefit from them. It is well and good to make as many educational resources as possible accessible to as many teachers and learners as possible. But, to borrow a line from the movie *Field of Dreams*, if we build it, will they come?

The answer, we believe, will be shaped by progress in two related areas. To deliver on the promise of open knowledge will first require concerted attention to conceptual questions about what kinds of knowledge can best contribute to educational quality. To put it simply, "they will come" if they find resources and insights they value and can use. Second, future prospects will depend on the development of policies and practices that support an ethic of openness in ways that are inclusive, inviting, and rewarding (in several senses of the word). These challenges are related, clearly, and are likely to be further complicated by the increasing calls for accountability faced by higher education today.

Like the vision of open education itself, these challenges can seem daunting. It is tempting to reach for shiny new answers that depart, radically sometimes, from what has gone before. Our instinct is to be more modest. The promise of open knowledge can best be met, we believe, by building on what is already underway, by not underestimating the value of small gains, and by balancing big ambitions with lots of small steps along the way.

Knowledge That Matters

Although the concept of "open knowledge" for higher education carries with it the ring of the new, it is worth remembering that knowledge about teaching and learning has not previously been "closed." The past several decades in particular have seen significant advances in basic research about how people learn. These advances are now making their way into the work of regular faculty through widely circulated reports such as *How People Learn* (Bransford, Brown, and Cocking, 1999). Journals and conferences dedicated to pedagogical exchange are long-standing in some fields and newly launched in others. For several decades, campus centers for teaching have provided opportunities for educators to sample the literature on teaching and learning and share what works in their own classrooms. In short, openness—quite apart from the technology that increasingly supports it—has been on the rise for some time now, and much can be learned from these ongoing efforts.

One important lesson from these developments is embodied in the emergence of the scholarship of teaching and learning, a set of practices through which faculty bring their habits and skills as scholars to their role as educators. The scholarship of teaching and learning draws on a variety of earlier lines and fields of work: educational research, classroom assessment, faculty development, and others. Its distinguishing feature, however, is the value placed on what teachers know and can learn from their own practice and their own students. In fact, one now sees faculty in every discipline and every type of institution approaching teaching as serious intellectual work, finding that it poses interesting questions about learning that invite inquiry and investigation, documenting their efforts, and sharing the results. In the process, they are contributing to the improvement of teaching and learning in their own classrooms and, importantly, beyond.

As we have seen through the Carnegie Academy for the Scholarship of Teaching and Learning (CASTL), this kind of knowledge is powerful because faculty often find as much to learn from work that remains close to the situated experience of other faculty as from studies done with methodologies designed to minimize the influence of context on research results. When such work enters the teaching commons, faculty can see how others manage complexity in the classroom and address real-world problems in situations they know how to "read." Faculty can identify a good question, a promising investigative strategy, an assignment or assessment design that they might try out or include in their own repertoire, and they are aided in incorporating it into their own work by their understanding of how the original context differs from their own. In short, the momentum that the scholarship of teaching and learning has established over the past decade clearly points to the value of pedagogical knowledge that is deeply contextual and closely tied to the particulars of classroom settings.

This is not to say that faculty can't also benefit from *basic* research on teaching or learning, and from the "best practices" literature that now circulates widely. But it would be a mistake, in higher education as it has been in the lower grades, to assume that findings from such research can be simply "applied" or "translated" to practice in any straightforward way. As the authors of a 1999 National Academy of Education report argue, it makes more sense to "view research production and research understanding as part of the same process" (cited in Shavelson and Towne, 2002, p. 156). In other words, *doing it enables one to use it*. Practitioners must participate in the effort if it is to have real consequences in the classroom. And it is in making available the work of practitioners—the knowledge embedded in and about practice—that the open knowledge movement can perhaps make its greatest impact.

Looking ahead, we see exciting opportunities to elaborate and fine-tune what we will call the "genres" in which close-to-the-classroom knowledge can be captured in ways that will travel to other settings. Again, there are lessons to be learned from developments already underway. While there is always likely to be a tension between local origins and broader usability, a number of current efforts point the way to a right balance. The great potential of the KEEP Toolkit, for instance, lies not only in its user-friendly technological features, but in the templates it offers for capturing pedagogical thinking and materials in ways that are readable. The "class anatomy" template, for example, calls for representations of course design and rationale as well as specific classroom activities and discussion segments. The "project template" reflects what Carnegie Foundation staff have learned about the evolution of a scholarship of teaching and learning, moving from an initial question, to results, to telling examples of student work. While these templates (and there are others) provide a good deal of flexibility, their common features make it easier for users to make sense of what they are seeing—and thus to adopt and use what they find most relevant.

Similarly, while the promise of the e-portfolio is partly its electronic availability—its openness—its power as a "genre" for making the intellectual work of teaching useful to others has been significantly advanced by efforts like that of Dan Bernstein and his colleagues in the national Peer Review of Teaching Project (Bernstein, Burnett, Goodburn, and Savory, 2006) to define the elements of a successful portfolio, thus providing a scaffold for both the makers and readers of portfolios. Additionally, the requirement that portfolios include evidence of student learning makes it possible for readers to make judgments about the effectiveness of the teaching that is represented. The genre of lesson study also comes to mind, with its carefully prescribed set of elements and steps, starting with a description of learning goals, moving through a detailed lesson design, evidence of student learning, and reflections on how the lesson might be revised; see for example the Lesson Study Project directed by William Cerbin at the University of Wisconsin-La Crosse (Cerbin and Kopp, 2006). Then there are the more familiar genres of classroom assessment tools, rubrics, and assignments, as well as more novel inventions like the "elicitation engine" proposed by Diana Laurillard in her essay in this section.

The idea here is not to standardize or limit what is available, nor to leave behind what has already been done. What is needed are small steps to open up possibilities and invite experimentation with evolving norms and forms for representing, reading, and reviewing pedagogical knowledge. This prescription is not simply one of common sense; it follows from the model of change implied in the open knowledge movement. Where traditional views of educational reform tend to assume a small number of approaches that can be "scaled up" and widely adopted, open knowledge (and, more broadly, open education) offers a different path to improvement, eschewing the "fat head" for the "long tail" (to use Chris Anderson's now well-traveled metaphor) in which many approaches find smaller groups of adopters and champions (Anderson, 2006).

In keeping with this view, the best bet for the future is, appropriately, to *keep open* the question of which knowledge genres, norms, and forms will have the greatest power to travel and make a difference, cultivating in teaching and learning the same kind of diversity that is so essential to the natural environment. This means making a space for good things in all shapes and sizes—and not only in online formats. True, knowledge about teaching and learning is much enriched and enabled by new technologies that give access to classroom materials, video, electronic portfolios, assessment instruments and rubrics, workshop and conference presentations, and other evolving genres, including those that facilitate collaboration. Most faculty recognize that much about teaching practice cannot be easily conveyed on paper, and important experiments using new media now exist that make it possible to represent teaching and learning in new ways. But, as many authors in this volume suggest, the promise of open education lies not only with technology but with individuals, relationships, exchange, communities of practice, and being open to the full range of possibilities for engaging as many people as possible.

Inviting and Maintaining Openness

The "stuff" of open knowledge for teaching and learning is on the rise, happily, both in supply and in the variety of materials and representations of teaching and learning. Pushing further in these directions is a *sine qua non* for important future work. But having good stuff is not enough. Those committed to this work must also push for policies and practices to ensure that what is open *stays* open in the fullest, most vital way. This means maintaining access, certainly, but it also means creating a culture in which people *want* that access, both as contributors to and users of knowledge in the teaching commons.

The first challenge in this regard is for the commons to remain open to educators from a full range of fields and disciplines who want—even if only occasionally and in modest ways—to contribute to pedagogical innovation and exchange. This requires more than just access to online or other outlets. As those involved in efforts to raise the profile of teaching on campus have documented extensively, it means support on campus for more and better occasions to talk about learning, informal working groups of faculty experimenting with particular pedagogies, time for departmental conversations about critical learning issues, and institution-wide seminars about important questions concerning the educational experience. On a wider scale, openness also requires that journal and newsletter editors, conference organizers, grant proposal reviewers, and the like recognize that scholars with different backgrounds, offering up widely ranging lessons, insights, materials, and studies can make valuable contributions.

Questions about who can (and can't) put what into the commons raise a second set of issues about ownership and access that will increasingly need to be faced. Open education does not necessarily mean "free"; there are, at the least, costs for the production of these resources. That said, the movement will need to grapple further with the prospect of forms of privatization and commercialization that unduly restrict access. Here it is useful to remember that in arenas as diverse as natural resources, the Internet, and scientific research, the notion of the commons has tended to be invoked—most famously by Garrett Hardin in his discussion of "the tragedy of the commons"—to mourn its passing or warn against its loss. For better or worse, David Bollier reminds us in *Public Assets, Private Profits*, history provides many examples of shifts from public to private control, from the enclosure movement in England in which the landed classes took over open fields traditionally managed by local communities, to the recent trend for business interests to seek greater sway over the use of public resources such as land, water, the airwaves, the Internet, and the results of federally funded research (Bollier, 2001). And, as the higher education community glimpsed in the early rush to e-learning in the 1990s, pedagogical work is potentially as vulnerable to enclosure as other intellectual and cultural resources.

This means thinking through the intellectual property issues involved in going public with work on teaching and learning: assuring that one is in compliance with current intellectual property practices and establishing appropriate incentives for contributors, but also seeking creative ways to keep access as open as possible. As MIT's OpenCourseWare Web site explains:

The intellectual property policies created for [OpenCourseWare] are clear and consistent with other policies for scholarly materials used in education. Faculty retain ownership of most materials . . . following the MIT policy on textbook authorship. MIT retains ownership only when significant use has been made of the Institute's resources. If student course work is placed on the [OpenCourse-Ware] site, then copyright in the work remains with the student.

No doubt there are many ways to negotiate these waters and a number of precedents to draw from. The key move, it would seem, is captured by Stephen Weber in *The Success of Open Source*: to configure intellectual property "fundamentally around the right to distribute, not the right to exclude" (2004, p.16).

But this raises a third set of future challenges that revolve around the need for practices, "regulating access and use of common resources" (Palumbo and Scott, 2005, p. 288). In particular, higher education needs habits and conventions for citing and building on the work of others—an essential ingredient in the recognition, reward, and motivation for such work. In a paper presented at the Modern Language Association annual meeting in 2004, Elliot Shapiro, a senior lecturer in Cornell University's writing program, criticized the lack of such incentives: "Colleagues who borrow from syllabi . . . are not obliged to acknowledge what they have borrowed as they would if, in their published work, they borrowed from articles published more formally." In short, he says, though "all teachers depend" on the commons, they tend to do so in ways that are "invisible" (p. 6). For the commons to function effectively, more visible, shared conventions need to be established for the citation of individual work and for the mapping and management of knowledge in order to organize a vast and diverse collection of information in ways that allow it to be used.

Open Knowledge in an Era of Accountability

Building the teaching commons will take energy and money to bring people together for exchange around important questions about teaching and learning, to develop new venues and outlets for exchange and collaborative scholarship, to create and maintain repositories and maps through which this work can be located and used, and to identify and resist restrictive modes of commercialization and privatization of pedagogical work. It will also require serious engagement with issues of quality.

Thus far, questions about quality in open knowledge (and open education, more broadly) have been framed in terms of provenance: good materials and reliable "knowledge" come from good places like MIT, Foothill College, Carnegie Mellon University, the Open University, and, more generally, from individuals with recognized scholarly credentials. That seems a perfectly appropriate consideration, but it is not, we would argue, finally a sufficient one. As the experience of other initiatives like MERLOT, Connexions, and even Wikipedia attest, conversations about quality and standards are clearly underway in the open education community that will add to the field's sense of how to sort the bad from the good, the misleading from the useful.

But in other circles, the conversation is much further along—and moving in directions that may run counter to what is needed to push ahead with the directions outlined above. In particular, we are concerned about how to maintain a space for educational experimentation and exchange in a period that seems headed for increasingly bottom-line forms of accountability, with its concomitant calls for institutions to make evidence of student learning outcomes available to the public, as found in the United States, for example, in the 2006 report of the U.S. Secretary of Education's Commission on the Future of Higher Education.

At one level, the value of evidence is something that any responsible educator would share. Faculty care about their students, and they want to know that the resources they find in the teaching commons will serve those students well. The danger comes when high stakes constrict people's ability or willingness to explore new pedagogical ideas (Shulman, 2007). We can see this negative dynamic at play already in the frequently documented trajectory of pedagogical innovation: those trying new approaches often find that their early efforts meet with dissatisfaction from students and suspicion by colleagues. The 2007 Harvard University report on teaching, for example, recommends steps to ensure that "the spirit of trial-and-error and adjustment" can flourish in Harvard's classrooms, "unconstrained by faculty fears that a new approach . . . might initially result in a depressed overall 'effectiveness' score" on the student evaluation form (p. 32). Without those first, risky efforts, it is hard to see how new and better approaches will come into being . . . and how the teaching commons can be kept vital and well supplied with creative ideas.

Perhaps the most interesting experiments now underway to improve and ensure the quality of open pedagogical knowledge are with peer review. In a multicampus experiment in which faculty created and reviewed course portfolios, Dan Bernstein and colleagues (2006) have built peer review into the process in a number of ways. First, a course portfolio is created in the company of other faculty who exchange a series of memos about content, method, and student work that eventually form the major components of their documentation. Second, the finished portfolios go through a process of external peer review, whether for purposes of improvement, formal evaluation, or both. Indeed, in their book on the project, the authors make a thought-provoking point about external review: Because academics are unaccustomed to sharing the intellectual work of teaching with each other, the project needed to provide guidance in the art of review and critique. Third, course portfolios are used to foster departmental and campus collaboration. And finally, in the spirit of field-building characteristic of the open knowledge movement, course portfolios are made available for larger groups of colleagues to use—and by implication, to review—through posting on the Web (See www.courseportfolio.org).

As educators gain experience in creating, critiquing, and building on each other's pedagogical work, understandings about quality will become better articulated and more widely shared. Still, for the near future, the open knowledge community will have to perform a delicate balancing act. Openness will be meaningless without attention to quality. If the teaching commons becomes a home for work that cannot gain the respect of peers, and has nothing to recommend it beyond the enthusiasm of its creator, it will soon be abandoned by those doing (and seeking) good work. But as is true in any field—especially in formative early days—the need for tough standards must be balanced with the need for incentives to experiment and to push into unknown territory. The commons must serve both as a repository and a seedbed. Open knowledge is not simply about making new pedagogical work available. It is about creating the conditions in which ever better ideas and models can come forward.

Modest Steps toward Big Ambitions

What's next for open knowledge about teaching and learning? Will the commons continue to thrive and become the vibrant, growing enterprise that its practitioners and friends would like it to be? John Willinsky, the author of *The Access Principle*, argues that "with a form of knowledge that is constituted as a public good, which is the case with research and scholarship, the knowledge should be circulated as widely and publicly as possible, especially as that wider circulation increases the value and quality of that knowledge" (Jaschik, 2005, p.1). As with other areas of academic thought and practice, the best chance for pedagogical knowledge to circulate widely and publicly will be the success of that knowledge itself. Will this work improve teaching? Will it help create better environments for student learning? Will it create a vision of what is possible that is compelling enough to attract colleagues to join in? The challenge for the open knowledge community is to realize that their big ambitions can best be pursued in concert with others who care about learning in higher education, and by taking the many small steps necessary to create an academic culture where the intellectual and creative work involved in teaching is understood, encouraged, and supported.

Acknowledgments

This article draws upon the authors' book, *The Advancement of Learning: Building the Teaching Commons* (2005), and their article, "Building the Teaching Commons," in *Change* magazine (2006).

References

Anderson, C. (2006). *The Long Tail: Why the Future of Business is Selling Less of More*. New York: Hyperion Books.

Bernstein, D., Burnett, A. N., Goodburn, A., and Savory, P. (2006). *Making Teaching and Learning Visible: Course Portfolios and the Peer Review of Teaching*. Bolton, MA: Anker Publishing Co.

Bollier, D. (2001). *Public Assets, Private Profits: Reclaiming the American Commons in an Age of Market Enclosure*. Washington, DC: New America Foundation.

Bransford, J. D., Brown, A. L., and Cocking, R. R. (Eds.). (1999). *How People Learn: Brain, Mind, Experience, and School*. Washington, DC: National Academy Press.

Carnegie Foundation for the Advancement of Teaching. KEEP Toolkit. Retrieved February 20, 2007, from http://www.cfkeep.org/static/index.html.

Carnegie Foundation for the Advancement of Teaching. The Carnegie Academy for the Scholarship of Teaching and Learning. Retrieved February 20, 2007, from http://www.carnegiefoundation.org/programs/index.asp?key=21

Cerbin, B., and Kopp, B. (2006). Lesson Study as a Model for Building Pedagogical Knowledge and Improving Teaching. *International Journal of Teaching and Learning in Higher Education*, 18(3), 250–257.

Hardin, H. (1968). The Tragedy of the Commons. *Science*, 162, 1243–1248.

Harvard University. (2007, January). Compact to Enhance Teaching and Learning at Harvard. Proposed by the Task Force on Teaching and Career Development to the Faculty of Arts and Sciences.

Huber, M. T., and Hutchings, P. (2005). *The Advancement of Learning: Building the Teaching Commons*. San Francisco, CA: Jossey-Bass.

Huber, M. T., and Hutchings, P. (2006, May/June). Building the Teaching Commons. *Change*, 38(3), 24–31.

Jaschik, S. (2005, December 20). "The Access Principle" [Interview with John Willinsky]. *Inside Higher Education*. Retrieved October 9, 2006, from http://www.insidehighered.com/layout/set/print/news/2005/12/20/access.

Laurillard, D. (2008). Open teaching: The key to sustainable and effective open education. In T. Iiyoshi and M. S. V. Kumar (Eds.), *Opening Up Education: The Collective Advancement of Education through Open Technology, Open Content, and Open Knowledge*, pp. 319–335. Cambridge, MA: MIT Press.

MIT OpenCourseWare. Frequently Asked Questions: Who Owns the Intellectual Property on the MIT OCW Web site? Retrieved February 20, 2007, from MIT OCW Help at http://ocw.mit.edu/OcwWeb/Global/OCWHelp/help.htm.

Palumbo, A., and Scott, A. (2005). Bureaucracy, Open Access and Social Pluralism: Returning the Commons to the Goose. In P. du Gay (Ed.), *The Values of Democracy*. Oxford, UK: Oxford University Press.

Secretary of Education's Commission on the Future of Higher Education. (2006). *A Test of Leadership: Charting the Future of U.S. Higher Education*. Washington, DC: U.S. Department of Education.

Shapiro, E. (2005, April 18). Collaborative Teaching and the Problem of Intellectual Property. Presentation at the Modern Language Association annual meeting, January 2004.

Shavelson, R. J., and Towne, L. (Eds.). (2002). *Scientific Research in Education*. Washington, DC: National Academy Press.

Shulman, L. S. (2007, January/February). Counting and Recounting: Assessment and the Quest for Accountability. *Change*, 39(1), 20–25.

University of Wisconsin-La Crosse. Lesson Study Project. Retrieved February 20, 2007, from http://www.uwlax.edu/sotl/lsp/.

Weber, S. (2004). *The Success of Open Source*. Cambridge, MA: Harvard University Press.

Willinsky, J. (2005). *The Access Principle: The Case for Open Access to Research and Scholarship*. Cambridge, MA: MIT Press.

Conclusion: New Pathways for Shaping the Collective Agenda to Open Up Education

Toru Iiyoshi and M. S. Vijay Kumar

At Carnegie's Open Education Summit in 2006, President Lee S. Shulman, referencing the Foundation's history of "wondrous successes and unintended consequences," commented that "as the Carnegie Foundation's leadership over the years reflects *anticipatory genius necessary to understand the unintended consequences,* so should our efforts have not just rear-view but forward-view mirrors." (personal communication, September 15, 2006). His remarks eloquently capture the spirit and intent of our efforts, and particularly, of the key messages we want to put forward in this closing chapter of the book.

It is indeed our hope that the reflections and recommendations contained in this volume not only enhance our preparation for unintended consequences, but also help to proactively construct new, tunable learning environments that can take full advantage of various aspects of open education. Our key messages here include recommendations as well as cautions to help accelerate the advancement of effective teaching and learning beyond the mere free dissemination of educational tools and resources. As we craft these recommendations, we are acutely aware that to a large extent we serve as "intermediaries" for our authors who have taken a variety of positions and articulated some important issues and suggestions for planners and practitioners to transform education. In addition, we are aware that we are not the only ones researching the emergence and growth of open education activities; recently there were reports on open technology, content, and practice released by organizations such as The William and Flora Hewlett Foundation (See http://www.hewlett.org/Programs/Education/OER/OpenContent/Hewlett+OER+Report.htm), Ithaka (See http://www.ithaka.org/strategic-services/oss/oss-organization-for-open-source-software-study/), and the

Open eLearning Content Observatory Services project (OLCOS), co-funded by the European Union's eLearning Program (See http://www .olcos.org/cms/upload/docs/olcos_roadmap.pdf). Yet, our understanding of the current landscape and our commitment to joining the community for expansion of opportunities and change bring us to the following recommendations.

Recommendations

1. Investigate the Transformative Potential and Ecological Transitions

Open education is a means to an end. However, as we noted in our introduction, one of open education's most critical questions—how can open educational tools, resources, and knowledge demonstrably improve education quality?—is rarely mentioned or explored. Unfortunately, this omission from the conversation and action mirrors the education community's serious lack of engagement in investigating the transformative potential of open education. In his presentation about the value of educational media at the Educom conference in 1992, Neil Postman, the NYU professor and scholar of media and culture, famously asked, "What is the problem to which headlamp washer wipers are the solution?" Postman challenged the relevance and value proposition of new media and technology for education in the face of what he believed was a societal submission to the seduction of technology. Postman's provocative query is perhaps a good starting point for us to better understand the implications of open education. We need a similar critical enquiry on its value and impact.

Does open education shed new light on the persistent, hard problems of education with respect to access and quality, and perhaps offer new solutions? Does it provide a fresh look at the practice of education, necessitated by the flatness and fortunes expected of the new global dynamics of mobility and emerging economies? And, at the very least, what new pathways for education's agenda of continuous improvement does open education offer?

As the idea and practice of open education expand, it becomes increasingly critical to undertake systematic and systemic studies to better understand and clarify the transitions from traditional roles of educators and institutions to those needed to be effective in this ecology of technology-facilitated open education. Many authors of this book have discussed the possibilities of employing technology that promotes community-based peer learning, as well as technologies that provide intellectual and cognitive support for individual learners and groups of learners. Open education is beginning to provide dramatically increased access to educational resources and opportunities for learning. However, there is not the interaction, adaptation, evaluation, and personalization that characterize dimensions of quality in traditional education.

A look at the landscape tells us that our efforts with open education so far have been largely confined to attempts at improving what we already do. While this is certainly valid, we encourage consideration of approaches that transcend traditional practices, organizations, disciplines and audiences. The reuse and remix of resources, as well as connected communities of exploration, illustrate the opportunity for innovative activities at the intersections of domains. We believe that the sweet spot for opportunities created by the confluence of open educational resources, network and multimedia technology enablement, and greater understanding of "social pedagogy" is in *blended* and *boundary-less* education.

One of the most significant aspects of the changes in front of us is the promise of *blended learning environments* that involve optimal combinations of the physical and virtual, and integrate conventional pedagogical methods with innovative network-based learning to deliver quality educational opportunities. These are not limited to esoteric applications such as augmented reality, as in superimposing virtual objects on real landscapes. This can include bringing "experts" in contact with learners or even situated learning experiences, such as laboratories, real and virtual, to supplement online access to content in distance education situations.

The use of technology to enable and extend traditional human teacher-intensive educational approaches in conjunction with open educational resources offers the opportunity to scale the benefits of quality education that were previously confined to traditional cloisters to new audiences and for a variety of contexts even in nontraditional and informal modes. But the emerging applications that some of our authors have described extend the notion of *boundary-lessness* beyond typical lines of geography and politics to cross disciplinary lines, inducing proximity between research and teaching, and in some cases helping bridge the divide between the learned and lay persons by making the output of research more widely understood.

Some of the larger implications of *boundary-lessness* are in the affordances for advancing thematic education (directing education toward an understanding of big problems) and integrative learning (pursuing learning in more intentional, connected ways across subjects). We urge that in the future, the energies and resources of initiatives, institutions, organizations, and foundations involved in educational strategy-setting be directed toward addressing these opportunities that may recast the role of the university and formal education in light of an open world.

2. Change Education's Culture and Policy

Rethink Resources, Relationships, and Rewards   True progress in open education requires changes in practice and policy reflected through a change in education culture. From the stories that our authors tell, we see a pattern of pedagogical and technological inertial frameworks in higher education which present real obstacles to realizing the potential of extending educational opportunity and quality through open education. These inertial frames are manifested in various ways—as inflexible teaching approaches and curricula, as an inability to share ownership of the learning process with students, or even as technology designs that constrain choice and flexibility.

Higher education also places a high premium on originality, whereas adapting or improving another's educational materials is rarely understood to be a creative, valuable contribution. Thus, while scholars are expected to build on the work of others in their disciplinary research, teaching is largely treated as a private, highly territorial enterprise, an attitude that robs the education community as a whole. If there are no incentives for faculty to use and enrich open educational goods to transform their teaching and student learning, pedagogical practice will always struggle to advance.

Open education demands a fresh perspective on resources and relationships available to education. Traditional assumptions of scarcity with respect to the extent and type of resources available to educators and learners, be it content or contact, are challenged. At the same time, recognizing and integrating the learner as an active, core participant in the creation and delivery of the educational experience is becoming necessary.

In order to take full advantage of a growing number of open educational assets, more institutional resources need to be allocated to build the capacity to support both faculty and students in best using these open educational tools and resources.

Recontextualize Roles and Values   As we look at educational strategy for the future, we will need to revisit the inertial frames in which education is operating not only in terms of resources and relationships, but also in terms of our dominant model of formal academic learning. We must not only understand the *invariants*, *core values*, and *purposes* of education, but also understand them in the context of changing technology, along with the marketspace of educational resources.

We urge a rethinking of our valuable and cherished roles in sense-making and certification. How can academic institutions function to best serve as sense-making entities in this new realm of technology-facilitated open education? In a world of extensive access to an enormous set of resources, the learner is faced with several challenges with respect to locating and evaluating pertinent information, not the least of which is the uneven nature of available resources. How can educators who function as coaches pointing out constructive learning experiences, as resource managers (we could perhaps call them "education concierges" or "education sommeliers") who help select from a variety of options, and as facilitators of group work, as well as providers of interaction environments, become agents of effective, responsive, and appropriate learning opportunities? Similarly, how can instructional design experts assist faculty and students in using an optimal set of tools, resources, and pedagogies/learning designs to maximize the educational effectiveness in their local context of teaching and learning? And in the wake of technology-enabled social learning, what support is needed to turn learners to become more like peer-teachers who can help each other's learning?

All of these questions are important and can help us articulate what ought to be done. But the most significant first step toward new models of education would be to start building an "open" mindset, that is, receptivity to open resources at many levels—institutions, administrators, faculty, support staff and students—through effective professional and leadership development.

Certification (which to some extent is a proxy for accountability) is derived from a set of coherently packaged educational experiences, and the general assurance educational institutions can give about the quality of the products (students) of the system. The extent to which online resources have an impact on the largely contact-based, situated experience becomes a new factor in thinking about certification. Then again, technology also offers new opportunities for continuous learning (lifelong learning), and this has implications for how we think about certification and warranties.

This new order, where there is a shift in the locus of control of educational production and practice, requires a reexamination of the economics and ecology of education-production function and investments in education, accountability structures, and the process of certification of education/learning.

3. Make Open Education Solutions Sustainable

Sustainability surfaced as one of the primary issues raised by our authors as they discussed the initiatives with which they have been involved. While the sustainability of the individual initiatives is certainly a central issue, we believe the more important discussion to be about the role of open education in delivering sustainable solutions and the impact on larger educational issues and challenges facing learners, educators, institutions, nations and society at large. With this more expansive perspective in mind, we identify the following as key dimensions for open education efforts to address:

Programmatic and Technical Integration   The centrality and connection of open educational initiatives to the core institutional (writ large) mission is increasingly discussed at our education establishments. While appearing to be largely motivated by resource allocation/economic considerations, it is clear that there are deeper considerations related to coherence, cultural, and contextual compatibility that are at play. To the extent that open education efforts are not tightly integrated with educational program priorities and the delivery infrastructure (technical and organizational), they will be marginalized and their value under-realized.

Synthesis and Synergy   The title of this volume explicitly shows our bias toward these twin dimensions of success. The early stages of the open education innovation cycle have witnessed the launch of several open initiatives across the world, focusing variously on different educational audiences and programs. At this point in the maturation of this movement, a focus on synthesis and synergy, rather than separation, is strongly recommended. As one of our authors observed at the Open Education Summit, practitioners in education place a disproportionate value on differentiating themselves rather than relating themselves to the whole. A shift away from this prevalent tendency is in order. We must look beyond institutional boundaries and connect efforts among many settings, and seek complementarities and productive combinations.

Glimpses of the powerful impact of synthesis and synergy can be seen through the linked efforts undertaken by institutions in the OpenCourse-Ware Consortium that allow access to a range of course and program offerings across institutions in any area. Similarly, the Sakai, MERLOT, and other open education initiatives coordinate the collaborative efforts of institutions, individuals, and vendors in developing and maintaining open source collaboration and learning environments. Foundations and sponsoring agencies can advance the sustainability of open education by directing support for multi-institutional initiatives and targeting resources for investigating organization and business models for sustainability and growth.

Governance   Governance is clearly one of the most important areas affecting the sustainability of open education initiatives, rendered challenging by the two significant defining characteristics of the open education movement, namely the *widely distributed nature* of the effort and *collectivity, both* so critical for value and viability. Issues related to locus of control, authority, boundary agreements, and processes for sharing, decision-making, resource allocation, and even certification become prominent with consortium and community efforts for sponsoring and supporting open efforts. Models of governance from past open source efforts, such as the XConsortium and the W3C (World Wide Web Consortium), as well as more recent consortia, provide valuable insights and learning. From our comments on the importance on integration, it follows that even in a narrower institutional context, governance considerations to advance coherence and efficiencies are critical.

We started our discussion on sustainability by pointing out the importance of placing the value proposition of open education in the larger space of educational problems and opportunity. In concluding this discussion, we want to emphasize that beyond the dimensions of sustainability discussed earlier, open education requires a structural surround, a scaffold if you will, to meet its potential for sustainable transformation. This scaffold is provided through developing human resources and structure—leaders and organizational processes that deliberately incorporate open education into current and new practice.

4. Make Practice and Knowledge Visible and Shareable

Transferring practical knowledge about how to use tools and resources, even if they are readily available, is not easy. Indeed, this kind of pedagogical know-how is notoriously hard to make visible and portable. While some might argue that such knowledge is already built into educational tools and resources—that a syllabus, for instance, already embodies what the user needs to know about using that syllabus—the vast majority of this kind of practical knowledge remains tacit and invisible in the experiences of the educator(s) who created and used the materials or the learners who used the materials. Thus, a crucial task before us is to build intellectual and technical capacity for transforming "tacit knowledge" into "commonly usable knowledge." Building this capacity is urgent, as the process of creating and sharing quality educational knowledge needs to catch up with the burgeoning availability of open educational goods.

Our authors have shared a variety of efforts to document and make portable such educational knowledge and experience: designing teaching and learning activities using pre-defined frameworks, telling stories about effective use of open technology and content, and capturing the critical aspects of teaching and learning using multimedia. We are encouraged by this plurality of methodologies for effective and meaningful knowledge representation and exchange, and suggest that valid approaches for linking and weaving these efforts together be explored.

There is great value in bringing peer sharing and review, specifically, and the conduct of research practice, in general, to teaching and learning through technology. As several chapters in this book illuminate, open education offers the potential of added dimensionality to the scholarship of teaching and learning by making diverse pedagogy visible, as well as through facilitating community enquiry and discourse. The growing worldwide interest in using electronic portfolios to document both the processes and products of teaching and learning is indicative of progress in this area.

We hope to see growing collections of representation of effective practice that contribute to open and global knowledge-sharing in education, through many disciplinary and interdisciplinary societies and communities, such as the International Society for the Scholarship of Teaching and Learning (see http://www.issotl.org), as well as in online forums and spaces.

5. Build the Commons through the Collectivity Culture

In order to collectively advance teaching and learning globally, we need to devise mechanisms to harvest, accumulate, and distribute locally created educational assets, pedagogical innovations, and wisdom of practice in a manner that can be reused effectively in different local contexts. As practice and experience is made increasingly tangible and transferable, we need to create a network of educational knowledge-bases that inspires and helps to inform future efforts.

The canvas of educational issues and opportunities is wide and varied—from national concerns about competitiveness to bringing more global perspectives to curricula. The ambitious and accomplished projects represented in this book and other open initiatives can provide even more powerful solutions to the large problems of education if they can effectively collaborate to maximize the collectivity of their individual efforts. For example, the vision of the Meta University, eloquently articulated by Charles M. Vest, president emeritus of MIT, as "a transcendent, accessible, empowering, dynamic, communally constructed framework of open materials and platforms on which much of higher education worldwide can be constructed or enhanced" presents the dramatic potential of synthesis and the collective (Vest, 2006).

Fostering the collectivity culture and harnessing its power will require the creation of conditions favorable to the spawning and sharing of new ideas and models. Making openness thrive will require policies and practices that entice and reward openness, as well as programs for supporting and monitoring diversity as well as quality. Technology-enabled solutions in teaching and learning often fail to last because "one of the greatest challenges in educational improvement is the immense difficulty of 'scaling up': adapting a locally successful innovation to a wide variety of settings while retaining its effectiveness" (Dede, 2005). However, not many large-scale attempts have been made to actually use technology to help education communities to build and share knowledge of effective practice.

The systemic nature of change requires that synergy among various open education efforts, along with the intersection with other initiatives, are explored for end-to-end delivery of quality education. By employing powerful multimedia, data mining and analysis, knowledge management, and social and semantic network technology, we should be able to help people around the world find and use appropriate educational tools, resources and knowledge of practice that advance their local learning and teaching. Ideally, this should also enable learners and educators to contribute back to an ever-growing knowledge-base of open education, thereby leading to a spiral of educational transformation efforts.

At the End of the Journey . . . or the Beginning?

In the introduction to this collection, we invited you to take a journey through the essays, savoring the diversity of initiatives to better understand the potential of open education to explore solutions to the critical challenges that we all face everyday as learners, practitioners, educational researchers, and planners. We hope the rich reflections and considerations that the authors provided helped you find, if not direct answers to these challenges, valuable clues for how we could approach them. Now as we arrive at the end of this journey, we would like to leave you with a simple but fervent plea to engage. We encourage all involved in any aspect of developing and delivering education to heed this palpable "open" movement that is afoot, presenting the opportunity to redefine, rethink and rearticulate educational practice at several micro and macro levels—courses, programs, institutions or even nations. At the very least, as a community we must actively seek ways to connect open education efforts to the ongoing educational improvement and transformation efforts at our institutions. Higher education, over the centuries, has found ways to adopt innovations through research, pilot projects, faculty and staff rewards, a system for revolving academic leadership, and other means. Our hope is that we will also vigorously investigate and actively consider the opportunity presented by this movement and its implication for the structure and practice of education.

Educational institutions, organizations and communities must understand that open education is not just about disseminating resources that can be localized in many ways to improve education in local contexts, but also about an opportunity toward broadening and deepening our collective understanding of teaching and learning. Difficult and unchartered as the terrain may appear, we anticipate at least three dramatic improvements over time: increased quality of tools and resources, more effective use, and greater individual and collective pedagogical knowledge. Ideally, all will occur concurrently, combining local innovations and learned lessons through global knowledge-sharing. This process also needs to be spiral so that we can continuously pursue "better-ness" in various aspects of education.

This effort is truly exciting since this worldwide, ever-growing work can be a collaborative effort by the creators *and* users of these tools and resources for a spectrum of purposes: from improving teaching and learning in a single classroom, to creating necessary educational capacity for nation-building. Our hope is that this volume represents a useful starting point for the consolidation of experience and knowledge that will enhance the robustness of the whole movement as well as bringing further prosperity to education.

Opportunity is knocking. Are we ready to help education open the door?

References

Dede, C., Honan, J. P., and Peters, L. C. (2005). *Scaling Up Success: Lessons Learned from Technology-Based Educational Improvement*. New York: Jossey-Bass.

Postman, N. (1992, October). *What is the Problem to which Headlamp Washer-wipers are the Solution?* Keynote Address given at the annual Educom Conference, Baltimore, MD.

Vest, C. (May/June 2006). Enabling Meta University. *EDUCAUSE Review*, 41(3), 18–30.

About the Authors

Richard G. Baraniuk is the Victor E. Cameron Professor of Electrical and Computer Engineering at Rice University and the founder of Connexions (cnx .org), a nonprofit start-up launched in 1999 that aims to democratize the process of writing, editing, and publishing scholarly materials. Baraniuk has received national research awards from the NSF and ONR, the Rosenbaum Fellowship from the Isaac Newton Institute of Cambridge University, the ECE Young Alumni Achievement Award from the University of Illinois, and the Eta Kappa Nu C. Holmes MacDonald National Outstanding Teaching Award. He is a Fellow of the IEEE and was selected as one of *Edutopia* magazine's Daring Dozen Education Innovators in 2007.

Randall Bass is assistant provost for Teaching and Learning Initiatives at Georgetown University, and executive director of Georgetown's Center for New Designs in Learning and Scholarship (CNDLS). An associate professor of English, Bass has also served as director and principal investigator of the Visible Knowledge Project, a five-year scholarship of teaching and learning project involving 70 faculty on 21 university and college campuses. For 10 years he has been associated with the Carnegie Foundation for the Advancement of Teaching, where he served, in 1998–1999, as a Pew Scholar and Carnegie Fellow, and currently serves as a consulting scholar.

Trent Batson is a researcher and consultant (eportfolios), writer (editor of Campus Technology's Web 2.0 Newsletter), and project developer who is currently working on a collaborative project to develop the concept of the Web 2.0 portfolio. Batson has won EDUCAUSE and Smithsonian Institution awards and recognition. He was chair of the Board of the Open Source Portfolio Initiative (Mellon-funded) and is still active in the Sakai/OSP community.

Dan Bernstein is professor of psychology and director of the Center for Teaching Excellence at the University of Kansas. Previously he taught at the University of Nebraska-Lincoln, where he directed a project on peer review of teaching. That project expanded into a five university consortium devoted to the development and review of electronic course portfolios. His recent writing has focused on the representation of the intellectual work in teaching. Bernstein was a Carnegie Scholar in 1998 and continues in the institutional program of the Carnegie Academy for the Scholarship of Teaching and Learning.

John Seely Brown   is a visiting scholar at the University of Southern California and advisor to the Provost. He is also the independent cochair of Deloitte's new Center for Edge Innovation. Prior to that he was the Chief Scientist of Xerox Corporation and the director of its Palo Alto Research Center (PARC)—a position he held for nearly two decades. He was a cofounder of the Institute for Research on Learning (IRL). His personal research interests include digital youth culture, new forms of communication and learning in the network age, and new models/modes of innovation for the 21st century.

Barbara Cambridge   is the director of the Washington office of the National Council of Teachers of English, consultant for the Carnegie Academy for the Scholarship of Teaching and Learning, and past president of the International Society for the Scholarship of Teaching and Learning. Cambridge coleads the Inter/National Coalition for Electronic Portfolio Research, serves on the boards of the Washington Internship Institute and the Teacher Education Accreditation Council, and edits the Journal of Teaching Writing. Cambridge is professor of English at Indiana University Purdue University Indianapolis. Her latest publications include edited books on electronic portfolios for students, teachers, and institutions and on-campus support for the scholarship of teaching and learning.

Tom Carey   is a professor of Management Sciences in the Faculty of Engineering at the University of Waterloo, currently also serving as visiting senior scholar in the Chancellor's Office of the California State University. At Waterloo, he recently completed a term as associate vice-president—Learning Resources & Innovation, where his mandate focused on enhancing learning through innovations in teaching and technology (http://www.learning.uwaterloo.ca). Carey previously served as founding director of Ontario's Cooperative Learning Object Exchange and as a researcher on knowledge mobilization in high-tech companies, and currently has ongoing leadership roles in several higher education advisory boards and collaborations for online learning resources.

Catherine M. Casserly   is director of the Open Educational Resources Initiative at the William and Flora Hewlett Foundation. Catherine manages the portfolio of grants and works to raise global awareness and coherence in the field across participants, projects and sectors. Casserly has a Ph.D. in the Economics of Education from Stanford University and a B.A. in Mathematics from Boston College. Prior to joining the Hewlett Foundation, Casserly was the program officer for Evaluation for the Walter S. Johnson Foundation and worked as a policy analyst for SRI International. After college, Casserly taught mathematics in Kingston, Jamaica.

Bernadine Chuck Fong   is president emerita of Foothill College and visiting scholar, Stanford Institute for Higher Education Research at Stanford University. Under her presidency, Foothill won numerous innovative, teaching, leadership, and architectural awards and established *ETUDES*, one of the first learning management and open source systems that is part of the Sakai open source platform and is used nationwide. She has served on multiple boards, such as the Stanford Board of Trustees and the Carnegie Foundation for the Advancement of Teaching Board of Directors. She also does executive coaching as part of the national *Achieving the Dream Initiative* for institutional transformation in community colleges.

James Dalziel   is professor of Learning Technology and director of the Macquarie E-Learning Centre Of Excellence (MELCOE) at Macquarie University in Sydney, Australia. Dalziel leads projects including: LAMS (Learning Activity Management System), including roles as a director of the LAMS Foundation and LAMS International Pty Ltd; MAMS (Meta Access Management System); AAF (Australian Access Federation); and ASK-OSS (the Australian Service for Knowledge of Open Source Software). Dalziel's work focuses on transforming education through Learning Design, and systems integration and interoperability to create seamless eLearning and eResearch infrastructure. Dalziel is an advocate of open source software, open content, and open standards.

Stephen C. Ehrmann   directs the award-winning Flashlight Program on the evaluation of educational uses of technology at the TLT Group, a nonprofit that helps colleges and universities to improve teaching and learning with technology. Ehrmann is also well-known as an author and public speaker. Before cofounding the TLT Group in 1998, he served for eleven years as senior program officer for interactive technologies with Annenberg/CPB, for seven years as a program officer with the Fund for the Improvement of Postsecondary Education (FIPSE), and for three years as director of Educational Research and Assistance at the Evergreen State College.

Richard A. Gale   is visiting scholar at Douglas College in British Columbia. From 2002–2007 he was senior scholar at the Carnegie Foundation, and served as director of the Carnegie Academy for the Scholarship of Teaching and Learning (CASTL) Higher Education Program. Gale has taught composition, interdisciplinary arts, playwriting, and theatre history at institutions ranging from University of California, San Diego and the University of Minnesota, to Bowling Green State University and Sonoma State University. His publications and research interests include aesthetic literacy, arts assessment, integrative learning, critical pedagogy, pedagogy/theatre of the oppressed, theatre and national identity, teaching excellence, and the scholarship of teaching and learning.

Gerard L. Hanley   is the executive director of MERLOT (Multimedia Educational Resource for Learning and Online Teaching at www.merlot.org) and senior director for Academic Technology Services for the California State University, Office of the Chancellor. At MERLOT, he directs the development and sustainability of MERLOT's consortium of higher education systems and institutions, professional societies, corporations, and other digital libraries. At the CSU, Hanley oversees the development and implementation of systemwide academic technology initiatives and integrated electronic library resources supporting CSU's 23 campuses. Hanley previously held positions in the CSU include professor of Psychology, director of Faculty Development and director of Strategic Planning.

Diane Harley   is an anthropologist and senior researcher at University of California, Berkeley's Center for Studies in Higher Education (CSHE). Her research focuses on the policy implications of integrating information and communication technologies into complex academic environments. Areas of investigation include digital resource use in the arts and humanities, the economics of educational technologies, cross border e-learning, the future of general education, and the relationship between faculty culture and emerging models of scholarly communication. She served as executive director of the Berkeley's Multimedia Research Center (BMRC), and has managed multimedia education projects with universities, publishers, museums, and software developers. She holds a Ph.D. in Anthropology from UC Berkeley.

Mary Taylor Huber   is a senior scholar at the Carnegie Foundation for the Advancement of Teaching. She has directed Carnegie's role in the Integrative Learning Project and the U.S. Professors of the Year Award, and works with the Higher Education Program of the Carnegie Academy for the Scholarship of Teaching and Learning. A cultural anthropologist, Huber has been involved in research at the Carnegie Foundation since 1985. Her most recent books include *Balancing Acts: The Scholarship of Teaching and Learning in Academic Careers* (2004), and *The Advancement of Learning: Building the Teaching Commons* (coauthored with Pat Hutchings, 2005).

Pat Hutchings   is vice president of the Carnegie Foundation for the Advancement of Teaching. She came to the Foundation as inaugural director of the Carnegie Academy for the Scholarship of Teaching and Learning in 1998, after serving as a senior staff member at the American Association for Higher Education. She has written widely on the investigation and documentation of teaching and learning, the peer collaboration and review of teaching, and the scholarship of teaching and learning. Her most recent book, *The Advancement of Learning: Building the Teaching Commons* (2005), was coauthored with Mary Huber. She holds a doctorate in English from the University of Iowa and was chair of the English department at Alverno College from 1978–1987.

Toru Iiyoshi   is a senior scholar at the Carnegie Foundation for the Advancement of Teaching where he serves as the director of the Knowledge Media Laboratory (KML). Since joining the Foundation in 1999, he has led research and development efforts that take advantage of emerging technologies to enable educational institutions, programs, and faculty to transform the knowledge implicit in effective practice into ideas, theories, and resources that can be shared widely to advance teaching and student learning. Iiyoshi also works with various national and international initiatives and organizations in an advisory role to provide vision and leadership in the development and diffusion of innovative use of technology in education. Iiyoshi holds a visiting professor appointment at the Graduate School of Interdisciplinary Information Studies at the University of Tokyo.

David Kahle   is the director of Academic Technology at Tufts University and a lecturer on education at the Harvard Graduate School of Education. Kahle's experience includes the design of networked learning environments in support of higher education, informal adult learning, and public outreach initiatives. His current research and development activities are focused on the creation of information systems and cognitive tools designed to increase access to and comprehension of digital information. Kahle serves as principal investigator for the Visual Understanding Environment, an information visualization project funded by the Andrew W. Mellon Foundation.

M.S. Vijay Kumar is senior associate dean of Undergraduate Education and director of the Office of Educational Innovation and Technology, Office of the Dean of Undergraduate Education at MIT. In this capacity he provides leadership for sustainable technology-enabled educational innovation at MIT and influences the Institute's strategic focus on educational technology. In his prior role at MIT as assistant provost and director of Academic Computing, as well at other institutions, Kumar provided leadership for units engaged in delivering infrastructure and services for the effective integration of information technology in education. Kumar was the principal investigator of Open Knowledge Initiative (O.K.I). He is a member of the MIT Council on Educational Technology and the Advisory Committee of MIT OpenCourse-Ware (OCW). Kumar also serves as an honorary advisor to India's National Knowledge Commission. Kumar's research, presentations, as well as his extensive engagement as advisor to academic and professional institutions, are directed toward strategy and planning for technology-enabled educational innovations.

Andy Lane is professor of Environmental Systems in the Technology Faculty at the United Kingdom Open University. His teaching and research spans the use of systems techniques, particularly diagramming, to help with the sense making, learning and decision making required in complex situations. Lane has authored or coauthored many papers and educational materials in these areas. Previously, as associate dean and dean in the Technology Faculty, he has been responsible for the planning and development of many new educational programs and practices. In 2006, he was appointed director of the Open University's OpenLearn Initiative that is making some of the University's large catalogue of educational materials freely available on the Web.

Diana Laurillard is professor of Learning with Digital Technologies at the London Knowledge Lab, Institute of Education; formerly head of the e-Learning Strategy Unit at the UK's Department for Education, and VP for learning technologies and teaching at the Open University. Her research is the substance of her book *Rethinking University Teaching*. She is currently on the Boards of the Observatory for Borderless HE, the Centre for Applied Research in Educational Technologies (Cambridge), and the UNESCO Institute for IT in Education; Laurillard is also currently external examiner at the University of Oxford; formerly on the Visiting Committee on IT at Harvard University.

Stuart D. Lee is the current director of the Computing Services at Oxford University, and also a member of the English Faculty at Oxford where he teaches medieval literature. His main areas of expertise are in e-learning (which he has specialized in for 16 years) and digital collections. He has written books on digital imaging, electronic collection development, and was the director of the award-winning e-learning project the Wilfred Owen Multimedia Digital Archive.

Steven R. Lerman   holds the Class of 1922 Professorship at the Massachusetts Institute of Technology. He is vice chancellor, the dean for Graduate Students and director of the Center for Educational Computing Initiatives, an MIT-wide research center devoted to studying the application of computational and communication technologies in education. He chairs the OpenCourseWare Faculty Advisory Committee. He was previously the chair of the MIT faculty from 2000–2002 and 2006–2007. From 1983–1988, Professor Lerman directed MIT's Project Athena. This project developed a campus-wide distributed system of advanced computer workstations at MIT.

Marilyn M. Lombardi   is director of the Renaissance Computing Institute (RENCI) Center at Duke University and senior information technology strategist for Duke University. She also serves as scholar-in-residence for the EDUCAUSE Learning Initiative (ELI), a national association of institutional leaders, policy makers, technology professionals, librarians, and faculty dedicated to advancing learning through IT innovation. In these various capacities, she provides strategic perspective on national trends, builds multi-institutional coalitions, and writes extensively on emerging technologies that promise to transform teaching, learning, and research.

Phillip D. Long   is the associate director in the Office of Educational Innovation and Technology at the Massachusetts Institute of Technology. He is responsible for research and evaluation of innovative uses of technology in the MIT education. He leads outreach and dissemination efforts for a variety of projects including technologies developed by MIT iCampus, which develops technology tools for active learning. Current research interests focus on designing learning spaces to support active, authentic learning, software to authentic and active learning pedagogies, and virtual worlds. Dr. Long's professional activities are numerous but are currently focused on the New Media Consortium (Board Chair), and the NMC Project Horizon.

Clifford Lynch   has been the director of the Coalition for Networked Information (CNI) since July 1997. Prior to joining CNI, Lynch spent 18 years at the University of California Office of the President, the last 10 as Director of Library Automation. Lynch, who holds a Ph.D. in Computer Science from the University of California, Berkeley, is an adjunct professor at Berkeley's School of Information.

Christopher J. Mackie   is the associate program officer for the Program in Research in Information Technology for the Andrew W. Mellon Foundation. A computational modeler and social complexity theorist by training, he has held positions in the corporate, not-for-profit, and academic worlds, most often managing, researching, teaching, or consulting on the intersection of information technology, social cognitive psychology, and organizational effectiveness. He holds Ph.D. and Master's degrees from Princeton University, a Master's degree from the University of Michigan, and an A.B. from the University of North Carolina at Chapel Hill.

Anne H. Margulies   is the chief information officer for the Commonwealth of Massachusetts and, formerly, the executive director of MIT OpenCourseWare

(OCW). OCW is MIT's initiative to publish the basic teaching materials for the entire undergraduate and graduate curriculum openly and freely over the Internet. Previously, Margulies held several senior positions at Harvard University, including assistant provost and executive director for information systems. Margulies serves on the Boards of the Sabre Foundation, Shelter, Inc., and the Massachusetts Courts Advisory. She also was a member of the National Academies Forum on IT and Research Universities.

Owen McGrath is a research consultant with the Knowledge Media Lab (KML) of the Carnegie Foundation for the Advancement of Teaching, where he has served as a technical advisor for development of the KEEP Toolkit. He has also worked for many years in educational technology at the University of California (UC) Berkeley where he has led development and support efforts in multimedia courseware, collaborative on-line tools, and more recently the Sakai environment. He has a Ph.D. in Education from UC Berkeley and bachelor's degrees in English and Computer Science.

Flora McMartin is a founding partner of Broad-based Knowledge (BbK), a consulting group focused on evaluating technology-assisted teaching and learning in higher education. She consults with digital libraries, open courseware providers, and online journals on evaluating services and helps them build user communities. Her research interests include: the impact of computer-mediated learning, online collaborations and communities on student learning and faculty roles, as well as organizational change resulting from innovative academic departments and programs. McMartin received her B.A. in Art and M.S. in Higher Education from Iowa State University, and her Ph.D. in Education from the University of California, Berkeley.

Shigeru Miyagawa served on the original MIT team that proposed Open-CourseWare. He is professor of linguistics and holds a chair in Japanese language and culture. His linguistics publications include several books and nearly fifty articles. His interactive media project, StarFestival, won the Best of Show at the MacWorld Exposition and a Distinguished Award from Multimedia Grandprix 2000. *Visualizing Cultures*, in collaboration with the Pulitzer Prize-winning historian John Dower, received the 2004 MIT Class of 1960 Innovation in Education Award. The educational technology magazine *Converge* chose him as one of twenty national "Shapers of the Future."

Diana G. Oblinger is president and CEO of EDUCAUSE, a nonprofit association dedicated to advancing higher education through the intelligent use of information technology. Oblinger has held positions in academia and business including vice president for information resources and CIO of the University of North Carolina system and IBM director of the Institute for Academic Technology. Oblinger is internationally known for her leadership in higher education and information technology, and is a frequent speaker and the author of several books and dozens of articles. Oblinger has received several awards for teaching, research, and distinguished service.

Neeru Paharia is currently in a doctoral program at Harvard Business School where she studies consumer ethics. Prior to starting graduate school, Paharia was the executive director, and formerly the assistant director of Creative Commons, where she worked from the organization's inception. Paharia is also the founder and director of AcaWiki, a new initiative that is working to make key findings from scholarly research both physically and intellectually available to the public. Paharia completed her Bachelors degree at University of California, Davis, and her Master's from Carnegie Mellon University. Paharia is a former McKinsey and Company consultant, Coro Fellow, and Public Policy and International Affairs Fellow.

Cheryl R. Richardson   is a research scholar with the Knowledge Media Lab (KML) of the Carnegie Foundation for the Advancement of Teaching, where she has been involved in research and strategic planning. She also has worked with other Carnegie Foundation initiatives, at Georgetown University, and as a consultant based in East Africa to document, understand, and improve classroom teaching and learning. She cofounded a nonprofit organization that supports and designs programs for improving higher education in sub-Saharan Africa. She has Ph.D. in Education from Stanford University and Master's degrees in history and education.

Marshall "Mike" S. Smith   is program director for education at the William and Flora Hewlett Foundation. Before that, he was acting deputy secretary and under secretary for education in the Clinton Administration. He also worked in the Carter Administration. While not in government, he was an associate professor at Harvard, and a professor at the University of Wisconsin and Stanford. At Stanford, he was also the dean of the School of Education. Smith has authored a large number of publications on topics including computer content analysis, early childhood education, effective schools and standards-based reform. He is a member of the National Academy of Education.

Candace Thille   has been the director of the Open Learning Initiative at Carnegie Mellon University since its inception in 2002. Thille's experience includes designing Web-based learning environments for higher education and for the private sector. Her current focus of research and development is in applying results from the learning sciences to the design, implementation and evaluation of eLearning interventions that produce a positive impact on learning outcomes. Thille also serves as a redesign scholar for the National Center for Academic Transformation and as a Fellow of International Society for Design and Development in Education.

Edward Walker   advises institutions, agencies, and foundations on investment and deployment for educational technology in his role as executive vice president of Consulting Services for Education. He has served as CEO of the IMS Global Learning Consortium, vice president of BBN Systems and Technologies, and principal research scientist at MIT. He was cochair of the MERLOT Advisory Board and is a member of the advisory board for the Curriki Foundation and the MIT Open Knowledge Initiative. Walker holds a Ph. D. in Psycholinguistics and graduated from the Greater Boston Executive Program in Business Management of the MIT Sloan School.

David Wiley is associate professor of Instructional Technology at Utah State University and Director of the Center for Open and Sustainable Learning. He has previously been a Nonresident Fellow at the Center for Internet and Society at Stanford Law School and a visiting scholar at the Open University of the Netherlands, and is a recipient of the US National Science Foundation's CAREER award. His career is dedicated to increasing access to educational opportunity for everyone around the world.

Index

ABAB design, 176
AcaWiki, 96
Accelerated learning hypothesis, 176–177
Access, 353. *See also* Communities
  availability and, 153–154
  boundarylessness and, 431–432
  changing model of, 107–108
  content and, 135–145 (*see also* Content)
  Creative Commons and, 94–96, 154, 162, 215, 235, 247–255, 259, 273, 382
  cyberinfrastructure for, 110
  design and, 32–35
  digital libraries and, 105–117
  ETUDES and, 403–404
  future policies for, 434–436
  iLabs and, 61–74
  information glut and, 89–91, 108–109
  informational vs. educational, 105–108, 117
  innovation and, 261–275
  learning management systems (LMSs) and, 48–55
  open access movement and, 105, 109–110, 389–398
  open and distance learning (ODL) and, 158–159
  OpenLearn and, 155–157
  participatory culture and, 149–163, 390–395
  raising teaching profile and, 422
  research and, 109–110
  rising costs and, 321–323
  widening participation and, 149–163
Access Principle, The (Willinsky), 426
Accretion, 295–297
Adobe, 235
Advanced Distributed Learning Laboratory (ADL), 82
Affinity spaces, 392–393
Agency, 5
  design and, 27, 30, 35–39
  teachers and, 107
Aktan, B., 62
Alt-i-lab events, 82
Aluka, 120
American Association for Higher Education (AAHE), 292, 359–360
American Association of Community Colleges, 402
American Council of Learned Societies, 110
American Council on Education (ACE), 362–363, 366, 372
Anderson, C. xvi, 242, 421
Anderson, H., 63
Anderson, J. R., 168
Andrew W. Mellon Foundation, 221
Apache community, xvi, 99
Apple Computer, 233
Architects, 29, 121
ARIADNE, 375

Arizona State University, 371
Arko, R., 187
Arnone, M. P., 406
Art History and Its Publications in the Electronic Age (Ballon and Westermann), 240
Artificial intelligence (AI), 242
ARTstor, 120
Association of American Colleges and Universities (AAC&U), 395
Association of American Geographers (AAG), 296
Atkins, D., 170, 234, 243, 262, 349
ATutor, 375
Australia, 294, 296, 370
Author Snapshots, 186–187, 345

Bacchetti, Ray, 359, 366, 368
Bagozzi, R. P., 238–239
Bailey, T. R., 401
Ballon, H., 240
Baraniuk, Richard G., 139–140, 229–246, 441
Barker, J., 141
Barr, R., 401
Barrick, J., 239
Bass, Randall, 281–283, 303–317, 441
Batson, Trent, 20–21, 89–103, 441
BBC News, 153
Becta, 323
Belcher, John, 344
Benjaminn, J., 304
Benkler, Y., 22
Bereiter, Carl, 358
Berners-Lee, Tim, 217, 242
Bernstein, Dan, 281–283
  future policy and, 421, 425
  open teaching communities and, 303–317
  professional background of, 441
Biggs, John, 378
Bishop, A. P., 115
BitTorent, 241
Bjerkedal, T., 243
Block, Peter, 361

Blogs, xii, 36, 241, 249–250, 329, 351, 390
Bly, S., 181
Bodington, 16–17, 52–53
Bollier, David, 423
Booz Allen Hamilton, 218
Borgman, C., 181, 205
Boud, David, 378
Bransford, J., 40, 168, 183, 188, 405–406, 419
Brooks, Lane, 63
Brown, A. L., 40, 168, 183, 419
Brown, John Seely
  Connexions and, 234, 243
  culture of learning and, xi–xvii
  openness and, 262, 295
  professional background of, 442
  research and, 170
  sharing culture and, 225
  sustainability and, 340, 349
  systemic change and, 357–358
  technology and, 22
Bruce, B., 20
Burnett, A. N., 421
Burrus, C. S., 236
Butler, D. L., 168
Buttenfield, B., 115

C#, 73
California State University, 86, 192, 361
Callen, D., 136
Cambridge, Barbara, 282, 284, 357–374, 442
Cambridge, Darren, 93
Campus Progress: Supporting the Scholarship of Teaching and Learning (Cambridge et al.), 370
Canada, 294, 296, 363, 370
Capella University, 257
Carey, Tom, 138, 181–195, 442
Carlyle, Thomas, 105
Carnegie Academy for the Scholarship of Teaching and Learning (CASTL), 357, 359, 419
  best practices and, 293

building on solid foundations and, 370

Campus Program and, 292, 363, 367, 370–371

capturing knowledge and, 339–340

communications support and, 368–372

disciplinary work and, 291

economic issues and, 293

emergent leadership and, 360

goal of, 292–295

Higher Education Program and, 290

Institutional Leadership Program and, 292, 294, 370

interaction effects and, 362–363

Knowledge Media Laboratory (KML) and, 341

learned helplessness and, 364

Mapping Project and, 365–366

national context and, 365–366

opportunities for change and, 300–302

peer review and, 300

Scholarly and Professional Societies Program and, 291

Scholars Program and, 291

signature approach of, 290

structural overview of, 291–292

sustainable leadership and, 297–299

Carnegie Foundation for the Advancement of Teaching, 5, 173, 289, 359

accretive building model and, 295–297

KEEP Toolkit and, 184, 296, 312

KML and, 173 (*see also* Knowledge Media Laboratory [KML])

Open Education Summit and, 429

Carnegie Initiative on the Doctorate (CID) project, 342–343

Carnegie Mellon University (CMU), xiv, 242, 270

accountability and, 424

community-based research and, 168

OLI and, 397 (*see also* Open Learning Initiative [OLI])

teacher support and, 175

Carnegie Workspace, 346–347

Carpenter, Joel, 69

Casserly, Catherine M., 140, 261–275, 442

Caudros, J., 181

ccMixter, 95

Cech, Thomas, 296

Center for Authentic Science Practice in Education (CASPiE), 68

Centre for Educational Research and Innovation, 320

Centre for Recording Achievement, 359

Cerbin, William, 306, 421

Cervenka, K., 232, 236

Chaiklin, S., 24

Chat, 92, 101, 369

CHEA Institute, 411

Chemistry. *See* Research

Chile, 170

China Open Resources for Education, 224, 396

Chronicle of Higher Education, The, 391–392

Civil Engineering, 64

"Claiming an Education" (Rich), 143

Clinton, K., 393

CNN, 247

Cocking, R. R., 40, 168, 183, 419

Cole, J., 398

Colloquium on the Scholarship of Teaching and Learning, 289

Columbia, 170

Commission on the Future of Higher Education, 425

Communities. *See also* Specific community

collaborative practice and, 305–316

content and, 95–96, 136–138, 165–177

digital libraries and, 105–117

for educators, 95

faculty cultures and, 200–206

Communities. (cont.)
 global society and, 395–398
 governance and, 435–436
 group management and, 112–113
 Learning Activity Management
  System (LAMS) and, 380–386
 learning through creating and,
  265–267
 middle ground and, 304–316
 multi-layered teaching, 303–316
 open educational knowledge and,
  279, 283–285 (see also Open
  educational knowledge)
 participatory culture and, 390–395
 of practice, 169–170
 research and, 96, 165–177
 social economy and, 161–162
 for students, 100
 supported learning and, 156–157
 systemic change for, 357–372
"Community is King", 241
Community source software (CSS),
  37
 open educational content (OEC)
  and, 122–131
 organizational production and,
  122–123
Composition, 91–92
Computer-Assisted Learning, 2
Computer-Supported Collaborative
  Learning, 2
"Confronting the Challenges of
  Participatory Culture: Media
  Education for the 21st Century"
  (Jenkins), 279
Connexions, 139–141, 258, 266,
  397, 408, 417
 accountability and, 424
 brand equity and, 238–239
 broadcast and, 241
 content and, 229, 232–244
 Creative Commons and, 235
 development of, 232–233
 economic issues and, 234–235, 240
 flexibility of, 234
 fragmentation and, 234–235

 future and, 241–242
 goals of, 232–233
 infrastructure costs and, 234–235,
  240
 intellectual property and,
  235–236
 lenses and, 236–237
 modules of, 233
 National Instruments and, 235
 QOOP and, 240
 quality and, 236–237
 remix and, 241–242
 reuse and, 172–173, 233–234, 236
 rich feedback and, 242
 subscriptions and, 239–240
 sustainability and, 237–240
 translation and, 233
 users of, 237–240
 Web 2.0 and, 241–244
 Web 3.0 and, 242–244
 XML format and, 234–235
Content. See Open educational
  content (OEC)
Context, 56, 136–137
Control theory, 242
Cooperative Learning Object
  Exchange (CLOE), 192–193
Co-ownership, 38
Copyleft, 217
Copyright. See Ownership
Copyright Licensing Agency (CLA),
  54
Corbett, A. T., 168
Cornwell, T., 187
Council for Higher Education
  Research and Development
  (CHERD), 294
Council on Undergraduate Research
  (CUR), 296
Course management systems (CMS),
  36
Coventry, M., 310
Cox, R. D., 405
Creative Commons, 273
 Connexions and, 235
 educational framework and, 94–96

Learning Activity Management
System (LAMS), 382
noncommercial licenses and,
247–255, 259
OCW and, 215
participation and, 154, 162
Crowther, Lord, 151
Cuddihy, E., 239
Cyber-terrorists, 253

Dalziel, James, 283, 328, 375–387,
443
Daniels, J., 151, 261
D'Arbeloff Fund for Excellence in
MIT Education, 345
Darling-Hammond, Linda, 339
Data-mining, 242
Davidson, C., 392
DeAngelo, T., 239
De Anza Community College, 409
Dede, C., 391, 394, 438
del Alamo, Jesus, 62–64
Department for Children, Schools
and Families (DCSF), 321, 326
Design, 15–16, 21
ABAB, 176
access and, 32–35
adaptation and, 29–30, 101–102
agency and, 27, 30, 35–39
behavioral, 42
choice provision and, 97–98
community-based research and,
167–177
distributed, 65–66
emotional, 42–43
evaluation and, 175–177
experience and, 42–44
flexibility and, 32–35, 97–98
glut of information and, 89
iLabs and, 61–74
innovation and, 261–275
KEEP Toolkit and, 341–348
learning design systems and,
375–386
learning management systems and,
32

Modulor system and, 29
motivation for, 28
ownership and, 15, 38–39
participation and, 39–42, 390–395
pedagogical know-how and,
375–386
as practice, 28
primacy of, 28–32
as problem solving, 28
quality concerns over, 27
reflective, 43
specific context and, 187–188
sustainable innovations and,
337–353
theory for, 28–30
universal, 33
values and, 28–29
visceral, 42–43
Visual Understanding Environment
(VUE) and, 30–35, 37
"Design for Learning" program, 332
Desjardins, R., 166
Dholakia, U. M., 238–239
Digg rating system, 247, 397
Digital Equipment Corporation, 217
Digital libraries
certifying learning and, 113
Connexions and, 220, 232–244
content and, 135–137
cyberinfrastructure for, 110
informational access vs. educational
access and, 105–108
learner challenges and, 111
limitations of, 109
meeting learner needs and,
114–117
MERLOT and, 182–194
National Science Digital Library
(NSDL) and, 135, 397
open access movement and,
109–110
ownership and, 109
recommender systems and,
115–116
researchers and, 109–110
social interaction and, 112–113

Digital libraries (cont.)
Teaching and Learning Commons
and, 351
tools for, 115–116
Digital Library of Earth Science
Education, 187
Digitization programs, 109
Discover Babylon, 267
Donovan, M. S., 188
Driscoll, M. P., 406
Duguid, Paul, 22, 208, 340, 358, 395
Duke University, 255
Dziuban, C., 390

Easy To Use Distance Education
Software (ETUDES)
access mandates and, 403–404
as breakthrough technology, 403
course design and, 403
faculty contributions and, 404–405
Foothill College and, 403–409, 412
locus of control and, 408–409
resource sharing and, 406–408
Eckel, P., 367
Eckstrom, D., 187
Economic issues, 198
affinity spaces and, 392–393
Carnegie Academy for the
Scholarship of Teaching and
Learning (CASTL) and, 293
commmmercializing inventions and,
217–218
Connexions and, 234–235, 240
D'Arbeloff Fund for Excellence in
MIT Education and, 345
developing nations and, 142
dot-com boom and, 217
evaluation and, 78, 82–84, 87
Great Depression and, 90
growing demand for higher
education and, 165–166
iLabs and, 62–64
infrastructure cost and, 231
MERLOT and, 189–190, 192
MIT Alumni Fund for Educational
Innovation and, 63–64
myth of online costs and, 321–322

OCW funding and, 220–221
open access and, 105, 389–398
participatory culture and, 394–395
private/public control and, 423
reform and, 327
skilled labor and, 395–398
social economy and, 161–162
teaching materials and, 105–106,
230, 240, 252, 269–270
Education
accelerated learning hypothesis and,
176–177
closed, 143, 150, 161 (see also
Open education)
course management systems (CMS)
and, 36
culture of learning for, xi–xvii
democratization of, 55
direction and, 101
formal vs. informal, xi–xv, 140
fundamental values of, 325
global society and, 395–398
glut of information and, 89–91
growing demand for, 1–2, 165–166
historical perspective on, 1–4
human rights and, 223
learning management system and,
48–55
literacy rates and, 320
mono-disciplinary approach and,
48
narrow concept of, 375–376
new systemic literacy for, xi
Observatory on Borderless Higher
Education (OBHE) and, 319
rising unit cost of, 321–322
SAT scores and, 168
skilled labor and, 395–398
supported learning and, 156–157
technology and, xiii (see also Open
educational technology)
traditional methods and, 150–151,
166 (see also Teachers)
universal design for learning and, 33
Educational capital, 359, 366–367
Educational Modeling Language
(EML), 377

Education Maintenance Organization (EMO), 257–258
EDUCAUSE Learning Initiative, 391
Educom conference, 430
eduCommons, 225, 226n5, 241
EECS, 63
Ehrlich, Tom, 359, 366, 368
Ehrmann, Stephen C., 20–21, 61–75, 173, 443
e-learning. *See* Open education
eLearning Framework, 86
eLearning Program, 430
Electronic Networks For Interaction (ENFI), 92–93
Electronic Portfolios: Emergent Findings and Shared Questions (Cambridge et al.), 370
Electronic Portfolios: Emerging Practices in Student, Faculty, and Institutional Learning (Cambridge et al.), 370
Elton, L., 324
Emotional Design (Norman), 42–43
Encyclopedia Britannica, 241, 265, 392
Entrepreneurial self, 93
Environmental issues, 1
ERIC Digests, 188
e-science. *See* Research
European Union, 319, 430
Evaluation
  accountability and, 424–426
  activities and, 80–82
  business models and, 78
  certification and, 5, 84, 92, 94, 99–102, 107, 113, 153, 197, 208, 272, 349, 401, 404, 433–435
  community adoption and, 86–87
  community source software (CSS) and, 121–131
  core value recontextualization and, 433–434
  data and, 82–84
  defined, 77
  economic issues and, 78, 82–84, 87
  errors in, 87

  immaturity of, 78–79
  interpretation and, 84–86
  judgment and, 124, 142, 166, 199, 393, 421
  justification and, 88
  knowledge networks and, 366–367
  meaning and, 79
  metrics for, 79
  open educational resources (OER) and, 175–177
  performance and, 83, 87
  portfolios and, 175–177
  production quality and, 77–78, 82
  proofs of concept and, 81
  reform and, 326–327
  strategic approach to, 79
  sustainability and, 77
  understanding users and, 197–210
  utility and, 81–82
Evans, K., 168
"Every Child Matters" campaign, 319
Experience
  design and, 42–44
  iLabs and, 70–71
  social interaction and, 112

Facebook, xvi, 115, 259
Feminism, 304–305
Field of Dreams (film), 418
Flexibility, 321
  access and, 33–35
  agency and, 36–37
  learning management systems (LMSs) and, 48–55, 58
Flickr, 57, 259
Fong, Bernadine Chuck, 281, 401–415, 442–443
Foothill College
  access mandate and, 403–404
  accountability and, 424
  Easy To Use Distance Education Software (ETUDES) and, 403–409, 412
  faculty collaboration and, 404–405

Foothill College (cont.)
   implications beyond classroom
      and, 410–411
   leadership and, 412–414
   online course adoption and,
      402–409, 412
   resource-sharing and, 406–408
   Sharing of Free Intellectual Assets
      (SOFIA) and, 408, 412
Fox, S., 182
Full-time equivalents (FTEs), 50,
   58
Futures Project, 396

Gale, Richard A., 283, 289–302,
   339, 362, 443
Gallery of Teaching and Learning,
   346–348
Gardner, Howard, 338–339
Garrett, R., 324
Gay, G., 40
Gee, J. P., 392
Gender, 143
George Mason University, 93
Georgia State University, 362
Geser, G., 149
Giaconia, R., 47
Gibbs, Graham, 378
Gilbert, S. W., 173
Giving Knowledge for Free: The
   Emergence of Open Educational
   Resource (OECD), 3
Glassick, C. E., 312
GNU Free Documentation License
   (GFDL), 253–255
GNU Linux, 229, 235
GNU Project, 216–217
Goldberg, K., 62
Golde, C., 291
Goldman, S., 24
Goodburn, A., 307, 421
Google, 36–37, 109, 136, 140, 201,
   204, 239
Gore, Al, 1
Graff, Gerald, 368–369
Great Depression, 90

Green, D., 201
Green, M., 367

Hadley, W. H., 168
Hammond, A. L., 170, 234, 243,
   262, 349
Hanley, Gerard L., 138, 181–195,
   443
Hardin, Garrett, 423
Hardy, Thomas, 47–48, 55
Harley, Diane, 139, 144, 181–182,
   197–211, 443–444
Harper, R., 31
Harvard University, 425
Harward, J., 65
Hatch, T., 315
Hedges, L., 47
Hembrooke, H., 40
Hendler, J., 242
Henke, J., 182, 205, 208
Hewlett Packard, 64
Higher Education Academy, 259
Higher Education Trial Licence,
   54
Hill, B., 367
History Scholarship of Teaching
   and Learning, 314
Holt, J., 47
Holzman, N., 187
Hong Kong, 370
Howard Hughes Medical Institute,
   296
How People Learn (Bransford,
   Brown and Cocking), 419
How People Learn: Bridging
   Research and Practice (Donovan,
   Bransford, and Pellegrino), 188
HTML, 241
Huber, Mary Taylor, 284–285
   communities and, 312–313
   future policy and, 417–428
   professional background of, 444
   systemic change and, 357, 370
   technology-enabled knowledge
      building and, 348–349
Huitt, W., 47

Humanities and social sciences
(H/SS), 199
Hutchings, Pat, 284–285
communities and, 306, 313
future policy and, 417–428
professional background of, 444
systemic change and, 359, 365,
370
technology-enabled knowledge
building and, 348–349
Hylén, J., 396–397

IBM, 217, 235, 256
iCampus Project, 61, 64, 72
Identity Management (IDM) systems,
57
IDEO, 414
Iiyoshi, Toru, xi, xiv, 173, 282
future policies and, 1–10, 429–440
MERLOT and, 184
open educational knowledge and,
289–290
professional background of, 444
technology-enabled knowledge
building and, 337–355
iLabs, 17–18
architecture of, 65–71
authentic tools and, 68
Civil Engineering and, 64
del Alamo and, 62–64
distributed design of, 65–66
economic issues and, 62–63
equipment use and, 62
experience and, 70–71
funding and, 63–64
iCampus Project and, 61, 64, 72
increased experimental capacity
from, 71
interface design and, 68–71
learning-centered application design
and, 70–71
limitations of, 71
minds-on access and, 73–74
open source software and, 71–74
pedagogical approach and, 70
remote labs and, 61–65

scalability and, 64–65, 71
Service Broker and, 67–68
Undergraduate Research
Opportunities Program and, 63
value and, 68–71
Web services and, 67–68
IMS, 82, 171, 377–378
India, 170
Indiana University, 346, 359, 365,
369
Individuals. *See also* Access
distributed cognition and, 391–392
participatory culture and, 390–398
Wikipedia and, 391–392
Information technology (IT), 22
active learning support and, 42
experience and, 43–44
glut of information and, 89–91,
108–109
iLabs and, 61–74
informational access vs. educational
access and, 105–108
innovation and, 337–338
intellectual property and, 38, 54–57
lack of effective tools for, 32
learning management systems and,
32
participatory design and, 39–42
Post-It notes and, 31
rising cost of, 321–322
Service Broker and, 67–68
toys of, 101
Visual Understanding Environment
(VUE) and, 30–32
In Pursuit of Loneliness (Slater), 90
Instant messaging (IM), xvi, 217
Institutional Leadership Program,
294
Institutions, 16–17. *See also* Specific
institution
barriers and, 20–22, 100–101
collaborative practice and,
305–316
competitive nature of, 57
discipline-oriented faculty
development and, 191–192

Institutions, (cont.)
  ecological model and, 357
  Foothill College case study and,
    402–409, 412
  future policies for, 429–439
  governance issues and, 435–436
  information glut and, 89–91
  Institutional Leadership Program
    and, 294
  intellectual property and, 55–57
  leadership development and, 294,
    297–299
  open sharing and, 217–218
  staying power and, 367–372
  traditional methods and, 105–108
  use/reuse challenges and, 170–174,
    188–193
Integrated Microelectronic Devices,
  63
Integrative Learning Project, 296
Intellectual property. *See* Ownership
Intelligent Tutoring Systems, 2
Intermediaries, 359–360
Inter/National Coalition for
  Electronic Portfolio Research
  building on solid foundations and,
    370
  communications support and, 358,
    371–372
  systemic change and, 358, 360,
    362–363, 366–367
*International Journal for the
  Scholarship of
  Teaching and Learning*, 296
International Organization for
  Standardization (ISO), 171
International Society for the
  Scholarship of Teaching
  and Learning (ISSOTL), 296, 314,
    357–359, 370–372
Internet, 162
  access and, 2–3, 135 (*see also* Access)
  global platform of, xii
  iLabs and, 61–74
  increased education by, 2–3 (*see also*
    Open education)

  semantic Web and, 242
  service brokerage and, 18
  Web 1.0, 241
  Web 2.0, xii, xv, 159, 208, 229,
    241–244, 296, 237
  Web 3.0, 229, 242–244
IP McCarthyism, 248
Ireland, 370
ISKME, 242
Ithaka, 429
Iverson, D., 182

Jaschik, S., 426
Java, 73
Jenkins, Henry, 279, 284, 393, 401
Jensen, M., 242
Jesse H. Jones Graduate School of
  Management, 238
Jesuroga, S., 187
Job, Bible Book of, 47
Jobs, Steve, 414
Johnson, D. H., 236
Johnstone, S., 396
Joint Information Systems Committee
  (JISC), 55, 82, 332
Jones, D. L., 236
JORUM, 54–55, 330
Journalism, 390
JSTOR, 120
Jude the Obscure (Hardy), 47, 55
Judgment, 124, 142, 166, 199, 393,
  421

Kahle, David, 15, 27–45, 444–445
Karabinos, M., 168, 181
Kastens, K., 187
Kearsley, G., 406
KEEP Toolkit, xiv, 184, 417, 420
  Carnegie Initiative on the Doctorate
    (CID) project and, 342–343
  Carnegie Workspace and, 347
  case studies of, 343–346
  Gallery of Teaching and Learning
    and, 346–348
  Knowledge Media Laboratory
    (KML) and, 341–348

MERLOT and, 345
OLI template and, 173
open educational knowledge and, 296
as representation tool, 341–348
snapshots and, 342, 344–345
tacit knowledge of practice and, 342–343
Visible Knowledge Project (VKP) and, 312–313
Kennedy, Donald, 296
Kerberos authentication system, 217
King, John, xv
Knowledge Media Laboratory (KML), 173, 186
Carnegie Initiative on the Doctorate (CID) project and, 342–343
case studies of, 343–346
CASTL partnership and, 341
communications support and, 368
future and, 351–352
KEEP Toolkit and, 341–348
tacit knowledge of practice and, 342–343
Koedlinger, K. R., 166
Kolb, David, 378
Koper, Rob, 377
Kopp, B., 421
Korte, S., 394
Krafft, D., 187
Kristensen, P., 243
Kuali, 99, 122
Kumar, M. S. Vijay, xi, 20–21
educational framework and, 89–103
future policies and, 1–10, 429–440
professional background of, 445

Labour Party, 47
LabView, 62, 73, 235
Lagoze, C., 187
Lane, Andy, 137, 149–163, 445
Language, xiii, 124, 201, 268–269
access and, 96
digital libraries and, 106
iLabs and, 65, 73
learning design and, 377, 382

Modern Language Association and, 424
systemic change and, 363, 369
Larson, R. C., 395
Lassila, O., 242
Laurillard, Diana, xv, 281–283
learning design and, 378, 381–383
professional background of, 445
sustainable education and, 319–335
Lave, J., 24
Lawrence, S., 182
Learned helplessness, 364
Learning 2.0, xv
Learning Activity Management System (LAMS), 55–56
case study of, 381–386
educator engagement and, 383
learning design and, 380–386
real design and, 382–383
reform and, 332
sharing and, 382
templates and, 382–386
Learning design systems
educator engagement and, 383
instructional design and, 377
instructivist experience and, 380
iterative planning and, 384–385
Learning Activity Management System (LAMS) and, 380–386
narrow concept of education and, 375–376
overview of, 377–381
pedagogical know-how and, 375–386
potential advantages of, 384
support and, 385
templates and, 382–386
Learning management systems (LMSs)
access issues and, 50–51
Bodington and, 52–53
controlled access and, 50–51
cultural barriers and, 53–55
full-time equivalents (FTEs) and, 50, 58

Learning management systems
(LMSs) (cont.)
Identity Management (IDM) systems
and, 57
information technology (IT) and, 32
Moodle and, 51
pedagogical principle and, 51–53
personalization and, 50
pigeonholing and, 49
privilege and, 49
Student Record System (SRS) and,
48–49
tasters and, 50
technological barriers and, 48–55
virtual issues and, 48–49
Le Corbusier, 29
Lee, Stuart D., 16–17, 47–58, 445
Leeds University, 16
Lees, S., 21
Lego, 233
Leicester University, 56
Leinbach, D. T., 401
Leinhardt, G., 168, 181
Lenses, 236–237
Lerman, Steven R., 139, 213–227,
408, 446
Lessig, Lawrence, 47, 233, 248
Lesson Study Project, 421
Libre License League (LLL), 253,
255, 258
Licenses. *See* Ownership
Life-wide learning, 92
Linux, xvi, 229, 235, 256
Lisbon Agreement, 319
Lombardi, Marilyn M., 281–284,
389–400, 446
Long, Phillip D., 21, 61–75, 446
Lorenzo, G., 390
Loverude, M., 182
Lovett, M., 177
LRN, 375
Lynch, Clifford, 21–22, 105–118, 446

McDermott, R., 24, 363
Mace, R., 33

McGrath, Owen, 13–26, 173, 184,
337, 341, 447
McGraw-Hill Higher Education,
409
McKeever, J., 238–239
Mackie, Christopher J., 22–23,
119–131, 446
MacLean, D., 324
McMartin, Flora, 135–147, 173, 182,
447
McNiff, J., 143
McSherry, C., 390
Maeroff, G. I., 312
Maher, M. W., 205
Mai, R. P., 47
Manduca, C., 182
Mapping applications, 49, 365
design and, 31, 34–37
future policy and, 424
knowledge paths and, 215, 266
Marguilies, Anne H., 139, 213–227,
408, 446–447
Mark, M. A., 168
Markoff, J., 242
Markus, G., 243
Marshall, C., 181
Marsick, V., 368, 374
Martin, E., 304
Massachusetts Institute of
Technology (MIT), 270
accountability and, 424
Alumni Fund for Educational
Innovation, 63–64
commmercializing inventions and,
217–218
culture of, 213, 216–218
D'Arbeloff Fund for Excellence in
MIT Education and, 345
EECS and, 63
GNU Project and, 216–217
iCampus Project and, 61, 64
iLabs and, 17–18, 61–74
KEEP Toolkit and, 344–345
Materials Science Department and,
63

OCW and, xiii, 99–100 (*see also*
OpenCourseWare [OCW])
Open Knowledge Initiative (OKI)
and, 41–42, 97–99
Project Athena and, 217
Technology Licensing Office (TLO)
and, 217–218
Undergraduate Research
Opportunities Program and, 63
Vest and, xiii, 29, 220, 437
World Wide Web Consortium and,
217
Massively multiplayer online games
(MMOs), xii–xiii
Masson, P., 383
Masterman, Liz, 383
Materials Science Department, 63
MathML, 234
Matkin, G., 198
Maust, B., 239
Mellon Foundation, 22, 240
Mellon/RIT, 120, 122
Mellon Scholarly Communication
Program, 120
Melton, R., 192
MERLOT, 110, 135, 237, 330, 417
accelerating course development
and, 190–191
accountability and, 424
analytic reviews and, 188
Author Snapshots and, 186–187
composition of, 183
content and, 138, 182–194
Cooperative Learning Object
Exchange (CLOE) and, 192–193
discipline-oriented faculty
development and, 191–192
economic issues and, 189–190, 192
ERIC Digests and, 188
evaluation and, 81, 84–85, 375
expert voices and, 187
future policies and, 141, 187, 435
institutional strategies and, 188–193
KEEP Toolkit and, 184, 345
Knowledge Media Lab and, 186

learning assignments and, 186
member comments and, 185, 187
Oklahoma State Regents and, 191
pedagogical content knowledge and,
183–188
peer review and, 186–187
personal collections and, 185, 187
reuse alignment and, 188–193
segmenting and, 184–185
shared governance and, 189–190
South Dakota Board of Regents and,
192
specific context design and, 187–188
success of, 375
system-wide collaborations and,
192–193
Teaching Commons and, 189, 192
Tennessee Board of Regents and,
190–192
MetaUniversity, 254–258, 437
Mexico, 170
Microelectronic Devices and Circuits,
63
Microelectronics Device
Characterization Laboratory, 63
Microsoft, 61, 63–64, 234
Middlebury College, 392
Middle ground
alignment and, 312–313
collaborative practice communities
and, 305–312
hybrid spaces and, 304–305
organization and, 313–316
Milana, M., 166
MIT Council on Educational
Technology (MITCET), 218–220
Miyagawa, Shigeru, 139, 213–227,
408, 447
Modern Language Association, 424
Modulor system of proportions, 29
Montaigne, M., 119
Monterey Institute, 270
Moodle, 51, 375
Moore, C., 401, 410–411
Morris, P. M., 73

MountainRise journal, 296
mp3.com, 241
MSNBC, 247
Music, 94–95, 234, 241, 254, 273
MySpace, xvi, 57, 115, 241

Napster, 241
Nardi, B. A., 38
Nathan, M. J., 166
National Academy of Education,
   420
National Academy of Sciences, 166
National Association for School
   Personnel Administrators, 359
National Chiao Tung University
   (NCTU), 170
National Committee of Inquiry into
   Higher Education, 325
National Council of Professors of
   Educational Administration
   (NCPEA), 236–237
National Instruments, 62, 235
National Postsecondary Student Aid
   Study, 402
National Science Digital Library
   (NSDL), 135, 187, 397
National Science Foundation (NSF),
   110
National Student Satisfaction Survey,
   153
Nelson, R., 394
Nesting, 296–297
Netherlands, 363, 370, 377
Networks, xii, 22, 296. *See also*
   Specific network
 accelerating capabilities of, 363–367
 affinity spaces and, 392–393
 building on solid foundations and,
   369–371
 building social, 358–363
 cocreation and, 390
 communications support and,
   368–369
 connections and, 393–394
 Creative Commons and, 96
 digital libraries and, 105–117

 distributed cognition and,
   391–392
 educational capital and, 366–367
 educator community and, 95
 emergent leadership and, 360–362
 evaluation and, 366–367
 expanse of, xvi–vxii
 expert guidance and, 114
 increased access and, 154–155 (*see
   also* Access)
 interaction effects and, 362–363
 intermediaries and, 359–360
 involvement invitations and,
   360–362
 knowledge building and, 358–363
 learned helplessness and, 364
 "Long Tail" of, xvi–xvii, 119,
   241–242
 multimodal interaction and, 391
 national context and, 365–366
 net-gen students and, 93, 101
 niche communities and, xvi–xvii
 participatory culture and, 390–398
 peer review and, 365–366
 power of, 390
 recommender systems and, 115–116
 researcher community and, 96
 scale and, 358
 social economy and, 161–162
 staying power and, 367–372
 systemic change and, 357–372
Network self, 93
Newman, John Henry, 363
New York Times, 220
"No Child Left Behind" campaign,
   319
Nonaka, I., 339

Oblinger, Diana G., 281–284,
   389–400, 447
Observatory on Borderless Higher
   Education (OBHE), 319
O'Connor, no name given, 312
O'Day, V., 38
OE 1.0, 241
OE 2.0, 241

OE 3.0, 242
OER Commons, 242
OER Mixter, 95
Oklahoma State Regents for Higher
  Education, 191
Open and distance learning (ODL),
  158–159
Open classroom, 89
Open Content Alliance, 109
OpenCourseWare (OCW) project,
  xiii, xv, 126, 375, 417
  alumni use of, 222
  challenges to, 225–226
  communication and, 219
  communities of practice and,
    225–226
  Consortium of, 141, 223–225, 230,
    241, 435
  content and, 139, 144
  contributors to, 213
  core values and, 219
  Creative Commons and, 215, 247
  culture of sharing and, 213–226
  development of, 213–215, 218
  digital libraries and, 111
  economic issues and, 220–221
  educational framework and,
    99–100
  evaluation and, 207
  faculty use of, 221–222
  future policies and, 141, 223–226,
    435
  infrastructure for, 219–220
  innovation and, 262, 264–265
  intellectual property policies and,
    423
  IP-clearance and, 215
  KEEP Toolkit and, 344–345
  launch of, 219–221
  Mellon and, 120
  noncommercial license and,
    247–250
  permanent status of, 220
  quality and, 142–143, 225, 232
  ramp-up phase and, 214
  senior leadership support and, 220

service learning and, 127
shared decision-making and, 219
success of, 375
teacher support and, 174–175
users of, 215–216, 222–223
Wiley "historical" account of,
  247–259
Open education
  accelerated learning hypothesis and,
    176–177
  assessment improvement and, 116
  barriers to, 47–58, 100–101
  certification and, 5, 84, 92, 94,
    99–102, 107, 113, 153, 197, 208,
    272, 349, 401, 404, 433–435
  core value recontextualization and,
    433–434
  defining, 2, 89
  design and, 27–44 (*see also*
    Design)
  ecological transitions and, 430–432
  effects of, 2–4
  evaluation results of, 77–88
  fragmentation and, 231
  future policies and, 429–439
  improving, 114–117
  increased educational access by, 2–3
  information glut and, 89–91,
    108–109
  learning from peers and, 93, 100
  learning management system and,
    48–55
  learning through creating and,
    265–267
  multi-layered teaching communities
    and, 303–316
  past efforts in, 5–6
  pedagogical know-how and,
    375–386
  quality concerns over, 27
  relevance and, 3
  remixing and, 171, 230–231
  sharing potential of, 94–95
  skepticism of, 27
  sustainability and, 3–4, 77, 232 (*see
    also* Sustainability)

Open education (cont.)
  time lag and, 230
  transformative potential of, 3–4,
    430–432
  ultimate goal of, 77
  understanding users and, 197–210
  as visible work in process, 91–93
  wake-up call for, 6–7
Open educational content (OEC), 6,
    22, 119
  broader recognition of, 159
  Campus Program and, 357
  communities and, 95–96, 136–138,
    165–177
  community source software (CSS)
    and, 122–131
  Connexions and, 229, 232–244
  context and, 136–137
  Creative Commons and, 94–96,
    154, 162
  defining, 135–136
  digital libraries and, 135–137
  educational innovation and,
    261–275
  electronic portfolios and, 92–93
  faculty cultures and, 200–206
  future of, 141–145
  as King, 136, 241
  MERLOT and, 138, 182–194
  MIT OpenCourseWare and, 213–226
  open and distance learning (ODL)
    and, 158–159
  Open Content Alliance and, 109
  open source software (OSS) and,
    119–131
  pedagogical knowledge and,
    183–188
  purpose and, 136–137
  quality and, 124–125, 142–143 (*see
    also* Quality)
  remix and, 140, 171, 241–242
  reuse alignment and, 188–193
  student-generated, 92–93
  sustainability and, 138–140,
    206–209

transforming access and, 135–145
UNESCO definition and, 135
use and, 137–139, 144, 170–174,
  181–182, 197–210
widening participation and,
  149–163
Open educational knowledge
  accountability and, 424–426
  accretive building model and,
    295–297
  affinity spaces and, 392–393
  capturing knowledge and, 339–340
  Carnegie Academy for the
    Scholarship of Teaching and
    Learning (CASTL) and, 290–302
  change for, 282–291
  cocreation and, 279–281
  collaborative practice and,
    305–316
  commonly usable knowledge and,
    289–290, 389–398, 436
  communication and, 284
  communities and, 283–285,
    303–316
  credibility for, 279
  distributed cognition and, 391–392
  educational capital and, 359,
    366–367
  emergent leadership and, 360–362
  experimentation and, 279
  future of, 417–427
  global society and, 395–398
  interaction effects and, 362–363
  intermediaries and, 359–360
  KEEP Toolkit and, 296, 341–348
  knower's role and, 358
  Knowledge Media Laboratory
    (KML) and, 341–352
  learned helplessness and, 364
  learning technologies and, 319–325,
    337–353
  limited innovation in, 323–325
  middle ground and, 304–316
  motivation for, 280–281
  myth of online costs and, 321–322

narrow concept of education and,
  375–376
national context and, 365–366
network building and, 358–363
participatory culture and, 390–398
pedagogical know-how and,
  375–386
portability and, 340, 394
potential of, 282–283
professional imperative and, 337
publishing and, 314–315
reform and, 326–334
research and, 282–283
reuse and, 281
scholarship of, 289–302
skilled labor and, 395–398
sustainability and, 284–285,
  319–334
systemic change for, 357–372
tacit knowledge and, 289–290, 436
understanding local knowledge and,
  338–339
useful knowledge and, 418–422
Visible Knowledge Project (VKP)
  and, 307–312, 315–316
wisdom of practice and, 289
Open educational resources (OER),
  90, 95, 138, 390
accelerated learning hypothesis and,
  176–177
barriers to, 273–274
community-based research and,
  165–177
Connexions and, 229, 232–244
evaluation of, 175–177
future policies and, 141–145,
  432–433
governance and, 435–436
immersive environments and, 267,
  269–270
innovation and, 261–275
learning through creating and,
  265–267
MERLOT and, 182–194
revolutionary potential of, 165

skilled labor and, 396
social economy and, 161–162
sustainability and, 138–140
time and, 182
understanding users of, 197–210
use/reuse challenges and, 170–174
widening participation and,
  149–163
Open Educational Resources (OER)
  Initiative, 261–262
Open educational technology, 6, 389,
  401
access and, 105–117 (*see also*
  Access)
barriers to, 47–58, 100–101
boundarylessness and, 431–432
communications support and,
  368–369
continuity and, 39–40
design and, 15–16, 21, 27–44
digital libraries and, 105–117
Easy to Use Distance Education
  Software (ETUDES) and, 403–409,
  412
effectiveness of, 320–323
evaluation of, 18–20
flexibility and, 32–35
Foothill College cast study and,
  402–409, 412
future policies and, 429–439
glut of information and, 89–91
Identity Management (IDM) systems
  and, 57
information glut and, 89–91,
  108–109
innovation and, 261–275, 323–325
institutions and, 16–17
KEEP Toolkit and, 341–348
Knowledge Media Laboratory
  (KML) and, 341–352
learning management systems
  (LMSs) and, 48–55
limited innovation in, 323–325
modern computer power and, xiv
need for, 319–320

Open educational technology, (cont.)
  new learning ecology and, 20–21
  OCW and, xiii, 213–226 (see also
    OpenCourseWare [OCW])
  open source software (OSS) and,
    71–73, 119–131
  pedagogical principle and, 51–53
  perspectives on, 13–14
  quality concerns over, 27
  reform and, 326–334
  results and, 14
  rising costs and, 321–322
  sustainable innovations and,
    337–353
  traditional approach and, 22–25
  Visual Understanding Environment
    (VUE) and, 30–32
  Web 2.0, 159
Open Education Summit, 5, 9–10,
  429, 435
Open eLearning Content Observatory
  Services (OLCOS), 430
Open games, 267
Open Knowledge Initiative (OKI),
  16
  educational framework and, 97–99
  Open Service Interface Definitions
    (OSID) and, 16
  participatory design and, 41–42
Open Language Learning Initiative
  (OLLI), 268–269
OpenLearn, 242, 266
  participatory culture and, 155–158,
    160, 225, 397
  sustainability and, 330
Open Learning Initiative (OLI), xiv,
  138, 141, 242
  accelerated learning hypothesis and,
    176–177
  community-based research and,
    166–177
  developing a community of practice
    and, 169–170
  evaluation of, 175–177
  KEEP OLI template and, 173
  mini-tutors and, 168

  participatory culture and, 397
  teacher support and, 174–175
  use/reuse challenges and, 170–174
Open Office, 234
Open Service Interface Definitions
  (OSID), 171
Open Source Portfolio Initiative
  (OSPI), 92
Open Source Portfolio (OSP)
  software, 346
Open source software (OSS)
  challenges facing, 119–131
  community source software (CSS)
    and, 121–131
  copyleft and, 217
  Easy to Use Distance Education
    Software (ETUDES) and, 403–409,
    412
  GNU Project and, 216–217, 229,
    235
  human resource systems and, 120
  iLabs and, 71–73
  limitations of, 120–122
  Mellon/RIT support and, 120,
    122
  open educational content (OEC)
    and, 122–131
  Project Athena and, 217
Open University, 86, 127, 137
  accountability and, 424
  enrollment of, 321, 324
  LabSpace and, 266
  learning design and, 377
  mediation and, 151, 153
  OpenLearn and, 155–158, 160, 225,
    242, 266, 330, 397
  quality and, 159–160
  success of, 321
  supported learning and, 156–157
O'Reilly, T., 241
Organisation for Economic Co-
  operation and Development
  (OECD), 3, 320
OWL, 37
Ownership, 39, 231
  balance and, 99

ccMixter, 95
  Connexions and, 235–236
  copyleft, 217
  copyright and, 38, 53–57, 94–96,
    109, 123, 126, 149, 154, 162, 203,
    215, 226n5, 239, 250–251, 262,
    423
  Creative Commons and, 94–96,
    154, 162, 215, 235, 247–255, 259,
    273, 382
  digital libraries and, 105–117
  economic issues and, 56
  GNU Project and, 216–217
  JORUM and, 54–55
  noncommercial licenses and,
    247–255, 258–259
  OCW and, 215
  Teaching and Learning Commons
    and, 189, 192, 313, 346, 348–349
  Technology Licensing Office (TLO)
    and, 217–218
Oxford Brookes University, 56
Oxford University, 56, 109, 383
  Bodington and, 16–17, 52–53
  learning management systems
    (LMSs) and, 51–55

Paharia, Neeru, 20–21, 89–103,
  447–448
Palucka, T., 181
Palumbo, A., 424
Participation, 39–42
  affinity spaces and, 392–393
  connections and, 393–394
  culture of, 390–398
  design and, 39–42
  distributed cognition and, 391–392
  economic issues and, 394–395
  multimodal interaction and, 391
  widening of, 149–163
  skilled labor and, 395–398
Paton, R., 161
PDF files, 234, 236
Pea, R. D., 43
Peer learning, 93, 100, 159, 160,
  186

Peer review, 186–187, 216
  Carnegie Academy for the
    Scholarship of Teaching and
    Learning (CASTL) and, 299–300
  Carnegie Workspace and, 346–347
  collaborative practice and,
    306–308
  future policies and, 436–437
  national context and, 365–366
  portfolios and, 306, 426
  teaching and, 306–308
  Visible Knowledge Project (VKP)
    and, 307–312, 315–316
Peer Review of Teaching Project
  (PRTP), 421
  building on solid foundation and,
    370
  multi-layer teaching communities
    and, 307–308, 310, 315
  systemic change and, 359–360,
    365
Peer-To-Peer University (P2PU), 100
Pellegrino, J., 188
Pelletier, R., 168
Perkinson, R., 395
Peters, G., 161
Pew Internet & American Life
  Project, 390, 406
Pew Learning and Technology
  Program, 82
Peyton, J. K., 20
Plugfests, 82
Policy
  adaptation and, 101–102
  best practices and, 420
  Carnegie Academy for the
    Scholarship of Teaching and
    Learning (CASTL) and, 290–302
  changing educational culture and,
    432–434
  commons building and, 437–438
  course management systems (CMS)
    and, 36
  design and, 27–44
  "Every Child Matters" campaign
    and, 319

Policy (cont.)
  Foothill College case study and,
    402–409, 412
  future, 101–102, 417–439
  gender privileges and, 143
  governance and, 435–436
  information glut and, 89–91
  intellectual property and, 423 (*see
    also* Ownership)
  Lisbon Agreement and, 319
  myth of online costs and, 321–322
  "No Child Left Behind" campaign
    and, 319
  Open University and, 151, 153
  recommendations for, 430–432
  reform and, 319–334
  rethinking education and, 99–101
  shareable practice and, 436–437
  sustainability and, 434–436 (*see also*
    Sustainability)
  United Nations and, 319
  W3C Accessibility Guidelines
    Initiative and, 33
Pope, D., 63
Portfolios, 102, 261–262
  accountability and, 426
  Carnegie Academy for the
    Scholarship of Teaching and
    Learning (CASTL) and, 301
  collaborative practice and, 305–316
  educational framework and, 92–93
  Inter/National Coalition for
    Electronic Portfolio Research and,
    358
  Open Source Portfolio (OSP) and,
    346
  peer review and, 306–308, 426
  research and, 175–177
  Teaching and Learning Commons
    and, 348–349
  Urban Universities Portfolio Project
    (UUPP) and, 357, 359, 361–362,
    366–372
  useful knowledge and, 420–421
  Visible Knowledge Project (VKP)
    and, 307–312, 315–316

Portico, 120
Portland State University, 346
Postman, N., 430
Poverty, 90, 274
PowerPoint, 53
President's Council of Advisors on
  Science and Technology, 166
President's Information Technology
  Advisory Committee, 166
Professional and Organizational
  Development (POD) Network, 296
Project Athena, 217
Prosser, M., 304
Public Assets, Private Profits (Bollier),
  423
Publishing, 89, 115, 230, 314–315
  affinity-based self-organization and,
    392–393
  blogs and, xii, 36, 241, 249–250,
    329, 351, 390
  cocreation and, 390
  distributed cognition and, 391–392
  multimodal interaction and, 391
  participatory culture and, 390–395
  Wikipedia and, 391–392
Purdue University, 346, 359, 365,
  369
Purushotma, R., 393

Qatar University (QU), 170
QOOP, 240
Quality, 142–143
  challenges of, 124–125, 231–232,
    236–237
  community-based research and,
    165–166, 169
  Connexions and, 231–232, 236–237
  future policies and, 424–426
  participation and, 153, 159–160
  understanding users and, 198,
    206–209
Quality Assurance Agency, 153

Ramsden, Paul, 378
Rathbone, C., 47
Raymond, E., 23, 229

RDF Schema, 37
Read, B., 392
Readings, B., 324
Recommender systems, 115–116
Reconnecting Education and Foundations (Bacchetti and Ehrlich), 359
Red Hat, 235, 274
Reform
  accelerating capabilities and, 363–367
  courage for, 364–365
  economic issues and, 327
  educational capital and, 366–367
  evaluation and, 326–327
  Joint Information Systems Committee (JISC) and, 332
  learned helplessness and, 364
  Learning Activity Management System (LAMS) and, 332
  limited innovation and, 323–325
  literacy rates and, 320
  national context and, 365–366
  SoURCE project and, 329–330
  sustainability and, 326–334, 367–372
  systemic change and, 357–372
  teaching technologies and, 319–325
Rehm, E., 181
Reigeluth, C., 30
Remote labs
  Advanced Distributed Learning Laboratory (ADL) and, 82
  community-based research and, 167–177
  iLabs and, 65–74
  IMS alt-i-lab events and, 82
  Joint Information Systems Committee (JISC) and, 82
  LabSpace and, 266
  Pew Learning and Technology Program and, 82
Research, 333
  community-based, 96, 165–167

content and, 138–140
digital libraries and, 105–117
distributed cognition and, 391–392
iLabs and, 61–74
innovation and, 261–275
Inter/National Coalition for Electronic Portfolio Research and, 358
mini-tutors and, 168
open educational knowledge and, 282–283
participatory culture and, 390–395
understanding users and, 197–210
use/reuse challenges and, 170–174
Wikipedia and, 391–392
Rice University, 232, 238, 240, 397, 408
Rich, Adrienne, 143
Richardson, Cheryl R., xiv, 173, 184, 282
  open educational knowledge and, 279–287
  professional background of, 448
  technology-enabled knowledge building and, 337–355
Robinson, A. J., 393
Roen, Duane, 371
Roll, S., 238–239
rSmart, 98
Rubenson, K., 166

Sakai, 86, 375
  Carnegie Workspace and, 296, 347
  collaborative learning environment and, 92, 122
  community source approach and, 98–99
  future policies and, 435
  portfolios and, 92
  reuse challenges and, 171
SAKAI code, 52
Salmon, Gilly, 378
Salzburg Research, 262
SAT scores, 168
Savory, P., 307, 421
Scanlon, T., 239

Scardamalia, Marlene, 358
Schneiderman, B., 406
Scholarship Assessed, 290
Scholarship Reconsidered, 290
Schroeder, W., 239
Science, technology, engineering, and
    mathematics (STEM) fields, 301.
    See also Research
ScienceDaily, 267
Science journal, 296
Scotland, 363, 370
Scott, A., 424
Second Life, 115, 273
Sellen, A. J., 31
Sen, Amartya, 142, 274
Shapiro, C., 239
Sharable Content Object Reference
    Model (SCORM), 171
ShareAlike, 251–252
Sharing of Free Intellectual Assets
    (SOFIA), 408, 412
Shavelson, R. J., 420
Shibboleth, 172
Shulman, Lee S., 24
  future policy and, 425, 429
  institutional leadership and, 404,
    412
  multi-layered teaching communities
    and, 306
  scholarship issues and, 289, 301
  technology-enabled knowledge
    building and, 337, 339, 348
Shulock, N., 401, 410–411
Sichel, D. E., 322
Siemens, G., 393
Silicon Valley, 402
Simon, Herbert, 165
Slashdot, 247
Slater, Philip, 90
Smart phones, 101
Smith, A., 205
Smith, Deryl, 365
Smith, J. M., 166
Smith, Marshall S., 140, 261–275,
    448

SMS, xvi
Snyder, C., 239
Snyder, W., 363
Social economy, 161–162
Social Life of Information, The
    (Brown and Duguid), 358
Social writing, 92
Society for Teaching and Learning in
    Higher Education (STLHE), 294,
    296
Software, Use, Reuse and
    Customisation in Education
    (SoURCE), 329–330
South Dakota Board of Regents, 192
Spool, J. M., 239
Spyridaki, J. H., 239
Stanford University, 109, 251
*Stewardship: Choosing Service Over
    Self-Interest* (Block), 361
Storey, J., 161
Student Record System (SRS), 48–49
Students
  Carnegie Academy for the
    Scholarship of Teaching and
    Learning (CASTL) and, 290–302
  collaborative practice and, 305–316
  communities for, 100 (*see also*
    Communities)
  electronic portfolios and, 92–93,
    102
  Foothill College case study and,
    402–409, 412
  independent study and, 108
  informational access vs. educational
    access and, 105–108
  innovation for, 269–273
  isolated learning and, 107, 117
  KEEP Toolkit and, 341–348
  Knowledge Media Lab (KML) and,
    173
  leadership development and,
    297–299
  learning design systems and,
    376–386
  MERLOT and, 182–194

middle ground and, 304–316
National Student Satisfaction Survey
   and, 153
net-gen, 93, 101
"No Child Left Behind" campaign
   and, 319
open and distance learning (ODL)
   and, 158–159
participatory culture and, 390–395
peer learning and, 93, 100,
   159–160, 186
portable skills and, 394
service learning and, 127
supported learning and, 156–157
Studio-writing approach, 92
Suber, P., 110
Success of Open Source, The
   (Weber), 423
Sumner, T., 188
Surowiecki, James, 337
Sustainability, 77
   Connexions and, 237–240
   content and, 138–140
   future policies for, 434–436
   governance and, 435–436
   institutional strategies and, 188–193
   leadership development and,
      297–299
   learning technologies and, 319–325,
      337–353
   long-term viability and, 232
   networks and, 367–372
   open educational knowledge and,
      284–285
   reform and, 326–334
   reuse alignment and, 188–193
   staying power and, 367–372
   synergy and, 351
   Teaching and Learning Commons
      and, 349–351
   understanding users and, 197–210
   user-centric, 238
Swenson, C., 406
Symonds, W., 324
Synergies, 408

future policies and, 3–6, 435, 438
indicators of, 9–10
MERLOT and, 189–190
sustainability and, 351
systemic change and, 362

Tagg, J., 401
Tagging, 241
Taiwan, 170
Taylor, S., 161
Teachers, 218, 281
   accelerating course development
      and, 190–191
   alignment and, 312–313
   best practices and, 420
   blind spot of, 166
   Carnegie Academy for the
      Scholarship of Teaching and
      Learning (CASTL) and, 290–302
   collaborative practice and, 305–316
   community for, 95
   discipline and, 191–192, 203–204
   "Every Child Matters" campaign
      and, 319
   faculty cultures and, 200–206
   Foothill College case study and,
      402–409, 412
   fundamental error of, 166
   information glut and, 89–91
   innovation and, 261–275
   instructivist experience and, 380
   KEEP Toolkit and, 184, 341–348
   Knowledge Media Laboratory
      (KML) and, 173, 341–348,
      351–352
   leadership development and,
      297–299
   learning design systems and,
      376–386
   learning technologies and, 337–355
      (*see also* Open educational
      technology)
   local knowledge and, 338–339
   locus of control and, 408–409
   MERLOT and, 182–194

Teachers, (cont.)
middle ground and, 304–316
multi-layered teaching communities
and, 303–316
National Association for School
Personnel Administrators and, 359
National Council of Professors of
Educational Administration
(NCPEA) and, 236–237
networks for, 92
OpenCourseWare and, 218–222
open and distance learning (ODL)
and, 158–159
participatory culture and, 390–395
pedagogical content knowledge and,
183–188, 375–386
peer learning and, 93, 100
peer review and, 306–308
personal collections and, 203
professional imperative and, 337
raising profile of, 422
support for, 174–175
system-wide collaborations and,
192–193
traditional methods and, 91–92,
101, 182, 207, 392
Visible Knowledge Project (VKP)
and, 307–312, 315–316
Teaching and Learning Commons
accountability and, 424–426
collectivity culture and, 437–438
future policies and, 417–418, 423,
437–438
MERLOT and, 189, 192
multi-layer teaching communities
and, 313
sustainability and, 346–351
Teaching Quality Information, 153
Technology. *See* Open educational
technology
*Technology Enabled Active Learning
(TEAL): Studio Physics at MIT*
(KEEP Toolkit snapshot),
344–345
Technology Licensing Office (TLO),
217–218

Telecommunications, 2, 268
Templates, 382–386, 420
Tennessee Board of Regents,
190–192
Tests. *See* Evaluation
Textbooks, 10, 100, 251, 408–409,
423
approved adoption lists and, 264
Connexions and, 233–235, 238, 240
cost of, 230, 240, 252, 269–270
digital libraries and, 107–110
linear form of, 229
online reuse and, 269–272
problem solving in, 167
research and, 167, 173
selection of, 123, 140
Thille, Candace, 138, 165–179, 448
Thinkering, 243
Third Morrill Act, 247–248, 255
TLT Group, 18
Towne, L., 420
*Transforming Physics Courses: From
a Large Lecture Classroom to a
Student-Centered Active Learning
Space* (KEEP Toolkit snapshot),
344
Translation, 124, 253, 298, 413, 420
Connexions and, 230, 233–234
culture of sharing and, 215, 224,
382
design and, 30
educational framework and, 90, 94,
96
evaluation and, 81, 87
innovation and, 265, 275n1
multi-layered teaching communities
and, 303, 310
research and, 170
Trigwell, Keith, 304
Trow, Martin, 205, 209
Truncated learning, 368
Tufts University, 15, 100
Twigg, C. A., 322

Undergraduate Research
Opportunities Program (UROP), 63

United Kingdom, 294, 363
  cultural barriers and, 47
  "Every Child Matters" campaign
    and, 319
  Higher Education Academy and, 259
  Joint Information Systems
    Committee (JISC) and, 332
  learning management systems
    (LMSs) and, 50–55
  National Committee of Inquiry into
    Higher Education and, 325
  National Student Satisfaction Survey
    and, 153
  OpenLearn and, 155–158, 160
  Open University and, 151 (*see also*
    Open University)
  participatory culture and, 397
  Quality Assurance Agency and, 153
  reform and, 326–327
  Teaching Commons and, 192
United Nations
  Declaration of Human Rights, 223
  Educational, Scientific and Cultural
    Organization (UNESCO), 3, 135,
    165, 275n1, 396
  millennium goal of, 319
United States, 360, 363, 417
  Department of Education, 394, 402,
    411
  gender issues and, 143
  National Association for School
    Personnel Administrators and, 359
  National Coalition and, 370
  "No Child Left Behind" campaign
    and, 319
  participatory culture and, 397
  Rehabilitation Act and, 33
  Secretary of Education and, 425
Universal design for learning (UDL),
  33
Universal design (UD), 33
Universia, 224
Universities, 23, 285
  attrition and, 324
  closed, 150
  collaborative practice and, 305–316

commmercializing inventions and,
  217–218
Cooperative Learning Object
  Exchange (CLOE) and, 192–193
corporate, 161
course management systems (CMS)
  and, 36
cultural barriers and, 47
formal vs. informal learning and,
  xiv–xv
intellectual property and, 55–57
learning management systems
  (LMSs) and, 48–55
MERLOT and, 182–194
mono-disciplinary approach and, 48
National Council of Professors of
  Educational Administration
  (NCPEA) and, 236–237
network building and, 358–363
raising teaching profile and, 422
traditional methods and, 150–151
Urban Universities Portfolio Project
  (UUPP) and, 357, 359, 361–362,
  366–369
University of California, 197–199,
  346
University of Illinois, 188
University of Kansas, 312–313
University of London, 383
University of Michigan, xv–xvi, 109,
  357
University of Minnesota, 346
University of Pennsylvania, 63
University of Phoenix, 161, 324
University of Queensland (UQ),
  68–69, 72
University of Wisconsin, 421
Unsworth, J., 29
Urban Universities Portfolio Project
  (UUPP), 359, 361–362
  assessing findings and, 366–367
  building on solid foundations and,
    370
  communications support and,
    368–372
  learned helplessness and, 357

Use
  Connexions and, 232–244
  context and, 206–209
  digital resources types and,
    201–202
  faculty cultures and, 200–206
  OpenCourseWare (OCW) and,
    215–216, 221–223
  open educational knowledge and,
    281 (*see also* Open educational
    knowledge)
  personal collections and, 203
  quality assessment and, 206–209
  reuse and, 170–174, 188–193,
    230–236, 262–263
  SoURCE project and, 329–330
  sustainability and, 206–209, 238
    (*see also* Sustainability)
  understanding, 197–210
  user demand and, 199–200
User interface (UI) design, 43–44
"User-Oriented Planner for Learning
  Activity Design" project, 332
Utah State University, 127, 249, 252

Valdez, G., 394
Van House, N., 115
Varian, H., 239
Vest, Charles M., xiii, 29, 220, 437
Virginia Tech University, 346
Virtual learning environment (VLE)
  access and, 51
  intellectual property and, 55–57
  learning management systems
    (LMSs) and, 48–55
Visible Knowledge Project (VKP)
  collaborative practice and, 307–312,
    315–316
  Crossroads Online Institute and,
    315–316
  design of, 308
  digital stories and, 310
  focus of, 308–309
  individual projects and, 309–313
  KEEP Toolkit and, 312–313
  open education and, 309
  triads and, 311–312
Visual Understanding Environment
  (VUE), 15–16, 30–32
  access design and, 33–35
  active learning support and, 42
  agency and, 37
  experience and, 43–44
  flexibility and, 33–35
  individual needs and, 37
  ownership and, 38–39
  participatory design and, 41–42
  portable client application and, 37
VOIP, 257

W3C Accessibility Guidelines
  Initiative, 33
Walden University, 257
Walker, Edward, 18–19, 77–88, 448
Ward, D. J., 394
Watkins, K., 368, 374
Web 1.0, 241
Web 2.0, xii, xv, 159, 208
  Connexions and, 229, 237, 241–244
  participatory culture and, 296
  remix and, 241–242
Web 3.0, 229, 242–244
Weber, Stephen, 423
Websites
  AcaWiki, 96
  Carnegie Academy for the
    Scholarship of Teaching and
    Learning (CASTL), 357
  Carnegie Foundation, 368
  ccMixter, 95
  Connexions, 172, 229, 266
  Copyright Licensing Agency (CLA),
    54
  Creative Commons, 154
  Discover Babylon, 267
  eLearning Program, 430
  Electronic Networks For Interaction
    (ENFI), 92
  ERIC Digests, 188
  faculty culture and, 205

Hewlett Foundation, 429
iCampus Alliance, 61
IMS, 171
Inter/National Coalition for
  Electronic Portfolio Research, 358
International Society for the
  Scholarship of Teaching and
  Learning (ISSOTL), 357–358
ISO, 171
Ithaka, 429
JORUM, 330
KEEP Toolkit, 342, 344
LabSpace, 266
Learning Activity Management
  System (LAMS), 55–56, 380, 382
lenses and, 236
MERLOT, 237, 330, 345
National Instruments, 62, 235
net-gen, 101
OCW, 230, 226nn1,2
OECD, 3
Open eLearning Content
  Observatory Services (OLCOS), 430
Open Knowledge Initiative (OKI), 97
OpenLearn, 156, 330
portfolios and, 426
Rice University Press, 240
rSmart, 98
Sakai project, 52, 92
SCORM, 171
Shibboleth, 172
surveys and, 208
Teaching and Learning Commons,
  349
UNESCO, 3
Universal Declaration of Human
  Rights, 226n4
University of Illinois, 188
Visible Knowledge Project (VKP),
  311
WikiEducator, 266
Wikipedia, 265
Wei, C., 239
Weigel, M., 393
Wenger, E., 24, 363

Westermann, M., 240
Western Governors University
  (WGU), 256–257, 272
WGBH, 266
Whitehead, J., 143
Wikibooks, 242, 253–255
WikiEducator, 266
Wikipedia, 265
  accountability and, 424
  Connexions case study and, 233,
    241, 243
  distributed cognition and, 391–392
  participatory culture and, 391–392
  Wiley "historical" account of, 253,
    255, 259
Wikiversity, 242
Wiley, David, 124, 135, 140,
  247–259, 449
William and Flora Hewlett Foundation,
  221, 254, 261–262, 429
Willinsky, John, 110, 426
Wilper, C., 187
Winne, P. H., 168
Winner, Langdon, 36
Wired magazine, xvi
Wolf, A., 144
Women, 143
World Bank, 165
World Population Foundation, 395
World Wide Web, 217
World Wide Web Consortium
  (W3C), 33, 139, 217, 435
Writing, 91–92

XConsortium, 435
XML, 234–235, 241, 381
X Window System, 217

Yale University, 270
Yaron, D., 168, 181
YouTube, 54, 57, 259
Yue, Richard, 218

Zajonc, R. B., 243
Zephyr, 217